Letters of
SIDNEY HOOK

Sidney Hook, 1902–1987. Photograph, from 1963, courtesy of Sidney Hook Collection/Hoover Institution Archives.

Letters of
SIDNEY HOOK

Democracy, Communism, and the Cold War

Edited by
EDWARD S. SHAPIRO

M.E. Sharpe
Armonk, New York
London, England

Library of Congress Cataloging-in-Publication Data

Hook, Sidney, 1902–
Letters of Sidney Hook : democracy, communism, and
the cold war / edited and introduced by Edward S. Shapiro.
p.   cm.
Includes bibliographical references and index.
ISBN 1-56324-487-X (alk. paper)
1. Hook, Sidney, 1902–   —Correspondence.   2. Communism.
3. Socialism.   4. Democracy.   5. Cold War.   I. Shapiro, Edward S.
HX40.H593   1995
335.4—dc20   94-43873
CIP

Printed in the United States of America

The paper used in this publication meets the minimum requirements of
American National Standard for Information Sciences—
Permanence of Paper for Printed Library Materials,
ANSI Z 39.48-1984.

BM (c)   10   9   8   7   6   5   4   3   2   1

In honor of Gwendolyn Goldstein Freishtat

and

in memory of Oscar Goldstein

Contents

Letters

(alphabetically by name of recipient)

Preface

The letters in this book were selected from the mammoth collection of Sidney Hook papers in the Hoover Institution Archives at Stanford University. This volume does not claim to be a definitive and complete edition of Hook's letters. It contains only those unpublished letters that discuss the critical issues of democracy, war and peace, pacifism and disarmament, communism, and the Cold War, and Hook's response to many of the most important events of his lifetime, including the Spanish Civil War, the Waldorf Conference, McCarthyism, and the Vietnam War. It is in these areas that Hook made the greatest impact on American life.

Hook also published many letters on these topics in the *New York Times,* the *New Republic,* and other places. Because of the constraints of space, these have not been included in this book. Nor, for the same reason, does this book contain any of Hook's fascinating letters on euthanasia, religion, pragmatism, and the campus turmoil of the 1960s. Finally, segments in the letters dealing with personal matters, such as health, finances, or family, have been deleted.

Hook's papers, well organized alphabetically and topically, consist of nearly four thousand folders that contain letters and manuscripts covering all aspects of his private and public life. Nearly three thousand of these folders contain Hook's correspondence from 1920 until his death in 1989. They are awaiting use by a future biographer of this remarkably prolific and energetic philosopher-polemicist. Hook's autobiography, *Out of Step: An Unquiet Life in the 20th Century* (1987), provides the historical context for his correspondence. It can be supplemented by the essays in the two festschrifts honoring Hook: Paul Kurtz, ed., *Sidney Hook and the Con-*

temporary World: Essays on the Pragmatic Intelligence (1968), and Paul Kurtz, ed., *Sidney Hook: Philosopher of Democracy and Humanism* (1983).

At no time did Sidney Hook, members of his family, or officials at the Hoover Institute attempt to censor the selection process, although the publisher and I are grateful to Sidney Hook's son, Ernest B. Hook, for granting us permission to publish these letters. In no sense is this an "authorized" volume. As is customary, I made minor cosmetic changes involving spelling, grammar, capitalization, and punctuation. In addition, I eliminated the inside addresses of both Hook and the recipients of his letters as well as "Sincerely," "Yours truly," and other endings. None of these revisions change the thrust of Hook's arguments. The original letters are available for consultation in the Hoover Institution Archives.

My research was facilitated by grants from the Research Council of Seton Hall University and from the Hoover Institution's summer grants program. The Hoover Institution provided a stimulating environment for research. The staff at the Seton Hall University library was invariably courteous and helpful, particularly Tony Lee and Richard Stern. I dedicate this work to my in-laws, who, while never having met Sidney Hook, shared his concern for the fate of America and the survival of freedom.

Introduction: Sidney Hook— "A Democrat First"

The first thing one noticed on entering Sidney Hook's small office on the third floor of the Hoover Institution was two photographs of his mentor, John Dewey. Next to them was a poster for a series of talks titled "What Is Living and Dead in Karl Marx?" which Hook gave in 1984. The room's bookshelves contained the collected works of both Dewey and Marx. Hook's place in American intellectual life is to be found precisely here, at the crossroads of the conflict between the democratic pluralism of Dewey and the totalitarian monism of Marx. Hook first came to the public's attention in the early 1930s, when he was arguably the leading American Marxist intellectual and certainly the most important American explicator of Marxian thought. But even at this time Hook's understanding of Marxism was shaped by a commitment to freedom and democratic pluralism.

Hook took the life of the mind quite seriously, and was never shy about vigorously exposing egregious errors of logic and common sense. He exhibited above all else a commitment to reason and intelligence, coupled with an unwillingness to conform for conformity's sake to the prevailing intellectual fashion. In his autobiography, *Out of Step: An Unquiet Life in the 20th Century* (1987), he emphasized that this commitment had put him out of step with those New York intellectuals whom Norman Podhoretz referred to as "the Family":

> I have always been somewhat premature in relation to dominant currents of public opinion. I was prematurely antiwar in 1917–1921, prematurely antifascist, prematurely a Communist fellow-traveller, prematurely an anti-communist, prematurely, in radical circles, a supporter of the war against Hitler, prematurely a cold warrior against Stalin's effort to extend the Gulag Archi-

pelago, prematurely against the policy of detente and appeasement, prematurely for a national civil rights program and against all forms of invidious discrimination, including reverse discrimination.*

With a consistency and continuity rare among intellectuals, Hook for over half a century opposed totalitarianism and upheld the values of freedom and rationality. He battled those infected by political fanaticism or double standards and those who condoned abhorrent behavior by appealing to some transcendent political or social ideal. His adversaries compromised a rogue's gallery of sloppy thinkers, the perversely blind, and those he felt were in thrall to leftist ideology, such as Corliss Lamont and Lillian Hellman.

Hook resembled a surgeon, skillfully dissecting the errors in his opponent's arguments. Whether he was writing a book, an article, or a letter, Hook never doubted that people could be swayed by reason, and he never stopped being annoyed by those who should have known better, whether they were the editorial writers of the *New York Times* or a Florida housewife. This faith in rationality emerged early in Hook's life. Even before he was a teenager he proclaimed himself to be an agnostic. It was simply irrational, he declared, to believe in the existence of a merciful and powerful God in the face of widespread human misery. Only the pleadings of his parents that he not embarrass them in front of relatives and friends convinced Hook to participate in a Bar Mitzvah ceremony on his thirteenth birthday. People frequently asked him in his later years what he would say if he discovered after death that God really existed. He answered that he would simply state, "God, you never gave me enough evidence." All knowledge, Hook never tired of reminding his readers, is "scientific knowledge."

Hook's devotion to the power of reason was vividly manifested in his correspondence. Virtually to the day he died, he was an active letter writer. Even when he was deluged with his obligations as a teacher, department chairman, author, father, and husband, Hook made time to answer promptly his voluminous mail. Strangers often wrote to challenge some point he had made in an article or book review in the *New York Times* or elsewhere. Hook never considered their views unimportant, or unworthy of a lengthy and vigorous refutation, if need be. His responses frequently filled ten handwritten pages or more. He relished every opportunity to engage in a dialogue and to make a convert. He always assumed that his correspondents were capable of intellectual redemption, and he frequently overestimated the ability and willingness of individuals to change their minds once confronted with evidence clearly contradicting their deeply held beliefs.

---

*Sidney Hook, *Out of Step: An Unquiet Life in the 20th Century* (New York: Harper and Row, 1987), 605.

This is best seen in his lengthy correspondence with Corliss Lamont, perhaps the leading American apologist for Stalinism during the 1940s and 1950s. Lamont had, among other things, defended the Moscow Trials of the 1930s, praised Stalin, and accused anti-communists such as John Dewey and Norman Thomas of "red-baiting." Hook never gave up hope of reforming Lamont. As late as November 16, 1966 (see page 292), nearly three decades after he had first condemned Lamont for being pro-Stalin, Hook wrote:

> The truth is, dear Corliss, that you may be angry with me but you don't pity me. You are angry with me because you know I am right, disinterestedly right, about you. You are really pitying and feeling sorry for yourself—for having lost the intellectual and moral respect of your fellows, you have lost your own sense of self-respect. Self-respect cannot be bought or won back by money but only by moral courage.
> I propose an act of moral courage to you. What about it?

Hook's passionate, time-consuming efforts to convince Lamont to repudiate his past were doomed to fail. If Hook had been less the rationalist, he would have realized that Lamont was no more able to repudiate that which gave his life meaning than an archbishop was able to disavow faith in the truths of Christianity. There was simply nothing that Hook could have done to convince Lamont to recant, but still he persisted in this touching but doomed effort. As his relationship with Lamont demonstrates, Hook never fully appreciated the extent to which politics during the twentieth century had become for some a quasi-religion immune to rational refutation.

This was particularly frustrating to Hook because of the great efforts he devoted to spreading enlightenment. Sociologist Edward Shils described Hook as "probably the greatest polemicist of this century."* There was nothing that Hook liked more than a good argument. "I've had a wonderful week," he once told a colleague; "I had a fight every day."† Hook took seriously his obligations as an American citizen, and his polemical energies were especially used defending American democracy against its internal and external enemies. Through his voluminous writings, Hook sought to educate the public regarding nuclear weapons, affirmative action, academic freedom, and other matters relating to the preservation of America and her democratic institutions. "With the exception of Bertrand Russell," the philosopher Henry David Aiken wrote in 1962, "no other living English-speaking philosopher has performed with comparable distinction the arduous Socratic role of public gadfly, and none has thereby run such a risk of

---

*Shils, "More At Home than Out of Step," 583.

†Edwin McDowell, "Sidney Hook, Exponent of Democracy," *Wall Street Journal,* May 22, 1972, 20.

becoming a public scapegoat."* Never having felt alienated from his native land, Hook was befuddled at the stance of estrangement common among other New York intellectuals. Irving Howe, for example, titled his autobiography *On the Margin* (1982). Hook, by contrast, never felt he was a marginal American. If he felt "out of step," it was only with the left-wing intelligentsia.

In his contribution to the famous 1952 *Partisan Review* symposium "Our Country and Our Culture," Hook emphasized that he was perplexed by the "laments about the 'alienation' of the creative artist in American culture." American intellectuals should not be apologetic "about the fact that they are limited in their effective historical choice between endorsing a system of total terror and *critically* supporting our own imperfect democratic culture with all its promises and dangers." Nor was it clear to Hook "why an appreciation of the values of American life is incompatible with vigorous criticism of its many deficiencies and with determined efforts to enhance both its chances of survival and the quality of its cultural experience by more enlightened domestic and foreign policies." The United States required "the critical support, the dedicated energy and, above all, the intelligence of its intellectuals if it is to survive as a free culture."†

Nor was Hook alienated from the middle class. For Hook, being a socialist was merely a political statement. He never thought of himself as a member of the proletariat. His values and demeanor were quintessentially middle-class. He was a traditionalist when it came to the family and relations between the sexes. His abhorrence of the counter-culture and the New Left during the 1960s and 1970s stemmed in part from their repudiation of the proprieties of bourgeois life, and in part from their contempt for rationality, their craving for a transcendent spiritual experience, their simpleminded moralism, their dogmatic pacifism, and their call for unilateral disarmament in the face of Soviet nuclear weapons. He also was unsympathetic toward the radical wing of the feminist movement, and he found bizarre the feminist claim that marriage and family were oppressive patriarchal institutions. "The traditional chivalry of men toward weakness and vulnerability," he warned in 1985, "has been undermined by false conceptions of equality that overlook biological differences that transcend social and cultural forces. Such a false view absolves many men of a sense of responsibility [to women]."‡

---

*Aiken, "Sidney Hook as Philosopher," 143.

†Hook, "Our Country and Our Culture," *Partisan Review* 29 (September–October 1952), 569–74.

‡"Sidney Hook," in *The Courage of Conviction,* ed. Philip L. Berman (New York, 1985), 105.

Hook came to his views on reason and the scientific method via John Dewey. For six decades, he was among Dewey's most enthusiastic and influential disciples. As a graduate student in philosophy at Columbia University during the 1920s, Hook was initially skeptical about Dewey's philosophy of instrumentalism. Within a year or so, however, he became a convert. Dewey was the mentor of Hook's dissertation, published in 1927 with the seemingly oxymoronic title *The Metaphysics of Pragmatism.* When some of Hook's friends produced a festschrift in 1968 on the occasion of his sixty-fifth birthday, they titled it *Sidney Hook and the Contemporary World: Essays on the Pragmatic Intelligence* and dedicated it "To John Dewey, the teacher of us all."

The life of John Dewey provided Hook with a model for his own. Dewey, Hook noted in *Out of Step,* continued until his death at age ninety-three "in defending the heritage of American democracy and in resisting the advance of totalitarian thought and practice. At a time when age and achievement had earned him the right to retire from active political life, he had devoted all his energies and most of his husbanded hours of leisure in the fight for freedom."* The same can be said of Hook. The citation of the Medal of Freedom presented to Hook by President Reagan in 1985 accurately noted that his "devotion to freedom made him one of the first to warn the intellectual world of its moral obligations and personal stake in the struggle between freedom and totalitarianism. Man of truth, man of action, Sidney Hook's life and work make him one of America's greatest scholars, patriots, and lovers of liberty."

Hook was also influenced by Dewey's attitude toward ideas. Hook resembled Dewey in being interested in the relationship of ideas to the world of politics. His field of expertise was what could be termed "applied philosophy." Hook did not make a significant contribution to formal philosophy, although he was undoubtedly capable of doing so. He was president in 1959 of the American Philosophical Society. In his review of *Out of Step,* Edward Shils asked,

> Would Sidney Hook not have done better to have devoted himself to scholarship and philosophical reflection than to the very exhausting political activities in which he participated? . . . Was it not all a waste of the time and energy of a man of a very rare acuity of mind and a no less moral and intellectual integrity? Would it not have been a gain for Sidney Hook's learning and achievements as a philosopher had he refrained from such busy polemical activity and concentrated instead on writing philosophical works? No definitive answer is possible.†

---

*Hook, *Out of Step*, 93.
†Shils, "More At Home than Out of Step," 584.

But Shils *did* believe that it was possible to give a definitive answer to the question of "whether American public life would have been different had Sidney Hook not participated at its margins for so long." His answer: "It would have been different and worse had Sidney Hook not done what he did."* For Hook (and Dewey), the purpose of philosophy was not to contemplate the world but to change it.

Hook's respect for reason and his image of the university as a place committed to science and rationality was responsible for his detestation of the academic radicalism of the 1960s. He respected students, believed they were rational beings who would respond to rational arguments, and assumed they were in college to cultivate the life of the mind. In 1968, he organized the University Center for Rational Alternatives to resist the campus violence of radicals, the denigration of academic standards, the intimidation of faculty and administrators, and the politicization of the university. He directed some of his sharpest criticisms at a spineless and guilt-ridden academic community that had committed "intellectual treason" by attempting to appease student and faculty "storm troopers." "The number of individual faculty members who protested these violations of academic freedom, due process, and the decencies of civilized discourse, who urged a principled stand against them by faculties and, if necessary, law-enforcing agencies," Hook lamented, was minuscule.†

Hook's most important and famous philosophical work occurred in the 1930s when he was America's leading authority on Marxism and one of the very few self-described Marxists teaching in an American university. The historian John Patrick Diggins described him as "America's most original Marxist thinker."‡ Hook was both a worker in the vineyard of American Marxism and a major Marxist theoretician. He signed the famous 1932 statement "Culture and Crisis," calling for the election of William Z. Foster, the American Communist Party candidate for president, and in 1933 he wrote the political program of the American Workers Party. He was also an editor of V. F. Calverton's *Modern Quarterly* and helped found the short-lived *Marxist Quarterly.*

In *Towards the Understanding of Karl Marx* (1933) and *From Hegel to Marx* (1936) Hook attempted the seemingly impossible task of reconciling Marxism with instrumentalism, and historical materialism with freedom and diversity. Lionel Abel described Hook as the St. Thomas Aquinas of instrumentalism. Just as Aquinas tried to reconcile Christianity with Aristo-

---

*Ibid.
†Hook, *Out of Step*, 549–50.
‡Diggins, *Rise and Fall of the American Left*, 159.

telianism, so Hook attempted to square Marxism with instrumentalism. The subtitle of *Towards the Understanding of Karl Marx* was *A Revolutionary Interpretation,* and the author noted that it "was not written by an 'orthodox Marxist.' " Hook argued that Marxism was "neither a science nor a myth, but a realistic method of social action." It was possible, he avowed, "to dissociate the Marxian method from any specific set of conclusions, or any particular political tactic advocated in its name."* This reflected Hook's own relationship with Marxism.

He had gravitated to Marxism because of its naturalism and ethics, not because of its supposed scientific approach to economics or politics. He had little interest in economics, and his political mentors were Jefferson and Dewey, not Marx. For Hook, Marxism was not an objective science, but a set of architectural drawings for the building of a just society. Marxism did not provide the proletariat with an infallible ideology, but with a plan for achieving its goals. Here Hook was reflecting the philosophy of instrumentalism, which believed ideas to be instruments to achieve objectives rather than dispassionate descriptions of reality. Hook did not believe that the Marxist dialectic taught that capitalism would inevitably collapse, but rather, to quote Diggins, "that truth arises out of experimental encounters with reality leading to the empirical verification of those encounters. Thus predictions about historical events must either be confirmed in actuality or revised in theory."† For Hook, Marxism was a philosophy of freedom "in which human activity could break from mechanical necessity once science was conceived not as the unfolding of laws or as the inexorable realization of ideals but the practical application of intelligence as the agent of social change."‡

The earliest communication in Hook's letters that refers to communism is a picture postcard dated June 24, 1929, which he sent to his family from Moscow while traveling on a Guggenheim fellowship. Written prior to his recognition of the true nature of Soviet rule, the postcard burst with enthusiasm for a society supposedly based on human solidarity.

> This is Moscow—bizarre and gorgeous—a city of startling contrasts—carrying ugly scars of the past and seeds of the future. Food is mean and clothes are rather shabby—but every brick, every road, every machine is a symbol of the new spirit. I have seen no Potemkin villages. Just mingling with the people has enabled me to tap veins of enthusiasm that run deep under the

---

*Sidney Hook, *Towards the Understanding of Karl Marx: A Revolutionary Interpretation* (New York: John Day, 1933), 114 and *passim.*

†Diggins, *Rise and Fall of the American Left,* 159–60.

‡Ibid.

surface of things. And just think of it! A country in which the red flag is the
national banner and the "International" the national anthem.

This zeal was short-lived. Within a very few years Hook had become one of
America's most prominent anti-Soviet intellectuals, and American Communists referred to him and his disciples as "Hook-worms."

In the 1930s, Hook attempted to disentangle Marxism from Stalinist
authoritarianism, the Hegelian dialectic, and the concepts of the dictatorship
of the proletariat, the infallibility of the communist party, the withering
away of the state, and the new socialist "collective man." In 1934, he
contributed "Why I Am a Communist (Communism without Dogmas)" to a
Modern Monthly symposium. "Only communism can save the world from
its social evils," Hook wrote.* But this demanded that Marxism be purged
of its dogmatic and authoritarian elements. As a pragmatist, Hook was
naturally skeptical of the deterministic elements of Marxist ideology, particularly its emphasis on dialectical materialism, and as a democrat he strongly
opposed the Soviet dictatorship and the rationalizations of communist sympathizers for Stalin's tyranny. Hook denied that communism necessarily
implied the denial of freedom of thought and speech. "No communism as I
understand it," he said, "would dream of denying the value of liberalism in
this sense." In equating communism with humanitarian social democracy,
Hook's understanding of communism (and Marxism) was idiosyncratic
and, as he later wrote, an "intellectual conceit."

Hook's attempt to reconcile Marxism and pragmatism was probably
doomed from the beginning. Respect for individual rights and democratic
processes found within the American liberal tradition was always more
important to him than socialism. "I am a democrat first, and a socialist only
to the extent that socialist measures achieve a more abundant life for free
human beings," he wrote in 1951 to a sympathetic critic (see letter 91).
"This means that I do not believe in total solutions; that my socialism is a
piecemeal affair, a matter of more or less to be decided in the light of the
scientific spirit and the democratic faith."

In his book *Speaking of Diversity: Language and Ethnicity in Twentieth
Century America* (1992), the historian Philip Gleason noted that Hook was
part of "a mighty democratic revival" during the 1930s and World War II
that saw the intelligentsia "invest democracy with the aura of the sacred and
exalt it to the level of a civil religion" (190–97, 219–21). This democratic
renewal stemmed, in turn, from a revived cultural nationalism, as intellectuals sought to differentiate America from Italy, Japan, and particularly the

---

*Sidney Hook, "Why I Am a Communist (Communism Without Dogmas)," *Modern
Monthly* 8 (April 1934), 143–65.

Soviet Union and Germany. More often than not, this "growing self-consciousness about the distinctiveness of American culture" led intellectuals to emphasize democracy as the defining element of American life.* Hook agreed. For him, democracy was not simply a superior political arrangement. It was the essence of the nation. Opponents of democracy were thus not merely misguided. They were traitors. The impulse that led Hook in 1940 to state that the enemies of democracy must "be swiftly dealt with" would not dissipate with the end of World War II.

In 1940, Hook suggested that Marxists look for inspiration to John Dewey, and he would repeat this suggestion on other occasions. "The most outstanding figure in the world today in whom the best elements of Marx's thought are present is John Dewey," he wrote in *Reason, Social Myths and Democracy* (1940). "They were independently developed by him, and systematically elaborated beyond anything found in Marx. If ever a democratic socialist movement succeeds in striking roots in American soil, it will have to derive one of its chief sources of nourishment from the philosophy of John Dewey."†

Towards the Understanding of Karl Marx had sought to rescue Marx from the Marxists, but by the early 1940s Hook had virtually given up on this salvage enterprise and could only by the loosest of definitions still be described as a Marxist. The publication of *The Hero in History* in 1943 made explicit his rejection of Marxian determinism. By then the contrast between Marxism and Deweyism was too stark to be papered over. Hook's 1947 *Partisan Review* essay "The Future of Socialism" formalized his break with Marxism:

> For the last twenty years I have presented an interpretation of Marx which has run counter to customary views and conceptions of his fundamental doctrines. . . . It would appear that if I were justified in my interpretation of Marx's meaning, I would be perhaps the last Marxist left in the world. This is too much for my sense of humor, and so I have decided to abandon the term as a descriptive epithet of my position. . . . Certainly if the Stalinists and their international salon of fellow traveling literateurs and totalitarian liberal politicos, whose deep ignorance of the subject is as broad as their dogmatism is deep, are Marxists, then I am cheerfully resigned to being non-Marxist.‡

In 1983 Hook published a collection of his essays with the revealing title *Marxism and Beyond.*

Hook's move away from Marxism did not surprise more orthodox Marxists. From the beginning, they had viewed his efforts to separate Marxism

*Gleason, *Speaking of Diversity*, 190–97, 219–21.

†Sidney Hook, *Reason, Social Myths and Democracy* (New York, 1940), 132.

‡Sidney Hook, "The Future of Socialism," *Partisan Review* 14 (January–February 1947), 25.

from Leninism, his questioning of dialectical materialism and materialistic determinism, and his attempts to accommodate Marx to American political and philosophical traditions as heretical rather than revolutionary. Will Herberg, then in his Marxist stage, accused Hook in the early 1930s of being steeped in the "outworn superstitions of democracy" and of being caught up in the "philistine worship of the abstract forms of democracy." Hook's Marxism, Herberg declared, was "the crudest sort of democratic fetishism disguised in a Marxist mantle." Hook, in turn, accused Herberg, the future author of *Judaism and Modern Man,* of "methodological thuggery" and of expounding a "Communist-Catholic theory of party infallibility."*

American Communist Party apparatchiks also assailed Hook. The *Daily Worker* described him in 1933 as a "philosophic hack" and an "insolent distorter of Marxism." V. J. Jerome, a second-rate Communist Party intellectual commissar, attacked Hook in an essay titled "Unmasking an American Revisionist of Marxism" (*The Communist,* January 1933). According to Jerome, Hook was a "renegade social-fascist" who employed "the tactics of the Second International opportunists." His Marxism was "crassly metaphysical," the "smugness-cult of a philistine bourgeoisie that feels it has 'arrived.' " A few years later Stalin himself personally denounced Hook as a "gangster of the pen" for criticizing the Moscow Trials.

By the 1940s there was little to distinguish Hook politically from those on the left wing of the Democratic Party. Old habits die hard, however, and he continued to refer to himself as a socialist or a social democrat. Certainly this was a clear case of "false consciousness." In a 1952 essay titled "The Philosophical Basis of Marxian Socialism in the United States," Hook predicted that "no matter what historical variant develops, if democratic traditions and institutions are preserved in the face of the current world-wide totalitarian crusade against them, they will acquire a more socialist content." He anticipated the emergence of a socialism that would combine instrumentalism with Marxian realism and "realize the highest traditions of American democracy."†

These were hardly prophetic words. After World War II, socialism had even less appeal to Americans than it had had prior to the war, and Hook seemingly had little interest in formulating a socialist alternative to capitalism and individualism. All his contributions to socialist thought occurred during the 1930s. He was too good a pragmatist to remain an ardent socialist. As socialism's relevance to the real world diminished, Hook's socialism

---

*Diggins, *Up from Communism,* 147.

†Sidney Hook, "The Philosophical Basis of Marxian Socialism in the United States," in *Socialism and American Life*, ed. Donald Drew Egbert and Stow Persons (Princeton, N.J.: Princeton University Press, 1952), 1:450–51.

became increasingly more muted, an occasional concession to youthful intellectual fancies.

The great postwar debate, Hook never tired of arguing, was not between collectivism and private enterprise but between democracy and its enemies, or, as he put it in *Political Power and Personal Freedom*, "between the absolutist and the experimental temper of mind."* His energies now focused not on domesticating Marxism but on fighting (and winning) the Cold War, whether in Europe, Asia, Central America, or in the court of American public opinion. There was hardly a *cause célèbre* of the Cold War in which Hook was not involved. He agreed with the verdicts in the Alger Hiss and Rosenberg cases (although he publicly opposed the execution of Ethel and Julius Rosenberg), he attacked unilateral disarmament and what he considered the excessive fear of nuclear warfare, and he favored a hawkish military strategy in Vietnam once the Johnson administration made the fateful decision to escalate America's military involvement.

Hook, however, differed from other advocates of democracy such as Walter Lippmann, who emphasized the doctrine of natural rights. For Hook, democracy was not metaphysically but empirically true because it provided more freedom, prosperity, and security than any other political system. Nor did his confidence in democracy stem from any belief in the goodness of mankind. He was too familiar with Stalinism to believe in that. Rather, he believed in the possibility of educating the citizenry. Hook's commitment to democracy partially explains his attacks on the Supreme Court of Earl Warren and Warren Burger. He believed the Court was arrogating to itself powers best left with the democratically elected Congress.

Because of his staunch anti-communism, conservatives were willing to overlook Hook's reflexive antagonism to religion and his vestigial democratic socialist sympathies. He played little role in the great social movements of the 1960s and 1970s such as civil rights and feminism. Those both within and outside of conservative circles came to view Hook as one of the gurus of the neo-conservative revival of the 1970s and 1980s, a description he did not welcome or believe was accurate. "No one has more clearly and consistently explained and opposed our century's totalitarian assault on civilization," William F. Buckley, Jr.'s *National Review* declared in 1973. "No one in academic life has stood more firmly against the intellectual, political, and moral diseases that have infected his own profession."† In fact, Hook became the American Right's favorite former radical. President

---

*Sidney Hook, *Political Power and Personal Freedom: Critical Studies in Democracy, Communism, and Civil Rights* (New York, 1959), 183.

†Editorial, *National Review* 25 (January 19, 1973), 74.

Nixon appointed him to the council of the National Endowment for the Humanities, and it was during the Reagan administration that the NEH selected Hook to deliver the prestigious Jefferson Lecture in the Humanities.

Former left-of-center colleagues of Hook in the trenches of anti-communism, such as William Phillips, Irving Howe, and Arthur M. Schlesinger, Jr., were dismayed by his new status. In his *New Republic* review of *Out of Step,* Schlesinger claimed that Hook's "obsession" with the communist issue had resulted in his becoming a peripheral figure in American intellectual life after the 1950s. Schlesinger had not always believed this. At a 1968 dinner in honor of Hook's sixty-fifth birthday, Schlesinger had praised Hook for having "enlightened a whole generation to the dangers of communism."*

Hook died in 1989, that *annus mirabilis* of recent history that saw the dissolving of the Soviet Empire and protests within China against Communist rule. Within three years the Communist Party in Russia had been outlawed, the Soviet Union had dissolved, the Cold War had ended, and many erstwhile Communists had become pariahs throughout Eastern Europe. One wonders how Hook would have responded to these developments.

Certainly he had not anticipated them. On the contrary, he was very skeptical that Communist governments could ever be overturned, whether in Europe, Asia, or Central America. Some American sovietologists, most notably Stephen Cohen of Princeton, were taken by surprise by the events of 1989 because they believed that communism enjoyed widespread public support. Hook, in contrast, attributed the staying power of communism to its totalitarian nature and to the role of Marxist ideology. Ideology, he believed, determined Communist behavior, and this ideology did not allow for the peaceful transfer of power to its enemies. As an intellectual, Hook perhaps took the commitment of Communist rulers to Marxist ideas too seriously. His image of communist totalitarianism had no place for the momentous events of 1989.

This emphasis on the power of ideology came naturally to Hook, who had first come to public attention as an explicator of Marxist thought. In failing to anticipate change within the Communist sphere, Hook ignored the possibility that Communist leaders (with the exception of those in Cuba and North Korea) might be pragmatic enough to abjure Marxist ideology as a solution to deep social and economic problems. This should not, however, blind us to his important role in American intellectual life. During the 1930s he took the lead among American intellectuals in warning against communism and the Soviet Union; during the 1940s and 1950s he vigorously defended America's efforts to contain the spread of Soviet power and at-

---

*Schlesinger, "A Life at the Barricades," 30–31.

tacked those who criticized America's nuclear deterrent; and during the 1960s and 1970s he staunchly vindicated academic standards and the integrity of academia against what he felt were the onslaughts of barbarians both from within and from without the university.

In the concluding paragraph of *Out of Step,* Hook noted that the greatest and most enduring sources of happiness in his life had been "the experience and excitement of clarifying ideas, of battling in a good cause, and of teaching a bright and questioning class of students." Indifference to politics was "a flagrant expression of moral irresponsibility. Those who profess such indifference owe the intellectual and cultural freedoms in which they luxuriate to the commitment and sacrifices of others."* This was an indifference Hook never exhibited.

Bibliography

Abel, Lionel. "Sidney Hook's Career (The Philosopher in Politics)." *Partisan Review* 52 (Spring 1985): 31–41.

Aiken, Henry David. "Sidney Hook as Philosopher." *Commentary* 33 (February 1962): 143–51.

Baumann, Fred. "Reason's Faithful Disciple." *This World* no. 18 (Summer 1987): 106–11.

Berman, Paul. "The Last True Marxist Is a Neoconservative." *Village Voice Literary Supplement,* March 13, 1984.

Best, Steven. "Hook, Sidney (1902–1989)." In *Encyclopedia of the American Left,* ed. Mari Jo Buhle, Paul Buhle, and Dan Georgakas, 332–33. New York: Garland, 1990.

Browder, Earl. "The Revisionism of Sidney Hook." *The Communist* 12 (1933): 133–46, 285–300.

Camporesi, Cristiano. "The Marxism of Sidney Hook," *Telos* no. 12 (Summer 1972): 115–28.

Capaldi, Nicholas. "Sidney Hook: A Personal Portrait." In *Sidney Hook: Philosopher of Democracy and Humanism,* ed. Paul Kurtz, 17–26. Buffalo, N.Y.: Prometheus Books, 1983.

Diggins, John P. *The Rise and Fall of the American Left.* New York: W. W. Norton, 1992.

———. *Up from Communism: Conservative Odysseys in American Intellectual History.* New York: Harper and Row, 1975.

Eastman, Max. *The Last Stand of Dialectic Materialism: A Study of Sidney Hook's Marxism.* New York: Polemic Publishers, 1934.

Edwards, Lee. "Sidney Hook, 'Philosopher Engagé.'" *World and I* no. 7 (July 1987): 449–54.

Epstein, Joseph. "Remembering Sidney Hook." *Commentary* 89 (November 1989): 41–47.

Falk, Julius, and Gordon Haskell. "Civil Liberties and the Philosopher of the Cold War." *The New International* 19 (July–August 1953), 184–227.

Feuer, Lewis S. "From Ideology to Philosophy: Sidney Hook's Writings on Marxism."

---

*Hook, *Out of Step*, 606.

In *Sidney Hook and the Contemporary World: Essays on the Pragmatic Intelligence,* ed. Paul Kurtz, 35–53. New York: John Day, 1968.

———. "The Pragmatic Wisdom of Sidney Hook." *Encounter* 40 (October 1975): 37–45.

Gleason, Philip. *Speaking of Diversity: Language and Ethnicity in Twentieth-Century America.* Baltimore, Md.: Johns Hopkins University Press, 1992.

Glick, Nathan. "Sidney Hook, Embattled Philosopher: On America's Leading Polemicist." *Encounter* 65 (June 1985): 28–32.

Jerome, V. J. "Unmasking an American Revisionist of Marxism." *The Communist* 12 (January 1933), 50–82.

Konvitz, Milton R. "Sidney Hook: Philosopher of Freedom." In *Sidney Hook and the Contemporary World,* ed. Paul Kurtz, 17–27.

———. "Sidney Hook: Philosopher of the Moral-Critical Intelligence." In *Sidney Hook: Philosopher of Democracy and Humanism,* ed. Paul Kurtz, 3–16.

Kramer, Hilton. "The Importance of Sidney Hook." *Commentary* 84 (August 1987): 17–24.

Miller, Stephen. "Sidney Hook: Fifty Years of Anti-Communism." *American Spectator* 17 (January 1984): 18–21.

O'Neill, William L. *A Better World: The Great Schism: Stalinism and the American Intellectuals.* New York: Simon and Schuster, 1982.

Pells, Richard H. *Radical Visions and American Dreams: Culture and Social Thought in the Depression Years.* New York: Harper and Row, 1973.

Purcell, Edward. *The Crisis of Democratic Theory.* Lexington: University of Kentucky Press, 1973.

Reck, Andrew J. *The New American Philosophers: An Exploration of Thought since World War II.* Baton Rouge: Louisiana State University Press, 1973.

Schlesinger, Arthur M., Jr. "A Life at the Barricades." *New Republic* 196 (May 4, 1987): 30–31.

Schrecker, Ellen W. *No Ivory Tower: McCarthyism and the Universities.* New York: Oxford University Press, 1986.

Schwarzbart, Elias M. "Always a Step Ahead." *Freedom at Issue* no. 97 (July–August 1987): 5–12.

Shapiro, Edward S. "The Sidney Hook–Corliss Lamont Correspondence." *Continuity* no. 12 (Fall 1988): 59–95.

———. "The Jewishness of the New York Intellectuals: Sidney Hook, a Case Study." In *American Pluralism and the Jewish Community,* ed. Seymour Martin Lipset, 153–71. New Brunswick, N.J.: Transaction, 1990.

Shils, Edward. "More At Home than Out of Step." *American Scholar* 56 (Autumn 1987): 577–86.

Outline of the Life of Sidney Hook

Born: December 20, 1902, Brooklyn, New York
High School: Boys High School, Brooklyn, New York, 1916–19
B.S.: City College of New York, 1923
M.A.: Columbia University, 1926
Ph.D.: Columbia University, 1927
Married: Carrie Katz, 1924; child: John Bertrand
        Ann Zinken, 1935; children: Ernest Benjamin, Susan Ann
Instructor: New York University, 1927–32
Guggenheim Fellow: 1928–29, 1961–62
Assistant Professor, Department of Philosophy, New York University, 1932–34; Associate Professor, 1934–39; Professor, 1939–69
Chairman, All-University Department of Philosophy, New York University, 1957–68
President of American Philosophical Society, 1959
Regents Professor, University of California at Santa Barbara, 1966
Senior Research Fellow, Hoover Institution on War, Revolution and Peace, Stanford University, 1973–89
Jefferson Lecturer in the Humanities, National Endowment for the Humanities, 1984
Presidential Medal of Freedom recipient, May 1985
Honorary degrees: Hebrew Union College, Rockford College, University of Utah, University of California, University of Maine, University of Florida, University of Vermont
Died: July 12, 1989

Books by Sidney Hook

The Metaphysics of Pragmatism. Chicago: Open Court, 1927.
Towards the Understanding of Karl Marx: A Revolutionary Interpretation. New York: John Day, 1933.

From Hegel to Marx: Studies in the Intellectual Development of Karl Marx. New York: John Day, 1936.
John Dewey: An Intellectual Portrait. New York: John Day, 1939.
Reason, Social Myths and Democracy. New York: John Day, 1940.
The Hero in History: A Study in Limitation and Possibility. New York: John Day, 1943.
Education for Modern Man. New York: Dial Press, 1946.
Heresy, Yes—Conspiracy, No! New York: John Day, 1953.
Marx and the Marxists: The Ambiguous Legacy. Princeton, N.J.: Van Nostrand, 1955.
Common Sense and the Fifth Amendment. New York: Criterion Books, 1957.
Political Power and Personal Freedom: Critical Studies in Democracy, Communism, and Civil Rights. New York: Criterion Books, 1959.
The Quest for Being, and Other Studies in Naturalism and Humanism. New York: St. Martin's Press, 1961.
The Paradoxes of Freedom. Berkeley: University of California Press, 1962.
Education for Modern Man: A New Perspective. New York: Alfred A. Knopf, 1963.
The Fail-Safe Fallacy. New York: Stein and Day, 1963.
Religion in a Free Society. Lincoln: University of Nebraska Press, 1967.
American Freedom and Academic Anarchy. New York: Cowles, 1970.
Education and the Taming of Power. La Salle, Ill.: Open Court, 1973.
Pragmatism and the Tragic Sense of Life. New York: Basic Books, 1974.
Revolution, Reform, and Social Justice—Studies in the Theory and Practices of Marxism. New York: New York University Press, 1975.
Philosophy and Public Policy. Carbondale: Southern Illinois University Press, 1980.
Marxism and Beyond. Totowa, N.J.: Rowman and Littlefield, 1983.
Out of Step: An Unquiet Life in the 20th Century. New York: Harper and Row, 1987.
Convictions. Buffalo, N.Y.: Prometheus Books, 1990.

For a complete listing of Hook's writings from 1922 to 1988, see Barbara Levine, *Sidney Hook: A Checklist of Writings* (Carbondale: Southern Illinois University Press, 1989). There is also JoAnn Boydston and Kathleen Poulos, "A Complete Bibliography of Sidney Hook," in Paul Kurtz, ed., *Sidney Hook: Philosopher of Democracy and Humanism* (Buffalo, N.Y.: Prometheus Books, 1983), 311–55.

1

The 1930s

Arthur M. Schlesinger, Jr., aptly noted that Sidney Hook's life had been spent "at the barricades." These barricades, by and large, were constructed in the 1930s, the formative decade in Hook's career as a political intellectual. It was then that his passion for political debate and intractable opposition to communism and the Soviet Union were honed. At the beginning of the 1930s, Hook had been a Communist fellow traveler. He supported a communist revolution at home and the interests of the Soviet Union abroad. In September 1932, Hook, along with Newton Arvin, Sherwood Anderson, Malcolm Cowley, John Dos Passos, Waldo Frank, Lincoln Steffens, Edmund Wilson, and some forty-five other leading American intellectuals and writers signed a statement calling for the election of the American Communist Party's presidential ticket of William Z. Foster and James Ford.

By 1932, however, Hook had already begun the metamorphosis that would transform him in a few short years into one of America's leading left-wing anti-communist and anti-Soviet intellectuals. He titled chapter 14 of his 1987 autobiography *Out of Step: An Unquiet Life in the 20th Century* "Breaking with Communism." In it he attributed his initial political "obtuseness" regarding communism to three factors. The first was "genuine ignorance of what was really occurring within the Soviet Union." This was not due to a lack of evidence of the true nature of the Stalinist regime, he claimed, but to an intense will to believe the best about the Soviet Union that characterized segments of the American Left during the 1930s.

Hook spent the academic year 1929–30 in the Soviet Union. His stay resembled a religious pilgrimage. "I had come to the Soviet Union with the faith of someone already committed to the Socialist ideal and convinced that the Soviet Union was genuinely dedicated to its realization." He was reluctant to discard that belief since it was "the only animating social ideal available to someone who had rejected the system of capitalism as it operated in

the hectic days of the twenties with its mad scramble for profit and place"
(*Out of Step*, 123–24).

The second reason for Hook's attraction to communism and the Soviet
Union was his revulsion from the horrors of World War I. The war, the Left
argued, stemmed from the struggle of capitalist nations for markets and raw
materials. By destroying capitalism, bolshevism would eliminate the international crises endemic to capitalism. This, in turn, would prevent any future
wars along the lines of World War I.

Finally, Hook believed communism to be the major barrier preventing the
triumph of fascism and nationalism in Europe. His major concern was Germany, which he had visited in 1929 and where he had seen at first hand the
activities of the National Socialists. "I assumed," he wrote, "that the Kremlin
in its own interests and that of the international working class, as well as in
the cause of humanity, would organize a revolution through its powerful
Communist political and trade-union affiliates in Germany," to forestall the
triumph of Hitler, (*Out of Step*, 176).

Hook was too good a pragmatist and too independent a thinker to remain
a fellow traveler for very long. His disenchantment was hastened by the
attacks of Communist Party hacks on his explication of Marxist thought,
particularly his volume *Towards the Understanding of Karl Marx*, which appeared in early 1933. If this book made Hook suspect in the eyes of the
Communist Party, the reaction to the book made the Communist Party and its
minions suspect in his eyes as well.

In 1933, Hook, A. J. Muste, and other independent radicals created the
short-lived American Workers Party. Hook's experience with the AWP was
humbling.

> I got to realize how little I knew about the nature of the country whose system I
> was trying to revolutionize. I acquired a sense of the nature of the difficulties of
> the men and women in the field. . . . Our hypothesis that the revolutionary
> attitude toward American institutions was doomed because it lacked a native
> garb and spoke in a foreign tongue was invalid. It was not the medium or form of
> the revolutionary message that was wrong. It was the message. [*Out of Step*,
> 195–96.]

Hook now confronted the question the German sociologist Werner Somb-
art had attempted to answer some three decades earlier—"Why Is There No
Socialism in America?" As difficult as the plight of American workers was in
the Great Depression, they looked for succor to Franklin Roosevelt and not to
the American avatars of Karl Marx.

Two events in particular during the 1930s intensified Hook's abhorrence
of communism and the Soviet Union. The first and most important was the
Moscow Trials and purges of 1936 and 1937. "I discovered the face of
radical evil," Hook recounted,

> as ugly and petrifying as anything the Fascists had revealed up to that time—in
> the visages of those who were convinced that they were men and women of

good will. Although I had been severely critical of the political program of the Soviet Union under Stalin, I never suspected that he and the Soviet regime were prepared to violate every fundamental norm of human decency that had been woven into the texture of civilized life. [*Out of Step,* 218.]

Hook learned that without moral values socialism was only "an ideological disguise for totalitarianism."

Hook contributed to a socialism of moral values by participating in the Dewey Commission of Inquiry. Organized by his teacher John Dewey, the commission was established to provide a forum for Leon Trotsky and his son Leon Sedov to answer the charges brought against them at the Moscow Trials. These accusations included attempting to assassinate Stalin and his most important advisers. Because of Dewey's advanced age—he was nearly seventy-nine at this time—Hook became the commission's leading spokesman not only for Trotsky's right to defend himself before the Dewey Commission but for his right to political asylum.

The involvement of the Soviet Union in the Spanish Civil War confirmed Hook's worst fears. The Spanish Civil War moved writers and intellectuals such as Hook, George Orwell, and Ernest Hemingway as no other event of the 1930s. Here the struggle between democracy and fascism seemingly appeared in its starkest form. And yet the Spanish Republic's plea for Western support was sullied by the involvement of the Soviet Union in the struggle against fascism. The Spanish Communists and fellow travelers, Hook wrote, "countenanced—and, on the whole, approved—extermination of anti-communist elements among the Loyalist forces by Stalin's goon squads" (*Out of Step,* 174). As they had in 1932–33, the Communists revealed that their major goal was not defeating the Fascists but destroying their socialist and anarchist rivals. By 1936 Hook had no illusions regarding the Soviet Union or the willingness of fellow travelers in America to exonerate and justify anything just so long as it was done in the name of socialist solidarity and anti-fascism.

1

Dear folks,[1]   Moscow
                                                                       June 24, 1929

This is Moscow—bizarre and gorgeous—a city of startling contrasts—carrying ugly scars of the past and seeds of the future.

Food is mean and clothes are rather shabby—but every brick, every road, every machine is a symbol of the new spirit. I have seen no Potemkin villages. Just mingling with the people has enabled me to tap views of enthusiasm than run deep under the surface of things. And just think of it! A country in which the red flag is the national banner and the "International" the national anthem.

1. Sidney Hook's parents.

2

Dean Munn,[1]   November 24, 1930

In conformity with the request of the Chancellor, I herewith submit a report of what transpired at the meeting of the Social Problems Club held Friday, November 21, at the School of Education Auditorium. The speaker was Mr. Hamilton Fish;[2] his subject, "The Red Menace."

I was asked by the president of the Social Problems Club to present the speaker and chair the meeting. The meeting, scheduled to begin at 1 P.M., was called to order at 1:20. In my prefatory remarks, after announcing a meeting of the New York University Philosophical Society for the subsequent Tuesday, I thanked Mr. Fish for his courtesy in consenting to address the students at Washington Square and for his public spirit in taking time from his other pressing duties to discuss contemporary problems with those about to enter public life. Mr. Fish gracefully acknowledged the introductory words to the applause of the students.

Mr. Fish spoke for thirty minutes and, from what I could observe, seemed to have favorably impressed most of the audience with his interesting account of the history and principles of communism. Towards the close of his speech, when Mr. Fish was describing the activities of alien communists in the U.S., a person sitting apart from the rest of the students in the rear of the room suddenly exclaimed, "It's a lie!" I sprang to my feet, cries of "Put him out!" came from the audience, and Mr. Fish came to a full stop. He made a gesture as if to leave the platform. I stepped forward, asked Mr. Fish to take my chair, called the meeting to order, and demanded that the person who had insulted Mr. Fish make a formal apology and withdraw. He flung back that he wasn't a student at N.Y.U., wanted to know "who I was anyway," and muttered something about "not being able to stand it anymore." Thereupon I told him that he had no business at the meeting, that as an outsider he was trespassing on school property, and ordered him out. Several members of the club made for him, but still talking incoherently to himself, he left of his own accord. He neither looked nor spoke nor acted like a N.Y.U. student. Although I afterwards made inquiries, I could find no one who knew him.

When Mr. Fish resumed his speech he said that he was glad that the disturber was not a student and that he knew that the students at N.Y.U. were too gentlemanly and intelligent to act in such unmannerly ways or even to countenance such action. The audience applauded vigorously. As a whole it was obviously sympathetic to Mr. Fish and indignant at the interruption.

Mr. Fish brought his speech to a close and was given a lively hand of applause. I expressed my sincere regrets to him over the incident and assured him that the students present resented the unfortunate interruption as much as I. I suggested that the meeting be adjourned without the customary question period. Mr. Fish laughingly insisted that "the trivial remarks of a trivial fellow" had not put him hors-de-combat and asked me to allow the usual time for questions. In order to insure an orderly meeting and eliminate the possibility of rude discussion, I requested that all questions be written out and handed to me. With Mr. Fish's permission, I selected the questions to be answered, omitting all those that were too obviously political or personal in nature. Mr. Fish gladly answered all the questions put and later commented upon the keen intelligence they showed. After all the written questions had been answered, Mr. Fish consented to answer questions from the floor. I called upon one student who started off with an incipient speech as an exordium to the question he wanted to put. I began to call him to order but Mr. Fish asked me to let him have his say. When he was finished Mr. Fish replied to him at length. There was one other question from the floor from a person who took issue with Mr. Fish's position on deportation of aliens. Mr. Fish answered with a jest, and I took advantage of the laughter to thank him once more in the name of the Social Problems Club for his kindness in addressing the meeting and declared the assembly adjourned.

The letter of Mr. Iskiyan is quite symptomatic of the resentment which the intruder provoked in the minds of the audience. It is this quite justified resentment which probably accounts for the curious misstatements of fact the letter contains. First of all, to speak of a plot against Mr. Fish is nothing short of silly. Mr. Fish was secured on Thursday afternoon to speak on Friday. It was at his own request that I permitted any questions to be asked at all, and Mr. Fish was glad of the opportunity to answer them. The intruder was not even a student of the University, no less a member of the Social Problems Club. He probably would have acted in the same irresponsible manner no matter under whose auspices Mr. Fish had spoken. Mr. Fish told me that it was not the first time Communists had tried to break up his meetings. Indeed, it was the members of the Social Problems Club who were most indignant at the interruption. Had the intruder, who seems to me to have acted like an irresponsible crank, not left of his own accord, he would have been forcibly ejected. I have so far chairmaned three meetings of the Social Problems Club, addressed by Professor John Dewey, Mr. Heywood Broun,[3] and Representative Hamilton Fish respectively, and can certify that all the members of the Social Problems Club known to me acted with decorum, good taste, and good sense. I have made inquiries among other members of the faculty who have addressed the organization and have found that although one thought that some members were too exuberant, none thought they were ill-mannered.

Secondly, the Social Problems Club is *not* a communist organization. It is devoted to an impartial and objective analysis of contemporary social theory and problems. It is true that some of its members have communist sympathies, but many more of its members, including its leading officers, are non-communists. The communists are a vocally obstreperous lot, but *so far as I know* none is politically organized and never have they attempted to disturb a meeting. I am told that in inviting Mr. Fish the non-communists stole a march upon their communist friends. I have been called upon on occasion to arbitrate differences between the various groups within the organization. At all times I have impressed upon them the necessity of sober analysis and a tolerant, experimental attitude instead of noisy sectarian loyalties and uncritical faiths. I have reminded them that enthusiasm is an easy gift of youth, clear ideas a hard-won achievement. The Social Problems Club could not close its doors to communists without depriving them of perhaps their only opportunity to get an education in tolerant discussion and straight thinking.

The statement that the Social Problems Club has produced an unpleasant impression of N.Y.U. upon those who have spoken under its auspices is unwarranted. I recall with pride Professor Dewey's remarks to me about the intellectual eagerness of our students at Washington Square, as well as the tribute of both Mr. Broun and Mr. Fish to their political interest and intelligence.

Mr. Iskiyan's suggestion that the Social Problems Club be suppressed is unjustified, inexpedient and decidedly unAmerican. And Mr. Fish would be the first to brand it as such. Such action would (1) be punishing the Social Problems Club for an incident which by no stretch of the imagination can be laid at its door; (2) it would be penalizing *all* the members of the club because of the political sympathies of a *few;* (3) it would give these few an opportunity to pose as martyrs; (4) it would give the University a great deal of unhealthy publicity in organs of public opinion; (5) it would be depriving some students of the opportunity for intellectual self-expression which is so necessary for the growing mind, and consequently tend to fixate them in their uncritical views; (6) most important of all, it would go counter to the principle of liberalism and tolerance of all shades of opinion in the student body, which has so conspicuously marked the policy of the University.

In conclusion I wish to state that it is a mystery to me how the press received an account of the story. I noticed no newspapermen present, and would have taken all possible steps to prevent a garbled report from being sent out if I had suspected that any were.

1. James B. Munn, dean of Washington Square College, New York University.
2. Republican congressman from New York.
3. Correspondent for the Scripps-Howard newspaper chain.

3

My dear Mr. Herberg,[1]   August 15, 1931

I am glad to be advised of your interest in my writings on Marx and Marxism. You are of course aware of the fact that I am cautious about identifying the two. For some time I have been hard at work on a two-volume book on the philosophy of Karl Marx but due to chronic poor health and the pressure of other interests I am barely through with the first volume (which completes the historical analysis: the second volume—the more important—is straightforward analysis). The writings with which you are acquainted will give you a general indication of my point of view with the exception of Part II of the review of Lenin's *Empirio-Criticism* which appeared in the *Journal of Philosophy*. At that time I had not clearly enough distinguished between the Kautsky brand of orthodox Marxism and the revolutionary variety. The criticisms are intended against the would-be objective sociology of the vulgar Marxists among whom I include not only Kautsky, Hilferding and Cunow but Bukharin as well.[2]

In addition to the article you mention, I suggest you look at my review of Eastman's book,[3] his reply and my rejoinder, all in the *Modern Quarterly* 1928 (Vol. 4, #4 and Vol. 5, #1). Also my attack on Frank in the last number.[4] The substance of the second chapter of the first volume of my book will be found in the third volume of *Columbia Studies in the History of Ideas* (to be published in January) under the title of *Hegel and Marx.*[5] This is a 25,000-word essay on the systematic and methodological relationship between Marx and Hegel. Part of this may appear in the next no. of the *Mod. Quarterly.*

The outline of the course on Marx which I gave at the New School you will find in the special course bulletin entitled *Courses in Philosophy and Education* issued Jan. 5, 1931. The material, of course, is in my possession and will be incorporated in my book. Considerable of the historical portions of it I gathered during a 14-month stay in Germany (including two more at the Marx-Engels Institute in Moscow) as a research fellow examining original documents and contemporary cultural source material, especially on the Young Hegelians (the Bauers, Ruge, Koppen, Hess, Stirner, Strauss, Engels and others)[6] about whom someday I hope to write a separate book. But my primary interests in Marx as in everything else are not historical but analytical.

For a general indication of my views on technical problems of philosophy I refer you to articles in the *Journal of Philosophy* for 1926, 1927, 1928, 1929, and 1930 (see index of bound volumes); the *Monist* (1927); *International Journal of Ethics* (1927 and 1930); and *Mind,* forthcoming October issue (1931); *New Republic,* Vol. 63, #811 and 815. For my view on current events see reviews in *Current History,* Oct. 1930; March, 1931; May, 1931.

That ought to keep you busy for a while.

1. Will Herberg, American Marxist theoretician and spokesman for the Jay Lovestone faction. The Lovestonites denied the imminence of an American economic collapse, but not its inevitability, and argued that political tactics effective in Europe might not be effective in the United States. In June 1929 the American Communist Party expelled Lovestone, Herberg, and Bertram D. Wolfe as traitors to the working class. The Lovestonites then became known as the Communist Opposition. In the 1950s Herberg would become religious editor for the right-wing bi-weekly the *National Review.*

2. These were important Marxist thinkers during the early twentieth century. Karl Kautsky was the most influential of all Marxist intellectuals at this time and was known as "the pope of Marxism." Rudolf Hilferding was an Austrian Marxist economist who wrote on finance capitalism. Heinrich Cunow was a German Marxist anthropologist and philosopher known for his rejection of philosophical idealism. Nikolai Bukharin, a Bolshevik theoretician and politician, was accused in 1938 during the Soviet purges of being a Trotskyite and traitor to the Soviet Union and was then executed.

3. Max Eastman, *Marx, Lenin, and the Science of Revolution* (London, 1926).

4. Hook, "The Non-Sense of the Whole," review of Waldo Frank, *The Re-Discovery*

of America: An Introduction to a Philosophy of American Life, in *Modern Quarterly* 5 (Winter 1930–31): 504–13.

5. Actually it appeared as a three-part series in *Modern Quarterly,* 1931–32.

6. Bruno Bauer, Edgar Bauer, Arnold Ruge, Karl Koppen, Moses Hess, Max Stirner, David Friedrich Strauss, and Friedrich Engels.

4

Dear Herberg,[1]   May 29, 1932

I have found your letter very interesting and I shall try to clear up some of the points you have difficulty with. Excuse me for taking an inconsistency in your own formulation to illustrate the problem. If I can get you to think of the issue independently of the political party overtones and to follow the argument along, I have no doubt that we can see eye to eye on the main line.

On page 1 you wrote: "Now, of course, it is true that the class struggle enters constitutively into the material of the social sciences ('social facts') while it certainly does not do so in the material of the physical sciences. But is it not also true that the *present* class struggle (the only class struggle in which we are involved) does *not* enter constitutively into *past* 'social facts'? Why then is it not possible to study social development as scientifically as, let us say, geological development?"

On page 2 you add: "Now I maintain that the 'leading principles' (the direction of my research, my scientific 'logic,' but above all, my interpretation of results) I use in studying 'social facts' are themselves socially determined (here enters the class struggle!); but is this not also true of physical science? Are you ready to maintain that the recent turn towards idealism (even Berkeleyianism) in physics and biology (Jeans, Haldane) is not to be traced back to social-historical factors?"

"Scientific logic" and "interpretation" are intrinsic to science so that the second passage really implies that there is a class base to the physical as well as to the social sciences.

Now to begin with, you surely will not maintain that the philosophical, religious, artistic or whatnot *uses* to which science is put are part and parcel of scientific systems! To be sure, no science is possible without some social organization of a given degree of complexity, etc., but this explains *at best* only *why* science is undertaken not *what* it discovers. What possible class attitude is expressed in the proposition that the pressure of a gas varies inversely with its volume? What part of Newton's *Principia* is his confession of faith in the Almighty who works through laws? What part of

Eddington's[2] *The Mathematical Theory of Relativity* is his Quakerism? What scientists do and say outside of the laboratory on anything else but science can be explained in socio-political personal terms. But it is not science. That is why *no agreement is possible* about the sundry themes which engage them from the locus of God to woman's place in civilization. Peirce[3] once defined science as a method of settling doubt. And it is precisely because science can appeal to objective criteria that no controversy remains unsettled for long. Because I draw a distinction between physical and social science, you imply that I am denying the existence and objectivity of "social facts." "Is it not true," you ask, "that social facts exist just as objectively (i.e., independent of my scientific activity in reference to these facts) as do physical facts?" Of course they do! But there is a far cry from a "social fact" to a social science! Just as there is a far cry from a physical fact to a physical science. A science is not a series of facts—even a series of organized facts (malgre Huxley). Otherwise a dictionary would be a science. What makes Boyle's law scientific (p.v. = k) is that it can be deduced from theoretical assumptions about the distribution, velocity, elasticity, etc. of molecules of a perfect gas. What makes metrology not a science is that its propositions (assisting facts) are not *systematically* related. A fact by itself is the poorest thing in the world. It is a fact that slightly more boy babies are born than girls; that the percentage of children with cleft chins who have an I.Q. of more than a 100 is greater than of children with ordinary chins; that there is less suicide among Jews than non-Jews; that 99% of college students believe and act upon at least ten superstitions. But these facts and the hosts of others gathered by sociologists do not constitute a science.

Not only however do social facts which are unorganized fail to provide a basis for a science; the very organization of social facts into a system differs from the organization of physical facts. *Selection* enters into all science but in social science insofar as it is systematized a value-judgment is part of the selection. You seem to overlook this when you ask, "is it not also true that the *present* class struggle (the only class struggle in which we are involved) does *not* enter constitutively into *past* 'social facts'?" No, the class struggle does not enter into the historical fact that Alaric sacked Rome in 4ll A.D. But historical chronicle does not make historical science! Why did Rome fall? Now, in your terms, how do you account for the multitude of interpretations of the fall of Rome from Augustine down to Rostovtzeff?[4] Each age, each class *rewrites* the history of Rome even when the facts have remained the same. The present class struggle *does* enter into our systematic construction of the past (If I can find a reprint of an old article of mine on a critique of the historic-genetic method I shall send it to you). I would even go further and risk a paradox to the effect that the interpretation of the past depends upon how we want to act in the future—that an historical cause is that factor which we feel we must *change* in order to get desired results. Otherwise how distinguish between necessary and sufficient conditions of social change when as Engels admits there is a continuous reciprocity of all factors?

Now it does not follow that because I see things from a class point of view that therefore I fall into a hopeless relativism or skepticism about truth. No, any more than because the apple is red from one perspective and purple from another, I cannot pass true or false judgments about its color. Objective truth is possible (even in so highly personal an experience as love or hate) but my point is that the *very meaning of what it is to be objective* varies as we go from physics to sociology, from sociology to art. When you speak of the truth-destroying effect of class bias you imply that in all fields there is an objective absolute truth which is *the* truth and which would be seen by all if they could lower the blinders of class interest from their eyes. This seems to me, if you will permit the expression, a bit naive. It is as if someone were to say that *the* real color of the table is independent of any perspective from which it is seen, that the appearances (red, green, etc.) are to be judged by the degree to which they reflect or distort that real color. But outside of perspective there is no real color, just as outside of class attitude there is no "real truth" about the function of law and the validity of an economic theory.

You cite economics as an example of a possible social science. How do you imagine the soundness of the Marxian analysis will be demonstrated? It seems to me only by the revolutionary overthrow of capitalism and the development of a socialist commonwealth. Why? Because social action is not a controlled experiment but an irreversible activity on the basis of a class need and choice. Please explain "welfare economics," "institutional economics," "psychological econ.," "descriptive econ.," "math. econ." from your point of view. How would you go about *proving* the objective truth (in your sense) of the labor theory of value?

Yes, I am willing to accept the correspondence theory of truth. That's a change! But what does "to correspond" mean? When do we know, and how, that our ideas correspond with things except when our ideas enable us to control things. When I can say that "the united front above would often be a justifiable policy" with what must this proposition "agree" in order to be true? Test these propositions: "x is reliable," "$H_2 + 0 =$ water," "Jump!," "Look out!," "You have nothing to lose but your chains."

I do not accept Calverton's[5] theory of social compulsives. It is too simple: but I think Landy's[6] attack was scandalous. Bukharin and Deborin,[7] it seems to me, are muddled, and from the point of view of logical coherence, pitifully innocent.

The next issue of the *Modern Quarterly* contains the second half of my Hegel to Marx article. The June issue of *Current History* has a review of *Science at the Crossroads* which may interest you.

I liked your criticisms of Wilson[8]—but the subject is a big one and this letter is already too long.

1. Will Herberg.

2. Arthur Stanley Eddington, British astronomer, physicist, and mathematician.

3. Charles Sanders Peirce, nineteenth-century American philosopher and one of the founders of pragmatism.

4. Michael I. Rostovtzeff, Russian-born historian and author of histories of ancient Greece and Rome.

5. Victor F. Calverton, American Marxist literary critic and editor of the *Modern Quarterly*.

6. A. Landy, one of the theoreticians of the American Communist Party. For Landy's attack on Calverton, see Hook, *Out of Step*, p. 149.

7. Abram Deborin, leading Soviet Marxist philosopher of the 1920s. He was purged by Stalin in the 1930s.

8. Edmund Wilson, America's most prominent man of letters and author of *To the Finland Station* (New York, 1940).

5

Dear Herberg,[1]   June 6, 1932

You are right about the futility of attempting to settle the point at issue between us by correspondence. This summer I shall be teaching at the Square[2] (after July 5) and I hope you will be able to drop in for lunch and conversation.

Meanwhile I want to point out that in your argument you are playing both ends against the middle. In the social sciences you are arguing for a cultural objectivity, i.e., reduction to a formal science, which seems to me impossible to maintain; while in the physical sciences you are arguing for a cultural relativity or social subjectivism which makes science and mathematics appendages to the social disciplines. Now it seems to me that if either one of these positions is true, the other must be false; and that as a matter of analysis, they are both false. Take the latter first.

You say that Newton's conception of God "was an essential part of Newton's system." This is an amazing statement. What is your proof? Newton's say-so in his letters to Berkeley, and the 3rd book of the *Principia*? The only possible proof is to show that the propositions of the *Principia* can be *deduced* from his belief in a first cause or to show that the denial of any proposition (theorem) involves the denial of the religious premises which are presumably part of the system. How does Newton introduce God in deriving the laws of planetary motion from the formula for gravitation? Can you name one single theorem in whose proof God plays any part? At the best your sociological interpretation explains why and when people become interested in science, or subsidize or attack it, etc., but it cannot explain the meaning and validity of the science which is discovered. To be sure, the tendency to extend determinism to the understanding of phenomenon is conditioned by the socio-political milieu, but the point is that science is nothing if not deterministic (Heisenberg's indeterminacy principle notwithstanding) so that all that is explained is why and when science arises—which is altogether irrelevant to the *truth-value* of scientific propositions.

In the so-called social sciences, however, the class bias which you admit to be constitutive makes impossible the same degree of objectivity. You missed the point of my analogy between "objective social truth" and "the true color." I do not imply that without perception there can be no social facts. I am not a Berkeleian. But what I have said is that color: perspective: social truth: class bias. In a class-society there can no more be a classless truth in the social sciences (descriptive correlations which are quite meaningless until interpreted) than there can be *the real color* of an object independently of a perspective. From the point of view of any one perspective or any one class position, propositions are absolutely true or false, but class value is just as much an axiom in social analysis as perspective is in optics.

You have not yet told me whether you regard *economic factors* as the necessary or sufficient condition of social change. If you embrace my active theory of causation then you will have to modify your position on the identity of the causal concept in the physical and social sciences. The reasons are obvious.

I have found your questions stimulating and hope to continue the discussion with you sometime in July.

1. Will Herberg.
2. Washington Square, location of New York University campus in Manhattan.

6

Dear Schappes,[1]   February 22, 1933

Excuse the delay in answering your letter. Things are happening so fast that I haven't opportunity often to read my mail, no less answer it.

I want to thank you for your suggestions as to how I can improve my statement answering Jerome.[2] All of them were adopted and a revised draft submitted. But "they" have refused to accept any changes at all. They don't want a discussion—they want a pogrom.

About my alleged misquotation. I am sorry to say that you miss the point completely. First of all, I nowhere say that because Marx represented the interests of the proletariat, he was not scientific in his analysis of capitalism. My point is that no *system* of political economy can be free from a class bias and that this is what distinguishes it from real sciences. To be sure, detailed descriptions of one phase or another of the economic scene may be judged true or false independently of evaluating class attitudes; but a set of descriptions does not give a science, does not answer the question what makes *this* description relevant and *that* irrelevant. Marx's economic analysis was bound up with a program of revolutionary action just as Ricardo's[3] was even in his most "scientific" period. In the social sciences there is no classless point of view, for social knowledge implies social action in one direction or another, and wherever there are two classes there will be conflict about the ends and direction towards which human beings are to go. This conflict is the source of the normative considerations which unifies the set of "objective" descriptions. This difference between real science and "social science" flows from the difference in the subject matter of the two and cannot be explained away without making nonsense of Marx's thought, more accurately, without interpreting it as an objective idealism or religion.

Of course, the political economy of one class, in addition to being partial, may be dishonest and cook the facts. Or it becomes openly apologetic by merely stating its class point of view without the proper analysis. That is what Marx accused vulgar political economy of. But does that mean that classical economy was an "objective science" free from class presuppositions? I don't see how any one can assert that who has read Adam Smith, and least of all Marx who in his address to the First International contrasts the political economy of the bourgeoisie and the political economy of the proletariat. I discuss this question in greater detail in my book.[4]

But even aside from all this, I do not see how the sentence you quote from the *Symposium* article[5] logically implies what you say it implies. It is directed not against Marx but against Engels.

I think your place is in the League[6] because intellectually it is a freer working group than any other. The worst danger to the movement today— in addition to its leadership—is the accession of intellectuals for whom the iron-ribbed orthodoxy of the party offers a *personal* salvation of personal difficulties and who have therefore poked their critical eyes out of their head if they have ever had any. Several important political problems are here involved which we shall discuss at some other time.

I look forward with interest to reading your essay on Eliot.[7]

1. Morris Schappes, leader of the Communist Party unit at the City University of New York. Schappes taught English at CCNY.

2. V. J. Jerome, an American Communist Party cultural commissar, attacked Hook in "Unmasking an American Revisionist of Marxism," *The Communist* (January 1933): 50–82.

3. David Ricardo, early nineteenth-century British economist.

4. *Towards the Understanding of Karl Marx: A Revolutionary Interpretation* (New York, 1933).

5. Hook, "Towards the Understanding of Karl Marx," *Symposium* 2 (July 1931): 325–67.

6. League of Professional Groups, an American Communist Party front organization.

7. The poet T. S. Eliot.

7

Dear Mr. Dutt,[1]   ca. Summer 1934

I have just come across your contemptuous reference to my book *Towards the Understanding of Karl Marx* in the July issue of the *Labour Monthly*. When John Strachey[2] was here, he told me you were an honest man and I am prepared to believe it. Whether you have read my book or not, your party affiliation would impose upon you the necessity of referring to me in the manner you did.

But this does not settle any issues. Your dismissal of my book will not convince anybody who has read it, and it may interest you to know that more copies have been sold in England than in the U.S.A. Why not begin a further discussion on a Marxist basis on the questions that my book raises? Draw in, if you want to, my articles in the *Modern Monthly,* particularly my critique of the theory of social-fascism in the July issue which expressed, I think, the Stalinist view, to which you also subscribe.[3] This, in other words, is a challenge to a discussion. You may be as fierce as you please. I shall answer you in the pages of the *Labour Monthly* or, if your party does not permit such freedoms—elsewhere. You owe me this criticism because, so far as I can judge, you too do not believe that "Communism is inevitable no matter what." It was for denying this that I ran afoul of your party comrades in this country.

I do not share Cole's[4] position, but I think your criticism of his book is very unintelligent, despite the rhetoric and vehemence, as for example, you have challenged the distinction between Marx's method and Marx's conclusions which Cole, after me, makes. I wish to point out the following: 1—the distinction does not involve separation. 2—the correction to any specific conclusion is made by the further application of the Marxist method. 3— Marx believed a) that peaceful change to a classless society was possible in England and America, b) that a social revolution would be accomplished before the end of the century, c) that Morgan's[5] anthropological conclusions can be generalized. If Marx's method and conclusions were indissoluble, as you believe, then since you reject the truth of these specific conclusions, you would have to discard his method too. But of course Marxists would say these beliefs are false on good Marxian grounds, and they get different conclusions today by still using Marx's method.

I shall wait until September 15 for a reply from you to this invitation. If you are unwilling to carry on this discussion, I shall fire the first shot with a piece on the Marxism of R. P. Dutt.

1. R. P. Dutt, English Communist and editor of the *Labour Monthly*.

2. English Communist and author of *The Coming Struggle for Power* (London, 1932).

3. Hook, "The Fallacy of the Theory of Social Fascism," *Modern Monthly* 8 (July 1934): 342–52.

4. George D. H. Cole, author of *What Marx Really Meant* (London, 1934).

5. Lewis Henry Morgan, prominent nineteenth-century American anthropologist who influenced Engels.

8

Dear Comrade Stiller,[1]   July 26, 1934

I have just received and read your long and interesting letter and I must confess at the outset that I am not convinced of the truth of your position on any of the points you discuss. Before discussing one or two of them, I shall say a few things about the AWP.[2]

To begin with, the work of the AWP is being held up by a great lack of funds. In several parts of the country the situation is just crying to be led and organized by us but we lack strength and especially resources. This bears upon such things as pre-convention discussion and the convention data. The Ohio ULC and National ULC[3] took money and time and the convention *had* to be postponed on these most relevant grounds: also the pre-convention discussion period. As a matter of fact, your proposals *were* brought before the P.O.C.[4] and all the technical ones strongly supported by

Burnham.[5] (I was not there.) I do know that the P.O.C. is *aware* of your position on the Int'l [International] question and Trotskyism through Muste's exposition. (I have not read the office correspondence nor was I aware of its voluminous character.) The only man on the P.O.C. whose position on the Int'l is similar to yours is Hardman.[6] Most of the others are definitely opposed—they characterize it as Lovestoneism—and the rest feel that unity with the CLA[7] is so necessary for mass work and so sure to rally *all* communist groups (outside of the CP[8]) and left-wing socialists into one party that they have not yet taken a theoretical stance. The field-workers and practicals especially are keener about mass work than they are about the question of internationalism. I probably am the leftest of them all on the question of the 4th Int'l or rather the *call* for one, but I am not propagandizing for it and am prepared to wait until the Stalinists themselves drive them over to it.

Now about your argument. I do not at all see why it is a contradiction to share T's[9] general position and disagree with him on a particular tactic unless you can show that the tactic follows from the general position—which you do not.

1) General premise of T. and myself: the CI[10] is no longer revolutionary and cannot be reformed from within. The CI, minus its other sections, is the CPSU.[11]

2) T's tactic. Therefore build new parties in all countries *now* including the USSR.

3) My tactic. Therefore build new parties in all countries except the USSR. These new parties will be the best guarantees that the CPSU will reform, if at all, in the future. We might even invite it to join when we have built up a new int'l.

4) It would be perfectly compatible with my general position to urge as a specific tactic that no new parties be formed *today* in Uruguay (because of local conditions) or in a country where the Socialist Party gives evidence of going revolutionary tomorrow. Tomorrow I may advocate changing the tactic if conditions change enough. Your logic here is patently false.

What you say about the efforts of forming a new int'l can just as well be said—and I understand are being said—about your idea of a World Federation. I'm willing to run the risk of being regarded as a counter-revolutionist by the Stalinists. Every decent man must be.

If I were to believe what you do about the policies of Russia there would be no way out for me but to crawl to Canossa,[12] i.e., either recant and join the CP, or quit politics. Believing in your position would make it impossible to organize a new CP in *any* country. But let's look at the argument again. It's not I who am begging the question, and your observation that a perspective of peace does not *necessarily* entail national bolshevism—who said it does?—convinces me that I must be more explicit.

Both Trotsky and Stalin *say* they are internationalists. Both believe that the CP must build socialism in Russia as much as it can. The question is to discover whether the building of socialism is to be carried out in such a way that the rest of the international working class is to be considered *as least as much* as the Russians or not. That is to say: is Stalin a nationalist prepared to sacrifice other revolutions for what he conceives the state interests of the USSR to be? That is the question.

Now, in order to find this out, let us draw other facts into consideration. You accept my point 1 that at least thirty years would be necessary to build socialism (I think a 100) in Russia and my point 2 that this is, according to Stalin, Russia's main task. Now my point 3, which you admit is the king-pin of the rest of the argument—and which, as I shall show, you do not even touch—is that a revolution in any country in Europe would mean war. "Why," you say, "would Stalin have any objection to a successful revolution—a successful one would help Russia." No, my dear fellow, Stalin would have no objection to a successful one. But for it to be successful, *Russia would have to fight.* And every one knows that if Russia fights, then it is not *certain* that the revolution will be successful. But now, you say—and here is where you beg the whole argument—that "if Stalin's analysis of the objective conditions, etc., etc. leads him to believe that the revolution will not be successful" then it would be for the interests of the workers in all countries involved to prevent the revolution. (See your answers to my point 3 on page 6 of your letter.) A terrible logical blunder *because what we are trying to determine is whether Stalin is a national bolshevist or an internationalist*; the "if . . . he analyzes and comes to the conclusion that the interest of the workers in all countries demand this or that" is to *assume* that he is an internationalist already and you have cooked your case. It is just as if I were to argue "even if a revolution in other countries would be ultimately successful Stalin would try to kill it because it would diminish Russia's commanding position in the CI and Stalin's influence." If I argued that way I would be begging the question because I would be assuming Stalin was already an NB,[13] something I had set out to discover. Your statement in answer to my point 3 assumes the point you want to prove that Stalin eyes the situation like a true internationalist. You can prove anything this way.

Here is where the empirical evidence comes in. Here is where you must discuss Germany 1923, China 1927, Germany 1929–33 to find out whether Stalin proceeded like the internationalist you say he is or like an NB. I didn't want to discuss these things because I thought you were acquainted with them. But take Germany 1923. I have yet to meet any political group in Germany (including conservatives and Reichswehr men) who do not concede that a communist revolution in Germany in 1923 would have had the overwhelming majority of the population behind it—all except the Brandler-Thalheimer[14] group who were made the scapegoats by Stalin later. The left wing of the CP at that time, over Thaelheimer's head, placed in Stalin's hands an account of what was going on. But Stalin was angling for Rapallo.[15] So strong was the sentiment for revolt in Germany that large masses including many CP members struck loose anyhow against the sabotage of the CP in 1923–24–25. The treaty of Rapallo was followed by military understanding (broken only when Hitler came to power) with the Reichswehr which was supplied with arms by Russia, especially in 1924. It was the Reichswehr which crushed the workingclass revolt in Germany with great slaughter.

But now go on to every other major situation and crisis in Western Europe and China since 1924. You will find the same pattern. Always a consideration of the *immediate* needs of the Russian state and not the ultimate ones of the workingclass. *Even the capitalist class sees this.* These cases justify like all empirical evidence only *probable* inferences— but man alive, that is the only kind of inference that history allows. (Permit me to say that your chief weakness as a Marxist—so far as I have observed—is that you argue like a chess player when you approach *historical* problems. I have a tendency to formalism myself—it is a beloved weakness—but you are almost like a Platonist in your demand that "mathematical proof" (almost) be given for things which by their very nature can only be judged *empirically*—as more or less.) Now read the rest of the points, and you will see the force of my position.

You can't frighten me by trying to make it appear that my position can *honestly* be interpreted as a defense of war. Only a fool pacifist is against all wars. Marx approved of some, etc. Russia will have to fight sooner or later if she remains a workers' state. She may as well choose her own time and ground. Certainly she couldn't fight at a moment's notice but she must fight before the thirty years required to build socialism in Russia are up. If she doesn't, the workingclass movement throughout the world will be destroyed and Russia herself will definitely abandon her characteristic as a workers' state, many signs of which are already appearing. To avert this calamity, one or two revolutions in the West, which the CP won't make, are necessary. If Russia doesn't fight when Poland or France marches in to put down a German revolution, it's all over.

You mistake the point about Russia's peace pact. There are always military agreements for mutual assistance between her and capitalist nations. Today she is selling tanks to Turkey and tomorrow she will be selling tanks to Poland. Against whom will tanks be used? And yet you can say that there are no contradictions between her policy and the interests of the international workingclass? Russia is not thinking of a war to be fought in the interests of the whole international workingclass. She is thinking about a war of defense. And how is she defending herself? By giving proper counsel to revolutionary movements in the world? Not at all—but by entering into pacts with capitalist powers. When the next war breaks out—even the Russians say this—Russia will be one of a bloc of capitalist powers fighting another bloc. And then 1914 will repeat itself. Communists will say *Our Workers' Fatherland* is in danger, to support the USSR we must support our government which has made a bloc with her. (Or they may do something stupidly provocative and let themselves be liquidated by their capitalist government so that they can have a clear (!?) conscience.)

Well, I can go on and on discussing every point you make and showing that all the time you are begging the question at issue, dismissing the empirical evidence and exhibiting an unconditioned reflex of positive tropism wherever Russia is concerned. This must have its source in something other than your critical intelligence. How do *you* analyze it? Don't simply negate these sentences and hurl them back at me for my views on Russia have, so to speak, cost me blood.

I can't discuss Soviet (. . .) workers democracy v. dictatorship of the proletariat here. Suffice it to say that I regard this question as the first question—far more important and fundamental than the international question, the USSR, or the existence of the AWP—if being a Marxist means to accept the dictatorship of the party as preached by Trotsky and practiced by Stalin, I am not a Marxist. There can be no socialism without freedom for workers of all kinds who accept collectivism in the means of production; and there can be no freedom with a party dictatorship. The trouble is that we always think of *ourselves* as exercising the dictatorship, and, therefore . . . with the "democratic support" (what a mockery is concealed in that phrase) of the masses behind us. As an individual I would rather die than not be able to say that Lenin was mistaken in much of his technical philosophy, that Marx acted like a petty bourgeois philistine on many occasions in his life and not as a lionhearted revolutionist, that Trotsky is religious, that Stalin is—well, I don't want to write a book. The freedom that workers have under capitalism doesn't mean much because of the existence of capitalism; but they must have no less freedom under what is called the dictatorship *of* the proletariat. Certain things are going on in Russia which worry me a great deal. Why close one's eyes to them?

I must ask you again to return this letter or a copy of it.

I do not wish to conclude without telling you that although I am in emphatic disagreement with you so far, I like your criticisms because they are at least *argued*—and sometimes very acutely indeed. You say in your letter you are quite young and I know nothing of your political antecedents and development. I do not mean to be presumptuous but I think it will help you, as well as the movement, if you try to get as much formal training as possible and spread out into other fields. Stay in the AWP at least until the convention and then if you break away (or I) and someday we meet on opposite sides of the barricade we will wrap our bullets up in arguments. At present you ought to publish more.

1. Allen Stiller.
2. Hook, Abraham J. Muste, and James Burnham organized the American Workers Party in 1934. Hook in his autobiography described it as "an authentic American party rooted in the American revolutionary tradition, prepared to meet the problems created by the breakdown of the capitalist economy, with a plan for a cooperative commonwealth expressed in a native idiom intelligible to blue collar and white collar workers, miners, sharecroppers, and farmers without the nationalist and chauvinist overtones that had accompanied local movements of protest in the past. It was a movement of intellectuals, most of whom had acquired an experience *in* the labor movement and an allegiance to the cause of labor long before the advent of the Depression."
3. Unemployment Leagues organized by the American Workers Party.
4. The Provisional Committee to Organize the American Workers Party.
5. James Burnham, independent Marxist scholar and professor of philosophy at New York University.
6. J. B. S. Hardman, editor of *The Advance,* the organ of the Amalgamated Clothing Workers of America.
7. Communist League of America, a Trotskyist organization.
8. Communist Party.
9. Leon Trotsky.
10. Communist International.
11. Communist Party of the Soviet Union.
12. Meeting place of Pope Gregory VII and Emperor Henry IV in 1077. Henry waited for three days before Gregory received him. The name Canossa denoted the submission of secular power to the Church.
13. National Bolshevist.
14. Heinrich Brandler and August Thalheimer, German Communist leaders who called off an October 1923 Communist uprising.
15. The 1922 Russian-German treaty by which Germany became the first major power to extend *de jure* recognition to the Soviet government. Germany also provided the USSR credit to purchase German industrial products. Other major Western nations, with the exception of the United States, soon followed Germany's lead in recognizing the USSR. The United States did not recognize the Soviet Union until 1933.

9

Dear John,[1]   August 30, 1935

   Mail comes slowly to this little hamlet in an out of the way corner of
Vermont, so that I have only just seen your review of John Dewey's *Liberalism and Social Action.* And for once I think you have gently nodded. As
you know, my own disagreements with Dewey on some things are very
considerable and I am not what you would call a "softy" on questions of
logical rigor, but I believe Dewey's book is the most remarkable piece of
political writing of our generation.

   The reason is simple. The book is an attempt to present a set of values
and a *method* of testing them which enables any intelligent person, i.e., one
who does not hold his beliefs as a priori dogmas, to evaluate between
various alternative social systems. Your review *seems* to suggest that the
choice between socialism, capitalism and fascism is an *arbitrary* one and
that there is no way by which we can establish the relative superiority of
one or the other on different points. To be sure, even on Dewey's theory,
there is an *arbitrary* element in our choice but it appears as an *ultimate*
element, after the critical evaluation of our ends, the means of our achieving
them, and the cost in the sacrifice of these ends has been completed. To
deny the essential difference between a social view arbitrarily asserted *before* reflection and one accepted *after* reflection is to overlook (a) the fact
that social views are often changed as a result of critical analysis, and (b)
that there must exist some set of values which guide the ultimate choice
when it is made.

   Let me state this a little differently in the form of an exception to a
sentence of yours. You maintain that the term *liberal* can only be used
adjectivally and not substantively—that there are liberal capitalists, liberal
socialists, liberal Fascists, etc., but that there is really no such thing as
liberalism. Now if liberalism were *only* an adjective characterizing some
political faith, then the question of *whether* and *why* one should be liberal
becomes one of mere expediency since it is decided by considerations
flowing from the political system it qualifies. But, then, how do we evaluate
between alternative social systems? Is it a matter of personal taste? Why
quarrel about tastes? Indeed, if only tastes are involved there can be no
quarrel since when we differ you are merely talking about your taste and
about mine—two different things. The implication of your views seems to
be that every social system is the judge of itself and that no normative

considerations are relevant except as judgments of proper means. Along that path there is no escape from the Hegelian dictum that "whatever is is right."

It seems to me that liberalism (as distinct from the economics of laissez-faire) represents a social, and in the last analysis, an ethical philosophy. It is a social philosophy with a varying content but relatively invariant form. Its fundamental values are respect for the intrinsic worth of personality, freedom of intellectual inquiry, intelligence, social democracy and what for lack of a better term might be called spiritual charity. There are conflicts between these values in concrete cases but this is true of every genuine ethical situation. The opposite of liberalism as a social philosophy is illiberalism whose values are exemplified today in Germany, Italy and in a lesser degree in Russia.

Lest you regard it as anomalous that a Marxist comes to the defense of liberalism in this sense, let me remind you that it was none other than Marx who proclaimed that "the proletariat regards its courage, self-confidence, independence and sense of personal dignity as more necessary than its daily bread." Socialism as an economic system simply extends the sphere within which liberalism as a social philosophy may operate. As you very properly point out, Dewey in his *Liberalism and Social Action* acknowledges himself to be a socialist. Of that there can no longer be any doubt. The chief difference which remains between him and the Marxists is one of fact, viz, whether the classes entrenched in

[Rest of the letter is missing.]

1. John Chamberlain, left-wing writer.

10

Dear Mr. Lindsay,[1]   June 29, 1936

A friend of mine has just sent me a clipping of your review of my book *From Hegel to Marx*. I do not know the address of *The Observer* and so I am taking the liberty of writing to you directly in answer to the objections you have raised.

(1) To begin with, I do not think it quite fair to me to imply that since I start "by assuming that the philosophy of Karl Marx was the last word of human wisdom, then those who contributed to producing that last word are of great importance." I do not believe that Karl Marx or any one else has

said the last word on anything, and I am puzzled as to the grounds upon which you impute this belief to me. In fact I am even willing to admit that from the standpoint of technical philosophy Karl Marx was no philosopher at all; but then it is easy to rule out most philosophers by arbitrary definitions of philosophy. All I have asserted is that a knowledge of the doctrines of the men who influenced Marx is of great importance to an understanding of the thought of Marx. Since there was nothing on the subject with which I was acquainted, I set myself to this task. I am a little shocked that you should take me to mean that before anyone can understand Marx, he must agree with Marx, or assume that his philosophy is the last word of human wisdom.

(2) A more important point is your criticism of the experimental theory of truth present *in nuce* in Marx's thought and developed, independently of him, by John Dewey. You allow that in the natural sciences an hypothesis ultimately involves the transformation of the materials of a situation in order to determine, on the basis of the *predicted* outcome, its relative probability as opposed to alternative hypotheses. I do not see that the logic of inquiry is any different from social affairs once allowance is made for the differentiating character of the subject matter. It is not the case that on the experimental theory the facts *to be known* are altered in the process of inquiry: the action is directed to those phases of the situation which must be transformed in order to yield the relevant data for a conclusion.

Take Marx's theory about social classes (your own illustration). This falls into two parts. (a) There is a class struggle, defined certain ways, which exercises a pervasive influence upon legislation, law, education, arts, morals, etc. (b) The liberation of human beings from the effects of this class struggle (a value judgment) can be effected only by the successful prosecution of this struggle until socialism triumphs. (a) is an hypothesis of fact which, once the terms are defined, is tested by investigation. In the course of this investigation, certain *operations* are performed. We read, we travel, we interrogate, we use questionnaires and other instruments of social science, and if the results are what we antecedently predicted them to be, our hypothesis is insofar confirmed. The results are not altered or cooked in the activity of testing; only the relevant phases of the situation are altered. After the experiment is over, one might say that "the hypothesis is and always has been true." But what does this mean? Was the hypothesis true when there were no classes? It is the hypothesis or statement which is declared to be true. But hypotheses and statements do not exist *in rerum natura*. They have implied temporal coefficients. Is there any more evidence that an hypothesis—which on the basis of the predicted consequences or experiment—we *now* accept as valid *has always been true* than there is that it *will* always be true? Laws of nature have histories. What is the operational meaning and scientific evidence for your claim that my hypothesis about matter of fact "is and has always been true"? A theory of truth to be intelligible must be a description of the way in which propositions are validated. In this lies the superiority of the experimental theory.

The second part of Marx's theory about social classes (b) states that *if* classes are to be abolished, the only effective way of doing it is such and such. This proposition asserts something to be true (makes a prediction) independently of whether one accepts the antecedent clause. A Tory will hold that classes should be preserved. That is a value judgment. Value judgments have causes about which true propositions can be made. But "values" are not true any more than preferences are "true." Values may be intelligent, i.e., chosen after reflection upon the probable consequences of believing and acting upon them. But after the reflection has been performed and we agree upon the probable consequences of espousing value "x" as opposed to "x^1", I do not see what sense it makes to say that " 'x' is truer than 'x^1'." Values are the objects of any interest. Interests *may* be altered by reflection: and interests *may* be common: but there is no necessity that they be.

I wish now to examine your illustration about Hitler and the Jews. What is the hypothesis to be proved? You do not make this clear. Is it (1) that the Jews *are* hateful or mad? Or (2) that if certain things are done, the German people can be made to believe that the Jews are hateful or mad?

How would you prove (1)? We must first define hateful. Roughly, an object or person is hateful if many people usually experience a feeling of revulsion to it (or him). How do we test the proposition that a certain group of people find the Jews hateful? By performing certain *operations*—psychological tests, questionnaires, etc.—i.e., by changing the *relevant* features of the situation, so that we can gather evidence of their reactions. We do not first infect them with anti-Semitism and then test their reactions to Jews any more than in testing whether a man has malaria we begin with infecting him with the disease.

(2) states that if the Jews are accused of horrible atrocities, you can make people hate them. How would one test this proposition? In the same way as we test the proposition that if we feed arsenic to a dog it will die, i.e., by carrying out the relevant changes in the situation suggested by the antecedent clause. But why should we accuse the Jews of horrible atrocities or feed arsenic to dogs? That is a moral question. Unfortunately, a great many truths are far from being edifying, Hegelians to the contrary notwithstanding. On the basis of past history and what Mr. Hitler has done I am prepared to grant the truth of the proposition that if the Jews are accused of horrible

atrocities, people will find them (or anyone for that matter) hateful. Because I believe this is true, I hold that the circulation of atrocity stories about Jews should be a penal offense. I do not believe, however, that the hypothesis "if the Jews are accused, etc., then . . ." "is and always has been true."

Where in all of this do you find "sauce for the Nazi gander?" On an implication that lies cannot be more powerful than truth, or that whatever is is right! I can show with cogency that it is Hegel's theory of truth, not Marx's, that might determines not only what is right but what is true.

(3) In my preface I argue against the irrationalist wing of current-day Marxism that the fact that philosophic doctrines are conditioned by social circumstances does not prejudice the question of their validity. False doctrines as well as true ones are socially conditioned; therefore the difference between truth and falsity cannot be socially determined. Otherwise Marxism itself would be in the same class as the doctrines it rejects. I do no merely "allow" this logical difficulty, I urge it as forcibly as I can.

To my surprise you reproduce this argument and direct it against me, implying that to prove that a philosophy is socially conditioned is to *discredit* it. Neither I nor (what is more important) Marx have asserted any such thing. If Marx believed this how could he accept certain elements of Hegel's method (and Aristotle's too) since Hegel's philosophy was conditioned by the social milieu? How could he have accepted the Pythagorean theorem and the Copernican hypothesis? The fact that a theory which is accepted as true is conditioned by its day and age does not prejudice its truth for another day and age. It *may* still be true; and if it is proven false it is not because society has changed but because either better instruments of precision have been discovered or the subject matter in question has changed. A great many truths have been discovered by philosophy which are on the same footing as scientific truths generally.

There is, however, an aspect of philosophy which concerns itself with values. These values are related to social interests, and as interests change, these values are no longer regarded as adequate, e.g., Aristotle's conception of the good life and his glorification of the high-minded or magnanimous man whose portrait resembles a prosperous Greek slave owner; or the ideals of Dante, Castiglione, Erasmus, Calvin, Bentham, etc. Even here we do not discredit these ideals by trying to explain them. And since there is a continuity in the social heredity of western civilization, since our language and education have created some social and individual interests which we imaginatively identify with the past, we acknowledge a relatively permanent element in some feature of the Greek, Roman and Renaissance ethos.

(4) I am afraid that my footnote reference to you as one among other neo-Hegelians who wrote patronizingly of Marx has been misunderstood.

No offense was intended. I have profited from your little book on Marx and acknowledged as much.[2] What I had in mind was your observation, repeated in your review, that Marx did not understand Hegel. *Won't you make explicit in what respect?* I ask not as a challenge but in genuine quest for enlightenment. I have studied Hegel for many years and am gathering material for a book on him. It seems to me that next to Gans,[3] Marx (and Lasalle) came closer to grasping the meaning of Hegel than any of the post-Hegelians.

(5) I agree that Bauer, Ruge, Stirner, and Hess (and Engels) were not distinguished thinkers. But you underestimate the intellectual force of Strauss whose mind was as sharp as a blade and the genial insights of Feuerbach.[4] These men belong in any history of philosophy independently of their relation to Marx.

(6) One last point in this already overlong letter. I could not escape the impression in reading your review that you identify my version of Marxism with the current Stalinist brand. To my way of thinking there are two irreconcilable cultural struggles in the world today. One is between Fascism and socialism. The other is between experimental democratic Marxism and dogmatic authoritarian Marxism which is now the state religion of Russia. As far as philosophy and freedom of intellectual inquiry are concerned, both Germany and Russia are charnel houses of the human mind.

1. Alexander D. Lindsay.
2. Lindsay, *Karl Marx's Capital: An Introductory Essay* (London, 1925).
2. Eduard Gans, a Hegelian philosopher whose lectures Marx attended while in Berlin.
3. Ludwig Feuerbach, nineteenth-century German student of religion who influenced Marx's belief that religion was the opiate of the masses.

11

Dear T. V. Smith,[1]   February 18, 1937

Just a brief line to point out that it is not necessary to be a sectarian to believe in the right of political asylum or to believe that it is important that the truth should be made known. As far as most of the members of our Committee[2] are concerned, and you know many of them, they are in perfect agreement with your sentiments of "Fie on both their houses." But it has nothing to do with this case, tra la, any more than the flowers that bloom in the spring, tra la.

I do not know whether you believe me to be a sectarian, but you certainly cannot believe that of men like Dewey, Kallen,[3] Franz Boas[4] and a score of others who have been in the forefront of the fight for civil liberties in this country.

As I wrote you last time, this Committee is interested in issues which far transcend in importance the warfare between sectarians. I know that if you had been asked to sign a statement asking for an open hearing for Galileo or even Jan Hus or Dreyfus, you would not have replied that to sign such a statement commits you to one sect rather than another.

I hope that you will reconsider your decision not to join our Committee. If the pressure of other work makes it impossible for you to join us, can you send us an endorsement of our declared purposes?

1. Professor of philosophy, University of Chicago, and member of the Illinois State Senate.
2. Committee for the Defense of Leon Trotsky.
3. Horace M. Kallen, American philosopher best known for espousing cultural pluralism.
4. Franz Boas, professor of anthropology, Columbia University, and member of the American Committee for Intellectual Freedom and Democracy, a Communist Party front organization.
5. Captain Alfred Dreyfus, imprisoned in France in the 1890s for espionage.

12

Dear Professor Davis,[1]   February 18, 1937

I have read your letter of February 15th with amazement. At present it is impossible for me to come to New Haven to talk to you, which I should very much like to do because I have plenty to say.

Until we meet, however, I should like to indicate the following. In my original letter, I wrote to inquire whether you had signed a statement by Miss Van Kleeck,[2] drawn up at the behest of the Communist Party, denouncing the American Committee for the Defense of Leon Trotsky, which includes in its membership scores of people known to you as valiant fighters on behalf of civil liberties here and throughout the world. In your reply you write as if I had invited you to join our Committee, and giving your reasons why you cannot do so. This is beside the point. What I should like to know is, not why you cannot join our Committee, but why you consider it necessary to lend your name to a shameful and disreputable attack upon our Committee and its purposes. It is this which puzzles many of your friends on our Committee, particularly those who have been fighting on the Davis case.[3]

If you subscribe to the statements expressed in Miss Van Kleeck's letter, you are impugning the integrity and honesty of men who have, until now, believed in your integrity and honesty. I should like to know on what evidence you make such grave accusations.

You may say that, as you understand it, "(1) Trotsky's right to an asylum is guaranteed; (2) he has complete freedom to present any evidence he has."

Your first statement is both false and disingenuous, for Trotsky's right to asylum is not guaranteed and secondly you imply that you favor his right to political asylum. If so, why did you not come out with a statement to that effect, particularly last Fall, when Trotsky was in acute jeopardy of being handed over to the Russian authorities? All the signers of Miss Van Kleeck's letter say that now that Trotsky has political asylum, the Committee should dissolve. How many of them have ever defended his right to political asylum? Not a single one! That is why I regard your first statement as disingenuous.

As for your second statement, you have misunderstood the purpose of our Committee, which is to urge the organization of a Commission of Inquiry before which Trotsky can answer the allegations made against him at the Moscow Trials. The Committee itself does not constitute such a Commission. What the liberal world wants is not to give Trotsky freedom to present "*any* evidence that he has," but to discover the truth about that evidence as well as the evidence which came to light in the Trials. You add: "The only thing that surprises me is that he has not presented this evidence before, if he has any." I overlook the peculiar logic and ethics implied by this statement. But to whom do you expect Trotsky to present his evidence?

Are not his evidential claims on (a) the Bristol and Sedov incidents;[4] (b) the Pyatakov airplane flight;[5] and (c) the Rome meeting, all of which Trotsky claims to have been mythical, sufficient to raise at least a doubt in your mind? All that the Committee desires to accomplish on these matters is to get a Commission of Inquiry going which will examine these questions and numerous others on which Trotsky claims to have conclusive evidence. Even if a person is convinced of Trotsky's guilt, he should be in favor of a commission to confirm the fact of his guilt, if it is a fact, and in this way allay worldwide distrust of the Russian government, which is being identified, unfortunately, with the Hitler government in fundamental respects.

But I return once more to the question of why you signed Miss Van Kleeck's letter, objectively serving, independently of your own intentions, as a tool of the Communist Party. You write to me, "I recognize there are two ways of looking at this and if you feel that you can secure the truth by having a Committee you, of course, should do what you think will help to bring truth." If you grant the right of the Committee to do what it thinks necessary to help bring out the truth, how can you, at the same time, denounce us as people who do not want the truth? I grant your right not to join our Committee, but I do not grant your right to slander our Committee and to assert, as the Van Kleeck letter does, that it is counter-revolutionary, anti-Soviet and indirectly aiding armed intervention into Russia and similar nonsense.

Under the circumstances, I think that if you will reflect, you will come to the conclusion that you owe it to yourself and to those like Dewey, Norman Thomas, Kallen, Franz Boas and the rest of us on the Committee, to disavow in the strongest possible fashion the allegations of the Van Kleeck letter. Believe me, my dear Professor Davis, the Van Kleeck document does not hurt me as much as it does its signers. It reveals them as ideological fellow travelers of totalitarian intolerance, and makes it impossible to give any credence to their professions of liberalism and humanism.

1. Jerome Davis, professor of sociology, Yale University Divinity School.
2. Mary Van Kleeck, social worker and director of industrial studies, Russell Sage Foundation.
3. In 1936 Yale University told Davis that he would not be reappointed due to financial restraints. Davis's supporters argued that this was a violation of academic freedom, and that Davis was in fact let go because of his politics, including support for the USSR and the American labor movement.
4. Soviet accusation that Leon Sedov, Trotsky's eldest son, met Soviet traitors at the Hotel Bristol in Copenhagen in 1932. He then supposedly accompanied them to Trotsky's apartment where Trotsky instructed them to commit terrorist acts against Soviet leaders. In actuality, the Bristol Hotel had been destroyed in 1917. Sedov died in France in 1938 under mysterious circumstances.
5. Georgy Leonidovich Pyatakov, Bolshevik economist and one of the architects of Soviet industrialization, was executed in 1937 for supposedly holding secret meetings with Trotsky and for plotting with the Nazis. One of the charges against him stated that he had flown from Berlin to Oslo for a secret meeting with Trotsky. These meetings never took place. He was exonerated by the Soviet Supreme Court in 1988.

13

Dear Professor Lovejoy,[1]   February 18, 1937

Thank you for your frank letter of February 16th. It has made me realize that my first communication was unclear in several important respects.

1. The American Committee for the Defense of Leon Trotsky has two objectives: (a) to help safeguard his right to political asylum, which has now been assured, (b) to urge the formation of a Commission of Inquiry, before which he can present evidence in his possession bearing on the

allegations made against him at the Moscow Trials. The American Committee is emphatically not to constitute itself the Commission of Inquiry. It merely urges the justice of having such a commission organized and will retire from the scene when such a commission comes into existence (assuming that the asylum issue does not become focal again). The members of this Commission will not be members of the Committee. It is hoped that men of the calibre of Bertrand Russell,[2] Charles A. Beard,[3] Zachariah Chafee,[4] etc. will consent to serve on the Commission of Inquiry. The possible exception to the foregoing might arise in the event that John Dewey or Franz Boas, who are at present on our Committee, may desire to serve.

2. I agree with you that the name of the Committee is rather unfortunate, but it is not a serious obstacle when it is understood that the Committee itself will not be the tribunal of inquiry. I joined the Committee after its name had been chosen, and I understand that the reason for the name originally was that the efforts of the Committee were concentrated upon defending Trotsky's right of political asylum—the first of the two objectives of the Committee. When the Committee was first organized, Trotsky was in great jeopardy of being handed over, even without extradition proceedings, to the Russian government. There are practical reasons which make it difficult to change the name of the Committee at present. This will be decided at a membership meeting in the near future.

I wish to stress the fact that it is possible for people to join the Committee who believe (a) that Trotsky is innocent, (b) that Trotsky is guilty, and (c) that suspension of judgment is necessary. The necessary and sufficient condition for membership on our Committee is the belief that it is desirable that the truth be established on a matter which transcends in importance the issues involved in the Dreyfus case[5] or the Reichstag fire trial.[6]

I am enclosing a memorandum of Professor Brissenden,[7] who shares your scepticism about the practicability of a Commission of Inquiry, but who feels strongly about its desirability.

If, upon reconsideration, you accede to your initial impulse to join our Committee, we shall be very gratified. There is no one in this country whose reputation for intellectual incorruptibility is greater than yours, and I am convinced that we will more surely carry out the purposes of our Committee if you will join with us in our common quest to make the truth known.

1. Arthur O. Lovejoy, professor of philosophy, Johns Hopkins University, and the first secretary of the American Association of University Professors (AAUP).
2. British philosopher.

3. American historian and author of *An Economic Interpretation of the Constitution* (New York, 1913).

4. Professor, Harvard Law School, and authority on civil liberties.

5. The controversy surrounding the imprisonment of Captain Alfred Dreyfus for espionage. See letter 11, note 5.

6. Burning of the Reichstag on February 27, 1933. By blaming Communists for the fire, the Nazis were able to consolidate their control of the government.

7. Paul F. Brissenden, professor of economics, Columbia University.

14

Dear Mr. Davis,[1]   February 25, 1937

This is to acknowledge receipt of your communication of 2/22. The statements contained therein lead me to believe that despite my long letter you have failed to grasp my meaning, perhaps more accurately, I have failed to make myself clear. So once more I am sending you an interim statement.

You write, "I do not believe that the Trotsky investigation will accomplish anything worthwhile. In this I may be mistaken." This is a sufficient reason for not joining our committee, although many people have joined in order to express their belief in the desirability of such an investigation. But my question to you was, "why did you attack our committee, consisting of so many people known to you, as faithless to their declared intentions, tools of Trotskyites, objectively enemies of the Soviet Union, etc." These are serious charges. And they are stated in almost so many words in the Van Kleeck letter which appeared in the *Daily Worker*. On what evidence? Did you make an attempt to check the evidence? You say that you interpreted the Van Kleeck letter differently. But by no canons of logic or exegesis known to me can you explain away the fact that you charged us, among other false and horrendous things, with (I quote from the Van Kleeck letter), "political intervention in the internal affairs of the Soviet Union with hostile intent." And all because we want to find out the truth about Trotsky's guilt or innocence, the truth about charges made against a man who formally has not even been tried and convicted. Don't you believe that it is worthwhile to try to find out the truth? And if you believe you already have it don't you believe that it is worthwhile to have it disseminated?

You believe, so you write, that "the men who were convicted in Moscow on their own confession were guilty." Does this mean that you believe that Trotsky who has *not* confessed and claims that the whole thing is a frame-up is also guilty? Perhaps he is. The Committee has no view on the matter.

All it holds is that the cause of humanity would be served if it were made known whether T. is innocent or guilty. I find myself bewildered that I should be arguing with *you* about this most elementary human right. Have fundamental principles become so blurred? The dedication of your last book is "to all whose faith in social justice impels to action." I could place hundreds of passages from your books into startling juxtaposition with the Van Kleeck letter.

As for the Van Kleeck letter and the proof for my statement that it was drawn up at the behest of the C.P. More about this when I see you. In the meantime let me remind you of something that everybody around these parts knows, particularly people in the S.P.[2] *viz.,* that this is no new role for Miss Van Kleeck. In 1934 when the Madison Square Vienna protest meeting[3] was broken up by the C.P., twenty-four intellectuals wrote a letter to the *New Masses* and *Daily Worker* condemning that action. The C.P. responded with a mass meeting denouncing the signers. Do you know who were the chief speakers? Earl Browder[4] and Mary Van Kleeck. Have you read the Civil Liberties Union report on that Madison Square Garden meeting incident? Please send for it. Do you know who the minority was which contended that the Socialist Party broke up its own meeting because it provoked the Communist Party by inviting speakers the Communists didn't like? Bob Dunn (a C.P. member and honest) and Mary Van Kleeck. With the change of line of the C.P. the lady was assigned to the liberal and labor front—particularly the American Labor Party. The tendency she represents in the Am. Lab. Party is well known here. Make your own discreet inquiries among people who are not under suspicion of being Stalinists or Trotskyists. Ask Mary Fox or Mary Hillyer or Waldman and the right-wing socialists or the local C.I.O.[5] people. Miss Mary Van Kleeck is what is known as a "Communist Party stooge," always in the position of denying that she is a member of the C.P. (she has no party card of course) but carrying out assignments according to C.P. directives. The Russell Sage Foundation letterhead and her *past* reputation take a great many people in. James Waterman Wise,[6] the other instigator of the letter against our committee, who although not a member of the C.P. makes no secret of his conversion to the Stalin brand of communism, is another "stooge." These people have a right to circulate any letters and call themselves anything they please. A statement may be true, even if the source is dubious. It is the statement in their letter which I object to, and which because you signed I hold you responsible for it also, and not the fact that *they* instigated the campaign of slander against our committee. They were doing their duty. You however did something which contradicts the whole tenor of your thought and life for the last 25 years.

Forgive what may appear as a personal note in this letter and in the last. I meant to be not "scathing," as you say, but merely frank. But perhaps the appearance of subjectivity may be accounted for by the following. Everybody known to me on the committee who was in a position to do so has rallied around the Davis case.[7] I, myself, to mention only one incident which comes to mind, spent my time at the Cambridge meeting of the American Philosophical Association circulating petitions, arguing with others (some of the Yale contingent were particularly adamant), etc. In the nature of the case you came to symbolize, by the natural process of association and substitution, the very principles of equity and justice for defending which you are now being victimized. What a shock to me, to Dewey, to many others to find you lined up with the forces of darkness; not merely differing with us, which is your perfect right, but attacking us for applying to another case, one at least as important as your own, the same principles of justice and liberalism to which you have sworn allegiance before the whole world. My mind cannot encompass the fact still.

My first guess was that either your name had been forged or that you had signed in carelessness, without the relevant facts at hand. I still believe the latter, despite the reasons you have offered. I know I am a poor psychologist. Perhaps the "reasons" are a result of the personal tone I have unwittingly permitted to creep into these lines. But there are some things which are more sacred to me than psychology or diplomacy, and I cannot compromise on them.

I am not presuming to suggest to you what you should do. One can only think and follow the inner light, if we have courage enough.

1. Jerome Davis.
2. Socialist Party.
3. Meeting in February 1934 sponsored by the Socialist Party to honor socialist workers in Vienna who had been shot down by Austrian troops. Communists, attempting to take over the rally, caused a riot.
4. General secretary of the Communist Party of the United States and Communist candidate for president in 1936 and 1940. He was expelled from the party in 1946.
5. Congress of Industrial Organizations.
6. A spokesman for the American League against War and Fascism, a Communist front organization.
7. See letter 12, note 3.

15

Dear Rabbi Wise,[1]   March 6, 1937

This will acknowledge receipt of your communication of March 3rd. I find the tone of your letter so puzzling and its contents so irrelevant to the invitation[2] addressed to you that I can only account for them on the hypothesis that you have misunderstood the substance of my first communication. Under the circumstances, I feel it is incumbent upon me to make the position of the American Committee for the Defense of Leon Trotsky so clear that nothing but deliberate will to misunderstand will be able to obscure its meaning.

You state that you fully concur with us in believing that the right of political asylum should be upheld and the truth should be made known. You assert, however, in answer to this point, that there is no reason "in view of Mr. Trotsky's present domicile in Mexico, to provide him such an asylum." You may not be aware of the fact that when the present Committee was organized, Leon Trotsky had no right to asylum, but was threatened with deportation, without extradition proceedings, to Russia. Our Committee was instrumental in securing a haven for him in Mexico. Among the reasons for activity in his behalf on this particular issue was the realization that, if the right to political asylum were not upheld in his case, it would not be safe in the cases of thousands of others throughout the world.

Now that Trotsky has political asylum, this issue is no longer acute, but there is no more guarantee that he will continue to have political asylum in Mexico than he had in Norway, a country which was compelled, by the economic pressure of the Russian government, to restrict the right of asylum which it had originally tendered. One cannot believe both in the general right of political asylum and in its inapplicability where Trotsky is concerned. Should a situation arise which requires a re-affirmation of the right of political asylum in the case of Leon Trotsky, can we count upon your public support in the matter?

Your comment on the second objective of the Committee can only have been made on the basis of a misunderstanding of our purposes. The Committee wishes to see an impartial commission of internationally eminent men established to discover the truth concerning the charges made against Trotsky. No matter what any individual believes concerning Trotsky's guilt or innocence, there can be no valid reason for denying to him an opportunity to answer these charges before a competent Commission of Inquiry, which will evaluate evidence and documents submitted by both sides and make its findings known to the public. Consequently, I fail to understand your retort that Trotsky is encountering no difficulty in making his views, whether or not they are the truth, widely known. Isn't it at all important to determine whether or not they are the truth? You comment that the "press of the world, notably its most reactionary elements, seems to have opened its columns to him with suspicious generosity" is hard for me to understand. There is no press in this country which has opened its columns to him and has not opened its columns to people like yourself. And since you say you have been following the controversy, you must be aware that Trotsky has expressly repudiated the illegal re-publication of his articles in the Hearst press and is at present suing them because of it. I mention it only in order to clarify the situation. In passing, I should like to know on what objective grounds you can assert, in the face of the world press coverage of the Moscow trials, at which Trotsky was branded an assassin and a traitor, that "The opponents of Mr. Trotsky have been far more hampered than he is in gaining access to the media of public opinion."

Most astonishing of all, I find your observations on the campaign of the Communist Party to discredit our Committee. I wrote that such a campaign could easily serve as a precedent for the Hitler government to attempt to threaten inquiries into its activities by American citizens. I agree with you that the Hitler government has hardly waited for such a precedent, but is it not clear that, unless the campaigns of agents of totalitarian governments to stifle open inquiry in this country is exposed, a time may come when the Hitler government and other Fascist governments may succeed here in choking off criticism of their acts, as they have succeeded in some of the non-Fascist European countries?

You add that to invite you to join our Committee on this ground "savors of Trotsky's own disingenuousness in introducing the Jewish issue into the present situation." I cannot imagine on what grounds you assert this and, after carefully perusing my original letter, I find no reference to Trotsky, the Jew, or to the danger that the Hitler government will prevent agitation against its Jewish policy. Your friends on this Committee, who suggested that I write you, were under the impression that you were interested not only in the anti-Jewish acts of the German government, but in its anti-human acts, and indeed, the anti-human acts of any government. The Committee, as such, makes no assertion concerning the character of the acts of the Russian government. It merely wants the truth established before the world, not as it affects Trotsky, the Jew, but as it affects Trotsky, the human being. Most of the members of our Committee are not Jewish, and you were not invited as a Jew, but as a liberal. You are perfectly free to solidarize yourself with the campaign of the Communist Party against the attempt to organize an international Commission of Inquiry, but I think it should be beneath you to seize upon a non-existent racial issue which I agree is totally irrelevant in the present question, as a pretext for your stand.

I have never had the pleasure of meeting you, and I sent my invitation to you at the suggestion of other members of our Committee. I think it is, therefore, unfair on your part to accuse me of disingenuousness.

A Committee whose objectives have been formulated by Professors John

Dewey and Horace M. Kallen, and whose members are of the rank of men like Professors Franz Boas, William Ellery Leonard,[3] Paul F. Brissenden, Gaetano Salvemini,[4] and others and whose purposes have been endorsed by Dr. Alvin Johnson,[5] Professor Morris R. Cohen,[6] Sinclair Lewis,[7] and many other outstanding liberals, if it cannot inspire agreement should, at least, inspire confidence in the sincerity of its efforts and the importance of the work it has undertaken.

1. Rabbi Stephen S. Wise, Free Synagogue of New York.
2. To join the American Committee for the Defense of Leon Trotsky.
3. Professor of English, University of Wisconsin.
4. Refugee from Mussolini's Italy and professor of history, Harvard University.
5. Founder of the University of Exile and managing editor of the *Encyclopedia of the Social Sciences.*
6. Professor of philosophy, City University of New York, and a formative influence on Hook.
7. Author of *Main Street* and other novels, and winner of the 1930 Nobel Prize for literature.

16

Dear Mr. Davis,[1]   March 6, 1937

I have been looking over our correspondence, and I wish to make one final comment from the very outset. I made a simple request, namely, that you present the grounds on which you charge the American Committee with a series of acts enumerated in the Van Kleeck letter. Your communication of March 3rd indicates that you still stand behind that letter. I, therefore, ask you to tell me what evidence you have that the American Committee has issued statements denouncing the Soviet government, that speakers, in the name of this Committee, have called for armed insurrection in Russia, that its activities constitute intervention in the internal affairs of the Soviet government with hostile intent, etc., etc.

I think you will admit that there is a difference between not joining our Committee and solidarizing yourself with the attacks of the Communist Party upon our Committee. You say that you think it is a good thing to raise the questions which are raised in the Van Kleeck letter. That letter not only raises questions, but makes charges. If these charges are true, our Committee is masquerading in false clothes, and over 135 men and women eminent in American liberal life, including many of whom you know, are abetters of Gestapo agents.

Nor is it a question of "writing our honest convictions to each other." I would have been glad if you had written me so that I could have set you right, and had you convinced me, I would have joined you. But it is a matter of *publishing* not so much honest convictions as alleged facts, and of the uses to which that publication is being put by your Communist Party friends.

The fact that I have gone to all these lengths in writing you is an indication of the friendly esteem I had for you until the publication of the Van Kleeck letter. I think the very least you owe me, and other members of the American Committee, is an unevasive reply to the questions I have asked.

1. Jerome Davis.

17

Dear Professor Einstein,[1]   March 10, 1937

To begin with, permit me to express my gratitude to you for taking the time to write me about the subject of my recent communication. We are all heartened by your expression of interest in the establishment of an impartial Commission of Inquiry to investigate the charges against Trotsky.

The question as to whether the hearings of the Commission should be public has been discussed at great length by our Committees and the tentative conclusions reached were as follows:

In the event that either one of the parties invited to appear before the Commission refuses to put in an appearance, secret sessions at which only one party is present would have no validity and be suspect in the eyes of the world. Further, the announcement that such sessions would be secret would provoke a storm of criticism, which would turn public opinion away from interest in the Commission.

The danger that Trotsky might use the open hearings for his own political purposes was, also, considered at length. The upshot of the discussion seemed to show that there were few people who believed that Trotsky, who now has every opportunity in the press to make propaganda for his political purposes, would seize this particular opportunity to do so. He would have nothing to gain by such procedure, for first, it would be irrelevant, and ruled out by the Commissioners and, second, its effect would be prejudicial to his own demand for justice on the specific charges made against him.

It is, also, clear that the Commissioners would take testimony bearing only upon the specific charges made (of where, when and how), so that in a properly conducted inquiry, even if Trotsky were foolish enough to attempt to make political propaganda, this could easily be checked.

Balancing the definite disadvantages which would follow the announce-ment that the hearings of the Commission would be secret, against the possible dangers that open hearings might be used for political purposes, the overwhelming sentiment of our Committee was in favor of the latter alternative.

Of course, once the Commission was established, it could adopt rules and regulations to guide its own procedure with a particular eye upon the dangers of a public hearing.

We would be very grateful to you if you would give these considerations some further thought and would make whatever suggestions or comments you believe might be helpful in the situation.

1. Albert Einstein.

18

Dear Professor Coe,[1]   March 24, 1937

Please excuse my delay in replying to your letter of March 5th. An injury to my eye deprived me of my vision until a few days ago.

I found your letter very heartening. It raises a great many interesting questions, to some of which I do not know the answer.

There is one point, however, on which I do see clearly, and that is that no work which the Commission of Inquiry can perform can be prejudicial to the real interests of socialism. As a matter of fact, the greatest harm to socialism has already been wreaked by the trials so far conducted. And if there were no Commission of Inquiry, liberal sentiment throughout the world will be able, as now, to point to Russia and say: "See the fruits of socialism." If Trotsky's guilt is established, the world will forget him. If Trotsky's innocence is established, we, who believe in socialism, can look others in the face and say: "Our socialism is not incompatible with truth, decency and the recognition of the essential dignity of man." There may be some people who will seize upon the findings of the commission, if unfa-vorable to the Stalin regime, as an argument against socialism as such. But these are the people who are sure to seize upon other things, in their minds just as important an argument, for the same conclusion. Indeed, these are the people who are now using the trials as ammunition against socialism. And it must never be forgotten that it was not Trotsky who began these trials, but the present Russian regime.

I agree with your statement that it is better to cooperate with Commu-nists than with liberals who are opposed to socialism or with liberals who have not broken with capitalism. But with one important provision. They must be genuine Communists in the sense that they accept the principle of workers' democracy as formulated by Marx, and do not believe in an unprincipled dictatorship of a clique which, when it assumes power, will promptly proceed to do precisely the same things that its predecessors did, except for little sprinklings of holy water. It is not only as Socialists, but as intelligent men and women of integrity, that we must eschew Russian chauvinism as much as American chauvinism.

In a genuine socialist society even of the traditional variety, workers must possess at least the same amount of freedom and critical expression as they possess under the most enlightened form of capitalism. Otherwise there is no assurance that the so-called transitional state will be transitional.

Meanwhile, I am happy to be able to say that liberal and socialist opinion is veering with ever greater force to our position. Before long, we hope to have some members of the Commission take preliminary testimony in Mexico City. The Commission is still in process of formation, and nothing would please me better than to get your permission to nominate you as a Commissioner. There are few people whose non-partisanship, long services to progressive ideals, and moral authority have been so firmly established.

1. George A. Coe, professor of philosophy and religious education, University of Southern California.

19

Dear Mr. Lovett,[1]   March 24, 1937

This will acknowledge receipt of your communication of March 14th. I am a little disturbed at the tone of your letter, particularly since my original letter was not so much an invitation to join our Committee as a query concerning the grounds for the charges made in the Van Kleeck letter. I have read the publications and attended the meetings of the Committee. I do not find the statements made in that letter substantiated in the slightest.

The Committee as such has taken no position either on Trotsky's guilt or innocence or on the Soviet government. Individual members of this Committee speaking for themselves may have been critical of some acts of the Russian government. This no more makes them guilty of "intervention into Russian affairs with hostile intent" (as charged in the Van Kleeck letter), than criticism of Roosevelt by you or me makes us un-American.

The most saddening sentence of your letter is the statement that you regard the issue involved in the Russian trials as irrelevant to the question of the new social order for which we are both working. Is it really irrelevant whether in the Socialist state citizens are to be victims of judicial frame-ups as charged by Trotsky? Is it really irrelevant to a Socialist state whether the right to intellectual inquiry and freedom of criticism are to exist? Is Socialism to achieve a security—and a precarious one at that—at the price of democracy, human dignity and intellectual integrity? I am *not* saying now that these things are true of Russia, but I am firmly convinced that whether or not they are true cannot be irrelevant to Socialists, indeed even to liberals, anywhere in the world.

What do you say to people who ask, as I have been asked, is the state of affairs in present-day Russia what you have in mind when you work for a new social order in America? It is precisely in the interests of a new social order that it is necessary to know the truth. And the only function of the American Committee is to establish the truth concerning the charges made against Trotsky—charges which have not been convincing to the larger sector of world liberal and Socialist opinion. Until the truth is known, the Moscow trials will haunt every Socialist as well as every Communist, just as, in a much smaller way, the Dreyfus affair cast its specter upon French national life.

I write you this letter not in order to urge you to do anything or to expostulate with you, but merely to raise a question which every candid person must now face. Principles are more important than organizations, and intellectuals owe their primary responsibility not to factions or personalities, but to the abiding values of the human enterprise.

1. Robert Morss Lovett, professor of English, University of Chicago.

20

Dear Mr. Bliven,[1]   April 15, 1937

This is to acknowledge your letter of April 8th. I frankly confess that I am at a loss to understand both its tone and its logic. In my letter to you of April 2 I stated as a fact that many people—not political partisans—believe that for the last two years the *New Republic* editorials and book reviews on Trotsky have revealed a consistent bias against him. You may dispute the fact that many people do so believe; you may deny that this bias exists. But I cannot see what point there is in your saying in this connection that "the first duty of American liberals is to fight for improvement of conditions here in this country." Certainly, but as the columns of the *New Republic* prove, even you do not believe that this is the *only* duty of American liberals. Otherwise your laudable concern with Spain, Brazil, and other European countries would be inexplicable. I find your reply particularly hard to reconcile with the publication of Mr. Cowley's[2] four and a half page recent book review of the Moscow proceedings in which Trotsky is attacked in the bitterest and most personal fashion. If the whole Russian matter is relatively unimportant, why isn't that borne in mind when space is assigned to criticism of Trotsky as well as when suggestions are made that Trotsky's side be presented to *New Republic* readers? The *New Republic* carried an article by Trotsky on the occasion of the Reichstag Fire trials: I cannot see why I should be regarded as "out of order" for suggesting that he be heard on his own "trial."

Knowing as I do your propriety in all matters where personal ethics are concerned, I am quite surprised at your intimation that I am among "those people who are hiding under the bed, these last two decades, when a great many other people were fighting for improvement here at home." In fact I do not know anyone interested in discovering the truth about the Moscow trials from John Dewey down whom this characterization fits.

I understand quite well that the *New Republic* is not a public forum or a debating society, and I heartily agree that you are not required "to publish a defense of Hitler, or of fascism in general, just because (we) had attacked Hitler and Fascism." But that you should have seen fit to make this comparison apropros of the suggestion that another view on Trotsky be presented is evidence enough that the *New Republic,* on this point at least, has fallen far short of the standards of critical detachment and scientific probity which characterize its attitude on some other issues. You have a right to refuse publication of a defense of Trotsky but only after you have established the fact that he is in the same class as Hitler.

I know that it savors of presumption on my part to offer this criticism. Please be assured that I have no political axe to grind in the matter. As a reader of and contributor to the *New Republic* for many years, I felt it was my duty to write you frankly about your stand on what, it is safe to predict, will be an international Dreyfus case. Silence would have been easier. But if my remarks have no other effect than to lead you to reconsider in a cool moment a policy which many others besides myself consider false to the best traditions of the *New Republic,* I shall be content.

1. Bruce Bliven, editor of the *New Republic.*
2. Malcolm Cowley.

21

Dear Mr. Eddy,[1]   June 17, 1937

I have just read your piece on the guilt of Leon Trotsky in the June issue of *Soviet Russia Today.* I cannot tell you how shocked I am at your abandonment of every vestige of scientific method in your analysis of the theme.

Radek's[2] own statement, which made such a tremendous impression upon you, should have been sufficient to make you pause before aligning yourself with the judgment of Stalin's murder courts. I mention only two things: First, his warning to everybody in Western Europe and in America who is in any degree critical of Stalin, that they will end up as spies of Hitler and the Mikado,[3] shows what the real motivation of the trial is, namely, to make it impossible for liberals, Socialists or dissident Communists to raise their voices against the abominable practices of repression to which *you* yourself have been calling attention for years. Secondly, Radek explicitly says, on page 543 of the verbatim report, that all of the testimony of the accused rests upon his (Radek's) testimony and Pyatakov's. The only alleged contacts with Trotsky were through Pyatakov's flight to Oslo and Trotsky's letter to Radek through Romm.[4] On both of these points the most compelling evidence has been turned up to show that they are utterly without foundation. If you have not seen the literature on the subject, I shall be glad to send it to you. Indeed, my general impression is that you have not examined any of the counter-evidence that has been made available by the Second International, the Que Faire groups, as well as by Trotsky himself. You might also consult *Letter of an Old Bolshevik* just published by the Rand School Press.

Precisely what words of Trotsky in his *The Revolution Betrayed* seem to you to confirm the evidence of the trial? When Communists in this country say they desire to overthrow the United States government, is that evidence that they are assassins, arsonists, and spies of foreign countries? Trotsky has never made any secret of the fact that, like Lenin (compare Lenin's "Testament"), he believed that Stalin should be removed from a position of power. But in what way is that evidence of the specific charges of which he has been accused?

You write: "If the countries of Europe each must have a leader today, in my judgment Stalin is the best living leader the Soviet Union could have." This is certainly not the Sherwood Eddy who claims to be opposed to Fascism and Communism. Is it merely Hitler whom you oppose, and not the whole system of Fascist leadership in Germany? It is merely Mussolini whom you oppose, and not the corporative state? And are the thousand-and-one crimes that Stalin's regime has committed against Russian workers and peasants, crimes to which you have so eloquently called attention, to be forgotten? In approving the man, are you now approving the system? I can hardly believe my eyes.

I write as one who is politically opposed to both Trotsky and Stalin, and who believes that no socialist society can be built on a foundation of lies, cruelty and systematic abuse of power. Despite our differences, I have always had a strong faith in your intellectual and moral integrity. Your capitulation to Stalinist pressure and propaganda indicates how important critical, scientific method is. Without it, even men with the best of intentions must betray themselves and their ideals.

Though I suspect that recent events in Russia in the last few days have given you no desire to engage in a discussion, I should be very glad to meet with you to analyze the evidence bearing on the Moscow trials.

1. Sherwood Eddy, spokesman for the Social Gospel and author of *The Challenge of Russia* (New York, 1936).
2. Karl Radek, member of the Comintern who accused Trotsky of treason against the Soviet Union. Radek himself was found guilty of treason during the Moscow trials.
3. Japanese government.
4. Vladimir Romm, former Washington correspondent for *Izvestia* and a defendant during the Moscow Trials, was charged with having plotted with Karl Radek and Trotsky to overthrow the Soviet government.

22

Honorable Sir,[1]   August 9, 1937

From the very outset of Franco's rebellion against the Spanish Government, I have been a strong supporter of the Loyalist regime. Together with Professor Franz Boas of Columbia University I have helped to mobilize sentiment against Fascist outrages in American colleges and universities, particularly when Leopoldo Alas's[2] life was at stake. I am a member of the North American Committee[3] and a sponsor of the Debs column.[4] I have given money and lent my name to send men to Spain to help the Loyalist government. I have spoken and written in its behalf.

The news which has been coming out of Spain is very disquieting to me and, I assure you, to a very large section of American liberal thought which until now has actively supported the Spanish government. The assassination of Nin[5] and others by armed gangsters of the Spanish Communist Party, the suppression of newspapers in any way critical of the Communist Party line, the imprisonment and torture of hundreds—several known to me by their writings as staunch friends of democracy—all point to the conclusion that in fact, if not in name, the Communist Party dominates the Valencia government. Its decrees are the laws of Loyalist Spain today. The methods which have been employed against dissidents of any kind, including the base calumnies of Caballero,[6] are not a whit different from the methods of Franco. No government using such methods, or even countenancing them, is entitled to the support of liberals, not to speak of socialists. In pledging support of the Madrid-Valencia regime, American liberals did not pledge support of the Russian OGPU[7] whose hand is quite visible in all the outrages committed against justice, truth and elementary decency by Communist Party members in the Spanish government.

There is no surer method of forfeiting the support of all people of good will than for the Madrid-Valencia government to permit these excesses to continue and allow their perpetrators to go unpunished. It seems to me, and I still write as a friend of democratic Spain (against both the Spanish Fascists and Spanish Communists), that nothing but a *public* repudiation by you or some leading member of your government of such events, followed by resolute action against those responsible for them, can prevent American liberal opinion, before long, from lumping Franco and your government together.

P.S. I am sending confidential copies of this letter to a score of outstanding American liberals. If your reply is not of a confidential nature I shall be glad to forward copies to them.

1. Fernando de los Ríos, Spanish ambassador to the United States during the Spanish Civil War. He failed to convince the American government to allow the sale of arms to the Spanish government.

2. Leopoldo Alas Arguelles, former rector of the University of Iviedo, was executed by Franco's supporters.

3. North American Committee to Aid Spanish Democracy.

4. The American Socialist Party called for the formation of a "Debs Column" to fight in Spain. Named for the leading American socialist of the early twentieth century, the column never materialized.

5. Andrés Nin, leader of the Partido Obrero de Unificación Marxista (POUM), was murdered by Communists during the Spanish Civil War.

6. Francisco Largo Caballero, left-wing prime minister of Spain who invited Communists to participate in his Popular Front government of 1936–37.

7. Soviet intelligence agency.

23

Dear Professor Knight,[1]   February 22, 1938

I have just received your letter and am writing in haste a tentative reply so that you may be able to read it before your discussion group on Feb. 25th. You may read this only on the condition that you read them your letter to me so that they have an idea what you are asking me to answer. And I must confess right off that if they have a clear idea of what you have in mind or even of the precise nature of the questions you are asking, they have the advantage of me. For with all due respect, and with all appreciation for the aroma of wry humor which pervades your letter, I do not understand what you are writing about. I do not understand what the questions are which you are asking, from what quarter you are asking them, what writings of mine you are referring to. Nothing is clear to me except that you are overwhelmed with bewilderment. Now when a person makes a demand for clarity and precision of analysis, I think it is only fair for him to make a beginning. As it is I can only guess at what you mean.

I take it that you are not referring to any specific view of Karl Marx; nor to the validity of my interpretation of any of Marx's views. You are asking me for the grounds of my own beliefs. Which beliefs and where expressed? So far as I can gather the most important belief you attribute to me—indeed "the crux" of the matter, according to you—is this notion that "the main if not the only fact or force which keeps us from having some sort of idealistic Utopia in Western civilization is the immoral selfishness of the privileged class and that the main if not the only thing requisite to be done is a certain amount of properly directed abolishing and liquidating." I do not know where you learned how to scan a text and what canons of analysis you apply but the belief you attribute to me is the rankest poppycock. I do not and never have believed in Utopias. I do believe that if we abolished private property in the instruments of production (I shall examine the phrase further) we may be able to adopt a social policy which will eliminate economic insecurity, unemployment and war. There will certainly be plenty of other problems and evils; and human beings *may* even go on fighting. A man may be stupid because he has a bone pressing on his brain. If I remove the bone there is no guarantee that he will be intelligent because other things may in the future cause stupidity. But that is no reason for not removing the bone. We are not dealing with necessities but with shifting scales of probability. I do not believe that the main reason which stands in the way of the changes I should like to see introduced is the immoral selfishness of the privileged class. Capitalists, bankers and their apologists are no more selfish than the workers and their allies and sometimes I think lots more intelligent. There is a whole host of factors which keeps us from the change I have indicated. Some are rooted in American traditions, psychology, the character of American press and education, and not least unintelligent and doctrinaire radicalism. Nor do I believe in the *necessity* of a certain amount of liquidating. But if a socialist government, that came to power by democratic means, were to nationalize some of the basic industries (presumably another ambiguous phrase for you) and a minority group pulled another Fort Sumter, then if I couldn't buy them off or head them off by negotiation, I'd fight them. And in the fight I wouldn't neglect to define my terms. In fact I'd insist upon it because the other side would probably be using large, vague and mouthfilling phrases. So much for what you regard as the crux of the matter. When you ask whether anyone *can* (your italics) believe such bloodthirsty nonsense, the answer is simply yes. Why should that make you suddenly lose your faith in human intelligence? Where have you been all your life? You act like a man who has been sleepwalking for the greater part of it. Nazism, Fascism, Stalinism, the doctrine of manifest destiny, Mohammedanism, and many forms of Christianity and Judaism are bloodthirsty nonsense, and a good deal of political economy and philosophy have been bloodless nonsense. But that doesn't prevent people from believing it. Should they? No. Do *I?* No. (For further details see my critical review of Thurman Arnold in the forthcoming issue, April, of the *Univ. of Chicago Law Review.*[2])

You write on page 2 "What I am more concerned with at the moment, i.e., in addition to the crux of the matter, is questions of expository procedure and methodology" meaning, as the context shows, definition. No offense is intended when I say that I find your remarks about definition, as is the case whenever you touch a philosophical or basic methodological problem, extremely naive. Not being a Thomist,[3] I don't believe in essential definitions. Definitions are reducible to two kinds—definitions in use, and nominal definitions. All terms are definable including the terms in the definiendum but depending upon the purpose and context of inquiry not all of these latter need to be defined. In fact only a fool would attempt to do it. Although some terms may be *taken* as indefinable, all terms can be defined, for all definition is ultimately circular and the difference between good and bad definitions (they are not true or false) is, to borrow a phrase from C. I. Lewis,[4] only "in the diameter of the circle." Certainly, in some contexts I leave some terms undefined. Who doesn't? But once a problem is stated, if difficulties arise about the undefined terms, we can go on from there.

Now I can't make out your questions on p. 2 because I don't know in the light of what problems (even of Marxian exegesis) you are asking for definitions. All I want to say in this brief space is this: I use the concepts of class and class-struggle because they enable me to explain and correlate more concrete social data than any other concepts known to me; class divisions as I have defined them are more "fundamental" than other social divisions for this reason. They are also more fundamental in the sense that I am prepared to show that a certain schedule of values—securities, freedoms, and opportunities—cannot be procured under the existing system of ownership, control and distribution for the preponderant majority of the population; that no program based on national, racial, religious divisions will enable us to procure them; and that a program which stresses class divisions and appealing primarily to those now deprived of the above securities, freedoms and opportunities, if certain other conditions are fulfilled, in a unified political movement will probably achieve them. The goal and postulates of action are ethical; the means, program, and analysis of the conditions under which successful action is likely are scientific. I have defined ownership, which may be public or private, and property, which may be personal or social ("instruments of production"). You lump all of these together. When you say that "in sound economic analysis" there is no other property but social (means of production) your crude theory of definition betrays you. On some analyses that may be so, but not for any analysis which recognizes certain kinds of distinctions in which I am interested, e.g., the kind of property whose use or abuse does not by and large affect other people's opportunity to work, eat and therefore live, e.g., my clothes, books, house, etc. and the kind of property, control over which gives me, quite literally, control over the lives of those who earn their living by it, e.g., a railroad, a mine, or factory. Nobody believes, i.e., nobody intelligent, that all property should be private or that all property should be public. The extent and degree to which property should be private or public depends upon two considerations: the abundance of personal goods which any particular scheme makes available for the population at large, the control which any particular scheme of ownership of things gives over men. (The more human freedoms the better.) The particular answer we give is a function of different historical conditions (level of the productive forces, science, etc.) and of our conception of the good life. I am prepared to argue that in the present historical epoch, public ownership of most social property is the only scheme of ownership which makes economic security and personal freedom *possible*. This is only a necessary condition but not sufficient, for public ownership must function within the framework of political democracy. Otherwise you may have a measure of security but no freedom, as in a jail. (E.g., Russia. In effect Stalin and his bureaucrats really own the instruments of production, and no one has security who disagrees with them. Political and social democracy presuppose each other. One cannot be genuinely present where the other is absent.)

You will excuse me for regarding your denial that there is any ethical antithesis between getting an income from "property" and "labor power" as simply funny. Examine your breakdown operationally and you will see you are using words in different senses each time. I know what it means to inherit an income from Uncle Andy's aluminum trust; I don't know what it means to inherit "labor-power." If you give the last meaning, it won't have the same meaning as the first. Besides I can give a purely formal ethical answer to the question, using concepts non-operationally so that you will understand them. People who inherit incomes without doing any socially useful work for it (leave out wages of superintendence) by definition are parasites. I abhor all parasites. The bad I define as that which I abhor after reflection. Therefore those who get their income without doing any work for it are bad. I am surprised that in this phase of your argument you didn't trot out the abstinence theory of capital, and the effort-waiting-and-sacrifice conception of real costs. After all, there is only a difference in degree between the sacrifice and pain which a billionaire must endure investing and not spending his money outright and the sacrifice and pain of effort of a lumberman who earns say a $1000 a year working in all sorts of weather eight hours a day. If the investment brings 5%, the pain suffered by the billionaire in waiting is just 50,000 times as great as the pain endured by the lumberjack, etc., etc. *Can* anyone believe anything of this sort?! Unfortunately, yes.

In conclusion I must again state my impression that you have not put your problems concretely enough; and further that you seem to believe that I regard my general principles as sufficient for settling specific problems, which I do not. And I cannot understand how anyone who has read Dewey, as I presume you have, can write about ethics as you do. There is some justification for my good friend Niebuhr[5] because his ethics, like that of most sky-pilots, is just poetry. It's not supposed to be applied. Where he deals with material which is empirically relevant to ethics, i.e., human psychology, his basic assumption is that man's nature is unalterable and unalterably bad. As I get him he believes that since man is by nature "sinful," he ought to live in the best possible society in order to discover that fact.

Well, this is already longer than I had intended, and it has been fun writing it. Pray don't take it amiss if you find any of the spinach sandy.

1. Frank H. Knight, professor of economics, University of Chicago.
2. "The Politician's Handbook," review of Thurman Arnold, *The Folklore of Capitalism, University of Chicago Law Review* 5 (April 1938): 341–49.
3. Follower of the philosophy of St. Thomas Aquinas.
4. Professor of philosophy, Harvard University.
5. Reinhold Niebuhr, professor, Union Theological Seminary, and leading neo-Orthodox Protestant theologian.

24

My dear Upton Sinclair,[1]   April 28, 1939

Your letter of April 21 leaves me positively breathless. So, the only thing you feel quite sure about in reference to General Krivitsky's[2] articles is that you are "not in a position to form a judgment." Yet when Littlepage's[3] articles appeared on what was going on in Russia, you definitely set yourself up as one in a position to form a judgment on not only the truth but the relevance of his charges to the question of the specific guilt or innocence of the Moscow defendants.

You also write that you can see "several other possible interpretations of some of the stories (Krivitsky tells)." I am curious. What other interpretations have you of the murder of A. Nin and other Poumists (which even F. de los Ríos, former Spanish Ambassador to the U.S., has deplored), the operation of the G.P.U.[4] in Spain behind the back of Caballero, the imprisonment and execution of vocal anti-Stalinists in the International Brigade?[5]

Dear Upton Sinclair—Do you not see what a position you are putting yourself in? You are a hundred percent apologist of Stalin's terror in Russia and out. The Stalinists throughout the world use you as a "front" behind which to cover up their Hitlerian techniques in fighting socialists, syndicalists, anarchists, and independent lovers of freedom everywhere, while in private they refer to you as "a sap" (in the past they used to do this publicly)!!

Is it too much to plead with you for a little elementary consistency? A few months ago you wrote: "When Hitler learns that the Soviet Union has become counterrevolutionary, he will reduce the ardor of his crusade against it. So also will the big business press of Paris, London, and New York. When that happens I will admit that Stalin has sold out the workers."

Well, in view of recent events, what are you waiting for? Shall I send you the recent clippings on Russia from the *London Times,* the *N.Y. Times,* and the Paris ?[6] Or Stalin's recent speech appeasing Hitler?

1. Author of *The Jungle* and unsuccessful candidate for governor of California in 1934.

2. General Walter Krivitsky, Soviet military intelligence officer, wrote a series of articles in the *Saturday Evening Post* detailing Stalin's courtship of Hitler, the Moscow purges, and Soviet involvement in the Spanish Civil War. He was found dead in February 1941 in a Washington hotel under suspicious circumstances.

3. John D. Littlepage wrote a series of unflattering articles on the Soviet Union in the *Saturday Evening Post* in 1938.

4. GPU (actually the OGPU) was the Unified State Political Administration, the dreaded Soviet agency responsible for suppressing internal dissent. It would be replaced by the NKVD (later MVD).

5. Name given to denote the international military formations fighting in Spain on the side of the Republic.

6. The name of the Paris newspaper is not given.

25

Dear Miss Kirchwey,[1]   June 8, 1939

I have just received your letter of June 6th. I am sorry you think my reply to your editorial is heated.[2] But for the *Nation* to attack us because we wish to make a principled defense against enemies of intellectual freedom (while it has kept silent for several years now about cultural crimes committed by the Communist Party and its friends against genuine liberals) came as a shock to me. I, too, don't want to fight with you. I have publicly recorded my great debt to the *Nation* for its formative influence upon me during the war and post-war years when it didn't pull its punches against any kind of injustice or oppression. But for the *Nation* to add its voice to the chorus of denunciation rising from the Stalinist, Trotskyite, Catholic, and crypto-Stalinist press (and now that we are coming out in defense of MacLeish[3] the reactionaries will join in), means that it has changed sides. Some of the members of the Committee for Cultural Freedom have welcomed your editorial because they said that it was excellent publicity for the Committee and exposed the *Nation*. Maybe so, but it is not the less shocking to one who like myself had identified himself for two decades with its general tendency. That was why I invited both you and O. G. Villard[4] to join us (Villard has!). And that my own feeling in the matter is not personal is evidenced in almost a score of letters I have received from *Nation* readers.

It is really hard to reconcile your plea for all-round disarmament with your attack on the Committee. I believe in all-round disarmament also but not in *moral* disarmament. Instead of imputing ulterior motives to us (or to me), why not judge us by what we do, fighting with us on the specific issues of which you can approve and against us if we turn out to be another disguised group of totalitarians?

In conclusion, if my rejoinder to your editorial is heated it is a measure of the relatively high esteem I had for the *Nation* before you so unjustly attacked the Committee for Cultural Freedom. I have not always agreed with the *Nation*'s policy on specific issues, the Lord knows. Differences are compatible with a common set of ideals and especially with a common method. But it is those ideals and that method which the Manifesto of the Committee for Cultural Freedom eloquently affirmed and which the *Nation*'s editorial in effect denied.

1. Freda Kirchwey, publisher and editor of the *Nation*.

2. Hook's letter, which appeared in the *Nation*, May 27, 1939, was signed by a hundred prominent American intellectuals and called for the creation of a Committee for Cultural Freedom.

3. Archibald MacLeish, American poet and playwright, was a firm opponent of both fascism and communism. He had just been nominated to head the Library of Congress.

4. Oswald Garrison Villard, former owner and publisher of the *Nation*.

26

Dear Miss Kirchwey,[1]   August 23, 1939

In the *Daily Worker* of August 14th, there appeared an Open Letter in which the Committee for Cultural Freedom is specifically named as part of a pro-Fascist, reactionary movement which aims to disrupt existing relations between the U.S. and the U.S.S.R. Among the signers are I. F. Stone and Maxwell Stewart. They are listed as "Associate Editors of the *Nation*." I am writing not to protest against this (because the CCF believes in freedom of speech and press even for the totalitarians who slander it) but to inquire whether this characterization of the Committee expresses the *Nation*'s judgment of it. Since this Open Letter, initiated by Corliss Lamont, Chairman of the Friends of the Soviet Union, at the behest of the Communist Party, is being widely circulated with the names of Messrs. Stone and Stewart, listed as Associate Editors of the *Nation*, the impression has been created that they speak for the *Nation*. Our members, particularly those who have been contributors to the *Nation*, would like to know if this is the fact.

P.S. I have checked the names of *Nation* contributors among our members.

1. Freda Kirchwey.

27

Dear Sir,[1]   August 25, 1939

In the *Daily Worker* of August 14th you are listed as a signer of an Open Letter in which the Committee for Cultural Freedom is characterized as part of a pro-Fascist, reactionary movement whose aim is to disrupt friendly relations between Russia and the Western democracies, particularly the U.S. In the interests of our members, many of whom are undoubtedly known to you because of their active membership in the American Civil

Liberties Union, I am writing to inquire whether the use of your signature was authorized. If it was authorized, we should like to know on what evidence you have publicly issued a statement which we regard as a deliberate slander of the purposes of our organization.

In the event that you have not seen the Declaration of Principles of the Committee for Cultural Freedom, I am enclosing a copy.

1. Dr. Harry F. Ward, Protestant minister, professor of Christian Ethics, Union Theological Seminary, and chairman of the American Civil Liberties Union.

28

Dear Sir,[1]   September 27, 1939

This will acknowledge your communication of Sept. 18th in which you reaffirm your endorsement of the Lamont Open Letter. In that letter the organizers of the Committee for Cultural Freedom, John Dewey, Ferdinand Lundberg, Frank Trager and myself, are called "Fascists and allies of Fascists."

Who the real "Fascists and allies of Fascists" are the Stalinist pact makes crystal clear.[2] But I wish to brand your characterization of the organizers of the C.C.F. as false and vicious. Such slanderous remarks are proof that you have no right to call yourself either liberal, socialist, or Christian.

1. Harry F. Ward.
2. Refers to the August 1939 Ribbentrop-Molotov neutrality pact between Germany and the Soviet Union.

29

Dear Sir,[1]   September 29, 1939

The text of the letter you signed calls me and my associates "Fascists and allies of Fascists." You have admitted that you signed this letter and I presume that you read what you signed. I refuse to believe that the Communist Party has blanket authorization to affix your signature to any document it sees fit to issue.

If you do not believe that we are "Fascists and allies of Fascists," why did you sign a statement which refers to us in these terms? If you are sincere in your disavowal of this slander, we would like to have a statement to that effect from you, because the Lamont Open Letter bearing your signature has been widely publicized. As a matter of elementary decency, this is the very least you can do. Particularly in regards to the more than a score of our members who are also members of the American Civil Liberties Union. I myself have resigned from the American Civil Liberties Union and its Academic Freedoms Committee (of whose Declaration of Principles I am the author) in protest against your action. At Roger Baldwin's[2] urgent request—he agrees that your action is most deplorable—I am reconsidering my resignation.

But make no mistake about it. We are not going to let anyone slander us with impunity. Or permit individuals publicly to call us Fascists and then privately assure us that that was not what they had in mind. There has been enough duplicity and dishonorable "stooging" in recent years. The cultural atmosphere has been poisoned by it. We are not interested in that part of the Open Letter you signed in which Soviet Russia is hailed as a great force for peace. We are interested in what that letter, signed by you, says about the Committee for Cultural Freedom and its organizers.

1. Harry F. Ward.
2. Director of the American Civil Liberties Union.

30

Dear Sir,[1]   October 16, 1939

Thank you for your invitation to subscribe to the *Protestant Digest.* Your prospectus was inviting, and I read it through. I was astonished to discover the name of Jerome Davis on your Editorial Board. Jerome Davis is one of the outstanding apologists of Russian totalitarianism in America. Time and again he has justified the same type of terror and repression in Russia which we have all condemned when it was committed in Germany. Jerome Davis is entitled to his sentiments and is free to publish his own magazine. You must indeed be naive to imagine that any informed person will take your prospectus seriously with a man like him on your Board.

Just as soon as we begin to make an exception in favor of one form of totalitarianism, we weaken the struggle against all forms of totalitarianism. I am sure you would not have a Hitler apologist on your board, or an apologist for Franco or the Mikado. Why, then, an apologist for Stalin? I am very puzzled, and I am sure others will be too.

I have condemned Yale for depriving Mr. Davis of his right to academic freedom (it was I who introduced the resolution in the Council of the American Association of University Professors condemning Yale for its action), and would not dream of denying to him any more than to Fritz Kuhn[2] or Earl Browder civil or cultural freedom. But when Mr. Davis refuses to condemn not merely the suppression of academic freedom in Russia but the physical liquidation of victims of the Communist Party-line, I do not see how sincere believers in your avowed program can sit on the same Board with him.

Of those I know on your Board, let me add, I have the highest respect for Professors Hocking[3] and Niebuhr. This letter is not an aspersion upon your Board but an expression of doubt and inquiry.

1. Editor, *Protestant Digest.*
2. Leader of the German American Bund, a pro-Nazi organization.
3. William Ernest Hocking, professor of philosophy, Harvard University.

31

Dear Waldo Frank,[1]   October 16, 1939

I am sorry you have an infected hand, among other reasons because I cannot decipher very clearly your handwriting. The general point, however, is clear enough. Naturally, I am grateful to you for the handsome things you say of me.

If you will re-read the Open Letter you signed, you will see that the organizers of the Committee for Cultural Freedom are specifically referred to as "Fascists and their allies." Surely, at the time you signed the Lamont Open Letter, you could not have been unaware that Dewey and I had played a leading part in its organization. Both Dewey and I, Dewey even more than I (despite his differences with you he never fails to speak kindly of you; more than once does he refer to your shrewd insights into the possible line of Russian development in the last part of your book on Russia in 1932) expected you to join with us rather than with our detractors.

When you read our Manifesto in the *Bulletin* I am enclosing, you will see that it does not speak of the social structure of the different totalitarian states but of their regimentation of the arts, letters, and sciences. It is this which primarily interests our members and which we are resolved to keep out of America. The Lamont Letter falsified the content of our Manifesto, not to speak of the scandalously inaccurate account Lamont gave of other aspects of Russian life.

You are one of the few creative writers in this country who attempts to think about things, and you have had some political experience with the people behind the Lamont Letter. That is why your responsibility in signing is greater than that of the Communist Party stalwarts, professional fellow travelers, and the innocents. For you really do not believe what that document says; nor do you approve the use which has been made of it. Surely, you know you will get no thanks from Browder and his crowd (they claim to be contemptuous of you but they really fear you): and you mystify and puzzle the people with whom you can have intellectual differences on this or that but with whom, on the question of cultural freedom, you belong.

The present period is the last one in which individuals can break with the C.P. and be believed. And make no mistake about it, Waldo, you are in the anomalous position of being considered, because of the Letter and other incidents, as a close fellow traveler of the C.P. everywhere *except in the C.P. itself.*

1. One of the founders in 1935 of the League of American Writers, a communist front organization.

32

Dear Roger,[1]   October 18, 1939

I have decided to withdraw my resignation from the A.C.L.U. and will send you my annual dues at the end of the month. As you know, although I have not been a heavy financial contributor, I have been proud of my membership in the Union. Most of my activity has been connected with the Academic Freedom Committee of the Union and I am, as you will recall, the author of its draft on Academic Freedom which was circulated to all college and university presidents.

It seems to me, therefore, that I have some justification for complaint against the behavior of Harry Ward, who is the present chairman of the A.C.L.U. On August 14th there appeared in the *Daily Worker,* and subsequently in other places, an "Open Letter" in which the organizers and a large part of the membership of the Committee for Cultural Freedom are specifically referred to as "Fascists and allies of Fascists" who are seeking to disrupt the unity of progressive forces in America. (The Declaration of Principles of the C.C.F. together with a clarifying amendment by Morris Ernst[2] will be found in the enclosed copy of our *Bulletin.*) The organizers of the C.C.F. are John Dewey, Ferdinand Lundberg, Frank Trager, and myself.

Norman Thomas was our first member. You will find by glancing at our membership list, that many of the leading members of the A.C.L.U. are also members of the C.C.F. To mention only a few: Dorothy Bromley, Ben Huebsch, Morris Ernst, Horace Kallen, William Kilpatrick, Jesse Newton, etc.

The letter denouncing us as "Fascists and allies of Fascists" was signed among others (175 names were made public) by Harry Ward, Chairman of the A.C.L.U. The grounds given for this characterization was our reference to Russia as a totalitarian state in which art, science, and education are denied cultural freedom. Mr. Ward is entitled to any views he has on Russia, even to the belief that it is, I quote from the Open Letter, "a consistent bulwark against war and aggression." But Mr. Ward as Chairman of the A.C.L.U. is not entitled to denounce publicly leading members of the A.C.L.U. as "Fascists and allies of Fascists." Mr. Ward knows that this statement is both false and scurrilous, and he knew it when he signed the letter. Were Mr. Ward merely a member of the Board of the A.C.L.U. one could pass over his action as another mystery in his peculiar theology. But Mr. Ward is not merely a member of the Board of the A.C.L.U., but also the Chairman of the Union. In virtue of that office, he receives considerable publicity in the press of the country. Now is it not passing strange that the Chairman of the A.C.L.U. should appear in the public eye as a calumniator of men like John Dewey, Norman Thomas and others who have worked hard and honestly to preserve civil liberties in this country? Is not the very struggle for civil liberties, so important today, compromised by his action? Has he not betrayed the trust of the Union by this action?

In many circles within and without the A.C.L.U. people are asking whether Harry Ward, its Chairman, is not more of a liability than an asset. More and more are convinced, just as I am, that if Mr. Ward is permitted to continue in his actions he will do the A.C.L.U. irreparable harm.

I will not go into other evidence in my possession which indicates that Mr. Ward works consistently with the Communist Party in this country to discredit and besmirch by the foulest means individuals who have spoken up in criticism of Russian terrorism. The evidence I cite is sufficient to indicate that Mr. Ward has neither the emotional balance nor the judicious mind which seem to be necessary for the post he holds. I was wrong in sending in my resignation from the Union as a protest against Mr. Ward's action, as you very properly pointed out. But I hope the Board will agree with me that Mr. Ward is unfit to serve as Chairman. Like all other people who follow the Communist Party line, there is no telling what he will do next. And there are some things that the members of the A.C.L.U. want to be sure about, and that is that their Chairman will not help circulate the baseless slander that they are "Fascists and allies of Fascists."

P.S. The facts about the Open Letter are very interesting. We have very interesting evidence as to who inspired it, where it was sent from, and at whose behest it was circulated. I shall be glad to send you this information.

1. Roger Baldwin.
2. Prominent New York civil liberties attorney.

33

Dear Mr. President,[1]   October 30, 1939

Knowing how great are the burdens of state, I have never written a letter to you before. There are two reasons, however, why I must write this one. First, it concerns a theme which we both recently discussed at the *Herald-Tribune* Forum. Second, and more important, it involves the abuse of your name in a manner which is sure to have public repercussions of a most unpleasant character to all liberal and progressive elements in the country.

The situation is briefly this. In Vol. VI, No. 1, p. 11 of the *Bulletin* of the League of American Writers you are referred to by the President of that organization as "an honorary member." The League of American Writers was organized some years ago by the Communist Party to engage in political propaganda on the literary front, and particularly to further the political line of the Soviet Union. This is apparent not only in its literature (a condition for membership, for example, is acceptance of the Popular Front embracing the Communist Party), not only in the fact that a majority of its board consists of Communist Party members and fellow travelers, but from the actual history of its founding which I shall be glad to put at your disposal.

The context of the report in which your name is triumphantly cited as a member includes a defense of the policy of the Soviet Union, an attack on the Committee for Cultural Freedom, among whose members are John Dewey, Norman Thomas, Ferdinand Lundberg, and two hundred other leading liberals and progressives (for its opposition to all forms of totalitarianism), and advocacy of the political policies held by the Communist Party at the time the report was given.

I have further information that the controlling Communist faction in the League of American Writers plans to use "the fact" of your application as a screen behind which to carry on its work. In this way the Communists hope together with the reactionary forces in this country "to smear" you and your administration as secretly sympathetic with red totalitarianism. I am fearful lest this strategy succeed and the progressive features of your administration be swept away in the storm of reaction which such a tactic is likely to evoke.

I am making bold to suggest that you publicly repudiate the League of American Writers and its claim that you are a member. In the event that you entertain the slightest doubt about the validity of my statements and the advisability of the course of action I suggest, I shall be only too happy to discuss them with you in person or with anyone whom you delegate to investigate the matter.

Enclosed with this letter is a copy of the Manifesto of the Committee for Cultural Freedom. It indicates what my own position is, as well as the position which the League of American Writers is attacking, using your name as a shield.

In closing, permit me to assure you that I have no partisan aims but am motivated by the sole consideration of what will best serve the interests of cultural freedom in this country.

1. Franklin D. Roosevelt.

34

Dear Mr. Davis, [1]   December 18, 1939

This is to acknowledge your letter of Dec. 16th in which you allege that I have not properly stated your views on Russia in my letter to the *Protestant Digest*. I should be the last one in the world to attribute views to you which you do not hold, and if I am convinced that I am in error I shall make private and public declaration of that fact.

Since you say that you have often and vigorously criticized Russia for its restrictions on liberty and unjustified violence, I shall be very much obliged if you will refer me to the published record of such criticism, since 1937, when in the public mind you became a fellow traveler of the Communist Party. All of your public statements since 1937 indicate unqualified endorsement of the Stalinist regime of terror. For example, in 1937 you signed the Communist Party–Van Kleeck letter which appeared in the *Daily Worker* denouncing the American Committee to Investigate the Truth about the Moscow Trials and charging it with abetting armed insurrection in the Soviet Union, etc., etc. In 1938 you signed the Communist Party–Lamont letter which appeared in the *New Masses* of May 3, giving a blanket endorsement to the Moscow Trials and bloody purges, etc., etc. There are other statements of a similar character to which you affixed your name. In every case in which an inquiry was sent to you, you confirmed the validity of your signature.

To be perfectly honest, Mr. Davis, my letter to the editor of the *Digest* was only a very mild indication of my opinion of the views you have expressed and the role you have played in recent years. Together with others I am pretty accurately informed not only of your published work but of many other things as well.

However, I believe that justice should be done even to those who do not believe in it themselves, just as I believe in academic freedom even for those who extenuate its absence in Russia. And so, again I ask: where, from 1937 up to the Stalin-Nazi Pact and the invasion of Finland, did you express publicly the sentiments you have voiced in your letter to me of Dec. 16th?

1. Jerome Davis.

35

Dear Mr. Davis,[1]   December 26, 1939

I really do not know what to make of your excited letter of December 20th. Won't you sit down in a cool movement and reason a little with me?

First of all, you refer to my "name calling." What "names" have I called you? I have described what I take to be your views on Russia, and have asked you for the evidence that the description is inaccurate. Instead of sending me the evidence which you assert exists, you fall back on your right to free speech—as if I were attacking it!—and characterize as "name calling" those very "honest differences of opinion" to which you are always appealing when you are the subject of these opinions.

The question is, Mr. Davis, what precisely are your opinions about Russian totalitarianism? I have only your public statements to go on, and since 1937 your public record of collaborative activity with Stalinist partisans (to mention *only* public things). These seem to me to more than justify the inference that I, together with every other *independent* observer in the liberal and labor world, have made about your social views and ideological allegiances.

Your letter of Dec. 20th raises a genuine doubt in my mind, for reasons I shall soon state, whether you yourself know what your opinions are. You ask me to tell you more about the Van Kleeck letter attacking the Committee to investigate the truth about the Moscow Trials, request that I send it on to you, and in one breath say "I do not here admit that I signed these letters" and, in the other, "you cannot fairly read into the letters something which honest and competent people did not mean by them."

This is positively shameless, Mr. Davis! Two years and ten months ago we had an extended correspondence about this letter. I sent it on to you, you acknowledged that you signed it, and on the basis of what Miss Van Kleeck told you, you defended the absurd charges it made. I have copies of the entire correspondence—four letters of mine and four of yours. If you have changed your mind since then, why not come out publicly and say so?

As for the other letter, I told you where you can find it. Your name is printed as a signer. Until now you never denied that you signed it. It is on the basis of such things (and of many others) that people have come to the conclusion that since 1937 you have been either a Stalinist or a full-fledged Stalinist fellow traveler. This is not calling you names any more than calling a man a Republican or a sympathizer with the Republican Party on the basis of his printed statements and public (and private) acts, is calling him names. How can anyone tell that you don't believe the things you sign? Don't you read them?

I must also confess my surprise that you should resort to such obvious evasion in answering my question: where and when, since 1937 (or say after the first Moscow trial) did you, as you claim, "repeatedly criticize the Stalin government for lack of liberty, for hostility to religion and for bureaucracy"? Please point to published evidence of the same kind as I have cited, in which, far from doing what you claim to have done, you have actually white-washed Stalin's terror. More specifically, where have you publicly criticized any of the following:

(1) The first Moscow trial, (2) the second Moscow trial, (3) the Russian purges, (4) the executions of the Red Army staff, (5) the third Moscow trials, (6) the export of Russian oil to Italy for use in Ethiopia and Spain, (7) the Stalin-Nazi Pact, (8) the invasion of Poland, (9) the invasion of Finland, etc.

Also (a) the absence of academic freedom in Russian universities, (b) the absence of a free press, (c) the intellectual terror against all who did not and do not hew to the party line in every field from genetics to astronomy, from the cinema to philosophy, etc.

I have deliberately restricted myself to Russia since that is the acid test of Stalinist allegiance or sympathy. The nature of your collaboration with the Shukotoffs, the Burgums,[2] and others of their ilk in the trade-union field, your disgraceful failure to endorse the defense of Fred Beal,[3] innocent victim of a Southern frame-up and a G.P.U. denunciation, and sundry other matters which concern you (and which, I understand, are soon to come out) I prefer not to discuss at this time.

Finally, you are entitled to any of your opinions on any subject. I am entitled to criticize you, especially where I believe your opinions wrong and your public actions perilous to the ideals of a decent social order. I am anxious to be corrected if I am mistaken about your opinions. I do not set myself up as anybody's censor or mentor, but I will not forego my right to speak up for victims of injustice and to call a lie—even if it is a lie about Russia—by its right name. Nor have I any personal feeling against you. As a matter of fact, I feel sorry for you because I am convinced that you have been duped by your own naivete and by the machinations of members of the Communist Party and the G.P.U.

1. Jerome Davis.

2. Arnold Shukotoff, professor at City College of New York, and Edwin Berry Burgum, professor at New York University. Both of these men were active in the teachers' union in New York City.

3. Organizer for the National Textile Workers Union who led the 1929 effort to organize textile workers in Gastonia, North Carolina. Tried and convicted for murder in North Carolina, Beal fled to the Soviet Union. Disillusioned with the USSR, he returned to the United States where he served five years in a North Carolina prison.

2

The 1940s

For Hook, communism and fascism, with their claim to ultimate truth and demand for total allegiance, were the most dangerous threats to freedom and pluralism. They were not, however, the only ones. During the 1940s Hook also attacked religion, particularly Roman Catholicism, and claimed that the same reason cited for excluding political totalitarians from academia applied with equal force to religious authoritarians. Neither group was able to follow truth wherever it might lead. On *a priori* grounds a Communist professor had to reject philosophical idealism and classical economics just as a Roman Catholic professor had to reject materialism and deism. If Hook's attacks on religion were less fierce, it was only because in the context of the 1940s religion was a less immediate danger than communism and fascism.

Hook's most famous assault on religion was prompted by a speech by the Thomistic philosopher Mortimer J. Adler in New York in 1940, a few months after German forces had overrun Western Europe. Delivered before the founding meeting of the Conference of Philosophy, Science, and Religion in Their Relation to the Democratic Way of Life, "God and the Professors" claimed that "democracy has much more to fear from the mentality of its teachers than from the nihilism of Hitler" and his armies. Hitler's nihilism was at least "more honest and consistent, less blurred by queasy qualifications" than the positivism, pragmatism, and relativism espoused by the West's intellectuals and professors. Only a commitment to metaphysics and absolutist values, Adler asserted, could meet the challenge of fascism and communism. "Until the professors and their culture are liquidated," he concluded, "the resolution of modern problems—a resolution which history demands should be made—will not even begin." Hook believed Adler was calling for an educational inquisition to eliminate, among others, anyone who had been influenced by John Dewey, Hook's revered teacher and mentor.

Hook answered Adler in "The New Medievalism" (*New Republic,* October

28, 1940) and "The New Failure of Nerve" (*Partisan Review,* January–February and March–April, 1943). Here and elsewhere Hook denied that democracy required spiritual foundations and philosophic absolutes. Hook also organized the Conference on Methods in Science and Philosophy to respond to the authoritarian and anti-scientific impulses inherent in the thinking of Adler and such intellectual bedfellows as Robert Maynard Hutchins, president of the University of Chicago. In *Out of Step,* Hook denied that he had ever welcomed a confrontation with Adler and his acolytes. "I engaged in this because most often no one else was willing to do so. Time and again after resolving to devote myself to the sweet uses of technical philosophy, I would be urged once more to enter the fray, often by the very people who had advised me previously that I ought to turn my back on politics and write books for eternity."

Certainly Hook needed no urging to become involved in the controversy surrounding the Cultural and Scientific Conference for World Peace held at the Waldorf-Astoria Hotel in New York in March 1949. Such a conference, the *Daily Worker* had declared in January 1949, was necessary because "the peace, living standards, and democratic rights of Americans are imperiled by the threat of war that exists today." The conference was part of a Soviet peace campaign, and it had been preceded by a peace conference in Wroclaw, Poland, the previous year marked by ill-tempered attacks on American foreign policy. At the Wroclaw meeting, A. A. Fadeyev had assailed American foreign policy and its literary supporters, whom he described as "hyenas who mastered the fountain pen." Fadeyev led the Soviet delegation at the Waldorf Conference.

The Waldorf Conference—the "last hurrah of fellow traveling in the United States"*—was sponsored by the National Council of the Arts, Sciences, and Professions, a group that included such prominent American fellow travelers and Communist Party members as Jo Davidson, Howard Fast, Lillian Hellman, Albert E. Kahn, Corliss Lamont, John Howard Lawson, and Paul Robeson. The NCASP was an offshoot of the Progressive Citizens of America, which had been established to support the 1948 presidential campaign of Henry Wallace. The astronomer Harlow Shapley, a prominent member of NCASP, director of Harvard University's Observatory, and a leading fellow traveler, was in charge of the Waldorf Conference.

After Shapley rebuffed his effort to speak before a plenary meeting of the conference, Hook organized the American Intellectuals for Freedom to protest the Waldorf Conference. The AIF was a who's who of the anti-communist American Left. It included Max Eastman, James T. Farrell, Horace Kallen, Robert Lowell, Dwight Macdonald, Mary McCarthy, A. J. Muste, Arthur M. Schlesinger, Jr., Norman Thomas, and Bertram Wolfe. The AIF predicted

---

*John Rossi, "Farewell to Fellow Traveling: The Waldorf Peace Conference of March 1949, *Continuity* no. 10 (Spring 1985): 2.

correctly that the Waldorf Conference would become "a platform for pro-Soviet statements, for defense of Soviet aggressive acts against her neighbors, and for one-sided attacks on the foreign policy of the United States."*

Hook persisted in his effort to be placed on the conference's agenda. He even went to Shapley's room at the hotel and in a face-to-face meeting with the astronomer demanded the opportunity to speak. Shapley maneuvered Hook into the corridor outside his room, backed into his room, and locked the door behind him. Hook relayed the event to the press. "If they had let me speak then they would have demonstrated that they wanted a fair and free exchange of information on the way to secure world peace," he told the reporters. In fact, the incident revealed the exact opposite. The organizers of the Waldorf Conference, Hook maintained, were solely interested in echoing Soviet propaganda. Addressing a meeting of the AIF on March 26, Hook stated that, in contrast to the Waldorf Conference, the purpose of the AIF gathering was to "tell the truth about the state of cultural freedom in our divided world."

Hook's efforts to open up the Waldorf Conference to opposing views won him few friends among its true believers. Hook believed that Shapley, until his death in 1972, blackballed his candidacy to become a member of the American Institute of Arts and Sciences because of the Waldorf Conference imbroglio. The poet Louis Untermeyer, who chaired a Waldorf Conference panel on "Writing and Publishing," called Hook "a dirty, four letter word." According to Howard Fast, he was a "baboon of imperialism."† Hook was not dissuaded by such insults. Considering their source, he felt they were badges of honor.

---

*Rossi, "Farewell to Fellow Traveling," 1–31.
†Ibid.

36

Dear Mr. Soule,[1]   January 3, 1940

This is to acknowledge your communication of December 26. I am not surprised that you should consider a discussion of the *New Republic*'s policy of recent years towards Russia a waste of time. After all, it has been the editors of the *New Republic* who for years have stressed the importance of Russian theory and practice for American progressives; and—make no mistake about it—it has been precisely the editorial attitude of the *New Republic* towards Stalin's terror and the critics of that terror which has alienated a large section of American progressive opinion.

Your charge that I am not interested in a "candid appraisal" is not only false but comes with poor grace from an editor of the *New Republic*. Not only do you refuse to permit a basic criticism of the *New Republic*'s policy to appear in its pages, but you have consistently refused even to consider the findings of the Dewey Commission of Inquiry. These findings flatly contradict the position you took on the Moscow Trials. One would imagine that editors interested in a candid appraisal would be the first to examine them on their merits, particularly since you professed skepticism of the Dewey Commission and characterized its members as "Trotskyists." (Incidentally, if as the editors of the *New Republic* now believe, it is libellous to assert falsely that an individual is a "Stalinist," why it is not libellous to falsely characterize individuals as "Trotskyists" as the *New Republic* has done?)

Your sudden discovery that the Moscow Trials are not "really important for our time" after you spent so much space and energy defending them is a shocking exhibition of editorial irresponsibility and moral cowardice. The Moscow Trials have at the very least as much importance for our times as the Sacco-Vanzetti trials which the *New Republic* still discusses.

Permit me, before closing, to make just two points in answer to the opening and final sentences of your letter. I have no personal quarrel with you. My quarrel is with the editors of the *New Republic* in the interests of truth and intellectual decency, not in the interests of factional politics. In the sense in which I have defined crypto-Stalinism, the policy of the *New Republic* since 1935 and up to very recently has been crypto-Stalinist. I believe I can demonstrate this to the satisfaction of every reasonable person. I also believe that the readers of the *New Republic* are entitled to a critical analysis of this policy. I am now writing a brochure on *Russia and the New Republic* which I hope will have the same healthy effect on progressive opinion that the *New Republic* supplement on *Russia and the New York Times* once had.[2]

You complain about the reception accorded your letter by me and the *New Leader.* I am not responsible for the policy of the *New Leader.* But I note that they printed your letter entire, a courtesy which those who have been criticized by the *New Republic* rarely enjoy at the hands of its editors. As for my own alleged misrepresentations, I assure you that I am perfectly willing to correct publicly any statement I have made about the policy of the *New Republic* which I cannot justify by pointing to cold print. Is the *New Republic* prepared to do the same in reference to its statements about the Moscow Trials, about the Dewey Commission, about critics of Stalin, and the Communist Party line in this country?

P.S. Your reference to my "partisans," Mr. Soule, may be unworthy of you personally but is quite in keeping with similar innuendoes by editors of the *New Republic* in the past. For your personal information, I add that I am not a member of any political party.

1. George H. Soule, Jr., an editor of the *New Republic* and author of *A Planned Society* (New York, 1932).

2. Brochure never appeared. For more on the quarrel between Hook and the *New Republic* regarding the Moscow Trials and the Dewey Commission, see Hook, *Out of Step,* pp. 230–33.

37

Dear Mr. Soule,[1]   January 8, 1940

The only hypothesis which can explain your letter of January 4th is that you do not read the *New Republic,* and are not aware of what goes on in its offices. You *have* accused people of being Trotskyists who are even further from Trotskyism than you are, and you have *not* retracted the epithet. In your issue of April 14, 1938 you referred to the Commission of Inquiry into the Moscow Trials which had just entrained for Mexico as "a commission consisting of prominent American liberals and Trotskyists." Who were the Trotskyists? John Dewey, Suzanne LaFollette,[2] Benjamin Stolberg?[3] Name one! No wonder your collective editorial consciences have been uneasy about the Dewey Commission and its work. (You assigned the *Proceedings* of the Commission for review to a well known political enemy of Trotsky—the author of the first official Communist attack in this country on Trotsky;[4] you did not even dare to send out the *Findings* of the Commission for review despite your editorial *parti pris* and Malcolm Cowley's[5] extended acclamations of each volume of the official Moscow *Proceedings* as they happened.)

It is not I who am mistaken, but you, about the *New Republic*'s refusal to print letters of correction in full, even shorter than your own. When Malcolm Cowley delivered himself of a false and unprincipled accusation against me apropos of my critical review of Kenneth Burke in the *Partisan Review*,[6] impugning my integrity as a reviewer (Cowley of all people!) and attributing a Trotskyist bias to me, my reply was refused publication because I declined to cut it. My reply was shorter than yours.

You persist in asserting that I have "promiscuously" labelled people as Stalinist. Whom? I have referred to you as "crypto-Stalinist," and I stand by the characterization in the sense and for the period I have indicated. There is only one member of your editorial staff who was an out and out Stalinist (although not a card-holder of the C.P.). My knowledge of his Stalinism is based not so much upon his writings in the *New Republic* as upon his activities and expressed sentiments in connection with matters outside the *New Republic*. As much as I deplore the crypto-Stalinism of the *New Republic,* I do not hold you responsible for it.

In your letters you have continuously asserted things about me for which you have offered no evidence. On the other hand, I have always cited chapter and verse to back up my statements. Don't you think you are under an obligation to do what you unjustly charge me with not doing?

1. George H. Soule.
2. LaFollette was active in anti-communist and feminist causes and helped found William F. Buckley's *National Review* in 1955.
3. Labor journalist and author of *The Story of the CIO* (New York, 1938).
4. Bertram D. Wolfe, "Trotsky's Defense," *New Republic* 93 (November 4, 1937), 79.
5. Literary editor of the *New Republic.*
6. Sidney Hook, "The Technique of Mystification," review of Kenneth Burke, *Attitudes toward History,* in *Partisan Review* 4 (December 1937): 56–62.

38

Dear Mr. Early,[1]   February 1, 1940

In response to your communication of January 20th, I am enclosing the copy you requested of Vol. VI, no. 1 of the *Bulletin* of the League of American Writers. The reference to the alleged fact of President Roosevelt's membership in the organization is made on p. 11 by the Chairman of the League, Donald Ogden Stewart, a member of the Hollywood colony notorious for his partisanship in behalf of the Communist Party and the Stalin regime. Incidentally, the League of American Writers is listed as one of the chief "front organizations" of the Communist Party in the Report submitted by Rep. Starnes of the Dies Committee[2] to Congress, Jan. 3, 1940 (p. 9, Report No. 1476). Although I am very critical of the procedures of the Dies Committee, its findings on this point are unexceptionable. I have underlined the names of those members of the National Board of the League of American Writers on p. 12 of its *Bulletin* who are definitely Stalinist either by membership or by willingness to execute the orders of the Communist Party.

Since this issue of the *Bulletin* of the League of American Writers has for various reasons become exceedingly rare, I shall be very much obliged if you will return it to me after the President has had an opportunity to see it.

I am pleased that the President appreciates the friendly interest which prompted me to write him, and on the strength of it hope he will forgive me for making the following suggestions. If the reference to the President's honorary membership in the League of American Writers is false, he should publicly blast this organization for its part in the campaign of the Communist Party to compromise the New Deal administration—a campaign which will help reaction. If the President is actually an honorary member of the League of American Writers by virtue of having signed some apparently innocent document, then he should carefully investigate the conditions under which and the intermediary through which his signature was procured. It is safe to predict that the intermediary—no matter who it turns out to be—is a trusted collaborator of the Communist Party. The necessity of some sort of prompt and decisive action is obvious since forces hostile to progressive policies can make deadly use of this typical piece of Communist Party chicanery.

Please assure the President that I am interested in this matter not for any political or factional reasons but out of profound concern for the state of cultural freedom in America. Whatever their differences in politics all citizens of a democracy should regard the principles of cultural freedom and integrity as part of their common heritage.

1. Stephen Early, secretary to President Roosevelt.
2. House Committee on Un-American Activities, chaired by Martin Dies, Democrat from Texas.

39

Dear Sir,[1]   May 3, 1940

This will acknowledge your utterly astonishing letter of April 23.

In my communication to you of April 16th I wrote asking whether you had signed the document of the Progressive (Communist) Committee to

Rebuild the Labor Committee in which, together with other members of the Labor and Liberal Committee to Safeguard the Labor Party, I am denounced as a factionalist, and in which it is falsely asserted that I, an enrolled voter in the American Labor Party, have "criticized it from the 'left' for many years." In the event that you signed this document (your name is listed in your capacity as Editor of the *Protestant Digest*), I asked for the evidence on which you based your remarks.

In your reply to me of April 23 you admit that you signed this document, a document which lists you as a member of the Executive Committee of the Communist insurgent group in the A.L.P. You do not meet, however, my demand that you offer proof of the statements concerning me contained in that document. Due to a missing semi-colon in my copy of the document, I was under the impression that I also had been included among the so-called "red-baiters." To which you reply:

"If they had said you were a red-baiter I feel that perhaps they might have been justified . . . (because) you took the trouble to criticize the inclusion of Jerome Davis on my editorial advisory board."

My letter to you about Mr. Davis concerned your prospectus in which you professed opposition to all forms of totalitarianism. My simple query was to ask how you reconciled that program with defense of Russian totalitarianism as illustrated until the time of my writing by Mr. Davis. When you declared that this letter of mine which assumed the good faith of your campaign against totalitarianism was "red-baiting," I knew that something was rotten in Denmark. I therefore worked through a file of the *Protestant Digest,* and it is clear what the trouble is.

I charge on the basis of your editorial line that you are a Communist Party fellow traveler deceiving both the members of your editorial board and your readers. Your line parallels the Communist Party line on every point except that it is not as outspoken.

1. You have defended in effect the Nazi-Soviet Pact.

2. You have extenuated the invasion of Finland.

3. You have held that England and France are mainly responsible for the European War (not the invasion of Poland by Germany and Russia).

4. *You have failed to criticize, by as much as a syllable, the totalitarian excesses in Russia, even though were your program sincere that criticism would be just as much in order as criticisms of Franco's Spain.*

5. You have shifted from friendliness to hostility towards Roosevelt and the New Deal, paralleling the shift of the Communist Party.

6. You have supported all the Communist Party causes in the cultural and political field, and have never supported any cause which the Communist Party has opposed.

7. Your membership in the Communist Party Committee in the A.L.P. indicates where your allegiance lies.

In our American democracy you have every right to defend any cause, even one hostile towards democracy. But you have no right to pretend to a democratic faith you do not hold, and to resort to duplicity in order to further the aims of a totalitarian power. In the interest of moral and political hygiene, you ought to sail honestly under your own colors.

To assert that you are the "voice of Protestant Thought and Action," as your masthead proclaims, is an arrant presumption: your magazine represents the voice of Communist totalitarianism on what the Communist Party cynically calls the Protestant Front.

1. Kenneth Leslie, editor of *Protestant Digest.*

40

Dear Professor Cannon,[1]   May 20, 1940

The evidence that the Medical Bureau to Aid Spanish Democracy was Communist-dominated is derived in the main from two independent sources: (a) from individuals who worked in the offices of the Bureau in New York City, both before and after its affiliation with the North American Committee; (b) from individuals who worked as heads of active units of the Medical Bureau in Spain.

(a) These individuals are persons who either did office work or fund-raising (Francis Henson), and who resigned or were forced out because of Communist pressure. According to them the leading office personnel of the Medicine Bureau in New York, those in active charge, were either Communist Party members or fellow travelers.

(b) Much more important is the testimony, documents, letters, and photographs furnished by Dr. John Jacobs Posner, outstanding oral surgeon in New York City (200 West 57th Street), who gave up his practice to become head of the second unit sent to Spain by the Medical Bureau, and his assistant, Miss Mitchell. They were in charge of the American Base Hospital at Villa Paz, near Tarancon. Both of these people, whom I have personally interviewed and whose materials I have examined, are prepared to lay their material before you either in N.Y.C. or in Cambridge, if the latter suits your convenience. Their material in itself is absolutely conclusive but they offer as substantiating witnesses who can furnish additional data Dr. Donald H. Pitts, general surgeon, of Floydada, Texas and Dr. Abraham Ettelson, brain surgeon, 30 North Michigan Blvd., Chicago, Illinois, both leading members of the unit in Spain who were driven out for protesting against Communist political malpractices in the unit. They also mention the name of someone whom they say is known to you, Thelma Erickson (Mrs. Albert Byrne) whose husband and father are (or were) both members of the Communist Party.

Dr. Posner and Miss Mitchell are completely non-political people who were interested only in rendering medical aid to the Spanish cause. They have documents of praise and thanks from the Medical Bureau for the work they did, including, significantly enough, an appreciation from Robert Minor, member of the C.E.C. of the Communist Party of the U.S.A., who was the liaison man with full authority in Spain between Dr. Barsky,[2] the Communist head of the first unit, and the Communist Party of Spain.

Both Dr. Posner and Miss Mitchell are surprised that you are at the present time uninformed about the nature of the Medical Bureau because upon their return from Spain they made a confidential report to the Steering Committee of the Medical Bureau with the understanding that it was to be submitted to the officers, including yourself. This report was made to Dr. Louis Miller, Dr. Jesse Tolmach, Dr. Segal and Miss Lipshitz, secretary (all Communists or Communist sympathizers) at the home of Dr. Miller. I have read the stenographic copy of this report, which gives an account of the Communist domination as well as of the inefficiency of the unit in Spain and appeals, in the name of the Spanish people, for the eradication of foreign political influences from medical, humanitarian work. Dr. Posner and Miss Mitchell did not make this report public because they feared that newspaper publicity would prejudice the cause of the Spanish people by making it appear that the Loyalist government of Spain was the creature of the Communist Party, which they did not believe.

The material which I have seen, and I have not seen all the documents they have, proves that the Medical Bureau to Aid Spanish Democracy was in reality a Medical Bureau to Aid the Communist Party. Dr. Barsky, its first head, was a Communist. Robert Minor, who coordinated medical activities in Spain and decided questions of medical personnel and assignment, is a leading Communist functionary. Miss Frederica Martin, the head nurse at Villa Paz, was a Communist Party member who took orders from her political leaders in priority to orders from her medical superiors. Mr. Al Stone, who was *officially* known and referred to as *Political Commissar* of the Villa Paz Base Hospital in Spain, was a Communist Party functionary. Any criticism of the Communists in Spain, Russia or America, made by non-political members of the Unit (which was overwhelmingly Communist in complexion because of prior selection in the U.S.A.), was sufficient to incur the suspicion, and sometimes the open charge, of Fascist sympathy. Regular official meetings of the staff were held, at which all members were expected to be present, which were addressed by Political Commissars, on platforms adorned by pictures of Lenin, red flags with the Russian emblem of the hammer and sickle, and, in the background, by a small American flag.

Whatever medical aid reached Spain from the Bureau was used *exclusively* in behalf of Communist Party forces and detachments, primarily those of the International Brigades. Attempts made by Drs. Pitts and Posner to make materials and services available directly to the Spanish government were frustrated by Communist Party members. According to Dr. Posner the Spanish government compelled the Medical Bureau to withdraw from Spain *before the war was over* because it discovered that it was functioning primarily as a political auxiliary of the Communist Party.

These are only the highlights of Dr. Posner's and Miss Mitchell's testimony. I have disregarded in this report the wealth of detailed authenticating evidence they presented. I strongly urge that you get in touch with them if you have any questions about their material.

I think it is clear that as National Chairman, you together with many other democratic minded Americans whose sole interest has been in giving non-factional support to the Spanish people in their struggles against Mussolini, Hitler, and Franco, have been systematically deceived by Communist Party members who have occupied strategic positions within the Medical Bureau.

1. Walter B. Cannon, professor of physiology, Harvard Medical School.
2. Dr. Edward K. Barsky, Joint Anti-Fascist Refugee Committee.

41

Dear Professor Hocking,[1]   June 4, 1940

This is to acknowledge your letter of May 31st.

A copy of my letter to Mr. Leslie[2] was sent to you as a member of the Editorial Board of the *Protestant Digest* since in that capacity you appear in the public eye as sharing responsibility for its editorial policy. I thought you would be interested in my analysis of that policy. Needless to say, I am not a little surprised by your response.

After I wrote to Mr. Leslie I received a copy of Professor Reinhold Niebuhr's letter of resignation from the Editorial Board of the *Protestant*

Digest, written independently of mine, which completely confirms my analysis of Mr. Leslie's crypto-Stalinist line. Do you think that he, too, is fussy and superstitious? In a telephone conversation with him, he quoted Rev. Herman Reissig, an ex-Stalinist, that the Communist Party was indirectly putting up money for the magazine. Whether it is or not is immaterial; the important thing is the nature of its line and whether it is playing fair with its readers.

My letter to Mr. Leslie detailed the reasons for my conclusion that he was fronting for the Stalinist line. I should have very much preferred an answer to these reasons rather than an airy dismissal of them. Particularly since you seem to be quite misinformed when you write that Mr. Leslie is not affiliated with any communist organization. He is a member of the Executive Committee of the so-called Progressive Committee to Save the Labor Party, which is 100% Stalinist.

I hope you will pardon me for my feeling that your defense of Mr. Leslie shows extreme political naivete. You write, "he does not believe that all Russia is black because some Russia is red,—in other words some good things can even come out of Russia." Of course! But isn't it just as true that not all Germany is black because some Germany is brown? This commonplace can be affirmed of *all* countries. Why then does Mr. Leslie praise *only* Russia whereas almost all other major powers, including our own country, are severely criticized? And as for the good things that have come out of Russia, do you mean Russian foreign policy, particularly the Stalin-Nazi Pact (which let loose the dogs of war, the invasions of Poland and Finland) *so ardently defended by Mr. Leslie in the pages of the "Protestant Digest"?*

I am firmly convinced that the struggle against totalitarianism is indivisible, that you cannot be against it in one country and for it in another. That is why I am not impressed by what Mr. Leslie is saying against anti-Semitism any more than I was by Hitler's plea for the liberation of all oppressed minorities or by the Russian hullabaloo, in which Mr. Leslie joined before the Stalin-Nazi Pact, against Fascism. For these are only opportunist tactics in the general totalitarian strategy.

I have been a close student of the philosophy, practice, and organizational structure of left-wing groups in this country for more than twenty years. I may of course be wrong about Mr. Leslie—although my hunch is that, if anything, I have understated the case—but I doubt whether I am "superstitious."

1. William E. Hocking (see letter 30, note 3).
2. Kenneth Leslie.

42

Dear Professor Cannon,[1]   June 15, 1940

I shall be very much obliged if you will let me know what the upshot of your inquiries are concerning the activities of the Medical Bureau to Aid Spanish Democracy. We have not yet sent our report on Stalinist Outposts to the press, and in the event that your own independent investigation confirms our findings, perhaps it would be best for you to issue a public statement. That would permit you to place the proper blame on the political partisans who compromised the worthy aims of the Bureau, and prevent unjust accusations against individuals connected with the Medical Bureau who are not Stalinists and whose good faith was so grievously abused.

If, however, you have uncovered evidence which impugns the testimony we have, we shall be very happy to delete any reference to the Medical Bureau in our report, and send a specific correction to those members of the Committee for Cultural Freedom who have already received it.

May I add that I was very glad to read your letter disassociating yourself from the statement issued by the Association of Scientific Workers? Although the present picture is not altogether clear, we have evidence which indicates that the organization was founded by Stalinists in Philadelphia and that its line, including changes and various emphases, has followed that of the Communist Party. Our information comes primarily from a former member of the Communist Party who is a physiologist in a large eastern university and who is also a member of the Am. Assoc. of Scientific Workers. I quote a sentence or two from his account:

> After the Nazi-Soviet Pact the AASW changed its political slogans and interests in exactly the same way as did the American Communist Party or the American Youth Congress. The boycott of German goods, their chief topic at meetings, the slogans "Fight Hitler" and "Collective Security" and related catch phrases were suddenly dropped like burning embers and silence on foreign affairs accompanied by Keep America Out of War campaigns took their place.

I presume that you also know that before the Nazi-Soviet Pact, the AASW, although quite vehement about persecution of scientists in Germany and Italy, carefully refrained from any criticism or protest against the just as ruthless persecution of non-conforming scientists in Russia. Since the Pact, it is silent about Germany, too.

I am sorry that our correspondence should have begun about matters of this kind, for I should have much preferred to write you about your work on emotions, which I have greatly admired and found, together with my students, extremely useful in some of my courses in philosophy devoted to a naturalistic theory of human behavior. My chief interests lie in philosophy, not in exposing totalitarian fronts which it would be best totally to ignore if they were not so dangerous, and if they did not constitute such a serious threat both to intellectual integrity as well as to our political democracy. I trust you will understand my feelings in the matter.

1. Walter B. Cannon.

43

Dear Mr. Ingersoll,[1]   July 23, 1940

I have just read Mr. Victor Riesel's[2] article on *PM* in *The New Leader* of July 20th. Since I am mentioned in the article together with Professor John Dewey and other organizers of the Committee for Cultural Freedom as among those who have been objects of attack by Communist Party members and fellow travelers allegedly employed by *PM,* I am writing to inquire whether Mr. Riesel's allegations are true.

As a firm believer in our Bill of Rights, I am in favor of extending it to all legally recognized political minorities, even to those who, like members of the Communist Party and their fellow travelers, are seeking to destroy the Bill of Rights. But this does not justify the use of misleading labels of "liberalism" and "progressivism" as protective coloration for totalitarian propaganda. *PM* has every right to stand for any political creed; but in the interests of moral hygiene and political responsibility, which are the presuppositions of the Bill of Rights, that creed should be openly proclaimed. If *PM* is being manned in important key posts by members and fellow travelers of the Communist Party, your reading public should certainly be informed of it. As your own editorial declarations recognize, it is impossible for these people to prevent their political prepossessions and allegiances from coloring their stories and reports. I am therefore keenly interested in knowing whether Mr. Riesel's allegations of fact concerning the individuals mentioned are true.

1. Ralph M. Ingersoll, founder and editor of *PM,* a left-wing New York newspaper.
2. Newspaper columnist specializing in labor-management issues.

44

Dear Mr. Ingersoll,[1]   August 17, 1940

Thank you for your letter of August 12th which has just been forwarded to me here where I am spending my vacation.

I know you are a very busy man and there is no reason why you should spend any time answering my questions. But I believe that my point of view as well as my questions about *PM* are representative of a large sector of liberal opinion, particularly in the colleges and schools generally. And it is to this sector of opinion that *PM,* as I understand it, would like to appeal.

In reply to the charges made against *PM* by Mr. Riesel, Mr. Lundberg,[2] and others, one can say either that they are untrue or, if true, they are irrelevant; but it is not clear to me from your letter whether you are denying their truth or relevance or both.

As for the truth of Mr. Riesel's statements, restricting myself only to the point where I am mentioned in his article, I regret that I must confirm what he has to say about Mr. Leo Huberman.[3] I have the issue of the *Daily Worker* of Aug. 14, 1939 in which that gentleman denounced the outstanding liberals and progressives who organized the Committee for Cultural Freedom as "Fascists and allies of Fascists," for referring to Russia as a totalitarian state. I have the March, 1938 issue of *Soviet Russia Today* and sundry issues of the *New Masses* containing documents issued by the Communist Party endorsing the Moscow trials, Russian foreign policy and the Communist Party line in general, which were also signed by Mr. Huberman. There is no doubt whatsoever that he is a very intimate fellow traveler of the Communist Party.

Well, what of it? Is it relevant, even if true? It certainly is relevant for as you yourself recognize, the standpoint or bias which selects and interprets material for publication is of primary importance. It would be the height of naivete to expect unprejudiced reporting from a person who follows the Communist Party line. And so far as I have been able to test Mr. Huberman's performance as a labor editor and reporter in the issues of *PM* I have read, he has carried on precisely as a person would who is following the Communist Party line, with just enough protective coloration to deceive the politically innocent.

I use the case of Mr. Huberman only as an illustration to make the point clear (there are others like Leone Zugsmith who have been active in the same way and who have signed the same documents). It seems to me that it is not "a question of past connections" of some members in the leading personnel of *PM*. It is a question of their present organizational sympathies and totalitarian ideology. Under our Bill of Rights these people are entitled to profess their views openly and publicly, and I am prepared to defend them in that right. But it is an altogether different matter for them to use an avowedly non-Communist newspaper like *PM* to evaluate labor and other news from a Communist Party angle. I am sure you would agree if fellow travelers of the Nazi Bund were active on *PM*. Your excellent editorials on Lindbergh show that. Why, then, the difference in attitude towards totalitarian fellow travelers of a different shade? I really am puzzled.

Perhaps I am wrong about the facts; and my reasoning may be open to question. If so I shall appreciate hearing to that effect from you.

1. Ralph Ingersoll.
2. Ferdinand Lundberg, secretary-treasurer of the Committee for Cultural Freedom.
3. Marxist economist and author of *America, Incorporated* (New York, 1940).

45

Dear Corliss,[1]   May 17, 1941

This will acknowledge your letter of May 16th.

It seems to me that only an infinite capacity for self-deception could have led you to write as you did. You try to make out that I refuse to discuss political issues in terms of argument and evidence, and yet for the last five years you have been running away from every offer I have made to hold a public discussion with you on your views about Russia, Stalin, the Moscow Trials, etc. At first you didn't want to discuss the Moscow Trials because "it gives me a pain in the neck"; then because "there are for me far more important ways to spend my time than discussing it"; then because "I want to wait and see"; then because "you have made up your mind already." The quotes are from your letters to me and conversations. In the meantime, while writing this way, you had solidarized yourself with the Communist Party attack on our committee, and the quotes above were in reply to my patient attempt to argue against your unreasoned and mistaken course. When you became the spearpoint of the Communist Party attack against the Dewey commission's attempt to uncover the truth about the Moscow Trials, I renewed my offer again and again to discuss the issues with you, but to no avail. When I wrote my article for the *Modern Monthly*[2] I insisted as a condition for publication that you be shown it in advance and given an opportunity to reply in the same issue. You refused. You have always refused.

To prevent you from deluding yourself about your willingness to discuss things in terms of reason, I herewith repeat my offer to publicly debate your views on Russia, Stalin, the Moscow Trials, the Stalin-Hitler Pact, the invasion of Poland, the invasion of Finland, and on whether you are, as you amazingly proclaim yourself, "politically independent" or whether you are, as the rest of the world believes, an integral part of the Stalinist movement. Surely there is one subject mentioned here which you will be willing to discuss in terms of reason.

How odd that three and a half years after the publication of the *Modern Monthly* article you should raise the question with me of its accuracy. Odder still that you should challenge the truth of the reference to you as "a friend of the G.P.U." Do you recognize these words of yours from your *Daily Worker* article attacking the Dewey Commission? "The Soviet regime and its achievements are indivisible; and we cannot believe its system of justice is completely out of step with its splendid accomplishments in practically all other fields." You wrote that speech—didn't you understand what you were saying? The use of reason should begin with our own words. The G.P.U. is part of the system of justice of the Soviet regime, integral to the indivisible achievements and the splendid accomplishments you hail. The G.P.U., as Stalin put it, is "the shining sword, the indefatigable guard" of the Soviet regime. How can anyone be a "friend of the Soviet Union" and not be, given your own words above, a "friend of the G.P.U."? And at the time you wrote this, you were Chairman of the F.S.U.,[3] defending the verdict of the Russian courts, of which the G.P.U., says Stalin, "is the punitive organ" as well as "a military political tribunal." To characterize you as "a friend of the G.P.U." is strictly descriptive and strictly true. I could have made it stronger and no less true by saying that you were a defender and apologist of the G.P.U. Can anything be clearer? I am prepared to go over every word of that article and demonstrate that, if anything, I was understating the case.

That you, of all people, should pretend disquiet that the descriptive epithets so accurately applied to you are abuse, beggars all comment. Who was it that called Dewey a red-baiter, dealing with "the chief stock in trade of the Fascists and reactionaries"? Who was it that called me in the *N.Y. Post* "a rabid red-baiter and leading partisan of Leon Trotsky"? You did not say that by the latter you only meant my position on the Moscow Trials. This is simply not the truth as *your own words* in that letter show. Here is what you wrote: ". . . the *political* intent and the *political* control behind the committee's actions are well shown in the fact that its chief spokesman is Sidney Hook, rabid red-baiter and leading partisan of Leon Trotsky" (my italics). The truth is, Corliss, that by "a leading partisan of Trotsky" you meant I was a political Trotskyite, as is further shown by your reference to the members of the C.C.F. as my "Fellow-Trotskyites," although the over-whelming majority of them never served on the Moscow Trials Committee.

Why should the plain truth be so obscure to you? If you are ashamed at last of the great wrongs you have done, why not say so instead of denying you have done them. It is more manly and more intelligent. Do you want me and others to believe that you don't understand the meaning of the words you use? In your notorious Open Letter of August 1939, you say that "the Fascists and their allies" are trying to destroy democratic unity, and cite as your only concrete evidence the C.C.F. by name. You now say that it is "pretty absurd" to discover in this document even an "indirect reference" to the C.C.F. as "Fascists and their allies." This is even a more shocking statement. I will prove it to you by reason.

a) The *Nation,* which itself was highly critical of the C.C.F., commented as follows in its editorial of September 2, 1939:
"Last week we printed a letter signed by four hundred persons sympathetic with the Soviet regime attacking the Committee of Cultural Freedom and denouncing as 'fascists and their allies' the persons who organized that group and drew up its manifesto."
The *New Republic* and other periodicals summarized in a similar way.

b) Goodwin Watson[4] circulated his letter explaining why although he agreed with your document and not with ours, he didn't sign yours: he knew we weren't fascists or their allies as your document said.

c) After the Stalin-Hitler Pact, John Dewey sent a personal letter to the signers of the Open Letter asking them if they still thought we were fascists and pointing out the dishonesty of such a designation. Not a single member of your "initiating Committee" so much as acknowledged his letter. A number of your signers recanted.

d) The Communist press, official and unofficial, hailed your denunciation of the C.C.F. as "Fascists," etc.

e) Although *you* were aware of the way your document was universally understood, you nowhere and at no time published a correction of what you now call a "pretty absurd " interpretation.

Ask any unbiased person—or ask Margaret[5] or your mother who surely bear you no ill will—what light this puts you in. Show them all the facts.

I do not want to take the time to prove as I can easily do that in every other relevant point your behavior has been of a piece with the above. As for your letter of resignation from the *Marxist Quarterly,* when you circulated copies to the editors, *you* made it public. Whenever *I* have quoted from it, I have quoted it properly and with direct reference to your untrue and immoral public statements that you are "independent" in your political sympathies. I am willing to debate this question with you also.

Do not try to hide your face from unpleasant truths by attributing any personal "bitter" motivations to me. It is your ideas and actions which I have criticized, not because they are yours but because they are wrong and vicious. Why, indeed, should I be bitter against you personally? Our friendship was pleasant, and while it lasted you had many evidences of the nature of my feelings toward you. Believe it or not, it is the memory of those feelings which has prevented me from disclosing certain information which would be extremely damaging to you personally. For example, I have incontrovertible evidence that you were made National Chairman of the Friends of the Soviet Union by the Communist Party faction in that organization on the given ground that you would be the most easily amenable to control; and that some of the officials of your organization engaged directly in certain activities which I do not want to put down here on paper but which I once briefly described to you.

It is really these feelings which have led me, against my better judgment, to answer your letter at all. For publicly you have so completely identified yourself with Stalinist theory and practice that no "front" can any longer hide behind your name. Everywhere you are regarded as an unofficial Stalinist spokesman. And you have brought this on yourself. Why, you even rushed into print to defend the Stalin-Nazi Pact (with its mythical escape clause!) before Earl Browder did. Read over my *Modern Monthly* article again. Every prediction I made about your development has come true and worse. All your inner resources are gone. No one pays attention to your feeble protestations of differentiation. Even you don't half believe them. You have tied your future to the fate of Stalin, the greatest mass-murderer in history. Your doubts will not down. Instead of facing them, you are trying to whistle them away.

Poor, poor Corliss. You will never find your way back again to the intellectual companionship of honest minds by leaning on props. Sheean,[6] Louis Fischer,[7] McGill,[8] or any one else—they will all fail you. You will have to go it alone. If by a miracle you ever find the courage to break with Stalin, you will have to take the hard way.

---

1. Corliss Lamont, wealthy son of Thomas Lamont, a partner in the J. P. Morgan banking company, was a Communist fellow traveler. He had been a classmate of Hook's in graduate school at Columbia.

2. "Corliss Lamont: 'Friend of the G.P.U.,'" *Modern Monthly* 10 (March 1938): 5–8.

3. Friends of the Soviet Union, a communist front organization.

4. Goodwin B. Watson, professor of education, Teachers College, Columbia University.

5. Lamont's wife.
6. James Vincent Sheean, writer.
7. Louis Fischer, writer specializing in the Soviet Union and Soviet politics.
8. Possibly V. Jerauld McGill, professor of psychology, Hunter College, and a member of the Communist Party in the late 1930s.

46

Dear Corliss, [1]   June 4, 1941

After some hesitation I have decided to reply to your letter of May 27th on the chance that some plain talking may lead you to drop your pose of complacency (which fools nobody), and that a proof of what your mind has become, since you let yourself be taken into tow by the Stalinists, may revive a spark of intellectual integrity or moral decency in you who were once my friend.

There is really no pleasing you. You complain that I refuse to reasonably discuss with you your views on Russia and Stalin, and when I offer to meet you anywhere and under any appropriate auspices, you say I am looking for publicity. But I meant what I said. I will meet you anywhere—in your own home, in the bosom of your family, in a classroom, even in the columns of the *Daily Worker* if you will get your friends to open them to me.

To charge me with a desire for publicity when I put myself out to meet your complaint is a cheap slur of a weak man. Do you really believe that I can get any helpful publicity by debating with you, that I am in need of it? I have gone long ways in my life to avoid it as you once knew. Your remark about publicity is indeed revealing. I think you ought to know that in non-Stalinist circles, including the Socialist Party, there are two theories about you in respect to your fellow traveling. These theories, I am told, are widely held by the Stalinist leadership, especially among the cadres that antedate the Popular Front; and I know myself how prevalent they are in academic circles. The first is that you are an extraordinary fool; the second that you are a publicity hound and can be had for the asking by any political group which will provide you with large audiences and media of public expression. When I would interpose other explanations, they would be waved aside as expressions of sentimentalism. I suggest, therefore, great caution in charging anyone with a desire for publicity. If you must have an excuse for running away from the discussion you said you wanted, find another. The simple truth is that you are afraid —afraid, not so much of me as of the crying weakness of your position which you have sustained by a faith as irrational as that of Tertullian but more ignoble and less wholehearted.

You assert that my justification for referring to you as a "friend of the G.P.U." is as weak as water, and imply that the grounds I gave would justify calling many decent people "friends of the F.B.I." Water, incidentally, is one of the strongest elements in the world; if you believe my arguments weak, why don't you indicate where and how? Here is the answer to your pathetic *tu quoque:* If the F.B.I. were to play the same role in the U.S. as the G.P.U. in the U.S.S.R.; if I were to justify grotesque frame-ups and murder of myriads of innocents in this country as you have done in Russia; if I were to condone inhuman torture of defendants and their dependents in this country as practiced in Stalinist Russia; if I were to applaud the same kind of universal terror and espionage in this country as is found in Russia; and if I were to add to this the statement that the American system of justice could not be much out of line with the meritorious technical achievements of the American economy—which is the precise equivalent of the statement you made about Russia—then, and *only* then, would it be justified to call me "a friend of the F.B.I." And if such an unhappy day comes, I would have the gumption to accept the label as deserved, instead of whining about it as you are doing when you are truthfully characterized or with nerveless fingers and dull mind try to twist the laws of logic.

But I shall be generous with you. You object to the phrase "friend of the G.P.U." Very well, write me a letter telling me that you are *not* a "friend of the G.P.U." and give me permission to make it public since everybody, including the Stalinists, thinks you are. Or to prevent you from saying that I want to make political capital out of it, make it public yourself. I renew my offer to discuss this point with you, as well as others, anywhere.

I hope you will not be offended when I say that since you made a religion out of Russia, it has saddened me to observe a distinct deterioration in your intellectual powers. The first shocking public exhibition of it took place at the New School at the opening session of the Conference on Methods when you threw the audience into merriment by retorting to my charge that there was no academic freedom or free intellectual inquiry in Russia, with the question: How is this possible in view of the fact that the Russian aviators flew over the North Pole?

(Speaking of academic freedom, I am somewhat mystified by your references to my ideas on the subject which so far as I know have not changed. I believe in academic freedom in all countries, i.e., the right of qualified teachers to investigate, publish and teach the truth as they see it no matter what their beliefs. The only valid grounds for firing a teacher is *conduct* or practice unbecoming a teacher established by a fair hearing. Membership in the Nazi and Communist Parties imposes by official provision (the documents are available) practices that are unbecoming a teacher, like anonymous attacks on colleagues in shop-papers, etc. This must of course be established in the particular institution. With what in this do you disagree? The principle or the allegation of fact? Incidentally, the Academic Freedom Committee of the A.C.L.U. is discussing a proper formulation of this very point. I also believe that even members of the Nazi and Communist Party are entitled to full judicial rights, but that if they are guilty of a crime, like perjury, they should be punished. Not only am I mystified about your reference to my beliefs on this subject, I am even more mystified why anyone like you, who condones the most outrageous system of juridical frame-ups and academic terror that the world has ever seen, should be concerned with my views. You can't whitewash murder of scholars suspected of heresy in Russia, and pretend a genuine interest in academic freedom here. No one believes you. As protective coloration it's no good; the stain is already too deep. And as salve for an uneasy conscience, it's no good either unless you stop thinking.)

I thought I was beyond being surprised by anything you did or wrote but the line in your letter "I really love people and all the people" floored me. How can you with your record dare to say this? Have you no shame? That you love Stalin I have no doubt; did you also love the victims of his purges? Do you love the millions in his prison-camps? You who love all the people, why did you refuse to sign a petition asking that the lives of the Moscow defendants be spared? Why have you never raised your voice, out of love of humanity, against the ghastly episodes of official Russian cruelty from the man-made famine of 1932–33 down to today? Why have you so unlovingly attacked every decent person from Dewey down who protested against Russian excesses? What horrible obsession moves you to write as if you were a cross between Smerdyakov and Uriah Heep?[2]

You great lover of humanity and defender of the crucifixion of the named and nameless Russian men, women and children—I pity you from the bottom of my heart. I must confess that I do not love all the people. I do not love those who are cruel. I cannot love Hitler and Stalin and other tyrants who in degrading human beings have degraded me.

It is with reluctance that I write you as I do. But you are in a bad way, Corliss, and you need help. I am trying to help you—for your letter is also a psychological S.O.S.—by telling you the truth. You will be able to live peacefully with yourself only by learning to live with the truth, no matter how much it hurts at the beginning. Nor is it my truths I would want you to live by. Heaven knows I have made plenty of errors. It is to the willingness to search for the truth that I want to recall you.

It is late, Corliss, but not too late. You can still fight your way back to the community of free minds and free men whom Hitler and Stalin can't defeat even if they win the war, for no one can be morally defeated who doesn't yield up his values. That is where the Corliss I knew belonged, and unless you have become a completely different person, it is only the respect and esteem of this community that will make you happy.

I was once your friend, among the very few who never tried to exploit you politically or otherwise, but who liked you for yourself alone. You will remember how I tried to save you from a political career, how I urged you to bear in mind that there were other modes of activity besides politics, how glad I was that you were beginning to make your way in some of them. I am not now the enemy of that Corliss; in fact, I would like to see him restored to life.

Of course, no one can escape political commitments in this world. But these must be compatible with moral values which make friendship and other ideal goods possible.

1. Corliss Lamont.
2. Pavel Smerdyakov, a misanthrope and murderer who ends up hanging himself in Dostoevski's *The Brothers Karamazov.* Uriah Heep is the hypocritical and fawning clerk in Dickens's *David Copperfield.*

47

Dear Corliss,[1]   January 9, 1942

This will acknowledge your strange and unsolicited communication to me of January 1. You claim that "the Nazi-Soviet war and its course over the past six months" have justified your defense of Stalinism during the last ten years and invalidated my criticisms. You invite me to reconsider my position on the Soviet Union and my attitude to you personally, since my criticism of the unsavory and pathetic role you have played in the American cultural scene, as you say, "stemmed primarily" from your defense of Stalinism and its regime of terror and purge. You conclude with the remark that despite your innate modesty you are compelled to admit that history has proved you right.

It is not a question of your innate modesty but of something more important whose absence cries out from every line of your letter.

To begin with, history cannot prove anything right except statements or predictions about historical fact. What predictions did you make which the Nazi-Soviet war verified? Your record of predictions about Russia is a rather dismal one. You predicted that the Stalin Constitution would extend democracy in Russia. It was followed by a blood bath. You predicted that Stalin would never sign a pact with Hitler. When news of it was announced, you predicted that it would have an escape clause. When its terms were made public, you predicted that even without an escape clause, the Hitler-Stalin Pact would save the peace of Europe, whereas it unleashed the Second World War. What the strength of Russian resistance to the German invasion does prove is that Hitler would hardly have undertaken a war in the west unless he was assured of Stalin's benevolent neutrality. Only if it were the case that *before* June 22nd you had predicted that Hitler would invade Russia and that after six months of fighting he would be two hundred miles from Moscow, would the record prove you right—and only on these points. I do not know whether you actually made these predictions: I do know that before June 22nd, like the Stalinists everywhere, you called this war an "imperialist" war. It was only after Hitler invaded Russia that you regarded the war as one in behalf of democracy. So far as I can see the only thing that the Nazi-Soviet War proves about you is that you are a June 22nd patriot.

About my own predictions I cannot claim any infallibility. Although I made no public predictions about the course of the Nazi-Russian War when it broke out, I admit gladly that I was mistaken in my estimate of the powers of resistance of the heroic Russian soldiers. But I did predict that the Stalin Constitution would serve as a cloak for further measures of repression. I predicted that Stalin-Nazi pact and its consequences. I predicted that, *if* he were given an alternative of war or peace, Stalin would not fight Hitler (Stalin and Molotov complained that they were not given an alternative); and that *if* Hitler were to invade Russia, you would change your line on the war overnight (as you did). I did not predict Hitler's invasion; neither did Stalin. And now for the record I want to make another prediction. *If Stalin signs a separate peace with Hitler, you will change your line once more about the war.*

What is truly astonishing about your letter is that you seem to believe that the Nazi-Soviet War has a bearing not only on specific predictions, but on everything which occurred in Russia during the last ten years. I say "astonishing" but I really should not be astonished. After all, you once claimed that the success of the Russian airmen in flying over the North Pole proved that there was freedom of scientific inquiry in the USSR. Presumably, if they had failed, this would have indicated the absence of free scientific inquiry. I thought then that this was an all-time low in *non sequiturs,* but in your present letter you surpass yourself. How and why does the Nazi-Soviet War bear on the question of whether Russia is a democracy, whether scientific and cultural freedom exist for those who do not accept Communist Party dogmas, whether the Moscow Trials were frame-ups?

Consider the last point. You believe that Hitler's failure to capture Moscow "proves" that the Moscow Trials were genuine. If Moscow had fallen, would you have changed you mind about the Moscow Trials? It would be downright silly in one case as in the other. The truth about the Moscow Trials can be learned only by examining the evidence. That evidence is available in the Official Reports of the Soviet government and in the record of the Hearings and Findings of the Dewey Commission. Similarly, the truth about the destruction of free trade-unions, the adoption of the internal passport system, the Draconian labor decrees which reintroduce feudal elements into the Russian economy, arbitrary arrests, deportation, executions, the introduction of capital punishment for children—the truth about these and other aspects of Russian culture does not depend upon the outcome of a military campaign. Is it possible that you do not see this?

Suppose an apologist for Nazism were to point to his predictions of Hitler's amazing military successes. Would that constitute an answer to the victims of the Gestapo? Would that justify Fascism? Have you always believed that might makes right? Or is it only that Stalin's might makes right?

Your reasoning is exactly on a par with the thought processes of one who were to say that since the U.S. is now fighting Hitler, this proves that Sacco-Vanzetti were guilty. If Mussolini were to become embroiled with Hitler, and the Italian soldiers were to put up a stiff fight, would you argue that this justified the assassination of Matteotti?[2] Do you begin to get the point? The answers to a question cannot be found except in a field which is *relevant* to the question in hand.

One might argue that all of Stalin's past crimes were necessary to make it possible for him to prevent Hitler from taking Russia. The evidence, it seems to me, shows that these crimes weakened Russia, and that a less Stalinized Russia would have crushed Hitler a long time ago. Instead it helped him come to power in Germany by the policy of regarding German Social Democracy as the chief enemy, dual trade unions, collaboration with the Nazis, etc. But *you* cannot even argue that Stalin's crimes were necessary to his victory, for when they were committed you called them acts of virtue.

For years now I have offered to discuss or debate with you the evidence of the Moscow Trials (or a related theme) on a public platform or in the press. You have always run away. I renew the offer once more. Surely you ought to welcome the opportunity to present the "proof," furnished by the Nazi-Soviet War, that you were right in your passionate defense of the Moscow Trials, despite the evidence presented by the Dewey Commission that they were frame-ups.

You realize, I hope, that you will need something more than "innate modesty" to make your case.

1. Corliss Lamont.
2. Giacomo Matteotti, socialist deputy in the Italian legislature and author of *The Fascisti Exposed,* was murdered by Italian fascists in June 1924. His murderers were either acquitted or given light sentences.

48

Dear Mrs. Salter,[1]   ca. 1942

I have been intending to write you about a number of things but I have had little time and it has been very hot and humid. But your last letter in the *Protestant* makes further postponement impossible.

The Clerical-Fascist press in this country sometimes sponsors "Fresh Air Camps for Children" or "Free Milk for Undernourished Children." What would you think of a lover of religious freedom and political freedom who contributes to a clerical fascist magazine and pointed to the worthy causes it was supporting, and then added that after all it wasn't an official organ of clerico-fascism although its other articles clearly revealed its character? Your writing for the *Protestant* is exactly analogous, and your plug for it is incredible political naivete and folly.

After all, I am assuming that it is not merely the *color* of the totalitarian strait-jacket you are objecting to but the strait-jacket itself. Murder, frame-up, suppression, systematic deception are what they are no matter who commits them, and if you extenuate in one country what you condemn in another, you can't expect to be taken seriously as a libertarian spirit. Compared to the crimes of Stalinism, national and international, the Pope is a piker; only Hitlerism is worse, and that is why, although abominating Stalin, one may support military aid to the Russian armies. But ideological support, such as contributing to a Stalinist publication, is inexcusable in principle.

That the *Protestant* is a Stalinist front magazine is evident from the very issue to which you contributed. Read the editorial by Leslie on "Alter *und* Ehrlich"[2] in which he befouls the memory of two Jewish socialist martyrs who were assassinated by Stalin on preposterous frame-up charges of being agents of Hitler. (Hitler kills people for what they are—democrats, socialist, Jews. Stalin kills them and then, together with his minions throughout the world, slanders them.) You must indeed be politically innocent not to realize that the *Protestant* is an unofficial organ of the Communist Party on the religious front. Every issue shows it. The fact that other well-meaning people like yourself are taken in by its anti-Catholicism indicates that they too are innocent and are used as window-dressing. Go back to the first issues of the *Protestant* (when it was still the *Protestant Digest*) and see how many times Leslie has had to change his Editorial Advisory Board. Its members keep on resigning from it as soon as they catch up with him. Now he is basking in the reflected glory of the Russian military victories and exploiting the popular confusion between Stalinism and a totalitarian way of life—much more totalitarian than Catholicism—and simple Russian patriotism. (See Max Eastman's article in the July *Reader's Digest* which is, on the whole, sound.[3])

I know it is important to get printed, but getting printed in the *Protestant* helps clerical fascism, it doesn't hurt it. Here in the East every politically informed person is aware of what the *Protestant* represents. If you think you can play ball with the Communists, you are much more mistaken than a libertarian would be who thinks that he can play ball with the clerical fascists like Coughlin[4] and others, e.g., the Communists used to be for birth control and legalized abortions, but ask Sanger[5] what happened after Russia abolished her social legislation on these matters. The party line changed overnight.

Now the joke is that the Communist Party is seeking an alliance with the Catholic Church. The news isn't altogether public yet but it will break before long. The Vatican and the Kremlin are now negotiating for a Concordat—the Pope because he sees that Fascism is in danger and he needs secular authoritarian support on the continent—Stalin because he wants to neutralize Catholic political opposition so that Russia can get more territory in the Baltic provinces, the Balkans, and Poland. Here in America the Communist Party has already come out in official support of Mayor Hague of Jersey City, N.J. Do you know who Hague is? If any man is a Fascist in America it is he. His history is a yard long and all black. Hague is an ardent Catholic who has the unqualified support of the church hierarchy. When the rapprochement between the Vatican and Kremlin becomes public, Leslie and the *Protestant* will drop their opposition to clerical fascism. They won't print you. If you get printed elsewhere they will call you a Trotskyist and agent of Hitler just as they call Dewey and Kallen and me.

But aside from all this, isn't it crystal clear that you cannot support—as you are in fact doing—one variety of totalitarianism against another without betraying your liberal ideas? I have been studying the ways of the totalitarian animal for more than twenty years, and if there is anything you can rely on it is this: Contact or a united front with totalitarian ideologies or organizations is a kiss of death to any cause or person who gets mixed up with them.

1. No information is available on Mrs. Salter.
2. Victor Alter and Henryk Erlich, leaders of the Jewish Bund in Poland, had fled to the Soviet Union to escape the Nazis and were executed there in December 1941 on orders of Stalin.
3. Max Eastman, "Stalin's American Power," *Reader's Digest* 39 (December 1941): 39–48. Eastman was a poet, journalist, and writer on socialism, communism, and the Soviet Union.
4. The Reverend Charles E. Coughlin, Royal Oak, Michigan, the "radio priest."
5. Margaret Sanger was a leader of the birth control movement.

49

Dear Sir,[1]   March 14, 1945

This will acknowledge your letter of March 12th. You have apparently sadly misunderstood both my criticisms of Mr. Lerner and my criticisms of Mr. Eastman.[2] I regard Mr. Lerner as an apologist for totalitarianism because of his attitude toward democratic rights in Russia, and specifically for his recommendation that before anybody be permitted to talk over the radio, his views are to be approved by a Board of Censors. There is nothing which I wrote in my reply to Mr. Eastman that implies a position anywhere near the position Mr. Lerner takes.

When I wrote that totalitarians who do not abide by democratic procedure, who do not fight fair, can be excluded with a good democratic conscience, I was referring to *actions,* not thoughts or ideas. I am firmly in favor of permitting anybody to express his opinions, no matter if they are undemocratic. But this does not give a man the privilege to *act* as a Fifth Columnist. There is a world of difference between Mr. Lerner's position and mine, aside from the fact that he makes the exception in favor of one brand of totalitarianism, while I refuse to approve of a political strait-jacket no matter what its color.

I hope this makes things a little clearer.

1. Harold Feldman, American serviceman stationed at Fort Myer, Virginia.
2. Max Lerner, professor of political science, Williams College, and Max Eastman.

50

Dear Mr. Mayer,[1]   July 30, 1947

I have just received the July number of the *Walden Round Robin.* The opening sentence reads: "The danger of war with Russia yet this summer is greatly increased by newspaper talk *which has led Truman's advisors to think that war may increase their hope of remaining in office."* (my italics)

I am sure that anyone dedicated to the natural religious life would not publish such a serious charge without possessing sufficient evidence. I am therefore writing to inquire of the names of these advisers of Mr. Truman who wish to embroil us into war in order to retain political office, and what the evidence is that this is their intention. The last time I heard a charge of this sort was in 1940 when Mr. Roosevelt was accused of seeking to embroil us into war in order to win a third term. The charge proved to be utterly contemptible and without foundation of any kind.

Your whole discussion of the danger of war with Russia seems to me to be marked by a complete lack of realism and a disregard of the obvious facts of Soviet expansion and organized terror in every country in which her henchmen have seized power. You mention not a word about Russia's refusal to accept the reasonable restrictions of the Baruch proposal[2] to control the sources of nuclear energy. Instead you speak of American "arrogance" and apparently regard the Marshall Plan as "another revolutionary step against Russia." Although you profess, in passing, opposition to Stalin, this is extremely unconvincing in view of your unqualified endorsement of Wallace,[3] who believes that we suffer from an "excess" of political democracy in the United States, that Russia is a genuine "economic democracy" (as if economic democracy were possible without political democracy!) and who has refused to join Norman Thomas[4] in condemning the vast system of concentration camps which spans the Russian land from the Arctic to the Caucasus.

Nothing you advocate is designed to prevent Russian aggression. At best they are necessary conditions to rally support in behalf of democracy; but they would no more be *sufficient* to prevent Stalin from reaching out, according to his express declaration, for world conquest than they would have been sufficient to stop Hitler.

You are, of course, perfectly free to hold these views but as a responsible editor the least you should have done is to publish at the same time another standpoint on these controversial issues.

All this, however, is incidental. I am writing primarily to find out the names of the miserable creatures whom you have charged with the most heinous crime a human being can be guilty of—plotting war in order to stay in office, and the evidence supporting the charge.

P.S. I am sending copies of this letter to the Editorial Associates of the *Walden Round Robin.*

1. Philip Mayer, professor, William Penn College, Oskaloosa, Iowa, and a religious humanist.

2. See letter 56, note 2.

3. Henry Wallace, secretary of commerce, opponent of the Truman administration's Cold War policy, and Progressive Party candidate for president in 1948.

4. Leader of the American Socialist Party and its perennial candidate for president.

51

Dear Professor Williams,[1]   August 16, 1947

Your letter of August 9th has just arrived. I am very much puzzled by it. If taxing an individual with plotting a war to remain in office isn't a "serious" charge, will you please tell me what you regard as serious? And when you go on to add that the charge is not without foundation because of some "general psychological principle of human motivation," ambition, or whatnot, I can hardly believe you are in earnest. If someone taxed you with burning your neighbor's house to play the role of a savior would you admit that the charge was not "without foundation" because of the "general psychological principle of human motivation?" All you are saying is that the charge is not impossible, but since when is a *possibility* evidence that something is the case when its opposite is just as possible?

Since anything a human being can do is explained in terms of "a general psychological principle of human motivation," it is completely irrelevant in establishing a charge that a person is guilty of a *specific* act—and planning a war to ensure reelection is certainly specific.

By the same logic you are using one can argue that "the general principle of human motivation" (in this case a desire for peace, rather than ambition) is a foundation for the statement that neither Roosevelt nor Truman would do anything to provoke a war.

And I am afraid that I can't see what bearing pacifism, the objectionable conduct of the House Committee,[2] and the other things you touch on have on the question of the political and moral decency of irresponsible charges such as Mr. Mayer made. To say that Truman's policy may lead to war is one thing. (It certainly *may;* but a policy of continued appeasement in all likelihood *will*). But to say that Truman's advisers are planning quite deliberately to embroil us in war in order to ensure his reelection, is—in the absence of concrete evidence—just as much a contemptible slander as if someone were to charge you or me with arson or theft on the ground of some "general principle of human motivation."

Frankly, it's not the seriousness of the charge that Mr. Mayer has made which I doubt but—with the friendliest feelings—the seriousness of your defense of him.

1. Gardner Williams, editorial associate of the *Walden Round Robin* and professor, University of Toledo.
2. Committee on Un-American Activities.

52

Dear Williams,[1]   August 22, 1947

I found your letter of August 19th very amusing, but it did convince me that you were serious. In fact anything you now say, even that the moon is made of green cheese, I shall have to interpret as meant seriously on the basis of your strange dictum—for a naturalist—that "the fact that anything is possible is evidence that it actually happens." This smacks a little like a variant of the ontological argument in politics!

I don't want to burden you but I have two brief and final questions. First, what American President (or his advisors) planned a war in order to insure his reelection. Wilson? Roosevelt? Lincoln? Madison? Rather bewilderingly, despite your general principles of human motivation, you seem to exempt Roosevelt and "probably" Truman. Well, who did? And if you can't find anyone, how do you know that your "general principle" applies? It seems to be as much of an *a priori* principle as that all men are always selfish.

Second, you missed the point when I asked you how on *your* logic you could escape admitting that there would be some evidence of the charge of arson against you (or me) on the ground that it was not impossible. Your reply is that you would have to be crazy to plan such a thing. But in this world anyone might go crazy. Indeed, you have just got through telling me "the fact that anything is possible is evidence that it actually happens." But let me change the illustration to a charge that you (or I) would not have to be deranged to be guilty of—say, theft or plagiarism. Now suppose someone charged you with planning or committing (the distinction is here immaterial) theft or plagiarism. And suppose that when asked for evidence he pointed to "general principles of human motivation," tendency to relieve economic distress, desire for fame, added that it was not unknown for professors to commit discreet thefts and plagiarize from others, and topped it off with the observation (to paraphrase you), "How pure do you think human beings are anyway?" If *that* was all the evidence he had, don't you think he would be morally irresponsible? In law such charges are regarded as libellous *per se*. How do you account for it? And if Mr. Mayer named names and couldn't provide specific evidence, he'd have a tough time of it.

Believe it or not I've actually read Santayana,[2] but I think Machiavelli would be a better authority for you although he is much more circumspect and scientific in his political judgments than you seem to be. And as for how pure I think politics is, I take the liberty of referring you to my *Reason, Social Myths and Democracy* (N.Y., 1940).

P.S. Don't forget to send Mayer a copy of your reply. Unless he can furnish the evidence I asked for, I don't propose to have any truck with him.

1. Gardner Williams.
2. George Santayana, professor of philosophy, Harvard University.

53

Dear Mr. Mayer,[1]   August 30, 1947

Your letter of August 26th has just reached me. I find altogether unimpressive—in fact, positively disingenuous—your claim that my query for evidence of your charge that Truman's advisors are plotting a war to stay in office, is not a legitimate method of democratic discussion. You say that Communists also write vociferous objections against statements they disagree with. What is undemocratic about that? Nor is it wrong to send copies of my letter to those members of your editorial associates whose addresses I knew. For your charge is so serious—and if unsubstantiated so irresponsible—that I think that your board for their own sake ought to be aware of it lest others attribute the same sentiment to them.

Even if I did misunderstand your meaning, it would not be undemocratic unless it were deliberate, which you can hardly believe since until recently my attitude has been sympathetic to your project despite my disagreement with the way in which you use language. But I did not misunderstand you. Your remark would be quite pointless unless you meant to imply that a desire to stay in office would lead Truman's advisors to help in some way to precipitate war. Look at the sentence immediately after the one I quoted from your editorial. "For our President to be surrounded by people to whom war means increased prestige, while peace means retirement is to be in an atmosphere where peace is next to impossible." This is a charge against specific individuals, against those who surround the President. Who are they? You obviously do not mean that this would be true for anybody who would be around Truman. Further, Williams, who, you say, answered me "better than I could have done," interpreted the sentence I quoted exactly as I did, as a charge that Truman's advisors wish to embroil us in war. He believes the charge is true because of his theory of human nature and that it would be true even if you and he and I surrounded Truman.

It seems to me that the charge that a personal letter asking for evidence is undemocratic comes with particularly bad grace from one who makes public accusations of heinous crimes against some public officials which turn out to be obviously wild and unsubstantiated. Such techniques employed by the Nazis and Communists in Germany helped bury the Weimar Republic.

Incidentally, that you should make Williams' defense of the truth of the charge your own seems to me intellectually scandalous for another reason. If you accept his theory of human nature as true, according to which such crimes as you allege follow merely from "general principles" of human psychology, you may as well throw your natural religion out of the window. It makes nonsense of everything you've preached and written all your life.

Nor do I find any more convincing your reasons for silence about Soviet Russia's crimes against democracy, freedom, and natural religion. You say that the reactionaries are doing a good enough job. But a few years ago the reactionaries were praising Russia to the skies, but I don't recall your making any criticisms. There hasn't even been a line in your paper. Personally, I'm not interested in whether the reactionaries praise or condemn Stalin's dictatorship. I'm interested in criticism of Russia from a democratic and socialist point of view. Newspapers and radios are *not* "performing that duty well enough."

I have never been able to understand why, when Hitler was terrorizing Europe, people who think as you do *never* said that we ought not to criticize Germany because "it diverted attention from dangers more imminent and more nearly our own concern," and why they only sing that tune when Stalin's terror is criticized. Today Stalin is a far greater menace to world democracy than Hitler was in 1938, and I presume you are interested in world democracy just as much now as you were then. I think your fundamental error lies in the fact that you conceive the world struggle today as "a struggle between Communism and Catholicism," as you put it in No. 31 of your paper (March, 1946). As one who has fought Catholicism as vehemently and as consistently as anyone, this seems to me a tragic mistake. The struggle is between Communism and Democracy, as imperfect as it is. There is no more difference politically between the Pope and Stalin than between Stalin and Hitler. None of them believes genuinely in freedom of the spirit. And those of us who do must direct our main fire against whatever enemy of freedom is strongest at the moment without neglecting the constructive task of rebuilding a democratic, socialist world.

You are at liberty to publish both of these letters if you wish—although I have not written them for publication—provided you publish them in *toto*.

P.S. It has just occurred to me that perhaps you are not aware of the nature of Stalin's Soviet regime. I suggest you read, say, three favorable and apologetic books, Hewlett Johnson, *Soviet Power,* Albert Rhys Williams, *The Soviets,* Stalin's *Problems of Leninism,* and three critical books, Kravchenko's *I Chose Freedom, The Dark Side of the Moon* (both published by Scribner's), and Dallin and Nicolaevsky's *Forced Labor in the Soviet Union* (Yale Univ. Press)—and then let conscience be your guide.

1. Philip Mayer.

54

Dear Mr. Mayer,[1]   October 16, 1947

Your letter of October 2nd has just reached me. I can see no justification for your continued charge that I have misrepresented your position. Your statement about Truman's advisors implies both a hope and intent on their part.

I am baffled by your statement that "the main direction of its (Russia's) controls has been to eliminate the economic and mental barriers which stand in the way of an intelligent solution to human problems." How can you believe that Russia's practices prepare the way for an intelligent solution of human problems in the face of your admission that Stalin is as ruthless as Hitler? May I suggest that you read Kravchenko's *I Chose Freedom* (Scribner's) and Dallin's *Concentration Camps in the Soviet Union* (Yale University Press)? Then read some apologetic justifications of Soviet practices by men like Hewlett Johnson, Ward, or Williams or other official literature. You will then realize that the alleged removal of economic and mental barriers to freedom is being accomplished by the most horrible "suppression of people."

That you are so upset with the alleged temporizing with Catholic superstition by our government and the Socialist Party (when? and where?) and so insensitive to practices that make St. Bartholomew's Eve seem a kind of Mardi Gras, makes me wonder about the consistency of your pacifist convictions. It was the vote of the Italian Communist Party which made the recent Concordat between church and state in Italy possible despite the opposition of Saragat and his group.[2] How is it you are not sensitive to that?

I confess that I am growing weary of individuals who become hysterical over the slightest abuses of democracy in our country and England, but who are silent about, when they do not abet, murder in Communist countries. To lump together these types of outrage and imply that the U.S.S.R. and the U.S.A. are equally undemocratic is like putting a headache on the same plane as a fatal cancer.

Your unqualified support of Wallace[3] is tantamount to support of the present international Communist line. And I would be much more convinced of the consistency of your pacifist sentiments if I had any evidence of your *public* opposition—in more than a passing phrase—to the totalitarian terror which you deplore privately.

Humanism is indivisible or it is a fake.

1. Philip Mayer.
2. Giuseppe Saragat, founder of the Socialist Party of the Italian Workers.
3. Henry Wallace.

55

Dear Williams,[1]   March 25, 1948

I cannot resist making a comment on your card. Of course you are right. It is absurd that we should believe that we have to choose between one color of a straitjacket and another color of a straitjacket. But if it did come to a choice, the only way you could make it would be on the basis of the empirical experience we have of tyranny like that of the Russians and that under Schuschnigg or Salazar or Peron, etc. The Black tyranny is bad. But in actual effects it doesn't begin to compare with the horrors of the Stalinist dictatorship. As one who has spent years fighting both, I think I am something of an expert on the degrees of infamy which they exhibit. Read a book like Kravchenko's *I Chose Freedom,* or Dallin and Nicolaevsky, *Forced Labor in the Soviet Union,* or T. S. Eliot, *The Dark Side of the Moon* and you will get a glimpse into what I mean.

Your comparison between hell-fire and cook-stove is apt, but I should a million times prefer being left to the punishment of a future hell-fire— which is a myth—then to be broiled slowly over a cook-stove which is a burning fact. But I am heartened to find at least one philosopher at Harvard who, in political affairs, hasn't got the Christian science attitude that Ralph Barton Perry[2] has been agitating for in relation to Soviet dictatorship. His advocacy of appeasement of Stalin has left all of us here gasping.

1. Donald Williams, professor of philosophy, Harvard University.
2. Professor of philosophy, Harvard University.

56

Dear Dr. Einstein,[1]   April 2, 1948

According to *The New York Times* of March 30, 1948, the National Wallace for President Committee claims that you have endorsed Wallace as a man who is "clear, honest and unassuming," and that you have declared yourself in agreement with the fundamental premises of his program for peace.

Because of the gravity of the issues involved I am taking the liberty of writing to inquire whether this report is accurate. If it is, I think it is nothing short of disastrous for the cause of genuine peace and cultural freedom with which your name has been until now indissolubly associated.

Proof in social affairs is notoriously difficult. But if anything is demonstrable it is that in his public utterances Mr. Wallace has not been intellectually honest or clear or unassuming. I need only cite here his distortion of the Baruch-Lilienthal proposals,[2] his willful refusal to repudiate an acknowledged error, his charge that the Communist coup in Czechoslovakia was a defense action against the interference of the American Ambassador, his deletion of all criticism of Soviet expansionism from his speeches, his refusal to protest against the vast network of concentration camps in the Soviet Union and its satellites, his declaration that the U.S. suffers from an excess of political or bill of rights democracy and that the Soviet Union enjoys "economic democracy" but not political democracy, as if you could have the first without the second.

All this would be comparatively unimportant if it bore only upon Mr. Wallace's personal qualities. But the issue is not personal but fundamentally political—and this is what makes the implied claim of the Wallace for President Committee that you are endorsing its candidate so momentous.

Politically Wallace today is a captive of the Communist Party whose devious work in other countries you are familiar with much better than most scientists. His speeches are written for him by fellow travelers. Its line is indistinguishable from that of *Pravda* and the *Daily Worker*. It expresses from the first to last the illogic of appeasement.

One does not have to be an unqualified supporter of American foreign policy or even of American culture—and as a democrat, a Socialist and a Jew, I, for one, am not—to recognize that, so long as the self-corrective procedures of the democratic process are left intact, the incomplete patterns of freedom in the Western world are infinitely preferable to the brutal totalitarianism of Soviet Communism.

If this premise is granted then it remains only to establish the fact of whether or not the Soviet Union is committed to a policy of expansionism or ultimate world-conquest, to derive the general line of policy for peace-loving democrats.

Three lines of evidence point to the fact that the Stalin regime is committed to a program of world expansion: (a) what it says; (b) what it does; (c) and how it is organized for work abroad.

a) The state doctrine of the U.S.S.R. makes it clear that its regime does not believe that it can be secure until all other forms of government—whether democratic or not—are destroyed. I shall be happy to cite chapter and verse on request.

b) What the regime of the U.S.S.R. has done is illustrated in its long list of treaty violations which surpasses in length that of Hitler; its forcible annexation of territory and people which never belonged to it; its use of the veto;[3] its refusal to support any feasible plan of international control of nuclear energy; its systematic defamation of all individuals who espouse a program of world government as agents of British-American imperialism.

c) The intensive use of Fifth Columns to overthrow democracies has been part and parcel of the Kremlin's policy from the very beginning until the present. You know how it operated in the Weimar Republic. You can see today how it operates in Czechoslovakia, and how it is girding itself for action in Italy and France.

Wallace is the Gottwald[4] of tomorrow. His policy is designed to put the U.S. and its allies in a position where before long the only alternative to internal chaos and the threat of external annihilation would be capitulation to Stalin—the road which Benes[5] took.

When we spoke last at Princeton on the occasion of the reception given by the Institute[6] for one of the Bi-Centennial Conferences, you professed skepticism that the Russians—"a half-savage horde," as you called them—could ever constitute a menace to the U.S. I can only repeat now what I said then. This "half-savage horde" by itself is not hostile to us but only their regime which unfortunately controls them. This regime with the help of its fifth column can take all of Europe and Asia, which they will undoubtedly do if Wallace's policy prevails. An organized Europe and Asia can within a decade mass such power that we in the West can have no chance for survival as a free people.

This letter is already overlong. I know how busy you are and how remote the chances are that I can come to talk to you—which I would dearly love to do—and bring you my evidence for the statements I have made. I do not believe my mind is closed to counter-evidence and argument, and I do not advocate as Bertrand Russell does a preventive war. But the *prima facie* case against Wallace's policy is so strong, that I hope you will reconsider your endorsement of it.

1. Albert Einstein.
2. American proposal named after Bernard Baruch and David Lilienthal to limit atomic weapons. It provided for inspection of atomic sites. All members of the United Nations accepted the proposal except the Soviet Union and its satellites.
3. Soviet use of the veto in the Security Council of the United Nations.
4. Klement Gottwald, head of the communist government in Czechoslovakia.
5. Eduard Benes, president of Czechoslovakia at the time of the communist coup in February 1948. In 1946, he had appointed Gottwald to head the government.
6. Institute for Advanced Study, Princeton, New Jersey.

57

Dear Dr. Einstein,[1]   April 7, 1948

What prompted me to write you was the use the National Wallace for President Committee was making of your praise of Wallace and his position, and my honest doubt as to the accuracy of the report. I regret it very much if you found my letter annoying in any way. We are all groping for the truth on matters of great moment, and in the past I have set some store on your political insight.

Naturally I am grieved that you should consider my judgment, for which I indicated the lines of evidence, so "rigid and one-sided" as to make oral discussion unfruitful. And knowing how limited your time is, I certainly cannot expect you to engage in lengthy correspondence. But I do hope you will not take offense if I tell you, as one American citizen to another, why I do not find your remarks convincing even though I have pondered over them for a long time. There are probably many others who think as I do, and since you believe us mistaken it may perhaps be of some interest to you to see what our assumptions and arguments are. If we are wrong, you will find it easier to convince us than the Soviet scientists.

The question is: which foreign policy on the part of the U.S. to the USSR is most likely to preserve peace and not the question of the internal regime of the USSR. The answer to the first question depends on how we assess the evidence which bears on the intentions of the Soviet regime. When you warned the world against the spread of Hitlerism on what evidence did you rely? On what Hitler *said*—not to Lansbury,[2] but to the Nazi Party—and on what Hitler *did*. I have pointed to the evidence which shows what Stalin believes—the regnant dogmas of the Communist Party—and the record of his actions. Together they reveal a program of world conquest.

You do not challenge this evidence. You do not present contrary evidence. Instead you ask: "Who has threatened his opponent to a higher degree by direct action—the Russians the Americans or the Americans the Russians?" This is a fair question. Reviewing in my mind the events that followed the end of the war, and considering America not as an isolationist but as part of the world community, I should say that the Soviet Union by her violation of the principles of the Atlantic Charter, by her violation of her agreements to permit free elections and a free press in Bulgaria, Romania, Hungary, etc., by the coup she inspired in Czechoslovakia, by her war of nerves against Finland, and now Norway and Sweden, by her behavior in Berlin, by her sabotage of the U.N. Commissions on Greece, the Balkans, and Korea, and almost all of its agencies—that by all this, the Soviet Union has been the aggressor.

What actions of the U.S. do you consider as direct aggressions of equal weight against the Soviet Union? Do you mean the Marshall Plan in which the Soviet Union was invited to participate?

In 1940 American isolationists used to ask us whether America under Roosevelt had not been guilty of more hostile acts against Hitler's Germany than vice versa. You will recall how we answered that. It seems to me that the actions of the Soviet regime warrant even more strongly the inference that it is actively hostile to the existence of American democratic institutions.

You point out that the military strength of the U.S. is much greater than that of the USSR. Since this has been denied by many "experts," I should like to know on what evidence this judgment is based. But granted its truth, I am a little puzzled as to what follows from it in the way of foreign policy. Should we weaken our military strength or increase it? Are not the official Baruch-Lilienthal proposals significant in this connection as an indication of our willingness to submit to an international authority? Those few Americans who talk about a preventive war against the USSR speak as individuals. What they say can be matched by equally inflammatory statements in the *official* Soviet press. It seems to me that American policy should be judged by our *official* words and actions and not by the words of private citizens. That policy proclaims the belief that we are more likely to have peace if the democracies remain strong than if they disarm or appease.

The internal character of the Soviet regime is not relevant to our discussion. There exists no Jeffersonian International to overthrow the Soviet Union comparable to the Comintern. But I must confess to a bewilderment at the qualified nature of your judgment about the Soviet Union. In estimating its nature the point is not whether you, the greatest scientist in the world, would or would not like to live in the Soviet Union. You probably would be treated no worse than Pavlov[3] if you remained silent about world government and similar matters. The point is how the average individual fares in the Soviet Union in respect to security of life, personal and political freedom. Have you any doubts on that score?

Nor do I understand your meaning when you write: "It is difficult to decide whether it would have been possible for the Russians to survive by following softer methods." Precisely what methods have you in mind? I am puzzled on what evidence anyone can assert that cultural purges and terror in astronomy, biology, art, music, literature, and the social sciences helped the Russians to survive, or how the millions of victims in the concentration camps of the Soviet Union, not to speak of the wholesale executions, contributed in any way to the Russian victory over Hitler. The Russians defeated Napoleon who relative to his time was even mightier than Hitler. But I don't believe you would find it difficult to decide that this in no way constituted an historical justification of serfdom.

P.S. I am enclosing an editorial from the *N.Y. Times* which seems to me pertinent to the discussion.

1. Albert Einstein.
2. George Lansbury, a pacifist and member of the British Labor Party. He met with Hitler and Mussolini in 1937 in an attempt to avoid war.
3. Ivan Petrovich Pavlov, Russian physiologist who popularized the theory of conditioned reflexes. Pavlov was treated very well in the Soviet Union. He held the position of director of the physiological laboratory of the Russian Academy of Medicine.

58

Dear Jim,[1]   September 15, 1948

Since no one else received my letters from Berlin I assume that the letters I mailed you from Berlin did not arrive. After my little imbroglio with the philosophers from the satellite countries at Amsterdam,[2] I received an invitation from General Clay's[3] office to come to Berlin. I did so, staking my head on the strength of my scientific prediction that there would be no war this fall. It was the most exciting week of my life. I was in the thick of things and worked very intensively. I had long talks with Clay, Murphy, Hayes, Riddleberger and Howley.[4]

It was amazing to see how the historic and political situation has educated these people. For immediate purposes, they have accepted my diagnosis of the situation in Europe. However, they feel that with the election of Dewey and the appointment of Dulles as the Secretary of State our policy in Europe will follow the French policy, which means throwing Germany into the arms of Russia.[5]

At any rate drop me a line if and when you get this, indicating where I can get in touch with you in the event that anything arises. Lasky's[6] office in Berlin, which arranged for my trip, is very eager for you to come over. Clay and Murphy also asked me to arrange for sending some top-flight figures to Berlin to see things for themselves. They particularly wanted Luce[7] and several other opinion makers.

Stalin isn't ready for war. We may have it even if he isn't ready. But he is getting readier every day. It's only a matter of time, although there is a chance that if he feels he may lose the war he will not start it. Incidentally, after six weeks spent in France preceding the International Congress of Philosophy, I have come to the conclusion that we may as well write France off as far as any effective resistance to the march of totalitarianism is concerned. The same is true for Belgium. England, however, is another story. But more of this later. It is only a few hours since I got off the Queen Mary and I've a mountain of work ahead of me.

With best cordial regards to Marcia and the children from all of us.

1. James Burnham, professor of philosophy, New York University.

2. The Tenth International Congress of Philosophy met at Amsterdam in August 1948.

3. General Lucius D. Clay, the American military governor of Berlin during the Berlin airlift. Hook's letter is written at a time when many feared that the United States and the Soviet Union were on the verge of war because of the Berlin blockade.

4. Robert Murphy, American political adviser for Germany; Paul J. Hayes, foreign service officer; James W. Riddleberger, chief of political section of the American military government in Berlin; Frank L. Howley, brigadier general assigned to U.S. military government in Berlin.

5. Most people assumed that Thomas E. Dewey, Republican candidate for president, would win the 1948 election. Had he been elected, he would have appointed John Foster Dulles as secretary of state.

6. Melvin Lasky, acting secretary of the Congress for Cultural Freedom and an employee of the Office of Military Government in Berlin.

7. Henry Luce, founder and publisher of *Time, Life,* and *Fortune* magazines.

59

Dear Jim,[1]   September 20, 1948

Our letters apparently crossed. I am so swamped by work that I haven't the time to write you a decent letter about Europe. But I hope that before you go down South you will stop off for a few days in New York. The correct line is terribly important, and although I think that Europe may well be lost, something can be done to prevent its total loss.

I am convinced that Italy, France, and Belgium will not lift a finger to withstand Russian aggression, and that any policy in relation to France on any other assumption is suicidal. Under certain conditions Germany may serve as a break-wall and of course England can be relied upon. The tragedy in relation to the Marshall Plan is that we are doing most for those countries which will help us least.

At any rate I look forward to seeing you before you fly South again. There are many things to discuss.

Our best to all of you.

1. James Burnham.

60

Dear Dr. Black,[1]   March 7, 1949

The enclosed letter to Mr. Mann[2] detailing my experiences with the Cultural and Scientific Conference for World Peace[3] is self-explanatory. Since writing it I have discovered by actual count that almost eighty notorious fellow travelers of the Communist Party are among the sponsors of the Conference. I am confident that your own sponsorship has been procured under false pretences.

I am writing you as a fellow member of the Ethical Society asking you to join with me in exposing this fraud upon the American public. It violates every principle that Felix Adler[4] and the Ethical Culture Society have ever stood for. The Society is directly involved because the newspaper publicity issued by the Conference explicitly identifies you as a leader of the Society and as a sponsor of the Conference.

As a test of the sincerity of the controlling group behind the Conference I suggest that you write air-mail or wire Professor Harlow Shapley[5] of Harvard demanding that a place be made for me on the program, and upon refusal resign with a ringing declaration. Dr. Davis of Smith[6] who is on the program committee has already written to Prof. Shapley making such a request, but in vain. In virtue of the traditions of the Ethical Culture Society its leaders command the highest moral authority in the eyes of the public. It is only fitting that their actions exhibit at all times an unambiguous integrity.

1. Algernon D. Black, religious leader of the New York Society for Ethical Culture.
2. Thomas Mann, German novelist then living in California.
3. Official name of the conference that took place in New York at the Waldorf Hotel on March 25 and 26, 1949. For more on the conference, see John Rossi, "Farewell to Fellow Traveling: The Waldorf Peace Conference of March 1949," *Continuity* no. 10 (Spring 1985): 1–31.
4. Founder of the Ethical Culture Society.
5. Professor of astronomy, Harvard University, and organizer of the Waldorf Conference.
6. Robert Gorham Davis, professor of English, Smith College.

61

Dear Mr. Mann,[1]   March 14, 1949

I am writing to you *once more* about the Cultural and Scientific Conference for World Peace which is meeting at the Waldorf Astoria, New York City, March 25 and 26th. I have been refused permission to present a paper by the controlling group of the Conference. In this paper I wished to defend three theses which seemed to me of the greatest importance today.

1. There are no "national truths" in science, and that it is only by its deficiencies that a science can ever become the science of one nation or another.
2. There are no "class truths" or "party truths" in science. The belief that there is confuses the objective evidence for a theory which, if warranted, is universally valid with the *uses,* good, bad or indifferent, that are made of it.
3. The cause of international scientific cooperation and peace has been very seriously undermined by the influence of doctrines which uphold the notion that there are "national" or "class" or "party" truths in science.

Not only have I been refused permission to present a paper at any of the sessions, but I have also been refused permission to lead the discussion at the plenary session. I requested at least fifteen minutes. And this despite the fact that some members of the Program Committee, including Herbert Davis[2] and Guy Emery Shipler,[3] requested Professor Shapley that I be given an opportunity to be heard.

Since your name is listed as a sponsor of this Congress, I am appealing to you to support my request that I be permitted to read a paper at the plenary session. No arrangements have been made, apparently, by the Program Committee to have the point of view which I represent presented to the Congress. Further, no person who has in recent years ever spoken a critical word against all varieties of totalitarianism, including Stalin's, have been invited to participate in the actual program of the Congress. Neither John Dewey nor Ernest Nagel[4] nor Horace Kallen[5] nor James T. Farrell[6] nor Dos Passos[7] nor Edmund Wilson[8] nor Meyer Schapiro[9] nor scores of others have been invited to this Congress for World Peace.

Professor H. Muller,[10] American geneticist and Nobel Prize winner, has *not* been invited but A. Oparin, Acting Secretary of the Biological Section of the Soviet Academy of Science who moved to expel Prof. Muller from the Soviet Academy of Science because of his criticisms of Lysenko,[11] *has been invited.*

The New York Times of March 4th reports the resignation of Professor Irwin Edman[12] of Columbia University from the Sponsoring Committee of the Congress on grounds that it is designed to promote "the Communist point of view or one closely approximating to it." I sincerely hope that this is not true. But the way this Congress has been organized and my experience with it suggest that it is on the order of Wroclaw-Breslau.[13]

P.S. Since writing the above I have discovered that the Americans who were appointed to the Continuations Committee of the Wroclaw-Breslau Communist peace conference last summer were Dr. Harlow Shapley, Howard Fast,[14] Jo Davidson,[15] and Albert E. Kahn,[16] a notorious card-holding Communist and member of the Executive Committee of the New York State Communist Party. All except Dr. Shapley accepted; all including Dr. Shapley are organizers and sponsors of the Cultural and Scientific Conference for World Peace. Further, I have identified by actual count more than ninety well known fellow travelers of the Communist Party line, of the order of Corliss Lamont and Harry Ward, in the list of sponsors as published on the official stationery of the Conference.

I am confident that although you are listed as a sponsor of the Conference, your name was procured under false pretenses. At any rate, it seems to me highly desirable for the sake of your own good name to insist that the point of view I have expressed in my paper be presented at the Conference and that a place be made for me on the program. I shall appreciate it if you will send me a copy of your communication to Dr. Shapley. I am asking you to send me a copy of any telegrams or letters you address to the Conference because Professor Edman's letter of resignation was suppressed by the Organizing Committee, and he was compelled to make it public himself.

It seems to me that the cause of peace would be better served if independent persons like yourself make the sharpest disassociation from any individuals or groups whose main interest is in furthering the interests of Soviet foreign policy.

1. Thomas Mann.
2. Herbert J. Davis, president, Smith College.
3. Editor, *The Churchman.*
4. Professor of philosophy, Columbia University, and close friend of the Hooks.
5. For Kallen, see letter 11, note 3.
6. American novelist and author of *Studs Lonigan.*
7. John Dos Passos, author of *U.S.A.*
8. For Wilson, see letter 4, note 8.
9. Professor of art history, Columbia University.
10. Hermann J. Muller, professor of biology, Indiana University.
11. Trofim Lysenko, Soviet biologist who propounded the theory that acquired characteristics can be inherited. Stalin made this theory part of Soviet scientific orthodoxy.
12. Professor of philosophy, Columbia University.
13. Meeting of World Congress of Intellectuals in Wroclaw, Poland, August 25–28, 1948, which echoed Soviet propaganda.
14. American writer, author of *Citizen Tom Paine,* and at that time a member of the Communist Party.
15. American sculptor.
16. Coauthor, with Michael Sayers, of *The Great Conspiracy: The Secret War against Soviet Russia* (New York, 1946).

62

Dear Rabbi Newman,[1]   March 14, 1949

I an enclosing a copy of my letter to Mr. Mann which I read to you over the telephone. Your reactions to my suggestion that you support my request for a place on the program of the Conference you have sponsored seem very puzzling to me. Dr. Herbert Davis, Dr. Guy Emery Shipler, and Dr. Blanding[2] wrote to Professor Shapley urging that I be given an opportunity to present my paper. You alone of all the members of the Program Committee to whom I wrote have refused. What is more, you have gratuitously and mistakenly charged that "this is a jurisdictional dispute between Socialists and Communists" and that you as a democrat will have nothing to do with it. As a democrat it seems to me that your task is quite different.

Since writing you, the following facts have come to light. The Continuations Committee of the Wroclaw-Breslau Communist Peace Conference of last summer appointed the following Americans to its Continuations Committee: Dr. Shapley, Howard Fast, Jo Davidson, and Albert E. Kahn, a notorious card-holding Communist and member of the Executive Committee of the New York State Communist Party who delivered a more vitriolic attack on the United States at Wroclaw than did Fadeyev.[3] All except Dr. Shapley accepted; all, including Dr. Shapley, are organizers and sponsors of the Cultural and Scientific Conference for World Peace of which you are a sponsor. Further, by actual count I have identified more than ninety well known fellow travelers of the Communist Party line, of the order of Corliss Lamont and Harry Ward, in the list of sponsors as published on the official stationery of the Conference.

The Conference has also been launched under the auspices of the National Council of the Arts, Sciences and Professions from which Harold Ickes[4] resigned as paid national director with the public charge that it was a Communist Party front.

So far as I can ascertain you are the only rabbi that appears on the list of sponsors. All of the publicity which has gone out about the Conference makes conspicuous use of your name and position.

When I mentioned some of these facts to you over the telephone you dismissed them as irrelevant. I do not believe that they are irrelevant. Genuine lovers of peace can more effectively work for their goal if they sharply disassociate themselves from a group which under the cry for peace is interested only in furthering the foreign policy of the Soviet government. In 1940 what would you have thought of a peace lover who joined and supported a front organized by the German American Bund, which also professed its desire to prevent another World War?

You are a figure in public life. You have a responsibility as a leader of Jewry as well as a citizen of the United States. Yet you see nothing peculiar in including your name as a cover behind which a subversive group, acting as agents of a foreign totalitarian power, perpetrates a fraud upon the American people. I do not think such behavior is ethical. I do not think it is wise. And I think it is positively scandalous that you should seek to extenuate your conduct by the miserable evasion that this is a "jurisdictional dispute between Socialists and Communists." Are John Dewey and Horace Kallen socialists? They, too, have been excluded from the Conference. What precisely is socialistic about the theses of the paper I proposed to read?

The issue is not jurisdictional but fundamentally one that concerns moral integrity. Your clear duty is to resign from this Communist-controlled Conference with a ringing statement of denunciation of the people who have deceived you. Professor Edman has done just that. If you remain in the Conference you will not be able later to plead that you were ignorant of the character of the Conference.

In behalf of your own good name and of your high responsibility as a rabbi of your people, I urge you to clearly disassociate yourself from this Conference. The organizers of the Conference suppressed Professor

Edman's letter of resignation and made it necessary for him to release it to the press himself.

I shall appreciate hearing from you about this and will be glad to receive copies of any communications you send to the officers of the Conference.

1. Rabbi Louis I. Newman, Congregation Rodeph Shalom, New York.
2. Sarah Gibson Blanding, president of Vassar College.
3. Alexander Fadeyev, Soviet novelist and general secretary of the Writers' Union of the Soviet Union. He also was a member of the Central Committee of the Communist Party of the Soviet Union.
4. Harold L. Ickes, secretary of the interior, 1933–46.

63

Dear Mr. Shipler,[1]   March 16, 1949

I am positively aghast at the discourtesy of your letter of March 11th. I wrote to you as a member of the Program Committee of the Conference, asking that I be permitted to read a paper in its Proceedings. You supported my request and wrote to Professor Shapley. But the controlling group behind the Conference proved adamant. They would not even let me participate in the discussion. They would not make a place for anyone to present the position expressed in the three theses with which, I am sure, you agree. Mrs. Dorner[2] even refused to send me a copy of the program.

In view of all this, and assuming that your request that I be heard at the Conference was sincere, I wrote you again, saying "It seems to me that it would be highly appropriate, in the event that I am denied permission to speak, for you to publicly resign in protest." And because I made this perfectly reasonable suggestion—again on the assumption of your sincerity—you charge me with being "un-American" and a user of "smear technique," and made other insulting innuendoes. Why? Even if you have your reasons for not resigning, what logical or ethical justification have you for using these opprobrious epithets about me?

I am not familiar with some of the other things you write about in your letter, particularly the *Churchman* dinner. What has that to do with me and my request to you? By your own account, the two things are utterly different. Some individuals tried to induce your guests *not* to speak; but I am asking you to induce the inner group of the Conference to *permit* me to speak. I want *every* group and point of view to be permitted to speak. By giving only one point of view the Conference is perpetrating a fraud on the American public, and I assumed, because you wrote Shapley in my behalf, that you did not wish to help. Imagine, then, my shock in receiving your letter.

After all, my dear Dr. Shipler, I have never called you a Communist or a Communist Party fellow traveler because—such is fame—all I know about you until our exchange was that you joined Horace Kallen, John Dewey, and me in fighting for Bertrand Russell against the machinations of the La Guardia machine and the Catholic hierarchy.[3] To find you therefore insinuating that I am a tool of the Catholic Church because I do not believe in national or class or party truths in science makes me wonder about you. Everybody has a natural right to be stupid but it is a privilege that should not be abused. When it is, there is something rotten behind it.

You seem to be unaware that I—such is fame!—have been fighting Catholic totalitarianism even longer than Communist totalitarianism, and during years when you probably were playing "footsie" with the Church. The opening essay of my article which caused such a storm a few years ago read: "Catholicism is the oldest and greatest totalitarianism movement in history." It is no longer the greatest. Hitlerism was greater; Stalinism is greater still. But Franco, Peron, and Dollfuss[4] show us what happens when the Catholic Church gets secular power. A democrat must fight on all fronts all the time but some fronts are more active than others.

You write that you are a peacelover. *But would you have lent your name to the German-American Bund in 1940 when they were propagandizing for peace?* Why do you lend your name now for exploitation to the Communist group in control of the arrangements for the Conference? You can fight for peace independently—like Christ whom you invoke, and who did not make a united front with the Romans against his own people. A. J. Muste and Henry Neumann[5] love peace at least as much as you do. But you don't find them hobnobbing with fellow travelers.

You report that Shapley writes he planned this Conference long ago. He forgot to inform the editor of *Pravda*, who describes it as one of a number of Peace Conferences being called throughout the world as a follow-up to the Wroclaw-Breslau Conference which, as you know, was an intellectual pogrom.

I don't know Birkhead[6] and have never seen his stuff. I do know Ickes. But do *you* know that Ickes publicly resigned as paid national director from the Council of the Arts, Sciences and Professions which is sponsoring this Conference, charging that it was stooging for the Communist Party line? Does that make Ickes "un-American," "a smearer," etc.?

Will you please send me the addresses of all the gentlemen to whom you sent carbon copies of your letter to me? I want to send them copies of this one. As a Christian clergyman you would not deny me the opportunity to defend myself against your defamations of my character and motives.

P.S. As soon as the pressure of work lifts I expect to go into this business of the attack on the *Churchman* and plumb it to the depths. Until now I had never thought of you as a "Communist fellow traveler"—a term to which I give a precise and verifiable meaning. But your letter to me has aroused very strong doubts. In the interests of public morality I shall go into the matter very thoroughly and hope you will give me better cooperation in this matter, which concerns yourself, than you have in my attempt to get a hearing at the Waldorf Conference. If you are a victim of a Catholic conspiracy, I shall speak up for you against everybody despite the fact that you seem to be your own worst enemy either out of defects of intelligence or character. But if I find you have been playing a double game and knowingly and willingly permitted the Communists to use your name, the Lord have mercy on your soul!

P.P.S. This letter is *not* for publication.

1. Guy E. Shipler, editor of *The Churchman.*
2. Hannah Dorner, secretary of the Waldorf conference.
3. See letter 132, note 4.
4. Francisco Franco of Spain, Juan Peron of Argentina, and Engelbert Dollfuss, chancellor of Austria during the 1930s.
5. Leader of the Brooklyn Society for Ethical Culture.
6. Rev. Leon M. Birkhead, a Unitarian minister, founder of the anti-Nazi Friends of Democracy in 1937 and an anti-communist.

64

Dear Professor Ashman,[1]   March 17, 1949

By this time I hope you have read my article[2] and letter in the *New York Times.* I am enclosing copies of some other letters which you will please return after you have perused them. That there is a danger to academic freedom from reactionaries goes without saying. That the danger is mounting may be true. But what you don't seem to realize is that the only way to forestall reactionary efforts to purge the university is for the teaching profession to establish and live up to and enforce the higher standards for itself. The labor movement cleaned its own house among other reasons to prevent the government from stepping in to do that work. My point is that the academic profession must do its own house cleaning. And it's about time it knew what the score is. T. V. Smith, who used to be in the Illinois and U.S. House of Representatives, tells me that on the basis of his legislative experience, legislatures would never consider taking any action if they knew that there was a strong professional organization actively dedicated to upholding the standards of professional decency.

I know what life must be like in a backward community. But there is no easy way of breaking down reactionary attitudes. One way to inflame them is to give protection to agents of foreign governments exploiting the schools. But I agree with you that the Communists are not the only enemy, and it is important to destroy the influence of the Ku Klux Klan and similar groups where they exist. You can rest assured that if you want to come out openly and denounce anti-Negro and anti-Semitic discrimination, I will mobilize the sentiment of the country in your defense and pledge myself to come to New Orleans to speak at a mass meeting in your behalf if disciplinary action is taken against you. I don't know the local situation in the South and I therefore am not in a position to give any advice. All I can do is to promise my support. Perhaps if every teacher in the South who felt as you do about anti-Jewish and anti-Negro discrimination spoke up publicly, these evils might come to an end or at any rate be mitigated.

Just because the reactionaries who have their own fish to fry are attacking the Communist fellow reactionaries, it is important for liberals to take the lead so that they can more effectively turn their fire upon the first group of reactionaries when the danger from the second disappears. May I add in closing that it would betoken a more scientific attitude of mind on your part if you familiarized yourself somewhat with the facts about Communist penetration into American culture.

I am glad my voice is loud enough for you to hear it. I only hope that your ear is keen enough to hear what it is exactly that I am saying.

1. Richard Ashman, college professor in New Orleans.
2. "Should Communists Be Permitted to Teach?" *New York Times Magazine,* February 27, 1949.

65

Dear Carnap,[1]   March 20, 1949

I have just learned from Dr. Jacobs of the Voice of America that your name has been cited (presumably abroad) as a sponsor of the forthcoming Cultural and Scientific Conference for World Peace. I hope this is not true. If you actually have enrolled yourself as a sponsor, I am confident that you are unaware of the real auspices of the Conference. It is being run by people whose first act, if they came to power, would be to liquidate you and people like you. The Conference is as much a Communist Party front as was the Congress at Breslau-Wroclaw last summer.

I am enclosing some materials which I earnestly beg you to read very carefully. My experience with this Conference is decisive.

I can very well understand how honest people can disagree with American foreign policy now as in 1940. But what would you have thought of anyone who in 1940 lent his name to the German-American Bund who were then agitating for peace? People will draw the same inference about you if you are a sponsor of the Waldorf Conference and remain a sponsor. If you want to agitate for peace there is no need to associate yourself with agents of a foreign power: you can do it independently.

This business is no ordinary thing, as you will learn by developments in the next few days. Anybody who is still a sponsor by the time the Party-line begins to sound off at the Conference will be marked for life as a captive or fellow traveler of the Communist Party. You are not a Communist, and you are not a political innocent.

Forgive me for writing so strongly. It is a measure of the respect I have for you and your life work. There are mistakes and mistakes. This one can be positively fatal if not rectified.

1. Rudolf Carnap, professor of philosophy, University of Chicago.

66

Dear Dr. Shapley,[1]   March 21, 1949

This will acknowledge your letter of March 18th in which you accuse me of making plain misstatements of fact to some sponsors of the Cultural and Scientific Conference for World Peace. According to you, neither Dr. Davis[2] nor Dr. Shipler wrote to you requesting that I be put on the program.

I have in my possession a letter from Dr. Davis dated February 24, in which he writes me, "I assume that you have probably written also to Dr. Shapley but I will send him a copy of this letter with my request that you should be given a full opportunity to present your views at the suitable plenary session of the conference." On February 25th I wrote you that I had received Dr. Davis' letter and asked you to indicate at what plenary session my address would be given.

I have also in my possession the copy of the letter which Dr. Guy Emery Shipler wrote to you requesting that I be put on the program. In the *Herald-Tribune* of March 20th Dr. Shipler makes full acknowledgment of sending his request to you.

It will be clear now as to who has made plain misstatements of fact.

After receiving a letter from the New York office of your Conference informing me that you had telephoned that there was no place for me on the program, *I* telephoned Mrs. Dorner. It took me two days to get her on the phone, and I have an exact record of our conversation. Among other interesting things, she told me that I would have no more opportunity to participate in a discussion than anybody else on the floor of the Conference, and that my speaking depended upon whether or not I was recognized by the Chairman.

So much for these misstatements of fact. Since you have undoubtedly informed others that I have been guilty of making misstatements of fact, when the precise opposite is the case, I see no alternative but to request you to send me an apology for making false accusations and to send copies of your statement to the individuals with whom you have communicated.

1. Harlow Shapley.
2. Herbert Davis.

67

Dear Dr. Shapley,[1]   March 23, 1949

[The first half of this letter repeats the substance of what Hook
said in his letter of March 21st. It concludes with the following:]

What am I to think, Dr. Shapley? As an astronomer you know that the probability of three independently written letters, mailed at different times about the same subject to the same person, being lost in the mails is indeterminately if not infinitely small![2] At the same time I am loath to conclude that you are deliberately telling an untruth although you have not scrupled to slander my integrity in charging me with plain and persistent misstatement of fact.

There is only one alternative explanation which plausibly accounts for your conduct, unexampled in scientific and academic circles. It is that you do not know what is going on within your own organization, that the inner Communist group are deceiving you to the point of suppressing letters sent to you which they do not wish to come to your attention, and that you have become the willing dupe of enemies of your own country as well as of the ideals of moral decency and scientific truth you profess.

Since you have probably sent copies of your letter to the sponsors of the

Conference who forwarded my communication to you, I demand either a public apology or the names and address of all the persons to whom you have sent your untruthful charge against me.

Needless to say I regard your conduct in this matter as unbecoming a teacher, scholar and scientist.

P.S. Since writing the above several places on your program became vacant, but no invitation to fill them was received by me.

1. Harlow Shapley.
2. In this letter Hook quoted from letters of Herbert Davis, Guy Shipler, and himself requesting that he be allowed to address the Waldorf Conference.

68

Dear Sir,[1]   March 28, 1949

This will acknowledge your letter of March 26th. Every sentence in it, after the first, reveals a complete misunderstanding of the purposes of the rally of Americans for Intellectual Freedom.[2] Even on the basis of newspaper reports, I cannot see any justification for the amount of misinformation you crammed into a few lines.

First of all, we are all in favor of cooperation between the United States and the Soviet Union, both in the United Nations (whose UNESCO the Soviet Union has refused to join) and outside the United Nations. Secondly, we are not opposed to a free and fair discussion with Communists or with anyone else. In fact, it was because we insisted upon free and fair discussion and because the so-called Cultural and Scientific Conference for World Peace was so set up as to make free and fair discussion impossible, that we conducted our own rally.

We invited Dr. Shapley to speak at our sessions, although Dr. Shapley denied me the right to participate in the program of his conference, *even though he had been specifically requested to do so by President Davis and Dr. Shipler.* We invited the Soviet delegates to meet and discuss with us the fate of artists and scientists both in the Soviet Union and the United States. We have issued a six point statement of principles of our organization which was reported in the major newspapers, not a single one of which concerned itself with foreign policy, on which our own members differ. The six points concerned the conditions of free and fair cultural interchange. For example, we believe that an honest conference and not one which is an organizational maneuver by the Communist Party would have invited Mr.

Stravinsky[3] to appear on the same program in which Mr. Shostakovich[4] denounced him.

For you to say that the belief in intellectual freedom, fair play and decency logically entails a belief that we, to quote from your letter, "sever all diplomatic and economic relations with Russia, cut off aid to Russia's allies, and declare war on Russia" indicates such colossal deficiency in elementary logical sense as to raise a question in my mind concerning your sincerity in writing me.

If I am wrong about this I hope you will hasten to correct me, and to supply the data upon which you make such outrageous assertions which I have found in only one publication, namely, the Communist *Daily Worker*.

1. Curtis P. Nettels, professor of history, Cornell University.
2. A group hastily organized by Hook to protest the Waldorf conference. It included Daniel Aaron, George Balanchine, Roger Baldwin, Adolf Berle, Bernard De Voto, David Dubinsky, James T. Farrell, Reinhold Niebuhr, A. Philip Randolph, Norman Thomas, and James Wechsler.
3. The composer Igor Stravinsky.
4. The composer Dmitri Shostakovich.

69

Dear Mr. Shanker,[1]   March 28, 1949

You may quote me as follows: I am unalterably opposed to any kind of legislation barring individuals from teaching or public employment on grounds of membership in any legally recognized political party. The standards of integrity in teaching, as in all other professions, must be upheld by the members of those professions themselves. The interference of the state in these matters is always productive of more harm than good. Just as labor unions can be relied upon to clean their house of racketeers, ordinary and political, without the interference of the government, so can all the professions, including the teaching profession.

1. Albert Shanker, student at the University of Illinois and future president of American Federation of Teachers.

70

Dear Carnap,[1]   April 4, 1949

Only now have I had a chance to reply to your letter of March 24th. If I had known that the "maintenance of peace is more important (to you) than civil liberties," I should have never written you in the first place. For whoever believes that has already left the democratic camp. If peace is more important than civil liberties, then you should urge that the United States apply for affiliation to the Union of Soviet Republics at once. Of course, we could have had peace without civil liberties by capitulating to Hitler in 1939 and saved much bloodshed. My own view as a democrat is that peace *without* the specific freedom of the Bill of Rights is *not* worth having.

Our differences are too deep on this question to be discussed by letter, but I wish to say a few words about some of the reasons you give for remaining as a sponsor of the Communist-dominated Waldorf Conference—reasons which are really superfluous in view of the position you state above.

(1) You say that there is a "risk" that Communists will get the upper hand at the Conference, and that if the liberal sponsors were to pull out "they would hand the meeting over to the communists."

It seems to me that the best way to diminish this risk is to have done one or two things. (a) Either to have come to New York to participate, to see what was going on, to examine the structure of the program, etc. or (b) to have insisted that the announced free and fair interchange of views be held if your sponsorship was to be continued. You could not very well have done the first but you could have done the second. Your failure to do so meant that your name was used as window-dressing for a Communist show. The minor concessions the Communists made to decency were the result of resignations by sponsors who protested against being deceived.

(2) What do you know about Shapley? Do you know that he refused to protest the liquidation of Soviet astronomers in 1938 for introducing "counterrevolutionary" ideas into astronomy, and that he uses the word "Trotskyist" like the Nazis used the term "Jew"? Ask Philipp Frank[2] about Shapley's political sentiments.

But I am really puzzled by your statement that Shapley's failing to put me on the program does not make the Conference undemocratic. What made the Conference undemocratic was not that *I* was barred from the program but that the point of view I represented was not given a hearing, that in fact, except for the last minute intrusion of Cousins,[3] not one single speaker who outspokenly opposed the Communist line was given a chance at either the plenary or panel sessions. Shostakovich attacked Stravinsky, Schoenberg, Hindemith—but Stravinsky was not invited to reply. No one replied to Rogge, Thackery, Fadeyev, and Schuman's[4] criticisms of American foreign policy. Will you please tell me what you consider a democratic conference? Do you think that *you* would have been permitted to criticize dialectical materialism in the science panel? Is it democratic for a conference devoted to *world* peace to adopt a resolution condemning violations of free speech in this country but to say not a word, literally not a word, about the total suppression of free speech in the Soviet Union? Suppose at a philosophy conference all the speakers attacked the logical positivists who were denied a place on the program and permitted only to ask a brief question (two minutes) in the discussion period *if* there were time, and *if* they caught the chairman's eye? Would you call that a democratically organized conference?

(3) You write, "Since our government is persistently refusing to extend good will and cooperation to the other side, I welcome the getting together of scientists and artists in an attempt to lift the Iron Curtain (which is chiefly caused by our military threats) and to show each other respect and good will."

This is very hard to understand. With all its defects and mistakes, the United States government has time and again offered invitations to Soviet scientists and artists to visit our country without demanding reciprocal privileges. Many universities have had the same experiences. Even friends of the Soviet Union have been rebuffed, e.g. Simmons[5] of Columbia. Last January, Shapley asked the Soviet Union to permit the astrophysicist Asbarzumian to give lectures at Princeton and Chicago but the Politbureau has so far said "No." What precisely would you call "good will and cooperation" along cultural lines? Shapley's conference was so arranged that *no critical interchange* was permitted. You don't seem to understand that it was just because we wanted free discussion and not a rigged and canned program that Shapley would have none of us.

President Blanding of Vassar was on the Program Committee of the Conference. When she resigned, she declared: "To my knowledge, no meeting of the Program Committee has been called." Don't you think this is significant?

As for the Iron Curtain being chiefly caused "by our military threats"—won't you please specify? Is the Marshall Plan a military threat? The Baruch-Lilienthal atomic proposal? And what would you call the Czechoslovak coup and the Berlin blockade? The Iron Curtain has been imposed by the Soviet regime to prevent democratic ideas from coming in and freedom-loving Russians from running out. I was in Berlin last summer and saw first hand the operation of the Soviet system. The cultural and political terror in the Soviet Union have grown progressively worse since 1918.

I cannot see that my prediction that your sponsorship of the Shapley Conference will be taken as evidence of your being a Communist fellow traveler indicates either hysteria or intimidation. After all, if you believe that peace is more important than civil liberties, it is perfectly logical for you to support this Communist-inspired Conference which pleaded for peace only on Stalin's terms. And it is perfectly legitimate for people to judge you by your beliefs and actions. All I can do is to offer the friendly advice to study the political program and practice of the people you are traveling with. The Communists of 1949 are not the idealistic zealots you knew in Germany in 1918–21; they are more like the political murderers of Rathenau.[6] Even if you surrender your civil liberties to them, I do not believe they will let people who differ with them about anything, as you do in philosophy, enjoy peace.

1. Rudolf Carnap.
2. Professor of physics, Harvard University.
3. Norman Cousins, editor, *Saturday Review of Literature.*
4. O. John Rogge, New York lawyer who often represented left-wing defendants; Theodore O. Thackery, editor, *New York Post;* Frederick L. Schuman, professor of political science, Williams College.
5. Ernest J. Simmons, professor of Russian literature, Columbia University.
6. Walter Rathenau, German Jewish statesman murdered by right-wing nationalists in June 1922. His assassins then committed suicide.

71

Dear Professor Nettels,[1]   April 4, 1949

For a historian and scholar, you seem to me to be rather allergic to relevant evidence. Nor is it clear to me what press reports you read. It sounds as if you based most of your information upon the *Daily Worker.* I should imagine that it would be the duty of an objective historian to make inquiries for course material before leaping to conclusions. And what conclusions!

First of all, the pickets at the Shapley meeting had no connection whatsoever with the Freedom House rally. In fact, we condemned such picketing, as reported in the press, because it was not conducive to orderly discussion. We also condemned the action of the United States government in refusing to allow delegates to attend from all countries.

You seem to be completely ignorant of the basis of our charge against the Shapley group. It held itself out as an organization desiring a free and fair interchange of different points of view. It did not hold itself out as a Communist inspired effort to further the foreign policy of the Soviet Union. Your analogy, therefore, with a group of Roman Catholics in the United States inviting Italian Catholics to come here is completely besides the point. If Shapley and his group had announced that they were Communist sympathizers welcoming other sympathizers, we would not have even raised a question. And we would have defended them to the bitter end in their right to hold their meeting and profess any views they pleased. What we opposed was the intellectual dishonesty of a rigged program which led President Blanding of Vassar, a member of the Program Committee, to resign with a telling declaration, "So far as I know, no meeting of the Program Committee was ever held."

Nor do I find your letter logically coherent. In one breath you urge us to restrict ourselves to problems in our own country. In another breath, you take us to task for not attacking the Marshall Plan because of its grants to the Italian government which pays the salaries of Roman Catholic priests. The English government pays the salaries of Episcopalian divines. I personally am opposed to all that and would like to see the evidence of your statement that Marshall Plan money was going to the churches of Europe.

You tell me that you appreciate my efforts to inform Americans concerning the Communist position in this country and its activities. I see no evidence of your appreciation, but on the contrary, I see almost a willful misunderstanding of my efforts at enlightenment and the insinuation that anyone who is critical of Communist duplicity is opposed to peace.

I yield to none in my desire for peace and freedom, and one of the reasons that I attacked the Waldorf Conference is that I believe its line, like the line of appeasement of Hitler, makes for war. No, I have not forgotten that attacks on Communism are often a prelude to Fascism, but you apparently have forgotten that Communist cries of Fascism are always followed by attempts to destroy democracy. For example, Czechoslovakia and other countries.

1. Curtis P. Nettels.

72

Dear Professor Hamlin,[1]   May 27, 1949

Please excuse my delay in answering your letter of April 25th commenting on my article in the *New York Times* on "fellow travelers."[2] It arrived when I was abroad and only now have I had a chance to read it. It is an eloquent statement from a non-Communist "fellow traveler," and I wish to discuss the points you make in hopes we can reach some agreement.

I shall begin with your last point first in which you explain why you overlook the "sins of Russia" and concentrate on the "dangers in our own country." About the first you say we can do nothing, whereas the second are our own responsibility. I find this extremely difficult to understand in view of the notorious fact that fellow travelers do *not* overlook the sins of *other* countries, particularly those which are at the moment objects of propaganda war by the Soviet Union. When you and your fellows were asked to protest against the sins of Franco, Hitler, Mussolini, Chiang-kai-shek, the Greek government, etc., did you reply then that "the sins of other countries" are not our responsibility? Why is it that only when you are asked to condemn Soviet terror do you make this response? Nor is it true that we can do nothing about suppressions of freedom in other countries. Every protest counts. We know this from Goebbels' diaries[3] and from Stalin's former lieutenants who tell us that the Kremlin regards it as a triumph when American fellow travelers remain silent when outrages in the Soviet Union are committed.

Perhaps the explanation of your inconsistency is that you regard Russian "sins" as comparatively minor. This is suggested by your reference to the necessity of removing "the beam from our own eyes." Presumably there are only "motes" in the eyes of the Soviet Union. I cannot believe that you are aware of the character of Soviet terror and its pervasive character [*sic*]. Our own imperfections and "crimes," if you wish to use that word, are bad enough. But to draw an equation between them and those of the Soviet Union is like confusing a cold with a malignant cancer.

Now, as for peace. If you believe that we must work for peace through the United Nations, then I cannot understand your tenderness to the Soviet Union, in view of its refusal to participate in many of its agencies, its unbridled use of the veto, its reference to the United Nations Committee's Report on Greece as, in Vishinski's[4] choice words, "a pile of garbage," etc. Or examine the Soviet attitude as revealed in the deliberations of the Atomic Energy Committee. It is the same story. You cannot have it both ways at once—support of the U.N. and of its chief saboteur.

You write that "we must do everything to avoid military conflict." Do you literally mean everything? Then why not capitulation? We could have avoided conflict with Hitler if we had capitulated. Would you have approved? (I assume you are not an absolute pacifist.) It seems to me that it is the "fellow travelers" who increase the danger of war, not the critics of Soviet foreign policy, because they encourage the Kremlin to believe that there is no will to resist aggression. If there had been an Atlantic Pact[5] in 1938, I believe Hitler would never have dared to embark on war. But he was emboldened by English pacifism and American isolationism. (Under separate cover I am sending you an article analyzing the strategy of international communism on this point.)

The most fateful declaration in your letter is your statement that you are still prepared, although you abominate communism, to join with Communists in organizations to further peace or any other good cause. This means one of two things. Either you do not accept the evidence I and many others have presented on how members of the Communist Party work, or you do not object to being exploited by self-declared enemies of your own country in behalf of a foreign power. If the first, I should like to know on what grounds you reject this evidence. If the second, why not accept the responsibilities of your commitments? Here, as on other questions, I suspect that you really are not acquainted either with Communist theory or practice.

Please do not misunderstand me. As a democratic socialist I believe I am even more critical of American institutions than you. Certainly no one has been more active in combatting American violations of civil and human rights than my good friend Norman Thomas, whose position is similar to mine and with whose activities I have long been associated. By all means—let your voice be heard on what's wrong with America. But when you join in organizations controlled or dominated by Communists who would destroy the whole structure of democratic life in America, you not only defeat your own purposes, your very ends become suspect in the eyes of others. There are plenty of non-Communist organizations in which to work.

What would you think if someone who opposed segregation joins an organization against segregation dominated or controlled by the Catholic Church (which, on the whole, fights segregation more vigorously than most other churches) although other non-Catholic organizations exist? What would you have thought of someone who believed in peace in 1940 and who joined a peace organization controlled by the Nazi-American Bund? Why should you regard it as a sign of hysteria that people should think the same things about those who work with Communists?

There are dangers and threats to freedom in American life. There are people who would use anti-Communism as a cloak for reactionary purposes. But their unwitting allies are the fellow travelers, not the critics of the fellow travelers. Labor unions are cleaning their own house of the advocates of a concentration camp economy—not Big Business. Is there no lesson in this?

1. Talbot F. Hamlin, professor of the history of architecture, Columbia University.
2. "The Fellow Traveler: A Study in Psychology," *New York Times Magazine,* April 17, 1949.
3. Louis P. Lochner, ed., *The Goebbels Diaries, 1942–1943* (New York, 1948).
4. Andrei Vishinski, foreign minister of the Soviet Union.
5. North Atlantic Treaty Organization.

73

Dear Dr. Clark,[1]   September 16, 1949

Please excuse my delay in replying to your letters of July 7 and July 22. I want to thank you for the kind comments that you made on my Dartmouth article.[2] Your comments make it all the more difficult for me to express my feeling that you have not met the argument concerning the issue of Communists and education. I notice that you express great admiration for my old teacher Morris Cohen. But there is one thing I learned from him and that was to meet the argument.

Instead of meeting the argument, you say that there are three things which seem to you "to close the matter or at least to contain the materials in the light of which it might be closed," and in your letter of July 22nd you make reference to a fourth matter. Please permit me to comment on all of them.

1. Will you please indicate specifically which one of Meiklejohn's[3] arguments in the *New York Times Magazine* appears conclusive to you? I must confess that I found his whole argument vitiated by elementary logical fallacies involving two senses of the word "free." Meiklejohn argues that if a man is free to join a political party his ideas are therefore free. This is obviously false for it confuses free in the sense of voluntary with free in the sense of reaching conclusions on the basis of evidence. On Meiklejohn's views it would be impossible to say that any man's ideas were determined for him, even if he were on the payroll of the N.A.M.,[4] since his act of joining or not joining was free, that is, voluntary.

2. The exchange between President Allen[5] and Dr. Meiklejohn I think showed that Meiklejohn had not done justice to the position of a majority of members of the Tenure Committee of the University of Washington who, although recommending the reinstatement of the two members of the Communist Party, held that subsequent membership in the Communist Party should be regarded as sufficient for exclusion. This principle is by far more important than the particular application in the University of Washington case.

3. You quote from Professor Commager's[6] statement that "we are now embarked upon a campaign of suppression and oppression more violent, more reckless, more pervasive, and ultimately more dangerous than any in our history." Commager gives no evidence of this. And I

should myself say that this is an historically false judgment. I know firsthand what the post–World War I repressions were like, and I have read enough about the treatment of abolitionists in the North to convince me that the most hysterical people today are those who are shouting hysteria and are making judgments of the kind which you quote from Commager. Such judgments are not only false but dangerous, since they disarm us in advance against the possibility of wholesale repression in the way in which cries of Fascism under Bruening, under Schleicher, under Papen, led people to think that Hitler would be no different.

4. You refer to Mrs. Lynd's article[7] in the *American Scholar,* and yet the article should have suggested some doubts to you because of the nature of her documentation, particularly in reference to quotations from Mr. Canwell's[8] speech. She puts other people's words in his mouth as if they were a direct statement. I have checked on this quotation and on some other matters, and I have found that Mrs. Lynd's "evidence" is made up of whole cloth. I am discussing this and related issues in an article entitled "Academic Integrity" in the October issue of *Commentary.*[9]

It seems to me that you have confused two different issues: 1) whether academic freedom gives a scholar a right to profess any conclusion he reaches on the basis of evidence, which no one in this discussion has challenged, and 2) whether academic freedom gives an individual a right to propagandize for a party line whether it is that of the N.A.M. or the Communist Party. In the *Saturday Evening Post* of September 10th[10] I have tried once more to state the main issues and the main arguments. I shall be really obliged to you if you will meet the argument instead of invoking in a vacuum the unanalyzed phrases of a ritualistic liberalism. I recognize that the whole question is difficult and that it is possible for genuine liberals to disagree with my view. But what I have found really surprising is the failure of liberals who disagree with the position taken to meet the argument with relevant evidence. What you say about the importance of the free exchange of ideas and about the absurdity of not permitting Shostakovich to play his music I agree with. But it is irrelevant to the issue, which is one of professional ethics.

I hope you do not mind my writing frankly because the issue is going to be very much alive in the next few years and clarity seems to me to be essential.

1. Wesley P. Clark, professor of classics, Montana State University.

2. "International Communism," *Dartmouth Alumni Magazine,* 41 (March 1949): 13–20.

3. Alexander Meiklejohn, founder of the American Civil Liberties Union.

4. National Association of Manufacturers, a conservative trade organization representing the interests of big business.

5. Raymond B. Allen, president, University of Washington.

6. Henry Steele Commager, professor of history, Columbia University.

7. Helen M. Lynd was the co-author, along with her husband, Robert S. Lynd, of two classic works in American sociology: *Middletown: A Study in Modern American Culture* (New York, 1929), and *Middletown in Transition: A Study in Cultural Conflicts* (New York, 1937). Lynd, "Truth at the University of Washington," *American Scholar* 18 (July 1949): 346–53. Lynd's article accused the University of Washington administration of violating academic freedom and of caving in to anti-communist hysteria.

8. Albert F. Canwell, chairman of the State of Washington Joint Legislative Fact-Finding Committee on Un-American Activities.

9. Sidney Hook, "Academic Integrity and Academic Freedom," *Commentary* 8 (October 1949): 329–39.

10. Sidney Hook, "What Shall We Do about Communist Teachers?" *Saturday Evening Post* 222 (September 10, 1949): 33, 164–68.

74

Dear Professor Kattsoff,[1]   November 7, 1949

Please excuse my delay in replying to your letter of October 27th. Some day I hope to discuss the question with you at greater length. But I am wondering whether you have read my *Saturday Evening Post* article of September 10th. In it I take up some of the points you make.

As I see the question, it is primarily a matter of professional ethics. I accept, as a presupposition of the responsibility of a teacher, the rule laid down by the New School for Social Research that in the interests of academic freedom and responsibility no member of the faculty can belong to any party or group which dictates to him what he must believe in matters of science or scientific opinion. The evidence shows that the Communist Party is such a group. Therefore there is a fair presumption that anyone who joins the Communist Party is aware of what he is doing. There is overwhelming evidence, in terms of the conditions of party membership, of what his *intentions* are. After all, a member of the Communist Party understands that he must be a "professional revolutionist" and that everything, but literally everything, must be subordinated to the political objective. This establishes a *prima facie* case against him of professional unfitness to teach, though it does not affect his political rights.

As a matter of common sense, if a person came to you declaring that he would cheat if he had an opportunity to do it, would you hire him and then say you must catch him in the act, or would you not agree that it would be justifiable to say that since he had declared his intention there was no reason why you should take the risk? Now a member of the Communist Party reads his official instructions—I have cited the literature—which tells him that he must take advantage of his position wherever he can without exposing himself to inject the party line. Why then should we take all the trouble to watch him? To do so would disorganize the University.

In my *Post* article I show that this is not an absolutely hard and fast rule, but that some rules are necessary. We then use discretion in certain specifications and prepare to grant the possibility of exceptions. But all working rules in life as distinct from mathematics have borderline cases.

But perhaps we can continue this when I come to Chapel Hill. I should like to make a visit during our winter and your spring if climatic conditions arrange themselves that way. I always imagine that when it snows up here the cotton fields are blooming in the South.

1. L. O. Kattsoff, professor of philosophy, University of North Carolina.

3

1950–1952

The years 1950–52 were among the most meaningful in Sidney Hook's political life. It was then that he became widely known outside the rarefied world of academia and the pages of *Modern Monthly,* the *Journal of Philosophy, Philosophic Abstracts, Partisan Review, Commentary,* and the *New Republic.* Hook took his responsibilities as a teacher and citizen seriously. He welcomed the opportunity of publishing in the mass media and frequently wrote to the editors of popular magazines suggesting essays. His articles in the 1940s and 1950s in the *Saturday Evening Post,* the *New York Times Magazine, Fortune,* and *American Mercury* made his name familiar among the general reading public, and he became one of the most prominent spokesmen during the 1950s for the anti-communist American Left.

The spreading of Hook's fame occurred at the height of the Cold War and McCarthyism. This was not coincidental. Hook's major concern during this period was to stiffen the resolve of the anti-communist American Left at a time when the rantings of the junior senator from Wisconsin were discrediting anti-communism. Hook worked to save anti-communism from the anti-communists and to make clear the distinction between legitimate heretical ideas and the conspiratorial activities of the Communist movement.

No activity of Hook's was more important during this period than his involvement with the American Committee for Cultural Freedom (ACCF), the unofficial American branch of the Congress for Cultural Freedom (CCF). Melvin Lasky was the key figure behind the establishment of the CCF in June 1950. Lasky was then attached to the Office of Military Government in Berlin, and he thought it both appropriate and convenient that the founding meeting of the Congress be in West Berlin. Although the Berlin airlift was no longer in effect, the city remained the symbol of the Cold War. Ernst Reuter, the beleaguered city's mayor, enthusiastically supported the holding of the Congress in Berlin.

Hook was deeply moved when Reuter personally invited him to attend the Congress, and he eagerly accepted. Many of the leading European and American intellectuals were in attendance, including Jules Romains, Ignazio Silone, Arthur Koestler, Boris Nicolaevsky, Franz Borkenau, A. J. Ayer, Arthur M. Schlesinger, Jr., and James Burnham. The Congress was among the most notable experiences in Hook's life. His description of the Congress emphasized the differences between it and the Waldorf Conference.

> The news of the invasion of Korea broke just before the initial session. . . . The meeting opened with a period of silence, memorializing those who had fallen in the struggle for freedom. It was followed by the strains of the overture to Beethoven's *Fidelio* played by the Berlin Philharmonic Orchestra. The music too had a symbolic significance, for there was considerable uncertainty whether the Russians would move against West Germany, in which event all of us would have been prisoners of the Soviet security forces within a few hours. Nonetheless West Berlin, defenseless in an iron ring of Soviet armor, remained outwardly calm. If anything, instead of being subdued, the delegates to the Congress responded with *elan* to the overhanging threat of the Korean events. It was reflected in the militant tone of the criticisms of the Soviet version of culture, in the appeals directed to the peoples of the satellite countries to support the program of the Congress, and in the Message of Solidarity sent by the Western intellectuals to their confreres in the East; the message affirmed a bond of friendship and respect. . . . With few exceptions . . . all the delegates realized that Mayor Reuter's opening remark "We greet you as fellow fighters in the cause of freedom" was no mere rhetoric. [*Out of Step*, 433–36.]

Hook was selected to sit on the Congress' executive committee. In view of his position as an insider, Hook's growing dissatisfaction during the 1950s with the direction of the Congress was significant. The Congress was, he believed, too timid in challenging communism, too fearful of becoming the target of anti-anti-communists, too committed to maintaining the political status quo in Europe. By 1956, Hook realized that the Congress would never fulfill the promise of 1950, and he ceased participating in its work. "My inactivity by this time was not unwelcomed," he recalled, "since I was regarded by the Parisian directorate as a representative of the obnoxious American Committee for Cultural Freedom" (*Out of Step*, 449).

Hook helped found the American Committee for Cultural Freedom in January 1951. The Committee's certificate of incorporation declared its goal was to "further the democratic way of life in all spheres of culture." Its original officers included Hook, James Burnham, Elliot Cohen, William Phillips, Sol Levitas, and Richard Rovere, with Hook serving as its first president. The Committee's membership included many of the same persons who a year and a half earlier had protested the Waldorf Conference, including Arnold Beichman, George Counts, Max Eastman, James Farrell, Mary McCarthy, Dwight Macdonald, Arthur Schlesinger, Jr., and Norman Thomas.

The ACCF soon became embroiled in a controversy over the proper stance to take toward Senator McCarthy. Some of its members, most notably Max

Eastman, defended McCarthy's anti-communist antics. Others, particularly Macdonald, Rovere, and Schlesinger, believed that any organization claiming to defend culture and freedom must repudiate McCarthyism in no uncertain terms.

During the six years of its existence the ACCF was, in the words of historian William L. O'Neill, "middle of the road in the fight against Stalinist culture. . . . The most active members . . . believed that the danger to cultural freedom came first from Stalinists, later from McCarthyites. They fought both, and, despite lapses of judgment and taste, their record was better than critics have been willing to admit."* The same could be said of Hook's most sustained political effort of the 1950s, his attempt to awaken the universities to the challenge posed to academic freedom by Communist professors committed to propagating the party line.

While supporting the removal of card-carrying members of the American Communist Party from academia, Hook also attacked McCarthy and called for a national movement to remove the senator from national politics. "By ignoring the basic differences among nonconformists, social reformers, independent radicals and revolutionists, on the one hand, and conforming Communist Party members and fellow-travelers on the other," Hook later recounted, McCarthy and his supporters "provided an opportunity for those who were disciplined members of a totalitarian fifth column to pose as innocent victims of political paranoia." The bulk of Hook's writings in the 1950s, most notably *Heresy, Yes—Conspiracy, No!* (1953), sought to undo the damage done by the McCarthyites.

---

*William L. O'Neill, *A Better World: The Great Schism: Stalinism and the American Intellectuals* (New York: Simon and Schuster, 1982), p. 308.

75

Dear Sir,[1]   January 18, 1950

I am moved to write you in protest against the publication, without editorial criticism or dissociation, of the article on "Recognition of Chinese Government" by Hilda Selwyn-Clarke in the January *Socialist Commentary*.

This article is a miserable piece of thinly-disguised Stalinist apologetics which makes a mockery of your professed ethical philosophy of politics. Whatever the evils of the Nationalist regime, the terror regime of the Chinese Stalinists is many times worse. It is pretty late in the day to picture Mao Tse-Tung as the leader of an agrarian democratic movement of protest. From the day the Chinese Communist Party was founded in the Kremlin down to the present, it has been a willing tool of Soviet foreign policy. The Nationalists showed considerable independence towards the Western powers, whereas the Chinese Communists have never criticized by so much as a word the appropriation of Chinese territory and property by the Soviet Union. The condemnation of Tito by the Chinese Communists is an indication of how much independence they will display in the future.

The article says that socialists who are more concerned with the struggle for the rice bowl than for the cold war will wish the Chinese Communists well. I am not so much concerned with this typical defense of terror by spokesmen of totalitarianism. But that *you* should have let it go unchallenged puzzles me. It is extremely dubious that Mao Tse-Tung will give the Chinese masses more rice than they have had previously—more dubious even than that Stalin has given the Russian workers more bread than they enjoyed under Kerensky.[2] But let us assume for the moment that the Chinese peasants and workers will get a little more rice. If this is a justification of the Communist dictatorship in the eyes of Socialists, why wasn't the fact that Hitler increased employment and the standard of living in Germany a similar justification? For years this kind of rationalization was heard in defense of Mussolini and Hitler by those who said that the destruction of all civil rights and freedoms was the necessary price to pay for economic improvements.

Why do you now by your publication of this intellectually dishonest article accept this position when you reject it for other varieties of totalitarianism? I should have thought you understood by now that Stalin's terror is everywhere as thorough and deadly, if not more so, than Hitler's terror. The "cold war" is a war waged by the Kremlin against all Western democratic institutions, whether its economy is capitalist or semi-socialist, and it will become a hot war just as soon as Stalin feels he can win it. The issue is not fundamentally economic in our age, but political and ethical, viz., between democracy (and all its imperfections, but including the possibility of moving towards a humanistic socialism) and the most ruthless system of despotism in all human history. Surely, your friends on the continent, especially those in the Eastern Zone, have informed you of the facts of political life there.

In calling for the support of the Chinese Communists—sending them greetings of good-will!—you should also send greetings of good-will to the hangman in the Kremlin to whom Mao Tse-Tung has publicly acknowledged his thanks for the support which was essential to his victory.

I am much more of a Marxist in my theoretical outlook than your group is, but I have always admired the incorruptible ethical integrity of Leonard Nelson[3] and his followers who have refused to make a fetish of a mythical economic necessity, and who have never woven garlands of flowers over the shackles of despotism and dictatorship. By publishing this article on China without critical dissociation, you have outraged every moral principle for which Leonard Nelson has lived and for which several of his students, and your colleagues, have died.

1. Editor of *Socialist Commentary* (London).
2. Alexander Kerensky, head of the Russian government that was overthrown by the Bolshevik revolution of 1917.
3. Nelson, professor of philosophy at the University of Gottingen, espoused a synthesis of Plato and Kant. He founded the Internationaler Sozialistischer Kampfbund and opposed Germany's participation in World War I. Hook admired the courage and ethics of Nelson and the members of the ISK, although not their political judgment. See Hook, *Out of Step*, pp. 114–15.

76

Dear Mr. Hibbs,[1]   February 1, 1950

I understand that Harold J. Laski[2] is due for another visit to the United States. Despite opinion to the contrary, he is a person of little influence in England, but of enormous influence in the U.S., particularly in academic, liberal, and editorial circles. Ever since Bertrand Russell characterized him as "a smart silly man," I have been thinking of writing a critical analysis of his ideas and what he stands for. He is the grandaddy of all "totalitarian liberals," and his recent paean of praise for Stalin is typical of the kind of apologetics he goes in for. Most of the time, however, he is not as crude as that. His usual line is that Communism is the Christianity of the 20th Century—concentration camps and all! Since he declares that he himself personally is not a Communist, this increases his effectiveness and tends to give him the aura of an "objective" political scientist.

I am wondering whether you would be interested in an article on "Portrait of a Totalitarian Liberal," without committing yourself, however, in any way.

1. Ben Hibbs, editor, *Saturday Evening Post.*
2. Prominent British left-wing socialist intellectual.

77

Dear Professor Nietmann,[1]   March 24, 1950

I have glanced through the paper which you sent me on March 5th, and in accordance with your request I am making a few suggestions.

First, I wonder whether it is historically justified to seek for the key to what we roughly call "the American way of life" in the amount of beef or bread or milk consumed. I think the starting point should rest upon our recognition that democracy implies "Civil Rights and Groceries," and the interrelationship between the two, both in respect to civil rights and groceries. Your description of the present situation in the U.S.S.R. could be presented in conjunction with the state of affairs before the Russian Revolution, five years after the Russian Revolution, and the present. It is widely claimed, for example in Manya Gordon's book *Workers Before and After Lenin* as well as in the writings of Dallin and Nicolaevsky,[2] that the real wages of the Russian worker before allowances are made for social services, etc., were actually higher before the Russian Revolution, and that as compared to the real wages of the Russian worker from 1927 to 1929, his present wage is lower. Even more important, however, is the curve in respect to civil liberties, since according to the Communist ideology coercion is a temporary measure which will disappear when the state disappears, that is when socialism has been introduced. And as you know, the official claim is that the state of socialism in the classless society already exists in the Soviet Union. The evidence seems to show that in respect to civil liberties, the opposition to the Czar enjoyed much more freedom, as limited as it was, than any group not in sympathy with the leading cadres of the Communist Party could enjoy in the Soviet Union today. Most significant from my point of view is the fact that there has been a steady increase of coercion since the Russian Revolution to the present—no other political parties, no groups permitted within the dominant party, total regimentation of all arts, purging of the scientists, etc.

I mention these matters not so much to indicate my own point of view, but to call attention to some methodological points which require, it seems to me, treatment in your discussion.

Naturally, as an experimental pragmatist I disagree with both your account and your criticism of instrumentalism. But I am glad that you have made your criticisms in such a forthright way since it sharpens some basic issues. I believe that despite the differences among the various philosophical traditions of the West, they have much more in common with each other than any of them has with that new authoritarianism which George Orwell described so well in his *Animal Farm* and his *1984*.

In a few days I shall mail to you a draft of my paper. The title of my paper will be "The Conflict Between Democratic and Communist Ideologies."

1. William D. Nietmann, chairman, department of philosophy, College of the Pacific.
2. David Dallin and Boris Nicolaevsky.

78

Dear Mr. Schwarz,[1]   March 29, 1950

My position on the question of permitting members of foreign Communist Parties to visit this country is briefly this: the decision should be made *ad hoc* at the discretion of the Secretary of State along certain lines indicated below:

First, let me point out that some Communists from the U.S.S.R. were permitted to enter the country last year to attend the Waldorf Conference. I think this was a wise decision, just as the recent refusal to permit Picasso and his communist friends to visit was unwise.

Second, to raise *all* restrictions on the entry of foreign Communists would be inadvisable because (i) it entails a revision of existing immigration laws (the revision should be made but not on *these* grounds), (ii) it might lead to a veritable influx of foreign Communists which would tax our supervisory facilities, provoke incidents if they interfered with our own domestic affairs (as they undoubtedly would), (iii) it would be hard to explain to non-Communist D.P.'s and other democratic elements in Europe who were eager to come here, why we kept them out, etc.

Third, the principles that should guide intelligent policy are (a) Foreign

Communists should be permitted to come for *specific cultural purposes* indicated in advance, even broad political purposes, but not, for example, as fraternal delegates to the conventions of the Communist Party. (b) Their stay should be limited to a fortnight except on scientific missions. (c) The personnel of foreign Communists should be restricted to cultural and professional persons, e.g. Picasso should be permitted to come but not Duclos,[2] secretary of the French Communist Party, etc. (d) The reasons for permission should be made public by the State Department always with an explanation pointing up the contrast between our policy and that of the totalitarian countries. We should try to make capital of our free institutions *before* the Communists come. (It is utopian to think that members of the C.P. will tell the truth about us when they return to their countries.) (e) We, or the cultural department of the State Department, should *take the initiative* in offering to send well known *democratic* writers, scientists and artists to Communist countries on an exchange basis, etc., etc.

Finally, although I believe quite a persuasive case can be made out along the lines I have indicated, I honestly wonder whether the topic is sufficiently important or "big enough" for an article in the *Times Magazine* section. Perhaps it should be discussed as one aspect of a larger question: "How U.S. Should Conduct Its Cultural Policy?" or "Cultural Policy as Part of Enlightened Foreign Policy."

I am working hard on my piece on "Liberalism in Crisis" etc.,[3] trying to distinguish between the right to heresy which we should defend and conspiracy which is something else again. Hope to have it ready by Monday.

1. Daniel Schwarz, assistant editor, Sunday *New York Times*.
2. Jacques Duclos.
3. This appeared as "Heresy, Yes—But Conspiracy, No," *New York Times Magazine*, July 9, 1950, 1, 38–39. Hook expanded this essay into a book, *Heresy, Yes—Conspiracy, No!* (New York, 1953).

79

Dear Professor Hildebrand,[1]   April 3, 1950

I have just read in the *New York Times* of April 2nd the account of the meeting of the Board of Regents of the University of California concerning the imposition of the special non-Communist oath.[2] I must confess that I am appalled by the short-sightedness and foolishness of the action.

I am wondering whether I can be of any help to the faculty in inducing the Regents to abandon their unreasonable demands. Last October I accepted an invitation to teach in the summer session at Santa Barbara College of the University of California. Do you think it would be of any help to you if I issued a public statement? In the event that disciplinary action is taken against any members of the faculty, I am prepared, if you or your group deem it advisable, to resign publicly my position for the summer with a statement to the press giving the reasons. Although this will involve considerable inconvenience to me, it is a slight thing compared with the basic issues which are involved.

I do not want to act on my own but in conjunction with the authorized spokesmen of the faculty. Perhaps there may be other individuals who feel the way I do, in which case it would be more effective if we act together.

I shall appreciate hearing from you at your earliest convenience. Newspaper accounts leave matters a little obscure, and I do not know whether visiting professors of the summer session are expected to sign a special non-Communist oath. I should like to act in conformity with the decisions of the academic senate in this matter.

1. Joel H. Hildebrand, professor of chemistry, University of California.
2. A loyalty oath imposed on all employees of the California university system. This precipitated one of the great controversies over academic freedom during what came to be known as the "Second Great Red Scare."

80

Dear A.J.,[1]   April 18, 1950

I am sorry that you think I am suffering from schizophrenia because of the view which I expressed in my *Times* article.[2] I do not think there is anything wrong with your sanity, but I do think there is something seriously wrong with your logic and naivete. To think that a man like you should be so ignorant about the nature of Stalinism—and after all your experiences, too!

Your pamphlet[3] is unconvincing in every respect. You assume that in dealing with people like Hitler and Stalin we are dealing with the same people that Gandhi dealt with. You assume that free public opinion is exercised within the USSR. You do not explain why Hitler was not appeased at Munich. You do not explain why the non-resistance policy of the Jews did not save them from destruction. You do not explain why the non-resistant attitude towards the German soldiers in some countries did not lead them to abandon their arms. You write that the Russian soldiers are now deserting and that, if we folded our arms and refused to resist Stalin, more Russians would desert. This is really silly. Russian soldiers are now deserting because there are democratic countries to which they can go. They don't desert in Poland or Romania, and if we followed your program of non-resistance, this country would become another Poland or Romania. You underestimate the ability of the Communists to portray their actions as a defense of war against "the enemies of the people." They would shut down and imprison people like you and use the press to convince those who couldn't be told different that you were guilty of poisoning wells, etc., etc.

I could go on for a long time pointing out the inconsistent assumptions, the ignored evidence, and the angelic optimism which is sure to lead to diabolical results. Absolute pacifism is a noble philosophy, but an impossible one. You have not drawn a lesson from the fact that whereas in a democratic country you are free to agitate and propagate your point of view, in any totalitarian country today you will be a dead duck, or worse, confessing under torture and dragged to murder and infamy. Man, wake up!

1. Abraham J. Muste, secretary of the Fellowship of Reconciliation, a radical pacifist organization.

2. "The Scientist in Politics," *New York Times Magazine,* April 9, 1950.

3. *Gandhi and the H-Bomb: How Nonviolence Can Take the Place of War* (New York, 1950).

81

Dear Miss Saran,[1]   May 12, 1950

This will acknowledge your letter of April 24 concerning my communication on the China article in your January issue. I am completely disarmed by the spirit of sweet reasonableness which pervades your letter. The issues are too complex to discuss by letter. There is only one point which I wish to make and that is that the article not merely advocated recognition of the Chinese Communist regime, which is bad enough, but expressed positive approval of what the Chinese Communists are up to. I myself cannot make any moral distinctions between terror and terror, and there is absolutely no evidence that the Chinese Communists are Titoists. In fact, they were the first Communist group outside the Soviet Union to condemn Tito. I am confident that events will bear me out. The refusal of the Chinese Communists to permit us to feed the millions of starving Chinese peasants is a sign of what to expect. But more of this some other time.

There is something ironical in the fact that I, a naturalist, should have to remind members of the Nelson Bund[2] of the Kantian principle that what is wrong for one government to do cannot be right in identical circumstances for another to do.

Cordially and with comradely greetings,

1. Mary Saran, member of the editorial committee, *Socialist Commentary*.
2. Leonard Nelson and his followers.

82

Dear Ed Wilson,[1]   July 28, 1950

I am letting my membership lapse in the American Humanist Association as well as my subscription to *The Humanist* because of the policy of cultivated ambiguity on the part of the Association and the magazine towards Communism, which today is the greatest enemy of humanism in the entire world. In one of your letters you ask for funds in order to push the sale of Corliss Lamont's book on humanism in which the terroristic, heresy hunting, concentration camp regime of the Soviet Union is praised as "humanist." That you should push the sale of such a book is an outrage and a moral affront to any genuine humanist.

I am confident that you would not push the sale of a book which praised the Nazi regime or philosophy and that you would not be taken in by any apologetics for "Catholic humanism." What is called "Soviet humanism" is as phoney as a Soviet "peace" campaign. And as a humanist group it is your duty to say so. There cannot be any "humanism" without political and cultural freedom, and on the key issue of *freedom,* where the Communist movement is concerned, your association and magazine speak with an uncertain voice. On this issue you cannot carry water on both shoulders.

It is not enough to print occasionally a piece which is mildly critical of Communism and then one which takes by indirection a Communist line. For example, side by side with Geiger's splendid review of Kallen[2] in the last number, you print a review which sympathetically compares Debs[3] with Harry Bridges,[4] a convicted Communist perjurer.

It is fine to print with a warm editorial send-off Hutchins'[5] introduction to Jerome Davis' *Character Assassination.* But where were you all these years when Jerome Davis' friends, the Communists, labelled Dewey, Kallen, and other leading democratic humanists "Fascists?" As Norman Thomas pointed out in his review of the book—a review which should have been printed in *The Humanist*—the vilest forms of character assassination in this country were initiated by Jerome Davis' fellow-workers, the Communists, with whom he actively cooperated. Yet there is not a line about Communist smear campaigns in Davis' book. He has always condoned them.

Why plug Davis' book and keep silent about Communist character assassination?

One can oppose authoritarian Catholicism, which internationally is a much weaker enemy of humanism than is Communism, without Communist allies like Lamont and other pseudo-humanists who would drop their opposition to Catholicism overnight if the Kremlin changed its line. One can learn a lot from the clean, hard way Mrs. Agnes Meyer[6] opposes clericalism—without entangling alliances.

Years ago Ed Fiess warned me that the Humanist Association and magazine were systematically appeasing the Communists by avoiding, wherever possible, outright criticism of the Soviet terror regime for fear of antagonizing so called "Communist humanists"(!). I have reluctantly come to the conclusion that he was right.

P.S. This letter is not for publication. I shall probably write an article on "Communism and Humanism" for the *N.L.* or *P.R.*[7] discussing the whole question.

1. Edwin H. Wilson, editor, *The Humanist.*
2. George R. Geiger, an associate editor of *The Humanist,* reviewed Horace Kallen's book *Patterns of Progress* (New York, 1950).
3. Eugene V. Debs, American socialist leader during the early twentieth century.
4. Harry Bridges, leader of longshoremen's union in Hawaii and the West Coast.
5. Robert Maynard Hutchins, associate director, Ford Foundation.
6. Wife of the owner of the *Washington Post.*
7. *New Leader* and *Partisan Review.* Article never appeared.

83

Dear Ed Wilson,[1]   August 14, 1950

Your letter of August 9 has just reached me.

Before hearing from you I sent copies of my letters to some friends of mine. Of course I shall not circulate your letter unless you wish me to, but I have absolutely no objection to your showing mine to anyone else. The only reason it is not for publication is that I expect to do a longer piece later on, carefully documented.

In your letter you say that you have sought to combat communism in such a way as not to help Fascists and reactionaries, and that I have chosen a different course. I find this very offensive. What is your evidence that my criticisms of communism have helped Fascists and reactionaries? Certainly not the clerical fascist press? And although criticizing communism I have kept up a steady drumfire against all other forms of totalitarianism as my article in the current issue of the *Partisan Review* shows.[2] This is more than can be said for *The Humanist.* What would you say if someone told you that your criticisms of authoritarian Catholicism helps the Communist attack against the Church? Even if true, would that make your criticisms of Catholicism less valid or justifiable? When I used to attack totalitarian Catholicism in the pages of *The Humanist,* liberal Catholics used to reproach me because the Communists would use my arguments for their own purposes. So I think it is in extremely bad taste for you to make this charge.

Your letter obviously confirms my contention that the magazine and the association have deliberately sought to sidestep the issue concerning the flagrant incompatibility between humanism, whose central doctrine is the freedom of the human spirit, and the contemporary communist movement. Dewey and Kallen, the leading American humanists, have been crystal clear about this. And it is an issue that cannot be compromised any more than the issue between humanism and Fascism. That was the whole burden of my letter.

I have no objection to your publishing Lamont's articles, but I do object to your association *officially* pushing his book without one word of critical dissociation. I have no objection to your criticizing McCarthyism. I have done so myself. But I do object to your plug for the Communist variant of McCarthyism. And make no mistake about it. Your republication of Hutchins' introduction is tantamount to an endorsement of Jerome Davis' book. You now offer me three hundred words to be buried in the letter column to balance the score. Why, the very least you could do is to print in bold black type on the first page of the next issue (in exactly the same place that Hutchins' introduction appeared) the relevant passages from the reviews of Baldwin, Spitz, and Thomas.

I know you have a difficult decision to make. I have no doubt whatsoever about your own personal devotion to democracy and abhorrence of totalitarian communism. If you take a forthright stand along your own personal lines you will undoubtedly lose some people and some support. And since you have almost single-handedly built the organization, you are naturally loath to do it and are bitter against people like me who seem to be imposing a hard choice on you. But it is not I who am imposing this choice but the logic of your own beliefs and the urgencies of what may be freedom's last desperate battle. Better no humanist movement than one flawed at the heart by equivocation. I am confident, however, that a strong stand by the magazine and the Association against totalitarian communism will ultimately strengthen the humanist movement if the world remains free.

1. Edwin H. Wilson.
2. "The Berlin Congress for Cultural Freedom," *Partisan Review* 17 (September–October, 1950): 715–22.

84

Dear Abe,[1]   October 6, 1950

I have read the piece which you have sent me and find it excellent. It is very timely and very necessary. It requires courage to take this position, but in the long run it would be suicidal not to take it. I have only a few suggestions to make:

1) I agree with you completely about so-called loyalty oaths. But I think you should stress as the main objection to them their futility.

2) I think you should stress the fact—I hope to do a piece on this sometime in the future—that it is extremely difficult, if not impossible, to prove that indoctrination is taking place in the classroom even when it is going on. For example, a secret member of the Communist Party can present very persuasively a party line. Even if it is reported, he can always say that he was just presenting the point of view of the other side, etc., etc. We must have absolute confidence in the integrity of the teacher and then let him alone. Observation in the classroom makes it possible at most to tell how effective a teacher's techniques are but cannot indicate the over-all and underlying content. But you know much more about these matters than I.

1. Abraham Lefkowitz, principal, Samuel J. Tilden High School, Brooklyn, New York.

85

Dear A.J.,[1]   ca. 1950

If I were a gifted writer I would write a novel in which you would be the hero. Its first and last pages would be the same with one difference. On the first page you would be a young minister trampled by the horses of policemen breaking up a labor demonstration you were leading. On the last page you would be a grey-haired churchman trampled by the horses of policemen breaking up another labor demonstration you were leading. From the first page to the last page would be the story of your gradual withdrawal from the church and your gradual return to it . . . whatever church it is but certainly not a Roman one.[2] The story would be the saga of a good man lost in the jungle of political life, because he had been using the wrong guidelines and had not followed his vocation for martyrdom.

I remember once your saying at a public or committee meeting—it was the nearest thing to a boast I ever heard you make—that in every crisis of your life, you always chose "to go left." "To go left" was the talisman of your political purity. Politically, or course, such a policy is and was disastrous because where you go depends upon who calls himself "center" or "right," and these terms are so shifting that no one could guide himself by them except into a state of bewildering circularity and ultimately political breakdown. At the time you said it—perhaps you were defining your position with respect to the Trotskyist French turn.[3] I no longer remember because when I realized what a bad match-maker I had been in helping to forge the union of the American Workers Party and the Socialist Workers' Party, I fled and returned to the higher grounds of philosophy. The French turn was after that—so you might have uttered the words at another crucial juncture or they may have been reported to me.

But as I look back over the years, I interpret your remark about always "choosing to go left" as meaning something vastly different, something not political at all but ethical. Whatever you chose to do, you chose with integrity and honesty. You never fought foul or played unfair even with those who traduced you. You never permitted your moral sense to become sophisticated by apologetics for history. Your moral sense, which to me defines your personality, rather than your theological commitment, was much wiser than your political sense. It saved you from the fate of the Cannons and Budenzes and Burnhams—not to speak of the unspeakable Stalinists with whom, alas! so many of our erstwhile companions in the political jungle had so much in common.[4]

It is this autonomy of the moral sense, even when everything is granted about its conditions and causes, which ennobles human life. Although without intelligence it is never a reliable guide in the political jungle, once it is extinguished, nothing good can ever be achieved in this world.

Although I believe that your present course of absolute pacifism is tragically mistaken, and would ensure the death of free societies under Communist terror, I am happy to see that you are still as "left" as ever—in the sense in which I define it. I honor you for it. Perhaps if people like you were permitted to survive under Communism, instead of being among the first who are liquidated, I might accept the risks of its brutal triumph to the risks of opposing it. But this, as you know, is a vain "perhaps"—and, fortunately, the risks of opposing Communism so far are much less than the risks of unilateral disarmament. The Communist leaders have no vocation for martyrdom, because nothing exists for them but history.

And so, dear A.J., I salute you on your birthday and wish that you live long enough to see a world not only at peace but universally free.

1. Abraham J. Muste. For more on Hook's attitude toward Muste, see *Out of Step*, pp. 190–91, 199–201.
2. Muste was at one time a Protestant minister. He became a labor organizer, pacifist spokesman, and revolutionary Marxist. See Jo Ann Ooiman Robinson, *Abraham Went Out: A Biography of A.J. Muste* (Philadelphia, 1981).
3. Reference is to the policy of Trotsky during the 1930s that his followers join the French Socialist Party.
4. James Cannon, Louis F. Budenz, and James Burnham, prominent figures in the Marxist ideological warfare of the 1930s. Budenz became an informer for the House Committee on Un-American Activities during the 1950s, while Burnham became associated with William F. Buckley's right-wing *National Review.*

86

Dear Professor Kantorowicz,[1]   December 11, 1950

Thank you for a copy of your pamphlet, *The Fundamental Issue,* which you sent me with your compliments. It makes very interesting reading and explains some aspects of the controversy I was not familiar with.

As you may know from my writings, I regard as the main issue in the controversy the nature and degree of control of the university to be exercised by the faculty. If I understand you, this is your position also.

However, there is another line of argument in your pamphlet that seems to me to weaken the force of the main argument. This is your insistence that the loyalty oath per se is incompatible with academic freedom. If this is true, then those who refused to take the oath on that ground should have, in all consistency, refused also to take the oath to uphold the national and state constitutions. Indeed, one argument I heard often used against the special oath was its superfluity, since it was a special application of what was generically implied in the oath to uphold the federal and state constitutions. There is no getting around the fact that these constitutions are political documents, and that subscription to them is a political test—and because of the multiplicity of the provisions they contain—a more comprehensive political test than a special loyalty oath.

My own point of view is that all oaths, including those to uphold the constitution, are *unnecessary* in educational institutions. They never achieve the purposes for which they are intended and therefore are foolish in the education field.

The decisive point, however, is that such oaths involve the violation of academic freedom only when they require an individual to subscribe to something he does not believe in. For example, if I were a convinced Platonist in political theory I could not consciously take an oath to uphold a democratic constitution. But since I am a democrat I can take this oath without violating my beliefs although I am convinced that the oath is unnecessary. However, I would never take an oath to uphold the constitution of a non-democratic country. Lumping the two together seems to me to blur the main emphasis on the autonomy of the educational enterprise. It is enough to say that one refuses to take the oath because it has been imposed by the Regents against the wishes of the faculty and that such actions of the Regents, whether in respect to an oath or anything else, are a violation of the conditions of academic freedom. But if the faculty itself were to be so foolish as to require an oath of its own members which did not involve a violation of their beliefs, this would not be *per se* a breach of academic freedom.

Further, in contradistinction to your Appendix F, I believe that the legality or illegality of a political party has nothing to do with the question of academic freedom. Any man who has been certified as competent by his peers and who has professional integrity—no matter what his beliefs: Communist, Fascist, Platonist, Seventh Day Adventist, etc., etc.—should be permitted to teach. But if an individual is a member of any group, legal or not, which acts on official instructions to "take advantage of his position in the classroom" to indoctrinate for a party line, to capture control of departments, rewrite texts according to instructions received from an outside source, etc., he is professionally unfit to be a member of the academic community. His present and active membership in such a group, no matter what group, is an action which clearly declares his intent to violate the elementary duties of the scholar and teacher. This declaration of intention is *prima facie* evidence of unfitness.

There is much more that one can say, but this is sufficient to indicate what my position is and why I think that the fundamental issue in the outrage of the Regents of the University of California against its faculty becomes obscured if any oath *per se* is regarded as a violation of academic freedom.

1. Ernest H. Kantorowicz, refugee from Nazi Germany and professor of history, University of California.

87

Dear Sir,[1]   December 13, 1950

I find it extremely difficult to understand why, in his recent letter in the *New York Times,* Mr. Ralph Barton Perry remains silent about the steady stream of invective, denunciation and downright lies pouring from the lips of Messrs. Vishinski, Malik, and Wu,[2] whereas he rebukes Mr. Austin[3] for his occasional tone of "annoyance and anger." If anything, Mr. Austin has been a model of judicious restraint. Indeed, evidence seems to show that forthright replies of the character delivered by General Romulo[4] at Lake Success[5] have the best effect in clarifying the basic issues.

A great Harvard philosopher of an earlier day, George Santayana, once remarked that those who cannot remember the past are doomed to repeat it. When Mr. Perry tells us that now is not the time to be talking of the "free nations" but only of the terrors of war, he brings to mind those who a decade ago used to assert that the issue was not one of freedom versus tyranny but merely, to use Mr. Perry's phrase, of "peace versus war." But the reasons which induced Mr. Perry a decade ago to recognize that the issue was indeed one of the survival of "free nations" are today even more weighty, for our enemy is much stronger than Hitler. By all means let us emphasize, as Mr. Austin actually has done, the disastrous consequences of war, but unless this is coupled with a reaffirmation of our ideals and principles, it may be a preface to capitulation.

Mr. Perry would have us continue our military preparations presumably in Europe, if not in Asia. But if the issue is not one of "free nations" why should we do so? Why should we arm at all? If peace is to be maintained at any price, all we need do is to apply for affiliation to the USSR or accept the status of the satellite states.

Like many others who warned against Hitler's moves toward world domination but who until yesterday were stubbornly blind about Stalin's, Mr. Perry fails to appreciate the significance of the U.N. stand in Korea even if its forces are compelled to evacuate as a result of Chinese Communist intervention. I was in Europe when the North Koreans invaded and spoke to nationals of many different countries. All of them were convinced that if the United States had not given evidence of a will to resist in Korea, most of Europe would have been lost in a rush to make terms with the Kremlin.

Together with Mr. Perry, I deplore Mr. McCarthy's[6] tirades against the State Department. But in the last analysis, Mr. McCarthy derives all of his strength and influence from precisely the kind of foreign policy Mr. Perry advocated in the past, the failure to recognize the errors of that policy, and its continuation in a new form. Happily the State Department at present disagrees both with Mr. McCarthy and Mr. Perry.

1. Editor, *New York Times.* This letter apparently was not published.
2. Andrei Vishinski, Soviet diplomat; Jacob A. Malik, Soviet Union delegate to the United Nations; Hsiu-chuan Wu, envoy sent by Communist China to the United Nations to negotiate an end to the Korean War.
3. Warren Austin, American ambassador to the United Nations.
4. Carlos Romulo, anti-communist Filipino leader.
5. Headquarters of the United Nations at that time.
6. Senator Joseph R. McCarthy, Republican of Wisconsin.

88

Dear Mr. Krock,[1]   December 22, 1950

Have you seen President Truman's warm letter of greeting in the 85th anniversary issue of the *Nation,* December 16, 1950? If you will read the articles by del Vayo,[2] its foreign editor, and Freda Kirchwey, its editor-in-chief, in the same issue, it will be clear that the *Nation* is now a 100% apologist for the Soviet line. During the last years it has become almost an unofficial organ for the Kremlin.

I am confident that President Truman wrote this letter without knowing what the *Nation* stands for and that someone in his entourage induced him to send it. Although the letter politely says he doesn't always agree with the *Nation,* its content and tone would be more appropriate if he were writing to the *New York Times* than to a mouthpiece of defeatism and complete capitulation to Soviet aggression.

I have learned that a strong public attack will soon be launched against the President because of this unnecessary and foolish letter for which I am confident he is not to blame since he probably acted on someone's advice. The country is divided enough, and I feel strongly that the national interest would best be served if the President or some spokesman repudiated the letter "in the light of additional information of which the 85th anniversary edition is part," thus avoiding another imbroglio at a time when we have to pull together.

I am taking the liberty of writing you because of the high esteem in which I hold your judgment in these matters and because a suggestion or inquiry from you to the appropriate persons would receive consideration if you deemed the subject of sufficient importance to the cause of national unity to act.

The President should be held responsible for his own letters, I feel, rather than for those some subordinate misled him into signing.

1. Arthur Krock, Washington correspondent, *New York Times.*
2. Julio Álvarez del Vayo.

89

Dear Rabinowitch,[1]   January 8, 1951

This is a personal letter—not for publication.

I want to protest the big play you gave to Kahler's[2] *political* article in the December issue of the *Bulletin.* Mitchell, Wallace, and Buck[3] are more or less competent *technical* contributions, and their viewpoints balance each other pretty well. But Kahler is prejudiced from first to last, and not qualified either as an economist or a student of political science, and to give him the lead with the longest piece of tripe you have ever published is hard to understand. Your editorial disclaimer is insufficient. Kahler's piece should not have been printed without an equally strong one replying to his stupidities and inventions. As if *we* were responsible for the "cold war" and the invasion of Korea! The other three pieces will be read in the light of the things Kahler says, and by the time you get around to printing another point of view in realization of your "hope"—it is not even a promise!—Kahler's lengthy diatribe against U.S. foreign policy may have an effect on some of your naive readers that may not be undone.

I am not objecting to publishing Kahler's piece but only to publishing it without some *other* political analysis at the same time. You could have found one to balance his. Mitchell's correction of some of his facts doesn't hit the main point. Why didn't you ask Karl Wittfogel of the University of Washington, who is an expert?

I have been going over all the issues of the *Bulletin* and it is definitely not true—so it appears to me—that on political questions you present a balanced presentation of different points of view. The political line has been consistently soft and wishful-thinking in respect to the threat of Soviet expansion.

Again I don't object to the publication of any material even if it comes straight out of *Pravda* (in fact I wish you would reprint some of the Russian pieces on science and politics), but all I ask for, as a reader and subscriber, is no loading of the political dice. God knows, scientists are naive enough about politics. Either keep away from politics or give them a balanced diet.

1. Eugene Rabinowitch, professor of physics, University of Illinois, and editor of the *Bulletin of Atomic Scientists.*

2. Erich Kahler, "Foreign Policy Today," *Bulletin of the Atomic Scientists* 6 (December 1950): 356, 359–62. Kahler was a refugee from Germany and professor of German literature at Cornell University. In this article he attacked the South Korean and Chinese Nationalist governments, said the North Korean government was led by agrarian reformers, encouraged the American government to recognize the Chinese communist regime, assailed colonialism and militarism, and praised the neutralist policy of the government of India toward the Cold War.

3. Clyde Mitchell, "Promises and Facts in Korea and China," *Bulletin of the Atomic Scientists* 6 (December 1950): 357–58; Henry A. Wallace, "The U.S., the U.N. and Far Eastern Agriculture," ibid., 363–64; J. Lossing Buck, "Fact and Theory About China's Land," ibid., 365–68. Mitchell was an agricultural economist at the University of Nebraska. Wallace was the former secretary of agriculture and secretary of commerce. Buck was an employee of the United Nations.

90

Dear Lester,[1]   April 6, 1951

You are right—it *is* nonsense to talk about cultural freedom to those who lack bread. By the same token—it is nonsense to talk about education, hygiene, cruelty to women and children, or even love of God—to those who lack bread. The one thing to do about those who lack bread is to feed them! (And our American Committee[2] is in the lead of the fight to get the wheat for India measure out of the Rules Committee.)

But unless one is talking about starving, the relation between bread, in the generic sense of standards of living, and freedom is not so simple. And as far as Western Europe and the two Americas are concerned, the question is not about "starving" but about degrees of poverty and degrees of freedom and how they affect each other. In the halcyon days of my socialist youth I used to think that an improvement in standards of living (bread), *automatically* insured the growth of political and cultural freedom, but reflecting on the abolition of unemployment and the rise of real wages in Germany under Hitler or on Peron's labor supported dictatorship shows how inadequate this approach is. Or consider the fact that when the big unions were first struggling for their life, barely able to win for their members a near subsistence wage, they were on the whole usually democratic. Today, after the unions have won far better living conditions than ever before, there is really little effective democracy left in them. (Lewis'[3] Mine Workers is a case in point. There are many others.)

As soon as one gets away from the level of actual mass starvation, as in India, the whole problem of the relation between bread and freedom must be rethought. Distinction must be made between political and cultural freedom (even though they are related). Why is it, that with all her austerity England in some ways has a healthier kind of cultural (and personal!) freedom than the U.S. with its comparative affluence? I find the whole subject bedeviled, not clarified by slogans and catchwords. I expect to sit down in a few days to write out my ideas under the classic title of "Bread and Freedom"—(or can freedom be bartered for bread?)

As far as the Committee is concerned everyone, of course, believes that bread is at least a necessary condition for freedom, but some of our members believe that capitalism, American style, is the best institution for distributing the bread, others believe it is the welfare state, others believe it is socialism, co-operatives or whatnot. If as a group we committed ourselves to one or another theory of how bread can best be distributed we would become transformed into another A.D.A.[4] or Young Democrat and/or Republican liberal political outfit. We don't want that.

We want a group in which, for all their differences, people like Sumner Slichter,[5] Lester Markel, Norman Thomas, etc. can belong; recognizing the interplay between bread and freedom, they nevertheless agree that after the minimum margins of life have been won, freedom has a strategic and *intrinsic* value that affects the existence and enjoyment of all other values.

P.S. In my mind at the moment, I feel that agreement on *process* is more important than agreement on any particular program.

1. Lester Markel, Sunday magazine editor, *New York Times.*
2. American Committee for Cultural Freedom.
3. John L. Lewis, president, United Mine Workers of America.
4. Americans for Democratic Action, a liberal lobbying group.
5. Sumner B. Slichter, professor of economics, Harvard University.

91

Dear Mr. Jessup,[1]   August 13, 1951

I have read your short comment on my article[2] which John MacDonald sent me. I do not object to your criticisms and appreciate the friendly spirit in which you make them. But there are a few phrases not essential to your argument that may be gravely misunderstood, one of which may do much harm to the cause of freedom, especially abroad.

On p. 1 you say I am "one of the most forceful spokesmen of the cause of American leadership to the still befuddled Socialists of Europe and the misty intellectuals of India (notably through the Committee for Cultural Freedom of which is he chairman)."

The Committee for Cultural Freedom has been falsely denounced by Communists and fellow travelers in Europe as a tool of American capitalism, and I am very much afraid—in fact I am certain—that your sentence will be picked up as "proof." As a matter of fact, I believe not in American leadership but American co-responsibility with other European democracies. Instead of "American leadership" would you say "spokesman of political democracy and cultural freedom"? And if you do not want to say this, will you please, please omit reference to the Committee for Cultural Freedom.

On p. 5, line 5 you recommend "the balance of Hook's article to businessmen." Would you add, if only in parenthesis, ("workers or anyone else concerned about freedom")? Otherwise it might appear that you are recommending me to businessmen not so much because what I say is true but because I can be used.

In the next paragraph you say I am willing to admit that economic freedom is an ingredient of freedom. This suggests that I believe in free enterprise which I do not. Would you put it this way: "is willing to admit as a *democratic* socialist that economic freedom in some fields may be an ingredient of freedom."

Similarly on p. 6, middle of second paragraph, "and if he is to befriend economic freedom," would you indicate in some way that I believe in economic freedom only in those sectors of the economy in which it does not give disproportionate power to a few; and within a democratic framework that makes morally primary the concept of public welfare along the lines advocated by the English Labor Party.

I am a democrat first, and a socialist only to the extent that socialist measures achieve a more abundant life for free human beings. This means that I do not believe in total solutions; that my socialism is a piecemeal affair, a matter of more or less to be decided in the light of the scientific spirit and the democratic faith.

1. John K. Jessup, editorial chief, *Life* magazine.
2. "Bread, Freedom, and Businessmen," *Fortune* 44 (September 1951): 117, 176–88.

92

Dear Lester,[1]   October 31, 1951

I have been thinking of a piece along the lines of "Who Should Be Our Allies and Why?" in the struggle for freedom. As I read affairs, I believe we are confusing the kind of allies which, willy nilly, we will have to use in the dread event of an all-out war, and the kind of allies we should choose in the *present* political fight for freedom that aims to prevent war. The present political struggle, particularly if it is aimed to win to our side the peoples behind the Iron Curtain, is more likely to be successful if we do not let our spokesmen be defenders of Czarist restoration, accomplices of Hitler, and the whole rag and bobtail pack of supporters of different varieties of dictatorship. (Nor do I see any need for the Vatican as a political ally insofar as we seek to appeal to the people of the Soviet Union or other Orthodox countries).

In the final showdown we may have to accept anybody in order to survive just as the American colonists, fighting for the ideals of the Declaration of Independence, had to accept military aid from the French Monarchy which was much more absolutist than England of that day, just as we fought with Stalin against Hitler, with Metaxas[2] against Mussolini, and just as we *may* have to fight with Tito and Franco. But in the present *political* struggle—which can be won if the masses behind the Iron Curtain are convinced that we don't wish to impose another form of totalitarian rule on them, cut their countries to pieces, enslave them, or restore a kind of capitalism they no longer remember—we don't need Tito or Franco or unreconstructed Nazis and their reactionary fellow travelers.

The long and short of the piece would be this: Stalin would love nothing better than to make his people and the whole of Europe believe that they must choose between Fascist totalitarianism or his own brand. If he succeeds he will have won the Cold War which will be followed by a total hot war—in which our chances of survival would be diminished. But if *we* win the Cold War, we have an excellent chance of avoiding the hot one.

What do you think?

1. Lester Markel.
2. Ioannis Metaxas, dictator of Greece, 1936–41.

93

Dear Mr. Tyson,[1]   November 6, 1951

This letter constitutes a formal acceptance of the invitation extended to me by the directors of the National Committee for a Free Europe, Inc. to serve as Consultant to the Director of the Division of Intellectual Cooperation. Because of my great interest in the work of the Committee, especially the Free Europe University in Exile, I wish to serve as consultant without any fee whatsoever so that the resources available to the Committee can be more directly applied to the valuable work it is doing abroad, particularly in Robertsau. I am therefore returning the check for $500.00 sent me by the directors of the National Committee for a Free Europe, Inc. as a consultant's fee for October, November, and December, 1951.

I deeply appreciate the view held by the directors of the National Committee for a Free Europe that in principle, professional consultant activity should be remunerated, but because the issues at stake—the preservation of a free world—is one to which I have devoted my life, I feel I should contribute my services, whatever they are worth, without any further return than the satisfactions to be gained in serving a worthy cause.

In communicating my decision to the directors of the National Committee for a Free Europe, Inc., which I hope will be acceptable to them, please transmit my assurance of continued willingness on my part to serve as a consultant and participant in any of their projects which lies within the sphere of my interest and competence, particularly the Free Europe University in Exile.

1. Levering Tyson, director, Division of Intellectual Cooperation, National Committee for a Free Europe, Inc. The National Committee for a Free Europe was a privately funded organization established in June 1949 that sponsored Radio Free Europe and other activities designed to restore freedom to Eastern Europe.

94

Dear Colonel Bing,[1]   November 21, 1951

To answer the questions you ask in your letter of November 14 would require a volume.[2] Just a few comments. I do not believe in a preventive war and conceive of political warfare without any overt military action whatsoever. Proper political warfare in behalf of democracy cannot be waged by any military organization. It must be conducted by civilians, trade unionists, educators, editors, professionals, etc. Incidentally, your own scheme cannot possibly be effective if its general ideas became known. One way of letting them be known is to put them on paper and to circulate them. I hope you have not done this in letters to other individuals. Although I know that you write in your own personal capacity and without stating any official position whatsoever, if any enemies of democracy ever pick up a copy of your letter or similar letters, they can make very effective and embarrassing use of them. Valid or invalid, ideas like yours should be spoken about, not written about. At most what you should write about is the degree to which we can find out what sections of the Russian people are anti-Stalin and what is the actual evidence that a Ukrainian insurgent army—an army no less!—really exists.

I hope you will forgive me for writing frankly but the subject is of such grave importance that the manner of treatment is as important as the matter itself.

1. Colonel Andrew J. Bing, Air War College, Maxwell Air Force Base, Alabama.

2. On November 14, 1951, Colonel Bing had written to Hook, suggesting that the American military equip and train refugees from Soviet-controlled territory. These persons would then be infiltrated into Eastern Europe and western Russia in order to liberate these areas from communist control. He believed this might even result in the overthrow of the Soviet government. The American air force would aid the insurgent movement by destroying the Soviet air force and checking the movement of the Soviet army.

95

Dear Ralph,[1]   February 14, 1952

I know you are a very busy man. This simple fact may be the ultimate explanation of your misunderstanding of my letter of August 28, 1951 which you interpreted as questioning your integrity. And so I am asking you to take a few cool moments in, or away from, your office to read this letter. For it will be at least as long as yours.

To understand my letter to you of August 28, 1951, you must read my letter to you of February 28, 1951 in which I protested against some disparaging personal remarks about me attributed to you on the grounds of my views about Communist Party teachers. I am enclosing a copy of that letter. Its receipt was never acknowledged. In it I refer to my letter of the previous year that accompanied my last articles—a letter which was also not acknowledged. By that time I had in my possession a memorandum from professors Ross and Dr. Van den Haag[2] about the fate of their manuscript arguing the case against the employability of Communist Party teachers. After they sent their article, they received no acknowledgment. They waited several months and sent a letter. No reply. Another letter, still no reply. A third letter registered. Finally they received a telegram from you saying that the manuscript had never been received. They then sent another copy. No reply. Still more letters . . . until finally a rejection.

I had also noticed that since the issue in question arose, you had not published or reprinted a single article differing with your position or that of Committee A on C.P. teachers.[3] On the other hand, you published many articles upholding that view—most of them confusing the issue of heresy with that of conspiracy.

Since I had received no word for the better part of a year as to whether you were going to print my article, which contained a few paragraphs expressing a position different from yours on C.P. teachers, I thought I was getting the same kind of treatment as professors Ross and Dr. Van den

Haag. I came to the conclusion that it was your policy not to print anything in defense of another point of view on the question. You have a right as editor, I suppose, to set editorial policy. I thought I had a right to criticize it. I wasn't reflecting on your motives in the slightest. I was challenging your judgment and asking for a clear-cut indication of the fate of my piece.

Now I think you will admit that the *Bulletin* has been overwhelmingly loaded with pieces whose general tenor supports the position of Committee A on C.P. teachers. Your own letter to a N.Y. chapter published in the *Bulletin* is an extended brief along the same lines. The public thinks that Committee A speaks for the members of the Association as a whole. I presume you know that this is the general public impression because you have often sought to correct it. Why in heaven's name, then, couldn't you reprint one solitary article giving the other side—presenting a view which many members of the AAUP hold? I still can't understand this.

The editorial bias on this question is apparent, and many members of the AAUP are puzzled by it. (As one of many other peculiar things that could be mentioned—I cite the fact that although Hutchins'[4] last piece which centered on the Communist issue appeared *after* my manuscript[5] was in your hands, you published it as a lead in the summer issue, while mine was published in an inconspicuous place in the autumn issue. The same thing occurred in relation to my previous article.)

I don't have to tell you that my reputation as a scholar and a writer doesn't depend upon my being published in the *Bulletin*. My only interest is that you publish a straightforward defense of a point of view on the issue of the C.P. teachers which disagrees with yours and Committee A's. Use someone else's article. You can get a good piece from Lovejoy.[6] All I am asking is for fair play in the discussion. Barth, Scott, Hutchins, Himstead to mention only a few on your side have had their innings. Why not someone on the other side in the *Bulletin* and as a speaker at a plenary session of the national meeting?

How necessary that presentation of the other side is becomes apparent from your claim on the basis of a paragraph from one of my articles that my position is not very different from the views of Committee A on this subject. If this were true you would still be under an obligation to publish the position of those who disagree with both Committee A and me. But it is not true. The paragraph you quote from me specifically says that "it is not necessary to link specific communists with specific activities undertaken by the communist cell officially functioning as a unit." This is explicitly denied by Committee A and again in your letter in which you imply that each and every C.P. teacher must be caught in the act of educational subversion before he is removed.

Despite the fact that you say that "members of Committee A are fully aware of the nature of Communism and of the Communist Party," it is demonstrable that neither they nor you are. Why, not long ago Committee A declared that it had not been conclusively established that the line of the C.P. was controlled by the Kremlin! Far from being "fully aware" of the nature of the C.P., Committee A is not even very well informed about how C.P. teacher cells function. It does not know what the mechanisms of control are by which the C.P. eliminates from its ranks those who do not carry out its party instructions. It has not reflected about the implications of the *act* of accepting instructions to subvert the educational process. It has never even mentioned the existence of these instructions in its voluminous literature on the subject.

You yourself say that "Nothing in the reports of Committee A gives countenance to infiltration of the profession by persons whose *purpose* is inculcation of the doctrines of Communism" (my italics). Well, I am prepared to show by documentary evidence that this is precisely the purposes of members of the Communist Party, and that since Committee A does not believe in barring members of the C.P., in effect it *does* countenance infiltration. You yourself say that Committee A has in mind only those members of the academic profession "whose political activities, if any, are open." I am not interested in the political but only in the professional, educational aspect of C.P. activity, but surely you ought to know that the political activity of every C.P. teacher *is anything but open.* For what purpose do you think he takes a concealed party name?

You say that Committee A and the Council "sought the views of many able scholars on the subject." Yet you never accepted my offer to present to the Council materials and analyses and arguments based on many years of study of this theme. Did you consult *anyone* who disagreed with Committee A?

Instead of meeting the arguments Lovejoy, I, and others have raised, you have kept on talking about "repression of thought" and "academic freedom," despite our reiterated assertion that we have no objection to the expression of *ideas* and *opinions* on communism or any other subject. The question is one of *professional* fitness by virtue of a voluntary *act* of affiliation with a group which instructs its members to subvert the educational process and which has mechanisms that rigorously exclude all members who do not accept its instructions. Do you or the Council or Committee A know anything about how the Control Commission of the Communist Party operates in relation to members? Don't you think it is relevant?

And what in the world has "guilt by association" got to do with the position of those like Lovejoy and myself who disagree with Committee A? We charge that members of the Communist Party are guilty of *voluntary cooperation* in an educational conspiracy which renders them profession-ally unfit. In the next number of the *Journal of Philosophy* (#4, dated February 14, 1952) there will be a number of articles critical of the position taken by Committee A (and one defending it). These articles, I am confi-dent, you will find highly instructive.

A few words about your reference to those who warned you against my views before I went on the Council. This is very funny. Since 1934, and even earlier, I have led the intellectual fight against the Communist Party in this country with strictly intellectual weapons. I have letters from you going back to my years on the Council thanking me for helping to expose the plans of the C.P. dominated Teachers Union "to take over" the AAUP. My speeches in the Council on this subject were literally applauded. Since I am not incapable of learning, some of my ideas have changed in the light of historical experience. I am not as gifted as some people who are born with the right ideas which they never have to change. But whatever my ideas were and are, I have never concealed them. I am puzzled, however, as to why you even mention this matter. What have *ideas* got to do with the question? I am prepared to defend the right of any colleague to defend even Communist *ideas* if he does it as a scholar, if he does it as a free intellectual agent on the basis of an objective presentation of evidence—mistaken as I think he may be. But a member of the C.P. is under willingly accepted instructions *not* to do this. Don't you know that "objectivism" is a party heresy which makes a member liable to expulsion just as much as "inactiv-ity" and "failure to obey instructions"?

It has been a matter of great regret to me that you never saw fit to accept my offer—on one occasion, telephoned to you—to have a personal talk on the whole question. Undoubtedly you have been the strongest single influ-ence in formulating Council policy over the years. I think you would have modified your position in the light of further discussion.

I am very much afraid that if Committee A continues to uphold the right of members of the C.P. to teach until they are actually found out subverting the educational process (if this is its line in the University of Wash. case),[2] great damage will be done to the Association.

I am glad that you still regard me as a friend, rumors to the contrary notwithstanding. The feeling is reciprocated. If matters come to a show-down and open controversy, I hope you will not permit our differences to cloud our relationship.

1. Ralph E. Himstead, general secretary of the American Association of University Professors (AAUP) and editor of its *Bulletin.*
2. Ralph Ross and Ernest Van den Haag.

3. Committee A dealt with matters of academic freedom.

4. Robert M. Hutchins.

5. Hook, "The Literature of Political Disillusionment," *American Association of University Professors Bulletin,* 35 (Autumn 1949): 450–67.

6. Arthur O. Lovejoy.

7. An investigation of the faculty at the University of Washington resulted in the dismissal of three tenured professors because of supposed communist affiliations. This is discussed in Ellen W. Schrecker, *No Ivory Tower: McCarthyism and the Universities* (New York, 1986), pp. 94–112.

96

Dear Professor Perry,[1]   March 31, 1952

Thank you for your note of March 26, which I am hastening to answer. I do *not* think it is logically possible to agree on the main issue both with Lowe and with Lovejoy and me. Several of the points you make in your letter make me feel that I did not succeed very well in communicating the chief points of difference between Lowe's position and mine:

1) First of all, I regard the issue as one of *professional,* not political ethics. This has nothing to do with whether membership in the Communist Party is a crime as defined by *legal* authorities. I have presented evidence, which no one has challenged, that members of the Communist Party are under official instructions to engage in unprofessional conduct, and that their actions are controlled by the Communist Party in such a way that continued membership is *prima facie* evidence of their professional unfitness. You will find references to some of these evidences in footnote 2 of my article "Mindless Empiricism."[2] I particularly refer you to my article in the *Saturday Evening Post* of September 10, 1949. Your statement that "membership in the Communist Party would usually *be taken to mean* adherence to a body of ideas rather than to an action group" puzzles me very much. My view is that anyone should be free to hold or profess any *ideas* he regards as valid. In the face of the evidence, everyone can be led to see that the Communist Party is first, last, and all the time an action group. On the campus, it is an action group designed to subvert those educational practices which are essential to honest teaching.

2) In my view the university or college should state as *a matter of principle* that anyone who is a member of any organization which instructs him to abuse his trust as a teacher is not qualified to teach. Once this is recognized in principle it should be admitted that each *situation* is to be judged in the light of all relevant considerations. Under certain circumstances we may decide to retain a member of the Communist Party. Just

as a hospital may sometimes decide to retain an untrustworthy person—untrustworthy because of his membership in a group dedicated to unprofessional practices—because some technical service he performs warrants the risk. But if the risk is too great, or if the individual is replaceable, he could not argue that he must first be caught in the act of dereliction before being dismissed.

3) The crux of the issue between Lowe's position, which is the AAUP's position, and mine is that Lowe and the AAUP believe that we are never justified in dismissing a member of the Communist Party unless we can establish *in his particular case that he has actually performed* the infamous tasks to which the Communist Party has assigned him and which, as his continued membership in the Communist Party shows, he has voluntarily accepted as his mission. This position really asserts that members of the Communist Party are to be treated in the same way as members of all other political parties. It overlooks the obvious fact that the Communist Party on the campus is an educational conspiracy, and as in the case of all other conspiracies, the *attempt* to commit conspiracy is sufficient in principle to make those guilty of it morally and professionally unfit to serve the ideas and institutions they are conspiring against.

The position of the AAUP is not only unrealistic on this question but in the long run will have an extremely mischievous effect on the intellectual life of this country. For unless we set up and enforce our own standards of professional integrity, the legislatures, pressure groups, and the wild men in the country, who cannot distinguish between heresy and conspiracy, will take over. I hope that before you send your memorandum to Himstead we may have a chance to discuss this matter further. If this is not possible, may I suggest that you request of Himstead that Lovejoy be invited to present a memorandum to the AAUP?

For years I have petitioned Himstead for permission to address the Council or national meeting on this subject. I have asked him to publish an article differing with the position of Committee A on this question in the *Bulletin*. Lovejoy also asked for a national poll of members after circulation of statements from both sides. All these requests have been refused.

You will note that my discussion has nothing to do with the *ideas* professors hold, whether they are *Communist* ideas or *Fascist* ideas. I have always stressed this in my discussions, and I am enclosing a reprint of an article three years old in which I bring home this distinction.

1. Ralph Barton Perry.
2. *Journal of Philosophy* 49 (February 14, 1952): 89–100.

97

Dear Richard Rovere,[1]   April 2, 1952

Thank you for the copy of your letter to Arthur Schlesinger.[2] I am sending him, and the other members of the Committee[3] mentioned in your letter a copy of this one.

Since I missed the morning session last Saturday I am dependent upon what other members have told me about what took place. So far I have found no one who agrees with Eastman's position and no one who even remotely suggested that "the most hysterical performance you could find anywhere" took place at the Waldorf on Saturday. On the contrary, I have been told that it was a most exciting meeting in which three of the speakers (you, Mary McCarthy,[4] Elmer Rice[5]) strongly attacked what you call McCarthyism and what I call cultural vigilantism. The following sentences from a letter from Harry Laidler,[6] who is no novice in these matters, seem representative of the general reaction:

> May I congratulate you on the success of the Saturday Conference. It was most stimulating and enlightening. That so many people attended all the sessions was a source of encouragement.

The office staff and administrative committee in charge of arrangements (in which incidentally I had no hand whatsoever—even the date wasn't cleared with me) informs me that Eastman in his speech maintained that there was no witch-hunt and that "the real threat to cultural freedom is the world-wide conspiracy to destroy all freedom everywhere." Zirkle,[7] the remaining speaker, was much more on your side than on Eastman's. In the discussion Eastman irresponsibly defended McCarthy by name to the overwhelming *disapproval* of the audience, including almost all of our members present. *No one identified Eastman's position on McCarthy with that of the Committee.*

This is the substance of the report I received.

If this is true, I am at a loss to understand your letter, particularly its tone. What would you have us do, prevent Eastman from speaking? No one knew what he was going to say when he was invited, but it was expected that he would differ with Rice and that you would take a position closer to that of the rest of us. One of the things we don't like about McCarthyism is his bullying attempt to shut people up who disagree with him. Shall we adapt the same procedure to Eastman, or to Rice?

Your letter gives the impression that the Committee has refused to take a stand on McCarthyism and that I and other members of the Executive Committee have been evasive on the issue because we fear a split. In a cooler moment I think you will realize how unjust this charge is. On the literature tables you could have found a pamphlet issued under the authority of the Executive Committee which contains two articles of mine, one on "Heresy and Conspiracy," the other on "The Dangers of Cultural Vigilantism." Everything that one can reasonably mean by McCarthyism is excoriated in this pamphlet.

You also know that at the Planning Conference last March which you attended not a single person defended McCarthyism. Several thought that McCarthyism was not as dangerous as Communism, but surely it is permissable to entertain different ideas about the relative degrees of danger involved in each *while being firmly opposed to both.*

The special question which troubled us was the rights, and limitation of rights, of members of the Communist Party to employment in government and non-government service. This is not an easy problem, and a meeting has been scheduled to discuss it because our action in specific cases depends upon the development of a Committee line. We have now added the question about a *formal statement* on McCarthyism to the agenda of the next meeting (which will be held on April 23—I asked for the postponement because I shall be giving a speech in Chicago on the 17th). But the point I want to make in this connection is that the question has now been put on the agenda because neither you nor anyone else raised it before in explicit form, whereas your letter implies that we have tried to avoid making such a statement. I am confident that if Eastman had not made his speech you would not have raised the question of a *formal statement by the Committee.* Your sense of "the desperate importance" of our Committee taking a formal stand on McCarthyism was born last Saturday. And if that is true, is it not unjust to tax me or anyone else with evasion on the issue? After all, as a member of the Executive Committee you were in a better position than anyone else to introduce such a resolution.

For myself a *general* resolution against McCarthyism is like a resolution against sin or a resolution against Communism or Fascism, and I can say this without misunderstanding, I hope, because I have publicly and repeatedly denounced the "irresponsible and morally scandalous methods of McCarthy." But I have no objection in principle to such a resolution. A resolution to have point and effect, however, should center on specific acts, particularly as they bear on cultural issues, as I believe our statement on Dondero[8] will do. That was the gist of my remarks to you about a resolution against McCarthy for attacking Wechsler[9] as a Communist. This suggestion came from *me.*

One final point and perhaps the most important. I am dismayed by the spirit of "ultimatumism" which your letter shows. If what we have in common is not enough to serve as a basis for reasonable discussion, or at least the assumption of good faith, then no agreement on any resolution means anything.

When the first Committee for Cultural Freedom was organized in 1939, a small group insisted that only under socialism was cultural freedom possible. Instead of trying to convince the rest of us that this was so, they split away to organize a "Committee for Cultural Freedom and Socialism." We survived it. The committee belongs to its members, and the influence of each member is limited only by his wisdom and his activity. Differences within the framework of the principles of the Berlin Manifesto are unavoidable.[10] To make these perfectly legitimate differences a ground for ultimata instead of a basis for discussion is to renounce the whole basis of our organization. This, I am sure, you do not want to do.

1. Liberal columnist and author of *Senator Joe McCarthy* (New York, 1959). This letter concerns a meeting in New York on March 29, 1952, of the American Committee for Cultural Freedom (ACCF). In a speech at the meeting, Max Eastman attacked Freedom House, the American Civil Liberties Union, and Americans for Democratic Action for being insufficiently anti-Communist. During the discussion, Eastman defended Senator Joseph McCarthy, saying that his only faults were an exaggerated sense of fair play and excessive honesty. The speech incensed Rovere. He wanted the ACCF to go on record as opposing McCarthy, and threatened to resign from the committee if it refused. See William L. O'Neill, *A Better World: The Great Schism: Stalinism and the American Intellectuals* (New York, 1982), ch. 10, and Hook, *Out of Step*, p. 427.

2. Arthur M. Schlesinger, Jr., professor of history, Harvard University, and a leading spokesman for the American anti-Communist Left.

3. American Committee for Cultural Freedom.

4. American novelist.

5. American playwright.

6. Author, economist, and New York City socialist politician.

7. Conway Zirkle, professor of biology, University of Pennsylvania.

8. Congressman George A. Dondero, Republican from Michigan, was a zealous supporter of Joseph McCarthy.

9. James Wechsler, editor, *New York Post*.

10. Manifesto of Freedom that was issued at the founding conference of the Congress for Cultural Freedom in Berlin, June 25–30, 1950. The Korean War began on the opening day of the conference. For more on the conference and the manifesto, see Hook, *Out of Step*, pp. 432–35.

98

Dear Dr. Einstein,[1]   April 22, 1952

Recent reports have indicated that the Communist Party press throughout the world has been playing up the recent charges of M. Joliot-Curie[2] that the United Nations forces in Korea have been waging germ warfare against China and North Korea. The scientific authority of M. Joliot-Curie is being exploited for narrow, partisan political advantage in disseminating an unproven and unlikely allegation of the most serious kind. The American Committee for Cultural Freedom is therefore taking the liberty of calling the attention of its members who are Nobel Prize winners in science, as well as of some Nobel Prize winners who are not members, to these facts in the hope that they will be willing to issue jointly the enclosed statement.

The American Committee for Cultural Freedom is an independent organization of writers, artists, and scholars and has no official connection with either the United Nations or with the United States government. It is dedicated to the defense of freedom in the life of the mind at home and abroad. Our interest in circulating the enclosed statement is motivated exclusively by a desire to establish the truth about the serious charges that M. Joliot-Curie has made and to make it known to all men.[3]

1. Albert Einstein.
2. Frederic Joliot-Curie, French Communist and Nobel Prize recipient.
3. The statement called for an objective scientific investigation of the charge of germ warfare. Einstein was the only American Nobel Prize winner not to sign the statement. Hook wrote to Einstein as chairman of the American Committee for Cultural Freedom.

99

Dear Dr. Einstein,[1]   May 6, 1952

You have every personal right to refuse to sign the letter to M. Joliot-Curie and to question its efficacy. But you have no moral right to cast slurs at the good name of the American Committee for Cultural Freedom by referring to this letter as a "counter-action promoted by politicians." Our Committee is not interested or active in politics from a narrow, partisan point of view. We speak for no political party. We are not a Communist front organization. We have not solicited your signature under false pretenses. We are interested in defending those values which are essential to the preservation of a free culture and the life of a free mind and, in this case specifically, in establishing the truth about the grave charges made by Communists the world over about the use of germ warfare by the United States.

As Americans we are concerned of course—if these charges are established as false—in clearing the good name of our country, but we are even more concerned with the question of moral responsibility and intellectual integrity involved in fanning the flames of war and hatred by accusations such as those levelled by M. Joliot-Curie.

We are also convinced that unless these charges are answered, the truth established and broadcast, the probability increases that some day bacteriological warfare will be used by some criminally irresponsible regime.

All we asked of you is that you join other fellow scientists in raising your voice in a request for an *objective inquiry into the truth* of these terrible charges. That you should have regarded this as a "counter-action promoted by politicians" both grieves and mystifies us. We find it all the more mystifying in the light of the fact that you have knowingly lent your name and great scientific authority time and again to many Communist front groups for exploitation here and abroad. The most recent one was the Communist Waldorf-Astoria "peace" meeting of 1949. Even if we are "politicians"—and perhaps, since we are as unalterably opposed to Communism as to Fascism, you may insist on so regarding us—we are at a loss to understand the double standard employed and why our proposal should not be considered on its merits.

Nor do we see the relevancy of the moral indignation expressed in your footnote about the absence of moral indignation by Nobel scientists at the military abuses of science. This is not the primary issue at the moment; primary is the issue of truth, atrocity mongering, and the use of the calculated lie to embroil peoples in war. The military abuse of science began centuries ago and culminated in the use of atomic warfare against the foes of democracy in the last war. We do not know whether Nobel scientists were ever collectively asked to protest the military abuses of science; we do know that some of them did not hesitate to urge upon their governments the possible non-military uses of the liberation of nuclear energy on the eve of World War II. If it is desirable for Nobel scientists to condemn the military abuses of science as you now seem to think, surely the action we propose at the very least can be considered a step in that direction. We, therefore, see no valid reason why, even believing as you now do, you should refuse to sign the letter to M. Joliot-Curie.

Under separate cover, I am sending you the Freedom Manifesto and other publications of our Committee so that you can determine for yourself the nature of our organization.

1. Albert Einstein.

100

Dear Dr. Einstein,[1]   May 12, 1952

In reply to the question with which you conclude your letter of May 7th, I am firmly convinced that the policy of silence is not the policy of wisdom in respect to the charges of M. Joliot-Curie. Nor, as the text of the letter to him shows, is the request made of Joliot-Curie likely to inspire hate among decent people. The letter is written in a sober, reasonable tone and asks only that he withdraw the charge or join the other Nobel Prize scientists in asking for an objective investigation by an impartial international body.

There are two assumptions in your reply which conflict with the evidence in our possession—viz., that we cannot reach the peoples behind the Iron Curtain, and that public opinion in democratic countries is not affected by the wild charges made against the United Nations and the United States. There are many ways in which the publication of the letter to M. Joliot-Curie can be brought to the attention of the satellite countries and even the population of the Soviet Union. We know that the events, for example, in which Madame Kosenkina[2] was involved in New York were known a few hours later in Moscow.

Much more important is the fact, attested to by a great deal of evidence from the press, that these charges about germ warfare are being given audience in Western European countries and Asiatic countries. This is unfortunate but true. Official denials by American authorities are brushed aside as meaningless. The letter of the Nobel Prize scientists cannot be so treated, particularly since it requests an objective investigation. Our French committee informs us that the letter made a great impression on French public opinion.

I feel you underestimate the effect of the calculated lie on public thought and feeling. When I was a boy in high school I was denounced as pro-German in 1917, and almost expelled, for challenging the universal belief among my teachers that the German army systematically cut off the hands of Belgian children, and that it used human corpses to derive much needed fat for industry. After the war, these tales were laughingly revealed as wonderful propaganda.

In consequence, when the first news come out about Hitler's cremation camps, Stalin's forced labor camps, and similar outrages against mankind, many people dismissed them as more atrocity stories.

They didn't turn out to be atrocity stories. The feeling now is that any piece of barbarism is possible and the Soviets are making excellent use of this new mood of credulity. The immoral thing about these carefully planted lies is that if they are believed they make people fanatical to the death in fighting those who are lied about. If the lies are finally exposed, the result is likely to be invincible incredulity to atrocities when they do occur.

That is why it is of the first importance to build up the moral authority of some international organization which can speak with the full weight of science and objectivity behind it. The world will listen to any group to which Nobel Prize scientists give support, especially on matters so close to scientific fact. In this way, in the terrible years which lie ahead, public opinion can avoid the extremes of credulity and incredulity for something closer to scientific skepticism.

I have been in Europe often during the last few years. I have been shocked to discover that because of Communist propaganda, the United States is hated and feared more than Hitler's Germany was in 1939. I am not denying that there may be, and are, other causes too, but it is simply incredible what lies are told about the United States and believed. I am old-fashioned enough to believe that truth is the best answer to the propaganda of the lie—not counter-propaganda. But I have learned enough from modern psychology to know that silence is no answer at all.

That is why, dear Dr. Einstein, I cannot accept your method of fighting for freedom and peace. Just as neither Christian love nor Trappist silence would have deflected Hitler, so they will fail with Stalin. The only thing that could have prevented Hitler from going to war was *both* an adequate defense in the West and making the truth known to the German people about what was happening in Germany and what Hitler had in store for them. And having studied Stalin's mind for twenty-five years, I am convinced that the only thing that will prevent him from giving the signal for war is an adequate defense in the West and knowledge of the *truth* about the West among the peoples of the Soviet Union.

It is as a contribution to the truth that the American Committee for Cultural Freedom endorsed the letter of the Nobel Prize scientists to M. Joliot-Curie.

1. Albert Einstein.
2. Oksana Stepanova Kosenkina, an anti-Soviet school teacher, had been taken from an anti-Soviet refugee camp in New York to the Soviet consulate on 61st Street in New York. Held against her will, she jumped out of a third-floor window of the consulate in August 1948. Over the protests of the Soviet Union, the United States offered her political asylum.

101

Dear Mr. Anastaplo,[1]   May 13, 1952

In reply to your letter of May 2, I have tried hard to read your mimeographed volume but the mimeographing is so bad I had to give it up after a while. But I have read enough of it to find the evidence that you are a very much confused young man—both philosophically and politically—with a large bump of self-righteousness that prevents you from seeing the relevant issues. I have sent you a couple of things of mine which will, I hope, make my position clearer to you since from your letter I judge that you haven't got the foggiest notion of what my position is, and confuse the most elementary distinctions.

First of all, I don't believe in loyalty oaths of any kind except for traditional ceremonial purposes. Secondly, I don't believe that a man's views on loyalty oaths, or whether members of the Communist Party should be admitted to the bar, are relevant to determining his "character and fitness." Thirdly, I am firmly convinced that members of the Communist Party, or of any other organization which instructs its members to prepare for the commission of actions incompatible with the performance of their professional duty, should not be admitted to the bar. Please note the distinction between holding communist or fascist ideas, however they may be defined, and membership in a Communist Party organization.

The question cannot be intelligently discussed unless one knows something about the Communist Party, how it is organized, its underground apparatus, etc. You don't seem to know very much about it, and pontificate blithely about conspiracy as if it were merely heresy. The activities of the House Committee on Un-American Activities apparently are "antics," irrespective of whether they are using the communist issue to smear the New Deal or whether they are exposing, under the fairest conditions, the nefarious work of a nest of spies like that of Hiss[2] and his friends. I don't think you are really competent to discuss the question of whether members of the C.P. should teach or be permitted to practice until you learn something about them.

On the philosophical issue you are all at sea. 1. There is no *political* right in a democracy to conspiracy or to overthrow the government by force or violence. A person who believes in democracy is justified in using force and violence against *a dictatorship*. You mix up both types of situations.

2. *Morally* human beings are free to use force and violence in any situation the conditions of which outrage their basic sensibilities. (But if the revolt is made against a functioning democracy, then both logical and moral decency forbid their calling themselves democrats.) In other words, there is a moral right to go to war for one's ideals against society but in that case one must take the consequences without whimpering, like John Brown. Your "rebel" sounds as if he would whimper. 3. It is not the *Euthyphro* which you should cite here but the *Crito*. Socrates is a heretic, not a conspirator, and takes his punishment, indeed insists upon it, because he still regards the community to which he belongs as his own. He is not at war with it.

Now the nub of the matter is this. Members of the Communist Party are at war with our society. They are all actual or potential agents of a foreign power. Consequently, I do not say that they should be imprisoned, but merely denied access to any positions where if they carried out their orders, they would create more damage than would the intelligent attempt to get rid of them.

Try to understand this position before you reply to it.

1. George Anastaplo, Chicago, Illinois. He responded to a newspaper report of a speech Hook gave before a conference of the National Education Association which advocated that Communists be ousted from the teaching profession.
2. Alger Hiss. Hiss was convicted of perjury in 1949 for denying that he had passed State Department documents a decade earlier to Whittaker Chambers, then a Soviet agent. He was sentenced to five years in prison.

102

Dear Sir,[1]   June 3, 1952

Your letter of May 27th[2] confirms my impressions of your first communication. I assumed, of course, that when you said you were a liberal you meant, among other things, that you were not a Communist. (You now call yourself a democratic socialist. Any sincere democratic socialist must be at the very least an anti-communist as well as an anti-fascist.) But what struck me was that you called Chambers a "stool pigeon." He has been referred to in that way only by Communists and only in Communist organs. That is why I was puzzled by your disavowal of Communism and your use of their techniques.

Any honest person knows that Chambers was not a "stool pigeon" sent in by the police to spy and report on the Communists. He was a convinced Communist who broke sincerely, and told his story under government subpoena. Why should any "liberal" or "democratic socialist" object to his telling the truth about the mortal enemies of liberalism and democratic socialism? Should he have perjured himself and *not* told the truth about the Communist Party? Did *you* object to Carlson's[3] telling the truth about his experiences with fascist groups in America? Did you call Carlson and others "stool pigeons"? Obviously not! Does this not suggest—I did not say demonstrate—the same kind of double-entry moral bookkeeping used by Communists and their stooges, some of whom attempt to pass themselves off as "liberal" and "democratic socialists"?

I did not of course refer to liberals as a "wolf-pack" but to those who were anti-anti-communists as a wolf-pack. Nor did I assert that you lacked an honest mind. I asserted that any honest mind, after reading conflicting reviews, would read the book[4]—not contentiously, in order to refute and scorn, but soberly, critically, and with a little intellectual humility, ready and willing to learn. It rests with you then to pass judgment on the honesty of your mind.

I predict that if you do read it and if you are a liberal or a democratic socialist, you will be thoroughly ashamed of yourself for calling Chambers a "stool pigeon."

1. John Maass, Philadelphia, Pennsylvania.
2. In his letter, Maass criticized Hook's "The Faith of Whittaker Chambers," a review of Chambers's autobiography, *Witness,* which appeared in the *New York Times Book Review,* May 25, 1952.
3. John Roy Carlson (pseudonym of Arthur Derounian), *Under Cover: My Four Years in the Nazi Underworld of America* (New York, 1943).
4. Chambers's *Witness* (New York, 1952).

103

Dear Arthur,[1]   June 6, 1952

Your letter of May 29th has reached me here in South Wardsboro, Vermont, and I am hastening to reply. First about Kristol's[2] election as Executive Secretary.[3] Since last January when Pearl Kluger resigned, we have been looking around for a successor. Pearl stayed on at our request as long as possible. The Executive Committee was informed of it, and I assumed that everyone knew we were looking for an able replacement. Pearl was invaluable, and I was frankly sorry she resigned but after she resigned, the Ex. Com. thought it would be desirable to have a cultural figure who could combine the executive and educational aspects of the work. I spent many days tracking down leads, and if you will reflect on possible candidates— and I should have written you but naively assumed that I probably was acquainted with all those whom you knew—you will see how few they actually are. Kristol is an able man, *his tenure of office depends on the pleasure of the Ex. Com.,* and I am confident that, despite whatever differences in emphasis exists between him and me and between him and you, he will serve with distinction.

Kristol had no hand in circulating the reprint of his essay.[4] It was part of a four article reprint (3 by members of our Committee) made available to us by *Commentary.* The Ex. Com. authorized its distribution, and a covering letter by Pearl Kluger called attention to the fact that these reprints did not necessarily represent the standpoint of the Committee. Dan James was in charge of promotion for a couple of months, and I never learned how the Kristol article appeared as a *single* reprint. But we *distributed* it: we did *not* pay for it. And when Dan James listed it as a Committee pamphlet, I insisted that it be listed only as one of a reprint series—and this at considerable expense to us, justified, I believe, to avoid giving a misleading impression. In this matter Kristol was not even consulted and if any mistake was made, Dan James and I (for not supervising him closely enough) were at fault.

I think your suggestion of another reprint, consisting of Rovere's piece[5] and various letters, is definitely worth considering, and I shall suggest it be explored at the next meeting of the Ex. Com. One problem will be money because for next year we will have to go on a very slim diet. Someone else will have to shop around for money; I'm fed up with it. The Hatters' Union expressed interest, and now that we are a tax-exempt organization, it may be easier to raise money.

Your letter rejoining to Kristol seems to me to make the point very effectively that the New Deal as such was certainly not interested in aiding Communism or Communists. Chambers' view here is quite definitely wrong, and I have just sent for *Commentary* to read Kristol's rejoinder. I shall be surprised to find that he shares Chambers' view. But on the basis of my own experience I know that *some* New Dealers, although by no means Communists, quite deliberately collaborated with organizations and causes dominated by the C.P. I gave Ickes[6] during the Spanish Civil War and Mrs. Roosevelt during the days of the American Youth Congress the evidence that some of the outfits they were associated with were C.P. controlled. Their attitude was—it changed later—that the C.P.'ers were left-liberals, that one could "talk and work with them." I wonder whether you know that Roosevelt himself until 1940 was a member of the League of American Writers. His membership was kept secret but Donald Ogden Stewart[7] spilled the beans in hopes of embarrassing Roosevelt vis-a-vis Willkie.[8] I wrote to Roosevelt warning him that the Republicans would play it big, and I understand that Roosevelt retroactively withdrew and claimed that deception had been practiced on him. Now, the real question, to which I never got an answer from Steve Early,[9] who told me that the President was grateful for tipping him off, was *who* enrolled Roosevelt in the League of American Writers. It probably was some idiotic New Dealer who didn't know his political arse from his elbow. But I don't see that the New Deal comes into the picture since men like Jerome Frank[10] caught on from the beginning. Thurman Arnold[11] *did* defend the Moscow Trials or at any rate didn't think it wrong to engage in juridical frame-ups. (Incidentally I have found him a completely unscrupulous person intellectually on *several* occasions. On one of them, at the *Life* roundtable on the pursuit of happiness, he sided with Father Walsh[12] against me in supporting the existence of Natural Law attributable to a supernatural origin—a doctrine he called *poppycock* a day before, talking to another group.)

The picture is complicated because different men connected with the New Deal caught on at different times about the nature of the Stalinist movement. Many people overlook the fact that fear of Hitler played a considerable role in inducing some to vote their *hopes* about Stalin's ultimate intentions, etc.

If the Republicans win—either wing—there probably will be an attempt to rewrite the history of the New Deal along the lines of Chambers' thesis. The sad truth about *gullibility* of some New Dealers at some time can be admitted. This is a far cry from treason and in no way validates Chambers' view.

I am confident that Kristol does not share Chambers' view. I think you are right in saying that the men he is talking about were the Popular Fronters—the writers for the *Nation* and *New Republic*. I am an expert on the famous letter of the 400 since it denounced the Committee for Cultural Freedom (at that time) as "Fascists and friends of Fascists." People like Max Lerner (who learned hard) who were known as New Deal supporters signed—those who at that time I dubbed "totalitarian liberals." I do not believe they were genuine New Dealers, although in some cases it was hard to draw the line.

But why the reference to the dear old, ineffectual, unread *Modern Quarterly*? That was a sectarian magazine bitterly opposed to the New Deal *and* the Popular Front from first to last. The last issue of the *M.Q.* (the memorial issue to V. F. Calverton) refused to publish my article on why socialists should support the war of the Allied powers against Hitler. You are mixing up your genres. But enough of this.

The fall will show whether there is enough *independent* intelligent life among American intellectuals for the Committee to live. Counts[13] turned down the nomination of Chairman (we need someone in New York City), and we are looking around for someone else. I myself want to get down to serious philosophical writing. Two years out of my life on ephemeral organizational matters are enough.

1. Arthur M. Schlesinger, Jr.
2. Irving Kristol. He became a leading neo-conservative intellectual.
3. Of the American Committee for Cultural Freedom.

4. Kristol's controversial essay " 'Civil Liberties,' 1952—A Study in Confusion," *Commentary*, 13 (March 1952): 228–36, blamed Joseph McCarthy's popularity on the lukewarm opposition of liberals to Communism. This infuriated Schlesinger and other anti-communist liberals.

5. Richard Rovere, "Communists in a Free Society," *Partisan Review* 19 (May 1942): 339–46.

6. Harold Ickes.

7. President of the League of American Writers.

8. Wendell L. Willkie, 1940 Republican presidential candidate.

9. Secretary to President Roosevelt.

10. Commissioner of the Securities and Exchange Commission in the late 1930s.

11. Assistant attorney general of the United States in the late 1930s.

12. Edmund A. Walsh, S.J., professor of government at Georgetown University and author of *Total Empire: Roots and Progress of World Communism* (Milwaukee, 1951).

13. George S. Counts, professor of education, Teachers College, Columbia University.

104

Dear Reverend McGirr,[1]   June 9, 1952

Your note of May 30 about my review of Chambers' book has reached me after some delay. When I referred to the Church I meant most American churches, *not* the Catholic Church. If I had more space I would have pointed out that the Catholic Church was always opposed to Communism: but I would also have to add that its opposition was not very effective. There were two reasons for this: (1) the Catholic Church did not oppose Communism on the grounds that Communism was anti-democratic. If it did, it would have had to oppose Mussolini and Franco, who were also anti-democratic—which it did not. (2) The chief spokesmen for the Catholic Church like Monsignor Sheen[2] argued or implied that if one began with Luther, one had to end either with Hitler or Stalin. This meant that Protestantism was in effect an unconscious ally of Communism. Such a doctrine cannot lead to a united movement against Communism in this country and is in fact deeply divisive.

My argument against Mr. Chambers' call for a *theologically* oriented politics will make clear, I hope, that although I believe that the Catholic Church can play a great role in the struggle against Communism, it must be on the basis of *moral* and *political* values which it shares with non-Catholics.

1. The Reverend P. J. McGirr, pastor, Blessed Sacrament Rectory, Brooklyn, New York.

2. Bishop Fulton J. Sheen.

105

Dear Reverend Reissig,[1]

June 9, 1952

Thank you for your letter of May 27, enclosing your communication to the Editor of the *New York Times,* which has reached us here. I enjoyed reading your sharp criticism of the review, but it is probably my obtuseness which prevents me from seeing the point you are trying to make. You admit that theological belief is not a sufficient condition for liberal social practice. And it is clear that it is not a necessary condition, as the life of Emerson, Dewey, and many others shows. What you must prove is that one cannot be a good Christian, theologically, and approve of slavery or nationalism or feudalism. When you do that you will have proved that Aquinas, Luther, Paul were not good Christians—which is a tall order.

Of course religion is bound up with moral principles *historically,* but you cannot logically derive a single moral principle from a religious one. It is morally wrong to inflict unnecessary cruelty or pain upon any sentient creature. From what theological principle does that logically follow? Wouldn't it be just as wrong to inflict such unnecessary cruelty even if God didn't exist? Would you absolve a man from the obligation of being honest because he lost his faith in the supernatural?

I have been arguing for the autonomy of the moral judgment—a commonplace of contemporary ethical humanism—and I can't see in what way it puts me in the same boat as Chambers.

About the fellow travelers of the '30s. If you believe "stupidity" is too harsh a term, what word would you suggest to characterize the attitude of those who brushed aside the *evidence* that the organizations with which they were connected were tools of Communist Party policy? I can cite you a long list of particulars. I have never denied that before Hitler came to power I thought the Communists, despite their suicidal theory of social-fascism, would wholeheartedly resist him. But after January 30, 1933, when the Communists still persisted in regarding the Socialists as their main enemy, it was quite clear to me that Stalin wanted Hitler to conquer Germany. From that time on, I fought them openly and showed that every one of their organizational activities was motivated by a desire to further the foreign policy of the Kremlin and that those who worked with them were their dupes.

There's nothing to be ashamed of in being fooled once. What is difficult to understand is the fact that some people rather enjoy being fooled over and over again and rarely admit that they have ever been fooled. What should one call them?

1. Herman F. Reissig, head of the office of international relations of the Council for Social Action of the Congregational Church.

106

Dear Rabinowitch,[1]   June 17, 1952

In the first place, I'm sorry I spelled your name with a Z. The natives of Wardsboro pronounce it that way. And that's about the only thing I can say I am sorry about, for I find your reply to my letter evasive and irrelevant. I didn't object to your publishing Kahler and Edgerton,[2] and I don't know what you mean when you say that "people who have once succumbed to Communist propaganda . . . exaggerate the danger of others succumbing to Communist or fellow traveling sirens, unless they are protected by ear plugs." I find it interesting that you should characterize Kahler and Edgerton as Communist or fellow traveling sirens, but I'm not asking you for ear plugs but for more and better music for intelligent ears. You seem to make a virtue of your editorial incapacity to supply it.

Nor do I object to your publishing Joliot-Curie. All I would expect a fair-minded editor to do in the event that Joliot-Curie attacked the U.S. with lies about our waging macrobial warfare would be to publish a piece by someone else exposing that nonsense. I would not expect the editor to excuse himself for his dereliction, if he failed to do so, by implying that former victims of Communist propaganda want to choke off Communists from being heard.

But I certainly do object to your setting yourself up as an authority as to what constitutes an acceptable article on foreign policy. You have neither the competence nor the right to do so in my opinion. It *may* be necessary in the interests of intelligent analysis to demolish Mr. Edgerton, as much as you don't like it. Do you lay down directives to Kahler and Edgerton, too, as to what position to take in their contributions?

Again I ask: who speaks for America in the pages of your magazine when foreign policy is being discussed? There are plenty who speak against her. I ask this question in no narrow nationalistic or partisan spirit for I believe that the best foreign policy for America is best for the prospects of freedom and vice versa. I really ask this question in the interests of a balanced education for American scientists who constitute the bulk of your readers. You have not been offering a balanced political discussion, and if you were objective you would admit it.

You ask me for the names of people who can write a thoughtful and constructive article on foreign policy. (You say you prefer Acheson and Kennan.[3] A good editor would have gotten them to write a piece by now.)

Here are some names of outstanding men selected on the basis of their writings, reputation, respect for evidence, capacity for analysis, and passion for freedom—and not on the basis of whether they please Mr. Rabinowitch or please me.

1. James Burnham
2. W. H. Chamberlain
3. Willmore Kendall (Yale)
4. David Dallin
5. Bertram Wolfe
6. J. Salwyn Schapiro
7. Hans Kohn
8. Peter Viereck
9. Norman Thomas
10. Bela Fabian

I don't agree with their positions but that isn't necessarily fatal. At least they know the nature of the enemy and believe in freedom. Each one of them is an intellectual giant compared to your Kahlers and Edgertons. Let's see what you do with this list. There are only two ex-Communists on the list.

No, my letters are not for publication. When I get around to writing to or about the *Bulletin*, it will be at greater length. And for heaven's sake, stop thinking of yourself as an authority on foreign policy. I hope that by now you have abandoned the view you expressed to me at Abba Lerner's house in Chicago when I reported that some people in Europe preferred to remain alive under slavery than to risk their life for freedom by opposing totalitarianism.

P.S. I hope you print in your chronicle column the letter replying to Joliot-Curie by Nobel Prize Winners in the U.S. and Germany.

I am also enclosing a reprint of an article of mine from *Fortune* which I think will interest your readers. The part on the American businessman was tacked on. Suggest you print it under the title of "Bread and Freedom" and make the corresponding emendations.

1. Eugene Rabinowitch.
2. For Kahler, see letter 89, note 2. William B. Edgerton was a member of the American Friends Service Committee. Hook was referring to Edgerton's article "A Quaker View of Politics," *Bulletin of the Atomic Scientists* 8 (April 1952): 111–15, which attacked the policy of military containment of the Soviet Union and China and praised nuclear disarmament.
3. Dean Acheson and George F. Kennan.

107

Dear Reverend McGirr,[1]   June 20, 1952

Thank you for your thoughtful letter of June 14th.

(1) I do not believe that the Catholic Church's teachings on communism were ignored. They were rejected because (a) of its failure clearly to distinguish between socialism and communism, and (b) its main criticism was *not* that communism was undemocratic but that it had a wrong or mistaken theology. Since all groups outside the Catholic Church have the wrong theology, this left the withers of most non-Catholics unwrung.

(2) The Church did condemn Mussolini's Hegelian philosophy and Hitler's racialism, but it emphatically did not condemn the *undemocratic practices* of either one. It gave the impression that if their theology had been found acceptable, their practices would have been found not unacceptable. Would you call the Lateran Treaty between Mussolini and the Vatican support of a democratic act? The Church wholeheartedly supported Mussolini's invasion of Ethiopia—because, among other reasons, the Abyssinians were Coptic Christians! Would you call *that* support of a politically democratic act?

(3) You completely miss the point about Franco. You tell me that Franco's *philosophy* was different from that of Mussolini. Granted. But my point was that Franco was as bitter and as bloody a political *anti-democrat* as Mussolini—in some ways worse. This cannot be denied by anyone who has respect for the facts; nor can it be denied that the Church supported Franco to the hilt. Ergo—this proves that the Church is not a bulwark of democracy, that it will support any political regime which will not molest it. The very fact that you write that Franco's philosophy was different from Mussolini's, as if that were relevant to the question of his political democracy, seems to indicate that for you, too, the acceptance of the proper philosophy or theology is more important than acceptance of a Bill of Rights democracy. It is flagrant inconsistencies and confusions of this kind which make many people believe that the opposition of the Catholic Church to the Kremlin has nothing to do with democracy, that if Stalin, e.g., gave the Catholic Church the same privileged position in the Soviet Union that Mussolini gave it in Italy, the Church would not oppose the politically undemocratic practices of communism.

It is demonstrably bad theology to say that Catholic dogma logically entails democracy or is incompatible with non-democratic systems of government. No one was a better Catholic than Aquinas. He was no democrat—aside from the fact that he believed in the death sentence for stubborn theological heresy.

(4) I have no objection to your showing my letter to Bishop Sheen. But I do not want to see it published.

My position is really a very simple one. I believe that all men of good will and moral probity—theists, humanists, naturalists, Jew and Gentile, East and West—can make a *united front* against communism. But I do not believe that *any* theological principle is a condition precedent therefore— just as all good and decent persons can live together in the community which we call American democracy independently of their theological beliefs or disbeliefs.

1. P. J. McGirr.

108

Dear Mr. Jongejans,[1]   July 2, 1952

Thank you for your thoughtful note about my review of Chambers. I have no objection to being consigned to someone's private hell if my civil rights are not in any way abridged. Logically—strictly logically— the denunciation of heresy as something beyond the pale is compatible with extending civil rights to heretics and orthodox alike. But *psychologically* and *historically* views like Chambers' have always been the premise for some discriminatory action against heretics—in politics, or education, or social life. People who think like Chambers, for example, would prevent, if they could, humanists from teaching. You draw too sharp an antithesis between pacifist, nonresistant theocratic totalitarians and the violent sort. I do not know of any theocratic totalitarian who is as genuine a pacifist as Tolstoy or Schweitzer. The fact is that historically all theocratic totalitarians who believe that heretics are in league with Satan, even when they live up to the *political* rules of the democratic game, move in one way or another towards cultural or educational repression of heretics. That is why without in any way abridging the political rights of theocratic totalitarians to participate in a democracy, the most vigorous criticism of their views is in order—a criticism of which they make use in criticizing humanists.

1. G. J. Jongejans, member of the Dutch embassy in Tokyo.

109

Dear Arthur,[1]   August 5, 1952

This is the first chance I have had to answer your letter about my experiences with Mrs. Roosevelt and Harold Ickes. I met Mrs. Roosevelt and spoke to her briefly at the *Herald-Tribune* Forum in the Fall of 1939. I was on the program. Ben Stolberg, who at that time was strongly pro-C.I.O. but anti-Communist, was also on the program. Mrs. Roosevelt, I believe, followed us. The speeches of all three of us are available in the *Proceedings,* Vol. IX (?). Stolberg was talking about Communist penetration of trade-unions and I on "The Trojan Horse Tactics in American Education." This was *after* the Hitler-Stalin Pact. Mrs. Roosevelt didn't like our speeches much. She ad libbed from her prepared address and gave the impression that anybody who objected to the C.P. control of organizations and the familiar techniques of duplicity and penetration was really opposed to "talking" to Communists, was afraid of ghosts and witches, etc. After it was over I spoke to her for several minutes and tried to explain what the issues were but she was in a hurry, seemed very impatient, and when I mentioned the American Youth Congress said she had every confidence in the young men and women running it, that it had not been taken over by the Communists, and even if it had "why be afraid to talk to them"—as if the talking was the issue. I offered to send her the *Bulletin* of the then Committee for Cultural Freedom and any data we had on front organizations, but she said it wasn't necessary. She was in the company of two rather elderly women who kept glaring at me all the time.

Ickes I saw as a result of a special appointment arranged for me by Frank Trager, who was co-chairman of the Ex. Com. of the CCF, through Saul K. Padover,[2] at that time one of Ickes' assistants, and who, I believe, was a member of our organization then. (Afterwards to my surprise Padover went *PM* in a big way, and was intensely pro-Soviet.) Dr. Posner and his assistant had come back from Spain and told me their story about running some of the Loyalist hospitals and in their naive unpolitical way—politically they were as innocent as can be—unfolded a horrifying picture of Communist machinations in the Spanish medical relief set-up. Ickes was chairman of one of the leading Spanish relief committees which the Communists had organizationally captured. I spent ten minutes with him. He said something to me about Norman Thomas having also reported something similar. He seemed mad and Padover at the time appeared pleased at what seemed to be the effect of my talk. (I dimly remember him saying at the time that someone—perhaps some other assistant of Ickes—was trying to cut him out from Ickes and picture him as a "nut" about communism.) Some time later I got a letter from Ickes telling me that Bishop McConnell[3] or somebody else who was an innocent front of the Committee in question had assured me that everything was all right and that the Communists were not in the prominent position in the medical relief set-up in Spain—which was false.

If you are writing a book on the subject, I suggest you find out who signed F.D.R. as a member of the League of American Writers. At that time also Mary Van Kleeck of Russell Sage who, if she was not a member was as close to the C.P. as any non-member could be and who debated with me the Moscow Trials (she took the Kremlin line 100%) on the radio, claimed to have the ear of Mrs. Roosevelt. I think Mrs. Roosevelt only began to catch on to the problem of Communist penetration after F.D.R. met some A.Y.C.[4] leaders at a meeting she arranged and after the Communists turned viciously on Joe Lash.[5] At that time I got the impression that both Mrs. Roosevelt and Ickes both regarded the Communists as important left-wing liberals whose hearts were in the right place.

My memory isn't what it used to be and some details may have escaped me. But the above is substantially correct.

By the way, I just read in the *Christian Register,* which is an excellent magazine these days, that you are a Unitarian. And here I was imagining you a great admirer of Niebuhr's *theology!*

1. Arthur M. Schlesinger, Jr.
2. Assistant to the secretary of the interior (1938–43), writer for *PM* (1946–48), and professor of politics at the New School for Social Research (1947–49).
3. Francis J. McConnell, Methodist bishop and supporter of the Spanish Republic.
4. American Youth Congress.
5. Protégé and biographer of Eleanor Roosevelt.

110

Dear Sir,[1]   August 14, 1952

I have finally read your letter and enclosure of July 18. Our agreements are quite superficial. A whole abyss separates us, for I find your letter and enclosure a compendium of almost all the major errors one can make about the Communist issue today. Anybody can be mistaken but to be *so* mistaken, and *so* certain that one is speaking in the name of Philosophy and oh! so "morally" superior to better men than oneself—all that is lacking is a prayer to God to forgive your tormentors!—is something unique in my experience, which has been quite varied. Pardon me for saying it, and if I am wrong your style is responsible for misleading me: you write like a person who either has a martyr complex or is an insufferable prig or both.

First in answer to your questions. I leave to each faculty the devising of the appropriate methods to carry out the exclusion of members of the Communist Party—or any other group pledged to subvert the presuppositions of free inquiry. *There are no fixed rules except the use of intelligence.* In most places because of the way the C.P. functions there will be found individuals and students expelled by the Party for refusal to obey orders. When an inquiry becomes necessary one leads to another. An intelligent faculty committee can tell when people are lying or telling the truth without benefit of general loyalty oaths.

Now about your own position. Your letter and enclosure make it clear that you regard it as wrong to inquire into a man's membership in the C.P. not only for lawyers but for teachers and judges. In fact you make the taboo quite general. Presumably if a man is a *current* and *active* member of the Ku Klux Klan or the C.P. you would not consider that fact as relevant in considering his professional qualifications to serve as a judge who is pledged to dispense justice independently of class or color or creed. Presumably if a man is a member of the C.P. you would not consider that relevant to hiring him for, or firing him from, (if you discovered his membership), an atomic research plant doing restricted work. *Mutatis mutandis* you see no justification in asking a man who wants to be a lawyer, who, if I mistake not, is considered an officer of the court, whether he is a member of an organization which seeks to destroy the state and the court, or a man who is supposed to be an objective teacher in pursuit of the truth, whether he is a member of an organization which instructs him specifically to violate every obligation of a good teacher. If one considers these cases carefully, especially the first two, one can hardly help concluding that to take a view like yours is a *reductio ad absurdum* of the position. But since there is no absurdity to which some people will not resort to defend another absurdity, I point out that your position demonstrably rests upon (1) ignorance of fact and (2) misunderstanding of the relevant principle in interpreting the facts.

(1) In your letter you say that you do not agree that members of the Communist Party are all actual or potential (you misread this word) agents of a foreign power. Excuse me for asking; and what do you know about it? Have you read Krivitsky, Valtin, Foote, Fischer, Gitlow, Rossi, Chambers,[2] the Minutes and Theses of the Congresses of the Communist International, the literature of the C.P., the Report of the Royal Canadian Commission,[3] the proceedings of the court trials and Congressional Hearings on the Underground Apparatus? You can't suck facts out of your fingertips. Why not

study the C.P. movement nationally and internationally before you declare yourself on whether it is organized as a conspiracy?

(2) But even though the party "may have some (sic!) conspiratorial aspects," you add that you cannot assume that "every member of a political party is to be charged with even the illegal acts of the party as a whole or that membership in any such group should establish a *prima facie* case against a character or educational employability."

(a) You have two principles here and you swing back and forth between them in the most unconscionable manner without realizing that the first does not apply at all. No one is saying that because some members of the C.P. stole atomic secrets or engaged in passport frauds, all members of the C.P. should be sent to jail. Even under the Smith Act[4] the government tries to prove for each and every defendant that he specifically is guilty of violating a law. A good deal of the moral fervor you work up is due to suddenly shifting from the question whether members of the C.P. should be permitted to teach or be lawyers to the question of whether they should be sent to jail just because they are Communists.

(b) The relevant principle is that the facts about the C.P. justify us in drawing a *prima facie* case against members in respect to employability or reliability for certain types of jobs—teaching, the military, government, service, the law. Now unless you contest the fact about the conspiratorial instructions given to C.P. members, there *is* a *prime facie* case, and you do not give one single reason either in your letter or enclosure against this *prima facie* case. All you say is that to make an inference based on membership is to exclude people because of differences with "their opinions or beliefs," etc. This is absurd. The inference based on present and active membership is that the individual is likely to carry out the instructions, which he has voluntarily accepted, and that the sensible thing to do is to prevent him from doing it.

Your position is so extreme you would even deny our right to refuse to *hire* a member of the C.P. no matter what the job is because we can't be certain he will carry out his dirty work. Of course we can't be certain, but we can make a fairly reliable prediction, particularly because we know— which you don't seem to know—that the Party Control Commission automatically drops inactive and recalcitrant members, especially those who do not carry out instructions. (I am asking my secretary to send you an issue of the *Journal of Philosophy,* containing a discussion which goes into the logic of the matter further.)

I can't spare any more time. Suffice it to say that there is hardly a page of your essay which does not contain some blunder of fact or egregious error in reasoning, especially when you write of democracy. No wonder, if you take Carey McWilliams' book as a guide![5]

To sum up. I don't believe in loyalty oaths even for candidates for the bar. I believe that a character committee (I don't know how they are elected: I assume they are intelligent) is completely justified in asking a candidate whether he is a member of the Communist Party or any other organization which instructs its members so to act as to destroy the very presuppositions of professional integrity. So long as a candidate answers the question, the fact that he regards the question as illegitimate and says so should not of itself be sufficient to bar him. He may be honestly mistaken, and the reasons he may give may show a high order of intelligence. Your refusal to answer the question whether you are a member of the Communist Party (assuming that you are not) does not bear on your character. But the *reasons* you give for not being willing to answer the question (even if you did answer it negatively) have a bearing on your fitness, if intelligence is part of fitness. I would question you closely on other points of law to find out whether the logical lacunae in your analyses were characteristic of all your discussion, or whether they cropped up only when you discussed the issue of Communist conspiracy. Only in the latter case would I regard you as fit to practice law without doing an injustice to your clients. And if I did come to the conclusion that your position on the employability of members of the C.P. was only a gentle obsession, and not evidence of generic and stubborn stupidity and admitted you to the bar, I would advise your friends or your wife to give you a kind of spiritual dry-cleaning and take some of the unctuousness and moral stuffiness out of you.

1. George Anastaplo.
2. Walter Krivitsky; Jan Valtin (pseudonym of Richard J. H. Krebs) author of *Out of the Night* (New York, 1941); Alexander Foote, former member of the British Communist Party, agent for the Kremlin, and author of *Handbook for Spies* (New York, 1949); Ruth Fischer, author of *Stalin and German Communism* (Cambridge, Mass., 1948); Ben Gitlow, Communist Party candidate for vice-president of the United States in 1924 and witness on communist subversion before the House Committee on Un-American Activities; Mario Rossi, author of *Marx e la Dialettica Hegeliana* (Rome, 1960); Whittaker Chambers.
3. Royal Canadian Commission on Communist Espionage.
4. Alien Registration Act of 1940, which made it a crime to advocate the violent overthrow of the government. After World War II, it was used to persecute leaders of the Communist Party.
5. McWilliams, *Witch-hunt: The Revival of Heresy* (Boston, 1950).

111

Dear Mr. Smith,[1]   September 4, 1952

Ann[2] found your letter so engaging that she asked me to read it and reply to it if I felt moved to do so. I am so moved. If you speak for the ordinary man in the street in England, it will be a great relief for those of us who consider ourselves friends and admirers of England and who have been puzzled, mortified, and often fed up with what we sometimes read about America in the *Nation and New Statesman,* the *Manchester Guardian,* and the book reviews in the *Times Literary Supplement.* You sound so level-headed and eminently reasonable even on matters on which we probably disagree! Perhaps you would like to know how things look like to us who are, so to speak, your opposite numbers in this country.

We, of course, are not representative of the man in the streets who probably would distrust us as "internationalists," too much impressed by English and European traditions. We know Europe first-hand by re-peated visits. For us the Atlantic community is primarily a cultural and spiritual notion. To some extent we are the opinion makers in the Ameri-can community, reporting, interpreting, and always pleading for under-standing of other peoples' positions. Our immediate circle has always felt very close to the British Labor Party—more sympathetic and im-mensely heartened by the refusal of the Trade Union Congress at Mar-gate to take Bevan's[3] line but almost as depressed by the volume, tone, and unreasonableness of the anti-American speeches of Morrison[4] and Bevan.

We have noted with sadness the growth of anti-American sentiment in Western Europe and especially England. I myself am convinced that most of this sentiment has been manufactured by the press. At any rate it is measured primarily by what appears in the press. This anti-Americanism is mostly abstract: I don't believe it is generated by personal contact with individual Americans. I say we are saddened by this growth of anti-Ameri-canism because we understand that a great deal of it is relatively inevitable, flowing as it does from an historical situation in which Western Europe and England (the Greeks) view themselves as dependent upon America (the Romans), and most of all from the basic fear of war. (Stalin has weapons compared to which the V2 is obsolete.)

Even if American politicians had the wisdom of the serpent and spoke with the voice of the dove, anti-American sentiment would be strong for the same generic reason that we sometimes dislike the innocent person in whose behalf we get into a quarrel with an offensive bully. If that person weren't there, maybe there wouldn't be a fight! Some people in Europe felt this way about the Czechs and Poles in 1939, and some Americans, very few, about England in 1940.

But the intensity and degree of anti-American feeling in Europe and England transcends what is relatively inevitable. And one thing you may be certain about. If the American man in the street ever became aware of the strength of this feeling, our nation would be carried away by a violent isolationism which would look on with equanimity as Stalin swallowed Europe piece by piece. I know that my friends and I play down the facts about European anti-Americanism to American audiences for fear of arousing that irrational reaction which leads to cutting off one's nose to spite one's face.

I shall mention only three issues on which needless anti-American feeling has developed abroad and which you have lightly touched on.

1. The Korean War. The initial reverses of American forces at the outset of the Korean War were greeted by English newspapers with ill-concealed jubilation, and one gets the impression that a considerable number of Englishmen are beginning to regret that the U.N. made a military stand at all. The recognition of Communist China *seemed* precipitate and hardly justified by its consequences. That action together with a number of others, whether right or wrong, hardly indicates that England has been acting like a "henchman" of the U.S.; nor do I believe that any responsible person expects England to be anything else but a partner in formulating policy. I think that U.S. military personnel, who are unusually naive politically, sometimes behave in a thoughtless way in relation to our Allies but, although field commanders have a great deal of discretion, the civilian government is still firmly in control. There is not a shred of evidence for the widely held belief in England that it was Attlee's visit which prevented the use by the U.S. of atomic bombs in Korea—a decision presumably made by our military. The very fact that negotiations have been conducted for more than a year, despite their use as a shield behind which the Communists recouped their forces, and despite strong popular impatience with the stalling tactics of the Kremlin's agents, is evidence of British influence on collective U.N. policy. It simply is not true that any responsible groups in the American government are itching to spread the war into an all-out World War III. Our government does want to end the Korean War, and it *may* have to consider as one means of doing this the extension of military operations. This *may* be a mistaken policy, but many people in England always seize upon a difference in a proposed strategy or tactic as evidence of war-mongering or reactionary hysteria which would blindly drive England into the abyss. No government desirous of war would have committed the folly of the American government a few years ago of urging upon Chiang Kai-shek a coalition regime with the Communists. The prime external responsibility, I admit, for the communist victory in China and the communist invasion of South Korea lies with the past policies of the American government. But these very policies should be evidence that the U.S. is not in the grip of war fever. We have moved more slowly against Stalin than Britain did against Hitler and in the face of greater provocation.

2. The so-called "witch-hunt" in America. Every segment of the English press refers to the American witch-hunt, and even the *Manchester Guardian* speaks of a "reign of terror" here. This belief in England reinforces the impression of many Englishmen that our foreign policy is of a piece with our domestic "hysterics." Now most of the talk about an American witch-hunt is poppycock. The subject is vast and I shall try to be brief.

By English standards the American scene always appeared to be one in which there was not sufficient acceptance of diversity. There is not much change in this respect except that a number of private groups are seeking to capitalize on the public revulsion against communism to discredit opponents of ideas or causes that are unrelated to communism. In addition, because of the evidence of communist penetration in high government positions which no one did anything about, despite its being quite generally known, many people support McCarthy despite his unscrupulous and demagogic methods of criticism and attack. Indeed, McCarthy has been the greatest boon to the Communists, and to be attacked by him now is almost equivalent to receiving a testimonial of good political health. But I am afraid that you miss the point when you say that in England you would rather have a dozen Red Deans preach communism than have one McCarthy. We too have our Red Deans[5] and their equivalents, but McCarthy lets them alone. His charges are directed against the administration. The charges are wild; they are exaggerated; they are irresponsible. But they were brought on by a most scandalous situation in which the administration countenanced the presence in sensitive positions of men identified as members of communist espionage groups. The administration has since learned its lesson, but you may recall that according to Truman, the Hiss case was a "red herring." Senator Nixon[6] is right in asserting that Trumanism was responsible for McCarthyism.

As far as the government is concerned the task is now to get rid of those whose primary allegiance is to a foreign government, i.e., the Kremlin. And unfortunately although there may be no witches, there *are* agents of the Kremlin who for years have carefully infiltrated into many strategic places. Sometimes I think that more Englishmen believe in the existence of ghosts than of conspirators. We are beginning to realize that the communist movement consists of fanatical zealots prepared to do anything—literally anything—to further their cause. From what I have learned about England, the feeling there is that Communists are merely rather unpleasant nuisances. No mistake could be more disastrous, and it is held in some high places.

Here is an illustration. I have an Italian friend who knew Pontecorvo[7] as a fellow-Communist from their Parisian days. When he met Pontecorvo here, the latter was unaware that my friend had broken with communism.

Without prying he learned from Pontecorvo both that he was still an orthodox Party man, and doing restricted work in atomic research. He thereupon
transmitted this information to American security officers who passed it on
to British security officers. Pontecorvo was permitted to leave England
months *after* this information had been made available. The irony of it is
that Attlee told the house[8] after Pontecorvo fled that it had been discovered
that one of Pontecorvo's relatives was a member of the C.P.! But Pontecorvo himself was a Party member, and Pontecorvo is a man of scientific
gifts much superior to those of Klaus Fuchs,[9] whose membership in the
German Communist Party was also known to British security officers. (The
odd thing about this is that there is a book by an Englishman, Alexander
Foote (who was a member of the British C.P. and worked as an agent for
the Kremlin), which tells in most convincing detail how members of the
C.P. in government service work. His book has been almost totally ignored
in England.)

3. But all this is subordinate to the assessment of Soviet Communism as
a danger to the world. Many of us believe that the English underestimate
the importance of the Communist ideology upon the Kremlin's program.
Logically, Communist ideology has no bearing upon practice, but *psychologically* it has enormous bearing. The same was true of Hitler's ideology.
Britain and America both erred most extraordinarily in their policy towards
Hitler. And I must note with regret that American liberals and English
Laborites especially helped generate a mood of pacifism, disarmament, and
sentimental wish-thinking *after* Hitler came to power which to some extent
emboldened him to carry out the program laid down in his *Mein Kampf.*
During the war Roosevelt, whose political naivete in foreign affairs cannot
be overestimated, went overboard. He actually believed that Great Britain
would be a greater threat to post–world war peace and freedom than the
Soviet Union. No statesman has ever committed a greater blunder—a blunder made worse because he had plenty of warning about the true state of
affairs from those who knew better. Chester Wilmot[10] is right about Roosevelt but wrong in whitewashing Churchill's own record of appeasement,
particularly in relation to Eastern Europe.

As the situation stands now, American policy makers are convinced that
the Kremlin will strike whenever it thinks it has a good chance to win. If
there is agreement about this, and a mountain of data supports it, everything
else becomes a matter of detail than can be settled by a little good will and
intelligence. Our main weakness is in the field of psychological political
warfare. That in part is due to the impression sedulously cultivated by a
very articulate group abroad that America is on the verge of Fascism and
that culturally there is little to choose for Europeans between the totalitarian

collossi of the U.S. and U.S.S.R. Even if this were true, in the interests of its own survival, England would be wise to accept the U.S. at least on the same terms that it accepted the U.S.S.R. when faced by Hitler. *But it is not true*—and so far from being true that some of us are extremely puzzled not only by the persistent way in which this is circulated but at the credulity of those who put stock in it. It is as if they wanted to believe it.

Please don't misunderstand me. There are many indigenous features in American life and some aspects of its foreign policy which weaken the struggle for democratic survival. But these, like the position of the Negroes, are slowly being improved. The very fact that the U.S. is a free culture makes it possible for all sorts of pressure groups, independently or in combination, to win support on some spurious issue or to influence Congress to give them some special protective legislation independently of its effect upon the economy of our allies abroad. Sectionalism is still strong in the U.S., and our system of balance of powers works very badly in times of crisis with Congress very often at loggerheads with the President. What seems like malice or a devilish design to gum up the works is much more likely to be stupidity or sectional pride in a coalition for diverse purposes. The consequences are bad enough, but there is hope that mistakes and even stupidity may be remedied.

Then again we have tens of millions of Americans who have strong personal ties to regions of Europe now being sacked by the Soviet Union. They have authentic information about the programs of planned extermination and total cultural terror that are being carried out there. This together with the more adequate coverage of foreign news by our press (not all of our newsprint is wasted—much of it is) accounts in part for the fact that the American public is much better informed as to what is going on behind the Iron Curtain than European communities except those that immediately adjoin Soviet occupied territory. It would hardly be an exaggeration to say that in consequence the American public is for the strongest possible measures, short of war, against Soviet aggression and regards the policy of Washington as bumbling, half-hearted, confused, and too sensitive to the wishes of other nations in the U.N. The edge of moral indignation has not been blunted by memory of total war.

Despite the readiness of the American public to support a firmer policy against the Kremlin, there is not a sufficient awareness of the price we must pay for this policy. There is not a sufficient awareness of the fact that the European and English economy cannot shoulder the burden of an armament adequate for defense, that their peoples have suffered much more than our own, that even our staggering taxes leaves us a margin of living which appears as luxury to the European masses.

I believe that the group, unfortunately small, to which I am closest is convinced that in one form or another the Marshall Plan must continue not as a dole but as a matter of justice as well as American self-interest, that we must buy more from Europe even at the expense of our own consumption goods industries, and that we must shoulder the main burden of European defense in the same spirit that the strongest member of a family works hardest for it. No American government can do this without the willing support of the American people. Our task is to convince the American people that this policy is just, as well as ultimately necessary for the survival of the West. We will keep at this no matter how high the tide of anti-American feeling rises. But our greatest fear is that when the full force of this feeling strikes the American public, anything we or those who think like us say will fall on deaf ears.

I have gone on at unconscionable length because as I was writing I thought I should like to use this letter to reach other English friends and acquaintances. Since your name happily is "Smith," I don't believe anyone will identify. When Ann and I are next in Europe we look forward to seeing you and Asie.

1. Will Smith, Wales, U.K.
2. Hook's wife.
3. Aneurin Bevan, militant trade-unionist and leader of the left wing of the British Labor Party.
4. Herbert S. Morrison, deputy leader of the British Labor Party.
5. Reference is to the Reverend Hewlett Johnson, dean of Canterbury cathedral in England and a communist fellow traveler.
6. Senator Richard M. Nixon, Republican of California.
7. Bruno Pontecorvo.
8. British House of Commons.
9. Klaus Fuchs, a British spy for the Soviets, received a fourteen-year sentence for espionage. He was released in 1959, after serving nine years. He remained a committed Communist and settled in East Germany.
10. Australian military historian of World War II whose book, *The Struggle for Europe* (New York, 1952), is quite critical of American military and diplomatic strategy.

112

Dear Dean Melby,[1]   October 22, 1952

Thank you for the reprint of your article on Progressive Education for the *British Yearbook*. I have read it with interest. My impression is that you exaggerate the amount of hysteria and repression in American education, and ignore the verifiable facts that American teachers have displayed more courage than they have at any other time in their history. When did faculties like those of California, Chicago, Pennsylvania, and Ohio ever actually oppose loyalty oaths in the past? Further, teachers as a group are more progressive than any other professional group. In the light of the gravity of the dangers, external and internal, to the security and survival of the United States, I think the educational situation, bad as it is in some places, is still marked by more freedom than we have ever enjoyed in the past.

I am taking the liberty of enclosing a pamphlet I have written on the general situation in which I try to put things, including the rash of cultural vigilantism, in proper perspective.

1. Ernest O. Melby, dean, school of education, New York University.

113

Dear Mr. Smith,[1]   November 3, 1952

1. I want to correct an impression you derived from my last letter—for which I may be at fault—that I believe the United States would be justified in *unilaterally* extending the Korean War. Nothing could be farther from my thought. This would obviously imperil the U.N. and our alliance with other nations. But when I wrote that our government may have to consider the extension of military operations, I conceived this, as my subsequent sentences showed, as a *proposal* to be urged upon all our partners in the Korean effort. And what I meant was that if our government, for example, were to *advocate* the bombing of Communist Chinese air bases in Manchuria, from whose sanctuary Chinese planes were inflicting sanguinary losses on U.N. troops, I am confident that a hue and cry would arise in England that we were intent upon unleashing total world war. Instead of soberly evaluating the chances that such an action would help bring the Korean War to an end, it would be greeted as a sign of militaristic aggression.

To some of us here it seems as if events which concern the U.S. are interpreted with a kind of *a priorism* of disfavor. There was more criticism of the American advance to the Yalu than of the Chinese Communist invasion of Korea, despite the fact that there is no evidence that if the U.N. troops had halted in the wrist of Korea the Chinese would have idly observed the North Korean rout. (The authority for my statement that some large English newspapers gleefully headlined early American reverses in Korea is the *New York Times*. I understand that the British Information Service here protested, and in the discreet sophisticated way the British do these things, this hostile tone was dropped for one more circumspect.)

This *a priorism* is illustrated in your comment on our continued support of Chiang Kai-shek in Formosa in which you see nothing but a proclamation of our intent to commit aggression against Communist China in the future. China is committing aggression against us right *now,* and instead of seeing in our continued support of Chiang Kai-shek (whatever may have been true in the past) an obvious move to bolster the U.N. position in Korea and the course of the U.N. in Asia generally, you interpret it as a sign of aggression to come—despite the whole history of American foreign policy in the Orient, which has been marked by less aggression than that of any other country, including Great Britain.

Nationalist China is still in the UN. Formosa is its territory. Just as the Kremlin was behind the North Korean attack against South Korea, so would the Kremlin be behind Mao's attack against Formosa. Mao can only attack and win Formosa with Soviet help. What would you have us do in that event—withdraw and organize a non-intervention committee in the way France and Great Britain did when Hitler and Mussolini helped Franco destroy the legitimate Spanish regime? Mao, who works more closely with Stalin than Franco ever did with Mussolini and Hitler, is a thousand times more dangerous to the survival of the free world than Franco. No, instead of withdrawing from Formosa at present, were my counsel asked by the UN I should propose to use, not Chiang's army officially, but Chinese volunteers from Formosa to fight in Korea. I can already hear the uproar in England at the notion. But I believe an excellent case can be made for this *proposal.* Aside from its merits, even if it is ultimately rejected in order not to wound Nehru's sensibilities, such a proposal would be construed in England today not as motivated by a desire to bring a pressure that would cause Mao and the Kremlin to cease hostilities in Korea, but as another illustration of American "war-mongering."

Even more incomprehensible to many Americans is the attitude of those Englishmen who go so far as to urge that we throw Nationalist China out of the UN and welcome Mao in, despite Mao's flouting of the basic decencies of international morality—and *at the same time* denounce the proposal of some Americans to permit Franco's Spain to enter the UN as evidence of growing Fascism in the U.S. This is really too much. Personally I would keep them both out, although Franco, who is not violating the peace, has a much better claim than Mao—perhaps as good a claim as Tito, one of Bevan's heroes.

2. The more I read about the American "witch-hunt" in the British press, the more evident it is to me that those writers have lost all sense of proportion. It is not true, despite your quotation from Justice Clark,[2] that communist ideas of government and economies are held to be criminal in America.

The Communist Party exists under various names in this country. It has a legal press, runs candidates, controls several unions, and engages in many diversified cultural activities. One can see Soviet movies glorifying the North Korean armies. This despite the fact that we are living under an official decree of national emergency, and that we are in a war which has cost us more that 125,000 casualties already. (If I recall correctly Great Britain arrested Mosely[3] and some of his close followers even before its casualties reached this figure.) No responsible person here considers the Communists by themselves a threat to American security. But no informed person regards them as existing by themselves but rather literally—and correctly—as a Soviet fifth column.

We take this warranted assertion—warranted by a mountain of evidence—as a premise for a policy which denies to fifth columnists, actual and potential, the right to hold positions in government service. Some nongovernmental services are just as strategic for our culture and economy. Those who are barred are not being deprived of their civil rights but only of their opportunity to carry out a subversion to which they are pledged. Even the former head of the American Civil Liberties Union[4] agrees that "A superior loyalty to a foreign government disqualifies a citizen for service to his own."

To what do you take issue—the facts or the policy based on them? I believe the policy is reasonable, given the facts, and that the errors, injustices, and stupidities which have attended the executive policy can be avoided by intelligent administration.

The House and Senate Committees on Un-American Activities and International Security respectively are part of the American Congressional system of committees. Their procedural faults are again part of the American system of committee procedure and unique to them only to the extent that their shifting personnel sometimes introduces extraneous issues. Congressman Dies,[5] for example, tried to use the Committee as a political weapon against the New Deal, and in its early years discredited the committee. But I still remember Congressman Vorhees,[6] an ardent New Dealer, telling me how surprised he was to discover the amount of Communist Party penetration when he joined the Committee. Under the whiplash of liberal criticism, the procedures of the House Committee improved to a point where even Alger Hiss, the object of the gravest possible political charges, received a perfectly fair hearing before it. I defy anyone who has actually read the hearings to deny this. When the House Committee succeeded in uncovering evidence of extensive espionage which the government had hushed up for almost ten years, it received in effect a popular mandate to continue investigation. It was partly as a result of the Committee's work that the government adopted its own loyalty program.

Why is it a "witch-hunt" to summon Communist Party movie stars and trade-union leaders before it in the quest for information? You do not seem to know in England that the House Committee cannot imprison people for refusing to testify to any question whatsoever on grounds of possible self-incrimination. But you may ask: why question them altogether? In the case of trade-union leaders, who can call strikes almost at will, I presume you will grant that it is desirable for members of the trade union movement (as well as others) to know which of their leaders is a Communist Party member so that they can look hard at any proposal which would convert the trade union into an instrument of the Communist Party. I am referring not only to politically inspired strikes but to the siphoning off of union funds into the coffers of Communist front organizations.

As for the movie stars, the Committee was not so much interested in the alleged attempts to control the political content of films, although there was some testimony on this point, but in the fact that one of the chief domestic sources of money for the Communist Party was Hollywood. I believe it is legitimate for a democratic government through duly constituted committees to make inquiry into the sources of the funds of fifth columnists intent upon destroying or injuring democratic institutions. Without approving of all the lines of questioning adopted by the Committee, I should maintain that uncovering information which is *accurate* and *relevant* to the problem which Congress is called to consider is perfectly legitimate. Where the need for information exists, the cure for the defects and imperfections of any existing committee is a better committee.

Pretty much the same observations must be made on the Senate Internal Security Committee's investigation of the Institute of Pacific Relations and of Owen Lattimore.[7] The Senate Committee set out to discover whether the Institute of Pacific Relations had influenced the policy of the American State Department in China, and the extent to which this I.P.R. was a Communist front. (Lattimore was a, if not the, leading figure in the I.P.R.) Is this not a legitimate subject of investigation? Nothing testifies so much to the opinionated ignorance about the United States on the part of many English magazines and newspapers as their conviction that Owen Lattimore is a well-meaning liberal martyrized by McCarthy[8] for telling unpalatable truths about Asia. The actual fact is, as anyone who goes to the trouble of reading both the hearings of the Tydings Committee and the Internal Security Committee, that Lattimore, at the very least, was a devious and skillful follower of the Communist Party line on Asian affairs. McCarthy's fault here is, as usual, asserting more than he could prove, although he had some witnesses to back him up. And although allegedly hunted as a witch, Lattimore is secure in his job, published a best seller, and still exercises a professional influence in the field of Far Eastern affairs greater than all anti-Communists combined. Some witch! Some witch-hunt!

Together with several other English correspondents you seem to me to judge the American Communist Party by what the British Communist Party *used* to be. When I was in Moscow in 1929 a Russian Communist ruefully quoted Lenin as saying that it was the most difficult thing in the world to make a Bolshevik of an Englishman—even of an English Communist. Well, it's been done. The hard core of the British Communist Party is growing—and it isn't measured by votes or even by membership figures. I judge this by my reading of the British Communist press and by following the careers of some Communist Party figures. As I wrote in my last letter, you infer from the *true* proposition that there is no *logical* connection (or entailment) between article of belief, doctrine or dogma and a form of behavior, overt or implicit, to the false proposition that there is no, or little *psychological* connection between ways of belief and ways of action. A Nazi who sincerely believed the lies Hitler told about the Jews was psychologically prepared to commit excesses against them as distinct from one who followed Hitler but was indifferent to the Nazi mythology. In general the likelihood that an individual will commit atrocities is directly proportionate to the degree of absurdity of his beliefs. When I observe university trained members of the British Communist Party swallowing Lysenko, echoing Zhadanov,[9] affirming with apparent conviction that Americans are conducting bacteriological warfare in Korea; when I read Maurice Cornforth's[10] references to Stalin's philosophic genius and his attempt to prove that John Dewey is a racialist—something which even the American Stalinists have not yet dared to repeat—then I know that the British Party has been Bolshevized. And I don't have to rely on Douglas Hyde[11] either. I sincerely hope I'm wrong, but I fear very much that "sleeping" and very much awake C.P. members and agents have infiltrated much more than the trade unions.

I gather from reading Rebecca West[12] that something about Pontecorvo is being held back from the British public. I am not surprised ever since I learned that some of the people who sent in "objective" reports on the situation in Yugoslavia when the British were debating whether to help Mihailovich or Tito were members of the British Communist Party. (One of them, Jack Klugman, was in British Military Intelligence and used the not very bright Randolph Churchill to put over the Party line about Tito being a great patriot and German fighter.)

3. All our disagreements really flow from our different estimates of Soviet aims, strategic and tactical. Despite the evidence of his *Mein Kampf,* his march into the Rhineland, his rearming, etc., many Englishmen asserted that "it would be a mistake to accept as a fact rather than a

supposition" that Hitler was bent on aggression. But the evidence that the Kremlin is bent on aggression is no less clear—not only from the *Mein Kampf* of Lenin and Stalin, both of whom believe that war with the West is inevitable, but from the whole pattern of Soviet expansion in Asia and Europe. They have made the Czars look like pikers!

To be sure there are differences between Nazi Germany and Stalin's Russia as there are between the first and Mussolini's Italy and the second and Tito's Yugoslavia. But the chief difference is all in Stalin's favor, for he commands devoted and fanatical fifth columns in the country of his enemies. His strength and source of confidence lies in the combination of his own power, his power in his enemy's countries, the confusions and hatred among his enemies, and their naive belief that when he cries "peace" and protests "encirclement" (Ah: that familiar echo!) he really means it.

You write that you can put yourself in the skin of the men in the Kremlin and find it easy to see all the western preparations for attack. I really doubt that you do find it easy. For on that hypothesis how would you explain to yourself the invasion of South Korea? And before that the provocative blockade of Berlin? And before that the coup in Czechoslovakia? If the West were looking for an occasion for general attack, any one of these events would have been seized as a justifiable ground. Conversely, in your imaginative identification of yourself with the men of the Kremlin how would you explain (a) American total mobilization in 1945—as a ruse or stratagem? (b) American willingness to include not only Western Europe but the Soviet Union in the Marshall Plan—a Plan accepted by Czech and Polish Communists before the Kremlin vetoed it? (c) America's willingness to surrender her monopoly of the atomic bomb in effect on the sole condition that it be not dropped on her? Do you really believe that Stalin would have offered to surrender the bomb to an international authority if he had a monopoly of it? I believe that we would all be dead or enslaved by now if he had it.

A concluding word. We were all heartened by the news that the British had exploded their own atomic bomb. And I for one am prepared to draw certain consequences from it. Churchill once said, truly I believe, that the only thing that stopped Stalin from overrunning Europe was America's possession of the bomb. And we *were* interested in preventing Stalin from overrunning Europe as much for Europe's sake as ours, for we can still fight in the dire eventuality of Europe's falling into Stalin's hands.

Now that England has the bomb and can defend herself and Europe, better has the time come for the U.S. to transfer its present military aid to the strengthening of Britain's atomic defenses. This would mean the withdrawal of American troops from England—whose presence has given such offense to anti-Americans—and possibly the relinquishment of American air bases whenever the British atomic stockpile seemed adequate as a counter-threat to give Stalin something to think about. How in your judgment would British public opinion receive these proposals? Wouldn't they lessen somewhat the fear of many Englishmen that the U.S. desires to drag Great Britain into the mad adventure of another war? Would the elimination of friction, almost inescapable when foreign troops are around, attenuate British irritation?

Several of my English correspondents have stressed the importance of building up the British export market in America and of international democratic planning in the allocation of the raw materials necessary both for defense and export production. I am in complete agreement and am urging the editors of various publications to explore these themes in their pages in order to develop a public opinion in support of executive action. As soon as the President moves in this direction some local trade group (sometimes with the help even of the trade unions) yells it is being liquidated for the benefit of foreigners. Most of the time it means only that their profit will be less: sometimes, however, there are, or could be, real causes of hardship. But these are matters that have to be settled on a piecemeal basis but in the light of general welfare, a difficult, obscure, but meaningful concept.

1. Will Smith.
2. Supreme Court Justice Tom Clark.
3. Oswald Mosely, British fascist leader during the 1930s.
4. Roger Baldwin.
5. Martin Dies, Democrat from Texas.
6. Jerry Vorhees, liberal Democratic congressman from California who was defeated for re-election by Richard Nixon in 1946.
7. Owen Lattimore, professor of history, Johns Hopkins University.
8. Senator Joseph McCarthy.
9. Andrew A. Zhadanov, pro-Stalinist chief of literary and cultural affairs in the Soviet Union in the 1940s. He died under mysterious circumstances in 1948.
10. Maurice C. Cornforth, English Communist philosopher and author of *In Defense of Philosophy: Against Positivism and Pragmatism* (New York, 1950).
11. President of Ireland, 1938–45, and historian, poet, and folklorist.
12. Author of *The Meaning of Treason* (New York, 1947).

114

Dear Dr. Einstein,[1]   November 10, 1952

Thank you for your letter of November 2nd.

I was very much moved by the noble statement you sent to *Kaizo*[2] and feel it is a pity that the full text was not released in this country, too.

The subject you discuss is the most fateful of our time. The position of Gandhi (and Tolstoy) has always seemed to me to be a live option, and I have often been tempted to embrace it when reflecting on the bitter cost of even the best victory. One thing has deterred me, viz., the realization that Gandhi could have been successful only with the British or a people with the same high human values. I am afraid he would have failed utterly with the Japanese military, with the Gestapo and S.S., and the Soviet M.V.D. What is even worse, the new methods of "scientific" torture would have reduced him to a broken-spirited, miserable wreck of a man, stuttering back the confessions suggested by a cunning and cruel prompter manipulating the coercions of hunger, pain, and crazed desire for sleep or even death.

I do not know whether you have read, or remember, Weissberg's book[3] on his experiences in the hands of the G.P.U., and how narrowly he escaped from becoming a groveling, crawling creature—a mockery of a man. This was twelve years ago or more, and since then the diabolical techniques of unmaking the mind and degrading the person have been perfected. No, I fear not even Gandhi could have withstood them, and few human beings have Gandhi's spiritual discipline.

When I think of how many millions of Jews permitted themselves to be slaughtered in what was in effect a passive resistance to evil, I find myself wishing that they had died like the Jews in the Warsaw ghetto. It sounds smug and hollow to say that when one must die in any event, one should do it nobly. Perhaps one should try not to die ignobly.

That is why I cannot accept a position which seems to be one of unilateral pacifism, in the face of an enemy who degrades before he kills. Even my good friend Norman Thomas recognizes that unilateral disarmament today would provoke Stalin to reach out his hands for the necks of all free men. And that is why if I were a scientist, and if I thought that the Kremlin had the remotest prospect of inventing a hydrogen bomb, with a heavy heart I would make the same decision you made in 1939.

And unless one believes life itself is an evil, surely your decision at that time was justified by the tragic events—was it not? The loss of life would have been no less, and perhaps more, if the bomb had not been used—although I never could understand why no demonstration was made on an uninhabited island as a warning to induce surrender. The Russians, anyhow, would have taken up the bomb where the Germans left it, even if we had not worked on it. You know what life under the Nazis was, and if you ever have spoken as I have in West Berlin to the simple Russian men and women who fled from the Soviet sphere, you would know that life there is not much different.

But forgive me for going on this way—I didn't intend to write at such length.

1. Albert Einstein.
2. A Japanese newspaper.
3. Alexander Weissberg, *The Accused* (New York, 1951).

115

Dear Mr. Aptheker,[1]   December 12, 1952

I would no more help build up an audience for you than I would for a member of the Nazi Party who offered to debate me to prove that Hitler was not really an anti-Semite. My evidence for characterizing the Communist Party as a conspiracy, and its members as professionally unfit to fulfill the vocation of a teacher, has been published many times. Subject to the laws of libel, you enjoy the freedom of the press in our country to answer that evidence—a greater freedom of the press, I may add, than would be extended to you in your own fatherland, the Soviet Union.

If you wish to reply to me I suggest as a medium the pages of the *Daily Worker* or *The New Masses and Mainstream* or *Political Affairs.* I shall read what you write with interest, for I am always prepared to re-examine my position anew.

But instead of beginning the debate with me, to convince *me* that as a member of the Communist Party you are capable of objective scholarship and teaching, you really must first take issue with the official views of your own party. For all of my sources were from official publications of the Communist Party or from declarations of its official spokesmen.

I shall cite a few of them. According to the *Daily Worker* of April 2, 1936, one of the conditions of membership is contained in the following pledge: *"I pledge myself to remain at all times a vigilant and firm defender of the Leninist line of the Party, the only line that insures the triumph of the Soviet Power in the United States."* Now I had always thought that the mark of an intellectually honest and objective scholar is his pledge to follow the line of *truth* no matter where it leads. What happens when this line contradicts the Leninist (or Stalinist) line of the Party? The objective scholar follows the truth. The member of the Communist Party, however, is pledged *at all times* to follow the Party line. How then can he make a claim to objectivity so long as he is a member of the Communist Party?

The demand that the member of the Communist Party "subordinate himself" to the Party line occurs again and again in official Communist Party literature. Here is a typical command. *The Resolutions of the Ninth Convention of the Communist Party of the U.S.A.* (Workers Library Publishers, p. 63) declares:

"In order to carry out their work effectively, and to win the respect and confidence of the workers, all Communists must *at all times* take a position *on every question* that is in line with the policies of the Party."

This means—does it not?—that if the Communist Party declares Roosevelt a Fascist in 1934; a Progressive in 1936 during the Popular Front; a war-monger and imperialist in 1940 during the Nazi-Soviet Pact; and a great democrat in 1941, after Hitler invaded the Soviet Union—a member of the Communist Party must go along on pain of expulsion. This absolute and unqualified acceptance of the Party line is certainly a sign of a disciplined party-hack. But what a quaint idea of objective scholarship!

But you also tell me that as a member of the Communist Party you live up to the ethics of honest teaching. Again I am puzzled. For in *The Communist,* the official organ of the Communist Party, which your own comrades at New York University asked me to read to find out how members of the Communist Party think and behave, I find the following:

"Party and Y.C.L.[2] fractions set up within classes and *departments* must supplement and combat by means of discussion, brochures, etc. bourgeois omissions and distortions in the regular curriculum. *Marxist-Leninist analysis must be injected into every class.*" (May, 1937, my italics.)

Now honest teachers do not inject Marxist-Leninist analysis into every class. Sometimes such analysis is irrelevant. Sometimes it is wrong. And when it is correct, they accept it *openly* as a contribution to truth, lower case, which is neither bourgeois nor proletarian. But how can any honest teacher, such as you claim to be, remain in an organization which instructs him to indoctrinate as follows:

"*Communist teachers must take advantage of their position without exposing themselves* to give their students to the best of their ability working-class education.

"To enable the teachers in the party to do the latter, the Party must take careful steps to see that all teacher comrades are given thorough education in the teaching of Marxism-Leninism. Only when teachers have really mastered Marxism-Leninism *will they be able skillfully to inject it into their teaching at the least risk of exposure* and at the same time conduct struggles around the schools in a truly Bolshevik manner."

The answer seems to me clear; no honest teacher can remain in the Communist Party, no Communist Party member can be regarded as an honest teacher. But perhaps you have protested against these outrageous official instructions to violate the basic morality of academic freedom and responsibility. Where and when?

I am particularly eager to know for the following reason. Writing in the *Communist* in 1938, your leader, William Z. Foster, published a very important article on "The Communist Party and the Professional" in which he said that *only* those individuals are selected as members "who show by practical work that they definitely understand the Party line, are prepared to put it into effect, *and especially display a thorough readiness to accept Party discipline.*"(p. 808)

He also said—and this affects *you*—that the Communist professional must introduce the Party line into his scholarly work. "Thus, our teachers must write new school textbooks and rewrite history from the Marxian viewpoints."(p. 809) You are an historian.

Now sworn public testimony exists that you, the Foner brothers of C.C.N.Y., Morais of Brooklyn College,[3] and several other Communist Party members who taught history actually met in the office of A. Trachtenberg, "the cultural Commissar" of the Party, a member of its Politbureau, its Central Control Commission, and liaison man with the Soviet G.P.U. in America, to carry out this assignment. The Soviet police not only progressively rewrite Russian history but apparently wish to do the same for American history through "good" Communists like yourself.

One illustration out of a hundred. For propaganda purposes the Kremlin decided that American Negroes were not only an oppressed race but an oppressed *nation*. It thereupon commanded the Communist Party to adopt the doctrine of "self-determination for the black belt" with the right of secession from the U.S. This infamous proposal would Jim Crow the American Negroes into a segregated state of their own. No American Communist, white or black, could reject this doctrine without being expelled. The party "historians" were ordered to ransack the materials of the American past "to prove" that the Negroes are an oppressed *nation*—and they still are hard at work on it as your own writings show, although the slogan of "self-determination" has been temporarily shelved with the Kremlin's permission.

Under the circumstances, my dear Mr. Aptheker, you will forgive me for doubting the sincerity of your professions of objectivity and honesty either as a scholar and/or teacher.

But perhaps all this, you will say, is only true of the past—and you have turned over a new leaf. It would be very difficult for me to tell, so long as you remained in the C.P. For I would need to have some evidence that you are not following Lenin's advice to members of the Communist Party on how to carry on Communist work in trade unions:

It is necessary to agree to any and every sacrifice and even—if need be—re-sort to all sorts of stratagems, maneuvers, and illegal methods, to evasions and subterfuges. . . . [*Selected Works,* Eng. Translation, Vol. X, p. 95]

But still it is not impossible that you *may* have experienced a conversion that the Control Commission knows nothing about. So here are two prelimi-nary simple tests of whether you are capable, as a member of the Commu-nist Party, of intellectual objectivity and honesty. On August 15, 1948 there appeared in *Pravda* as part of a letter from Professor Zhebrak the following: "As long as our Party recognized both tendencies in Soviet genetics . . . I persistently defended my views which at some points differed from the views of Academician Lysenko. But now, since it has become clear to me that the basic theses of the Michurin school of Soviet genetics are approved by the Central Committee of the All-Union Communist Party, I, as a mem-ber of the Party, cannot defend positions which have been declared mis-taken by the Central Committee of our Party." (Complete text on pp. 211–14 of Counts,[4] *The Country of the Blind*)

Now will you please tell me whether you regard this as a proper way of objectively determining scientific truth and settling scientific issues? Professor Zhebrak is a good Bolshevik. Is he an honest teacher or scholar? You cannot answer affirmatively and claim to have turned over a new leaf. If you disap-prove of this Communist Party procedure, will you say it *publicly?*

Secondly, something like an official pogrom on a high level has been begun by your comrades in Czechoslovakia with Nazi-like slanders against the Jewish people and the state of Israel.

Already the dread signs of planned extermination are appearing in Com-munist countries. According to the *New York Times,* Nov. 27, 1952, "A report reached Vienna today that the doors of Bratislava houses and apart-ments tenanted by Jews bore chalked inscriptions saying: 'Down with capi-talist Jews!' 'Jews live here,' or simply 'Jews.' "

Tell us whether as an objective historian you agree with the *Daily Worker*'s claim that the framed Slansky trials[5] have no anti-Jewish aspect whereas the Rosenbergs, charged and convicted of a most heinous crime against the United States, are being punished merely because they are Jews?

I am sending a copy of this letter to the *Daily Worker* to which you are a leading contributor, and am relying on your good offices to induce them to print it, together with your reply, if any. Or you may publish it in *Masses and Mainstream* of which you are an editor. If the readers enjoy our corre-spondence, I shall be glad to present the evidence for my statement that the American Communist Party is a conspiratorial fifth-column in the interest of the most total despotism in history.

1. Herbert Aptheker, American Communist, historian, and author of *American Negro Slave Revolts* (New York, 1943).
2. Young Communist League.
3. Philip S. Foner and Jack D. Foner and Herbert M. Morais.
4. George S. Counts.
5. Rudolf Slansky, Czeckoslovak Communist Party secretary, and thirteen other Czech Communist Party members were tried in 1952 for treason. Of these fourteen, eight were Jews. Slansky and seven others were executed. Of the eight executed, five were Jews. In order to deflect attention from the anti-Semitism permeating these trials, American and European Communists claimed that Julius and Ethel Rosenberg, who had been convicted of passing secrets of the atomic bomb to the Soviet Union, were victims of American anti-Semitism.

4

1953–1959

No question involving communism in American life was more important to academicians during the 1950s than the status of suspected Communists and fellow travelers within the university. This issue involved a host of other questions, including whether Communists and Communist sympathizers should be allowed to retain their academic positions, whether the professoriate should be subjected to loyalty oaths, whether universities should cooperate with congressional and state legislative committees in ensuring the loyalty of their employees, and whether academicians should be fired for refusing to reveal to these committees the names of those whom they knew to be members of the Communist Party. The anti-communist liberal-Left intelligentsia was sharply divided on these questions. Arthur M. Schlesinger, Jr., for example, argued that the actions of professors, and not mere membership in the Communist Party, should determine fitness to teach. It was one thing if a Communist Party member used his position to propagandize, and something else if his political prejudices did not affect his performance in the classroom. Schlesinger also distinguished between academicians in fields such as history, economics, and sociology, which were conducive to political propagandizing, and the hard sciences, where political issues were unlikely to arise.

Hook, by contrast, took a much harder line. For him, the mere fact that a person was a member of the Communist Party was *prima facie* evidence of unfitness to teach. The distinguishing characteristic of a true academician—the unwavering search for truth—was simply incompatible with participation in a conspiratorial political organization that required its members to follow faithfully and automatically the zigs and zags of Communist Party strategy and to subordinate their own quest for truth to the dictates of party ideology. Membership in a political organization which demanded that biologists reject Mendel, that philosophers repudiate philosophic idealism, that literary scholars condemn Thornton Wilder, Thomas Wolfe, and the New Criticism, that historians accept the primacy of historical materialism, and that political scientists spurn pluralism was inconsistent with an academician's obligations to his students, his institution, and his colleagues to be a truth-seeker. Hook rejected the assertion that his reasoning would also exclude Roman Catholics from the teaching profession. "There is no evidence whatsoever of the operation of Catholic cells in nonsectarian universities which impose a party line in all the arts and sciences that must be followed by all Catholic teachers on pain of excommunication."*

Hook realized that a person might have joined the Communist Party for family, social, and other reasons. The question was whether that person was a dedicated Communist, committed to the carrying out of party directives, or whether he or she was simply a Communist Party hanger-on or a believer in Marxist ideology without being controlled by the party. Membership in the Communist Party, he argued, should result in an investigation by that person's academic peers—not by politicians—to determine the extent to which he or she was under the control of the party. If it was determined that he or she was, in fact, a party lackey, that person did not belong on a college campus, or in an elementary or high school for that matter. Believing in heretical ideas was one thing; participating in a conspiracy was something else. This was particularly so in a democracy such as the United States, in which every citizen had the opportunity to participate in the political process. By attempting to do secretly what they were unable to do openly—change the government—Communists were engaged in a conspiracy.

Finally, Hook, an American patriot, was outraged by a political organization which openly proclaimed that in a conflict between the United States and the Soviet Union its first loyalty was to Russia. He had in mind such things as the statement in the September 1947 issue of *Political Affairs,* the theoretical organ of the American Communist Party, that it was an undeniable "fact" that the policies of the Soviet Union have invariably "corresponded to the best interests of the American people."

Hook's position on the incompatibility of membership in the Communist Party or Communist sympathies on the one hand and a position in academia (or in elementary or secondary schools) on the other was the most controversial aspect of his long public career. The Englishman David Caute attacked Hook in his book *The Great Fear.* Hook, Caute argued, had contributed to the atmosphere of fear permeating America during the early 1950s. It was ironic, Caute wrote, that Hook, a pragmatist, "was short of evidence that Communist teachers actually indoctrinated their pupils, but argued deductively from a few dated Party texts."†

---

*Sidney Hook, "Should Communists Be Permitted to Teach?" *New York Times Magazine,* February 29, 1949. For a rejoinder to Hook, see Alexander Meiklejohn, "Should Communists Be Allowed to Teach?" *New York Times Magazine,* March 27, 1949.

†David Caute, *The Great Fear: The Anti-Communist Purge under Truman and Eisenhower* (New York: Simon and Schuster, 1978), p. 406.

The historian Ellen W. Schrecker agreed. Schrecker's *No Ivory Tower** is the most comprehensive study of the impact of the Second Red Scare on academia. It is also a forceful indictment of Hook's fundamental premises— that membership in the Communist Party was *prima facie* evidence of a person's unfitness to fill a teaching position, that there had been a significant Communist presence in the university during the 1940s and 1950s, and that the university had a responsibility to purge itself of Communist influence to save itself from political McCarthyism. In fact, Schrecker observed, the academy "did not fight McCarthyism. It contributed to it." Universities "conferred respectability upon the most repressive elements of the anti-Communist crusade. In its collaboration with McCarthyism, the academic community behaved just like every other major institution in American life."† Schrecker claimed Hook bore partial responsibility for this disgraceful situation, even though there was no proof that Communists on campus had attempted to indoctrinate their students. There was no proof, Schrecker concluded, "because there was no indoctrination. . . . Communists teachers, both for professional and prudential reasons, did not try to proselytize in class."‡

Hook, in response, believed Caute and Schrecker to be both naive about the actions of Communists and uninformed about the nature of communism, particularly the demands the party placed on its true believers. University officials agreed with Hook rather than with his detractors. By the time the campaign to remove Communists and Communist sympathizers from the campus had spent itself in the mid-1950s, hundreds of party members and fellow travelers had been dismissed from academia and hundreds more were never hired in the first place. Hook remained convinced to his dying day that his position on this issue was the only sensible one.

---

*Ellen W. Schrecker, *No Ivory Tower: McCarthyism and the Universities* (New York: Oxford University Press, 1986).

†Ibid., p. 108.

‡Ibid., p. 340.

116

Dear Hacker,[1]   February 13, 1953

I want to tell you that your personal attack at the Civil Liberties panel on individuals who disagree with you on the employment of Communist Party teachers as "Savanarolas," who presumably wish to burn books and people, as men "who are inviting the McCarthys and Congressional Committees to our campuses," represents an unscrupulous misrepresentation of their position, and a deliberate resort to abuse instead of argument. I say "deliberate" because nothing could be clearer than the dissociation which Marshall, Norman Thomas, Jack Childs,[2] Lovejoy, I, and numerous others who hold this position have made from those who believe in suppressing dissent. Long before you decided to add your voice of opposition to McCarthyism, the individuals whom you maligned had sounded the alarm in numerous articles and speeches.

Your attack on me as someone who wished to introduce loyalty oaths when all I said was "that faculties should adopt a statement equivalent to the Hippocratic oath of the medical profession—and I don't mean anything like loyalty oaths"—is the retort of a demagogue, not of a man who wished to engage in a dialogue to clarify ideas. This is all the truer because you went on to restate in a paraphrase of my own words what such a dedication to honest scholarship and teaching would involve. (To make clear what I meant I read from the foreword of the New School catalogue.)

To cap the climax you tore a passion to tatters, berating James Marshall for saying that faculties should "police" themselves—"To think," you said in your concluding discussion, "that educators would corrupt the educational process by calling on universities *to police* (your voice emphasis) themselves!" This is an unexampled piece of gall because you used the identical expression in your own prepared text. I quote from *your* speech: "In the final analysis, universities, faculties, and academic societies must police themselves—never compromising the rigorous standards of first-class performance."

This position is no different from Marshall's and my own—although I carefully refrained from using the verb "police." Yet you sought to score on Marshall simply because he employed in passing the word "police" in the discussion.

You have every right to hold that Communists (members of the Communist Party) are entitled to teach on the same terms as "Keynesians or Freudians or Deweyites." While I criticized your preposterous equation between party liners and free inquirers, I commended your courage in publicly disagreeing with the former President and the Trustees of Columbia University. But there is such a thing as the ethics of intellectual inquiry which gives no man a right deliberately to distort and misrepresent the position of those who disagree with him. Your discussion before the final summing up, to which I had no chance to reply, violated the basic presuppositions of honest inquiry.

You may continue to believe that the present concern about members of the Communist Party on campuses—a concern which I have criticized as exaggerated—is a result of the thinking of scholars who have adopted the position of the New School on the issue.[3] But any informed person knows that the Rapp-Coudert Committee[4] appeared on the scene not because of the thinking of these scholars but because of the *activities* of the Communists in the City Colleges; and that the Senate Committee began its investigations after the *activities* of Hiskey,[5] Weltfish,[6] and their fellow Communists became a matter of public record. A position like yours which, for all your talk about self-policing, refuses to implement the "standards of first-class performance" and intellectual integrity against members of the Communist Party will not keep investigating committees away. Indeed, it is only too likely to invite them. But whatever its practical consequences in this respect, it has no bearing on my argument which centered exclusively on the question of *professional ethics*—an argument you pointedly ignored. In your prepared text you quote with approval President Conant's[7] position opposing governmental investigations of colleges—a view shared by *all* the panelists. Intellectual honesty, however, would have required a person interested in the relevant truth to mention at this point that President Conant does not believe that any known member of the Communist Party should be permitted to teach. He took this position as a member of the Educational Policies Commission of the National Education Association! (*American Education and Internal Tensions,* June, 1949, p. 39)

1. Louis Hacker, professor of history, Columbia University.
2. Jack Childs, professor of education, Teachers College, Columbia University.
3. The faculty of the New School of Social Research in New York City adopted the following credo:

> The New School knows that no man can teach well, nor should he be permitted to teach at all, unless he is prepared "to follow the truth of scholarship wherever it may lead." No inquiry is ever made as to whether a lecturer's private views are conservative, liberal or radical; orthodox or agnostic; views of the aristocrat or commoner. Jealously safeguarding this precious principle, the New School strictly affirms that a member of any political party or group which asserts the right to dictate in matters of science or scientific opinion is not free to teach the truth and thereby is disqualified as a teacher.

4. A special committee of the New York state legislature which in 1941 investigated subversives teaching in New York City's public colleges. It was named for Assemblyman Herbert Rapp and Senator Frederic R. Coudert. The committee's investigation resulted in the largest purge of professors in American history until the McCarthy era of 1953–54.

5. Clarence Hiskey, professor of chemistry, Brooklyn Polytechnic Institute.

6. Gene Weltfish, professor of anthropology, Columbia University. In 1953 Columbia did not renew the contract of Weltfish, an ardent feminist and radical who had accused the United States of conducting germ warfare in the Korean War.

7. James B. Conant, president, Harvard University.

117

Dear Arthur,[1]   March 18, 1953

Many thanks for your letter of March 11th which I found when I got back from Washington. I am beginning to despair of getting what I say *understood* without personal discussion. For your comments seem to assume that I support the general rule of "Automatic exclusion on the grounds of party membership alone." But I specifically dissociated myself from this position (see top of p. 4 second column in *New Leader* of 3/9/53 where I take issue with Eisenhower's formulation),[2] and *have always done so*. All I have ever argued for is that this membership constitutes *prima facie* evidence with action to be taken by the faculty committee after investigation of the specific *situation*.

This investigation, however, is not to be into classroom practices for reasons I gave at great length and which I believe are sound. The "crass cases" I referred to were cases which involved activity of some kind on or off the campus relevant to professional fitness, e.g. circulation of leaflets, cooperating with the C.P. to exploit a position at the university to disseminate lies about the U.S. using bacteriological warfare (Weltfish), etc. The faculty committee would consider the *total picture* before recommending action one way or another. On my view *if* Furry[3] did not lie to a faculty committee and admitted he was a member of the C.P., all of the things you mention about him would be relevant to determining what should be done. Personally, I would weigh the fact that he is in the physics department as more important than you: but even here if he were kept out of certain physics laboratories he *might* be retained. But whether retained or not, his membership in the C.P. *because of the nature of that organization and its educational directives* is an unprofessional commitment which leaves, so to speak, the burden of proof on him that he is not carrying out his C.P. assignments.

I am rather puzzled why you don't regard this last as very significant. Lovejoy, the first secretary of the AAUP and one who ought to know, tells me that when the AAUP was organized no one would have dreamed that cooperation with a group like the C.P. with its political and *educational* objectives was covered by the principles of academic freedom. And membership in the C.P. is cooperation. I am not arguing that membership is *ipso facto* an infallible sign of obedience to the C.P. on *everything*, but a highly reliable sign, especially today, of professional unfitness to be a member of the academic community, at least as much as demonstrated *willingness* to accept instructions from the N.A.M. to take advantage of the classroom to indoctrinate according to directives received from its public relations director, etc.

Perhaps the main issue between us is the probable consequence of adopting your formulation or mine.[4] I have just come back from Washington. I am convinced on the evidence I have that the adoption of the New School formula will lead to the elimination of public and Congressional interest in the matter, and that the whole subject will become *passe*. On your formulation, an attempt will be made to discover from *activities* who are Communists—and *that means an unending hunt for them.* On my formulation you do nothing until a person has been identified or proved a present member of the Communist Party on *other* grounds. This for many obvious reasons is going to become increasingly more difficult. The committees are running out of cases. The faculties don't have to look for them. They are in an unimpeachable position of saying: When you show us a member of the C.P. (or Klan, etc.) we will judge the entire situation in accordance with our general (New School) rule. Isn't this Conant's position, too? Last summer he said he agreed with me.

I had a half hour's discussion with Taft[5] on the subject. He is in McCarthy's camp, and I am very much surprised that Dick[6] gave him a plug in the *New Yorker* and, since you know Washington so much better than I, that you wanted the Committee[7] to quote him. It would have killed us. That remark, by the way, was in the context of Taft's *defense* of Congressional inquiries. He told me that originally he led a movement to fire Emerson[8] (on what seemed to me completely unjustifiable grounds). He lost the fight, and I gather he was looking for a formulation that would prove he wasn't too reactionary. He knows nothing about the details of C.P. organization, instructions to teachers, etc. Ickes was right when he said that "Taft has a very good mind until he makes it up." I know that even if Taft agreed with me on this one point about *prima facie* unfitness, I wouldn't quote him because of his outright support of McCarthy. No matter what he says, he is all the way over on the other side.

I hope you don't think me naive when I say I still believe we can reach an agreement on an intelligent and liberal formulation of the issue.

1. Arthur M. Schlesinger, Jr.
2. Hook, "Indoctrination and Academic Freedom," *New Leader,* 36 (March 9, 1953): 2–4. Eisenhower declared that no known Communist should be allowed to teach and that it was the responsibility of the university president and trustees to assure this. For Eisenhower's position, see the *New York Times,* January 17, 1953.
3. Wendell Furry, professor of physics, Harvard University. Furry, a Communist fellow traveler, refused to tell the House Committee on Un-American Activities whether he was a Communist Party member.
4. Schlesinger proposed making performance and not belief the determinant as to whether Communists should be allowed to teach. He opposed having the American Committee for Cultural Freedom support the automatic exclusion of Communists from teaching solely on the grounds of party membership.
5. Senator Robert A. Taft, Republican from Ohio.
6. Richard Rovere.
7. American Committee for Cultural Freedom.
8. Thomas I. Emerson, professor of law, Yale University Law School. There is no evidence that Emerson was a member of the Communist Party.

118

Editor, New School *Bulletin,*   May 26, 1953

In his letter to the *New York Times* (partially reprinted in the New School *Bulletin* of May 25), Mr. Ralph B. Perry fails to do justice to the moral and educational implications of the invocation of the Fifth Amendment by teachers and scholars when questions are asked bearing on their professional fitness to serve in an academic community. The academic community, of course, should be the sole judge of the qualifications of its members. But under certain circumstances an individual's qualifications may be seriously impugned even when he exercises a constitutional right. Under the protection of the First Amendment a man may plagiarize from some writing in the public domain with complete legal immunity. But he thereby gravely compromises his position as an honest scholar. The legal question is here completely irrelevant.

Much discussion has overlooked the significance of the observation of Professors Chafee and Sutherland[1] that: "A privileged refusal to testify is not an admission of guilt *for the purposes of criminal prosecution.*" (my italics) Mr. Perry forgets that our proper concern as educators is not whether an individual is legally guilty for purposes of criminal prosecution. We are not lawyers, judges, or prosecuting attorneys. Our concern is only with the question of educational integrity and professional qualifications insofar as they are affected by refusal on the ground of self-incrimination to answer inquiries bearing on vocational fitness and trust. To this question Mr. Perry pays altogether insufficient attention although it is of the very essence.

The sole *educational* issue, therefore, posed by the invocation of the Fifth Amendment by a member of the academic community bound by the obligations of honest inquiry and teaching, is whether such invocation ever carries with it implications bearing on the moral and professional fitness of an individual to *continue* as a member of the community.

An illustration will make the point clearer. Suppose a teacher is asked whether he accepted money from a corporation "to cook" his scientific experiments, and he invokes the privileges of the Fifth Amendment. Legally he may be completely justified, whether he is criminally guilty or not. But morally and professionally, his refusal to answer the question, which affects the whole rationale of the scientific and scholarly enterprise, is highly culpable because he has struck a blow at the very foundations of the academic community and undermined public trust and confidence in the integrity of his institution. Although legally in the clear, his refusal to answer is morally damaging not only to himself but to his colleagues.

For as President Dickey[2] of Dartmouth has argued in the case of teachers who refuse to answer a question about membership in the Communist Party on the grounds of the Fifth Amendment, such a man "either genuinely believes his words may incriminate him or he is using the privilege improperly. On the first assumption he, by his own action, avows the existence of what can reasonably be regarded as disqualification for service in a position of respect and responsibility; on the other hand, if he has invoked the privilege without truly believing that he needed its protection, he has acted falsely toward his government. Either way you take it, it seems to me we must say as a matter of general policy that such a person has compromised his fitness to perform the responsibilities of higher education, and unless there is clear evidence of peculiar circumstances in the particular instances which would make application of this policy unjust and unwise, the normal consequences of such disability must ensue."

It is precisely these considerations, ignored by Mr. Perry, which are in the forefront of public concern today as a consequence of teachers refusing to answer questions about their membership in the Communist Party—an organization which explicitly instructs its members to violate basic tenets in the moral and professional code of the honest scholar and teacher. Mr. Perry is altogether too cavalier about the character of the Communist Party as well as about the demoralization which would ensue if faculties sought to supervise members of the Communist Party to see whether they were carrying out their dishonorable tasks.

It is not necessary to rehearse here all the evidence which establishes the conclusion that membership in the Communist Party is incompatible with the fulfillment of the scholar's and teacher's proper function. At the very least, such membership establishes a *prima facie* presumption of unfitness to remain in the academic community. And if this is so, a question designed to elicit a truthful answer about such membership is preeminently relevant to our concern as educators, although it would be preferable if *educators* made such inquiries.

The grounds usually offered for the notion that an individual who is not a member of the Communist Party and truthfully answers that he is not, may still incriminate himself by his truthful testimony, are altogether untenable. It is sometimes said that such an individual refuses to answer because if he answered truthfully he might subsequently be "framed" by perjured testimony. The palpable absurdity of this claim is apparent from the fact that it could be used as a grounds to refuse an answer to any question whatsoever. Even if the wild possibility of subsequent indictment for perjury existed— and the evidence shows that it is members of the Communist Party who are under party instructions to commit perjury and not those who testify against them—it would be illegal to invoke the Fifth Amendment as a protection against that possibility. For in such a case it would be *other* persons' words which would incriminate oneself, not one's words.

A second reason given for the refusal to answer truthfully a question about membership in the Communist Party on grounds of the Fifth Amendment is that if a person admits his membership he will be questioned about the membership of others. But it is patent that if an individual refuses to answer a question because he does want to incriminate others, he cannot justify himself by invoking the Fifth Amendment. For he is not incriminating *himself* by his own words but others. And, in fact, it is illegal to invoke the Fifth Amendment on this ground. As Professors Chafee and Sutherland put it: "A sense of sportsmanship toward suspected associates is not an excuse. The Fifth Amendment grants no privilege to protect one's friends. If a man feels that he has a personal code compelling this reticence, he must pay for his scruple by standing the punishment society prescribes."

It should be noted carefully that all this in no way prevents any individual from following the dictates of his conscience and protesting against what he believes is a violation of his moral and legal rights by any Congressional committee. He may refuse to answer a question bearing on his educational fitness without prejudice to himself, his colleagues, and his institution, so long as he does not *invoke the Fifth Amendment*. In that case, he is in the position of a heretic, and it is up to the courts to determine whether he is legally justified or not, or whether he should be punished or not. An individual whose *conscience* commands him to defy a legislative committee and who refuses to answer its questions may be an honorable man, innocent of any wrong doing, and free of presumption of educational unfitness. But refusal on the grounds that one's own words will incriminate oneself, although legal, is not ethical from the point of view of professional morals. Such procedure is presumptive evidence that a man is an educational conspirator, not an honest, educational heretic, and constitutes a valid ground for further investigation.

I conclude by calling attention to the gravity of the issue. The life of the mind depends for its continuous functioning upon candor, openness, and the disclosure of relevant information, in the process by which truth of fact and wisdom of policy are reached. By deliberately withholding the truth on a matter which affects the very pride and honor of our vocation as scholars and teachers—particularly when other avenues of protest are open to men of honest conscience—those who invoke the Fifth Amendment are destroying academic freedom in a free society, not defending it.

1. Zechariah Chafee, Jr., and Arthur E. Sutherland, professors of law, Harvard University Law School.
2. John S. Dickey.

119

To the Editor of *Freedom and Union,*   June 8, 1953

I have read all sorts of weird things in my day but the following sentence in Mr. David C. Williams' review of Viereck's[1] *The Shame and Glory of the Intellectuals* in *Freedom and Union* for May, 1953 deserves a booby prize:

> Indeed, even for the minority of intellectuals who joined the Communist Party, and the tiny minority who, like Alger Hiss, engaged in espionage for the Soviet Union, the weakness of Western leadership must bear a large share of the blame.

The weakness was the failure to challenge Hitler early in his career, e.g., when he marched into the Rhineland.

(1) There is not the slightest empirical evidence that the intellectuals who joined the Communist Party were influenced by the failure of Western

statesmen to use a show of force against Hitler. On the contrary, up to and even after the very time Hitler marched into the Rhineland in contravention of the Treaty of Versailles the Communist intellectuals, like the rest of the Communist movement, were denouncing *both* Hitler and Western statesmen as war-mongers. The League Against War and Fascism organized by the Communist Party took the lead in this campaign. Hiss joined the Communist Party at the close of the Third Period when the Communists were still denouncing Roosevelt in this country and Social-Democrats abroad as Social-Fascists. It was only after Spain and the Popular Front had been established that the Communists demanded a strong hand against Hitler, and even then they were careful to say that they did not wish any war-like actions to be taken. The only two public figures who called for military action by the West against Hitler when he marched into the Rhineland were Pilsudski[2] and Trotsky, both of whom were violently denounced by the Communists.

(2) Not only did the conservative Western leadership in Europe fail to move actively against Hitler, but honesty demands that we acknowledge that the Socialist movement in Europe and this country was also opposed to such action. The English Labor Party was shot through and through with pacifism until Munich and even later. George Lansbury's extreme pacifism was held by few, but by and large the Labor Party was very far from urging actions that could be regarded as determined moves against Hitler. In this country, the Socialist Party and even many liberals opposed sanctions against Mussolini when he invaded Abyssinia for fear that such action would bring war. The dogma of the Left at that time was that a war against Hitler would either destroy the world or result in domestic Fascism.

(3) The falsity of the statement that intellectuals joined the Communist Party because Western leadership did not oppose Hitler is apparent from the fact that most of them clung to the Communist Party—especially the spies—even after the Hitler-Nazi pact. This disproves the allegations of some of them that Hitler's anti-Semitism drove them into the arms of the Communist Party.

(4) It was the mythology of the Soviet Union which attracted the intellectuals, not the failure of Western foreign policy. For these intellectuals were not at all repelled by the gyrations of the Communist parties which stood on their head at the command of Stalin who had been playing Hitler and the West against each other since 1932. For a time even after Hitler came to power the Communist Party of the Saar through the mouth of its leader, Niebergall, proclaimed: "And even if we Communists stand under the gallows—our program was, is, and remains: 'Back to the German Fatherland.'" The Communist Party of the Saar was under direct control of the Com-

intern. Why didn't this attitude repel the intellectuals from the Communist Party?

(5) But most fantastic of all is the implication that even the Communist spies and espionage agents are to be explained by the weaknesses of Western leadership. Were there no Soviet spies when Western leadership was stronger? As a matter of fact, it was when Western leadership under Churchill and Roosevelt was strongest in the fight against Hitler that Communist espionage was most extensive and most infamous. And how does Mr. Williams explain the large number of intellectuals who, dissatisfied with Western leadership, did *not* join the Communist Party or become Communist espionage agents?

Mr. Williams doesn't seem to understand that basic Soviet policy towards the West remains unaffected by the changes in strategy and tactics it develops. Those intellectuals who in the thirties joined the Communist Party may have been influenced by the fear of Hitler, but most of them rejected democracy in principle as unable to preserve peace and prosperity. If Western leadership indirectly contributed to the rise of Fascism, how much more so did Bolshevik leadership which boasted of its role in the political murder of the democratic Weimar Republic.

Mr. Viereck's metaphysics may be jejune and his defense of conservatism, new or old, a defense of a lost cause. But as an historian of Nazi-Soviet relations and the betrayal of the intellectuals who flocked to the Communist Party after Hitler and Stalin destroyed German Social-Democracy, his analysis is in the main sound and completely free from Mr. Williams' fantasies.

Political wisdom depends upon the ability and willingness to acknowledge errors when they are made. This holds for liberals as well as for others.

1. Peter Viereck, professor of history, Mount Holyoke College.
2. Josef Pilsudski, Polish minister of defense during the 1930s.

120

Dear Dr. Lynch,[1]   February 17, 1954

Thank you for your kind letter and the copy of *Thought* containing Professor Donahue's discussion of my book.[2] Considering how fundamental are our differences, his criticisms are on the whole temperate, more temperate than any other criticisms of my views I have ever read coming from a Catholic source.

But I do find it ironical that my attempt to show that Catholic teachers in secular schools do not operate like Communist Party teachers should, because of a few phrases, be taken as evidence of egregious blunder and misunderstanding of Catholic doctrine and practice on my part.

I say ironical because up and down the country liberal audiences have been throwing into my teeth the charge that Catholic teachers are like Communists. Denial that this is so often provokes opprobrious epithets and denunciations of me as a "Catholic lover" and as someone who is "compromising" with clerical reaction. Why only last Christmas at the meeting of the American Philosophical Society at Rochester the audience burst into frenzied applause at the charge of one of my critics, in the course of a discussion on academic freedom, that teachers who are Catholics are just as much conspirators as teachers of the Communist Party.

I have been expecting some Catholic thinker to answer that charge at much greater length and with much more authority than I have done. So far, however, nothing has been published which I have seen. Such an article should be published soon in view of the widespread belief that Catholic and Communist Party teachers are equally suspect.

And now Professor Donahue charges me with bad scholarship and gross misunderstanding for saying that (a) in Catholic colleges academic freedom does not exist in the sense in which I believe it does and should exist in secular institutions, and (b) that in the event Catholics become a majority in the community, education would in all likelihood lose its secular character. (In this last case if it did so, there is good theological warrant for excluding from the school system heretics whose ideas were critical of religious dogmas.)

(a) What I meant by saying that academic freedom does not exist in Catholic colleges was a very simple thing. I was not talking about attempts to proselytize students or refusal to permit free circulation of books on the Index. All I meant here is that there was no academic freedom for a teacher to profess views which were critical of Catholic dogma, just as, *mutatis mutandis,* there is no academic freedom for a teacher in a Hebrew yeshiva to criticize certain Jewish religious dogmas. If I am mistaken about this then I am prepared to publicly proclaim and recant my ignorance. Is a professor at Fordham permitted after honest inquiry to challenge the validity of the argument for the existence of God, or the argument for the immortality of the soul, or the doctrine of papal infallibility or any other fundamental proposition in natural or sacred theology? Can he teach according to the light of his natural reason that Catholicism is a false religion?

In secular colleges, academic freedom would require that a professor, once certified as competent, be permitted to reach any conclusion on such subjects, if these questions arose relevantly in the course of his pursuit of the truth in courses in philosophy and allied disciplines. Maritain[3] would enjoy academic freedom at Columbia. John Dewey and William James would not at Fordham.

(b) What I meant by saying that if the Catholics constituted a majority of the population they would abolish secular education is clear, even if undeveloped. I meant to say that in the light of the papal encyclical *Libertas* of Leo XIII, Catholics have theological justification in their own eyes for proscribing any beliefs in religion or philosophy which seem to them incompatible with revealed truth. They might suffer the propagation of religious views different from their own on prudential grounds, but as Ryan and Millar[4] make clear they do not in principle believe in tolerating propagation or teaching of false views on matters of faith and morals. (I have discussed these questions in my critique of Maritain in my book *Reason, Social Myths and Democracy* (1940) and in my article "The New Failure of Nerve" in *Partisan Review*, January–February, 1943.)

Professor Donahue will probably disagree with my views on education even if he understands them better. But I do not identify scientific method with the method of the laboratory. I specifically repudiate this view. I take scientific method very broadly as empirical method of which laboratory techniques are only one species. Further, I do *not* exclude the study of religion as part of cultural tradition from the subject matter of study in secular schools. I discuss this and similar questions at length in my *Education for Modern Man* (1946) which contains, among other things, a critique of the neo-Thomistic philosophy of education. If Professor Donahue wanted to discuss my educational philosophy, that is the place to find it. I would be grateful to him for criticizing it in its developed form and not on the basis of snippets from my last book. When he criticizes it I am confident he will not be able to attribute to me the view that "a secular education is presumably one where all serious consideration of religious thinking is omitted." Since I believe that philosophy should be a *required* course of study for all students and since no course in philosophy is adequate which does not seriously consider the argument for the existence of God, freedom, immortality, as well as the rivals, substitutes, and alternatives to scientific, empirical methods of reaching truth (authority, intuition, revelation), the precise opposite of what he attributes to me is the case.

This letter is not for publication, but I shall be glad if you will send it to Professor Donahue.

1. The Reverend William F. Lynch, editor, *Thought*, a Thomist journal published by Fordham University.
2. Charles Donahue reviewed Sidney Hook, *Heresy, Yes—Conspiracy, No!*, in *Thought* 28 (Winter 1953–54): 528–46.
3. Jacques Maritain, French Thomist philosopher.

4. Monsignor John A. Ryan and Father Moorhouse F. X. Millar, *The State and the Church* (New York, 1922).

121

Dear Mrs. Eager,[1]   May 17, 1954

This will acknowledge your letter of May 8th. I have no use for Senator McCarthy and believe he has pretty thoroughly discredited himself in the public eye. But I do not believe that this constituted a vindication of the way Senator Tydings[2] conducted the "Tydings Committee Hearings." I have read the record of the hearings and also of the McCarran Committee hearings on the Institute of Pacific Relations and Lattimore. On the strength of them I am convinced that Senator Tydings not only lost an opportunity to take the ball away from McCarthy by conducting a sober investigation into Communist infiltration into the Department of State and other agencies allegedly infected, but that his failure to do so contributed to building up McCarthy. The function of the Tydings Committee was not merely to examine McCarthy's exaggerated charges, but to establish the truth with respect to the existence or non-existence of loyalty and security risks *past* and present. Senator Tydings' report was justifiably interpreted as a partisan whitewash by anyone familiar with the history of the Communist movement in this country. It is a great pity all the more so because he created a mood of distrust in the country which McCarthy demagogically exploited. His responsibility is very heavy, indeed, and is not affected by the fact that he was the victim of an unscrupulous campaign.

1. Kathryn Eager, Chevy Chase, Maryland.
2. Senator Millard Tydings, Democrat of Maryland, a critic of Senator Joseph McCarthy.

122

Dear Milton,[1]   May 17, 1954

Thank you for the carbon of your letters to Sol Stein.[2]

1) The policy of the A.C.C.F. as I understand it is to act openly, but on some occasions it has to act discreetly—like the Anti-Defamation League. We do not dispute the right of Communist front groups to hold meetings, etc., but we believe that in the public interest deception should be exposed.

Our objection to an organization like the National Lawyers Guild is not that it appears on the Attorney General's list—personally I have criticized the way this list was drawn up—but that as Adolf Berle[3] put it when he resigned, "it is not prepared to take any stand which conflicts with the Communist Party line," and that this is due to the fact that it is under the control of individuals who have consistently followed the C.P. line. Felix Cohen[4] is my authority for saying that soon after it was organized it was taken over lock, stock and barrel by C.P. partisans. I believe we ought to apprise that person of the public evidence (like Berle's statement) so that he knows what he is doing. Sometimes we take a *public* stand when many individuals are involved. But where only one or two persons are concerned, it is not feasible to issue statements. I do not see any conspiracy involved in Thomas[5] writing to a speaker. After all the speaker normally would and could have informed the organization from which he was withdrawing of the source of his information. He was not asked to hold any communication confidential. Some of our own members often write to us for guidance. Suppose you had consented to speak under the auspices of an organization not knowing who they were. Would you feel it was inappropriate if a letter apprising you of the facts were sent to you? If the facts were accurate, wouldn't you be glad to get them? Where's the conspiracy?

2) In the next number of *Confluence* I have an article on "Security and Freedom"[6] which I believe will answer your question.[7] Twenty-five thousand people—not to speak of the close periphery of the C.P.—constitute not an immediate political danger but a *security* problem. There are far graver problems than security, but until that problem is met the far greater ones will not be met. In France and Italy the C.P. is not only a security problem but a clear and present political danger. Most government services are infilterable, according to my advices, from top to bottom. They can't solve the problem short of open civil war. They can only live with the problem so long as *we* survive as a free and strong nation. That is why our security problem is one that affects the whole world. Part of that security problem is not only *prevention* of espionage and subversion, but protection of the innocent from bureaucratic idiots who are self-righteous about their idiocy because ritualistic liberals deny that there is or ever was a security problem. To my way of thinking, Truman had considerable responsibility for producing the climate of opinion which McCarthy so demagogically exploited. But more in my article.

1. Milton Konvitz, professor of industrial and labor relations, Cornell University.
2. Executive secretary of the American Congress for Cultural Freedom.
3. Professor of law, Columbia University Law School. He served as assistant secretary of state from 1938 to 1944 and as American ambassador to Brazil, 1945–46.

4. Son of Morris Raphael Cohen, Hook's teacher at the City University of New York.

5. Norman Thomas. Hook was commenting on the fact that Thomas had informed a person about the pro-communist sympathies of an organization that was sponsoring a meeting at which he was scheduled to speak.

6. "Security and Freedom," *Confluence* 3 (June 1954): 155–71.

7. Konvitz's question concerned whether American Communists constituted a security or political threat, or both.

123

Dear Mr. Washburn,[1]   March 10, 1955

Thank you for your letter of March 8th. As you can imagine, my mail is very heavy, but I find certain things in it which move me to take time from pressing chores to reply to you at some length. I do so all the more because your letter is a paradigm of the almost willful blindness of ritualistic liberals who substitute slogans for analysis and thereby play into the hands of cultural vigilantes like McCarthy. The spectacle has made me heartsick for years.

To begin with, take your comment on my statement that first evils come first and that communist fanaticism is a greater evil than clerical fanaticism. It is clear that I regard clerical fanaticism as an evil and have written extensively about it. But all I am saying is that *today the most urgent threat* to your freedom and mine and the freedom of all mankind comes from the Kremlin, not the Vatican. After all, the Pope hasn't got any atomic bombs—neither has Franco or Tito, tyrants both. But the Kremlin has! "Were the Inquisition still flourishing . . ." you say. Yet it is not the Inquisition which is flourishing today but a murderous machine infinitely worse. How can you then equate the excesses of the Catholic Legion of Decency in California or Massachusetts or Catholic refusal to permit open Protestant worship—actions which should be severely criticized—with purge trials, concentration camps, organized liquidation? It is like equating a headache with a deadly cancer.

At the same time there is an intellectual insincerity in the argument. In 1941 when Hitler threatened the world, I urged, because first evils come first, that even Stalin be helped to withstand the Nazi scourge. At that time clerical fanaticism was even more virulent than it is today. But did you and those who think like you maintain during those years that the Church was almost as great a threat to freedom as Hitler? Did you protest then against the statement that Nazism was the greater evil?

The only charitable hypothesis for the lapse of logic and ethics in a position like yours is that you really do not know very much about Communism. Every line of your letter indicates it. "As between a reactionary dictatorship (like Rhee's[2] or Chiang's) and a Communist one," you write, "the bulk of the common people will choose the latter every time."

How do you know this? Can you cite any evidence whatsoever that in a *free* election the masses of Asia have anywhere chosen a Communist dictatorship? The only evidence we have contradicts your easy assertion. The vast majority of the Communist and North Korean prisoners *refused* repatriation. How do you explain this? How do you explain the movements of millions in Korea and Indochina *from* Communist territory to the territory held by "reactionaries?"

As bad as Chiang Kai-shek and Rhee are, they permitted more opposition than the Communist regime. They oppressed their inhabitants less, and allowed some opportunity for the criticism which could eliminate abuses. Formosa is far freer than the mainland. An opposition press to Rhee exists, and Rhee's party suffered defeat in the last election. To equate the role of Chiang and Rhee with the total terror of the Communist regime is like saying that there is little difference between a corrupt Tammany machine, which can be turned out, and a Fascist dictatorship. Would anyone with common sense draw such an equation?

You say you "never approved of our involvement in Korea." Presumably you *do* approve of the U.N., and you *did* disapprove of the failure of the League of Nations which invited Fascist aggression by not acting against it when it first manifested itself. Why the difference?

I am not at all impressed with your aside "Of course, Communism is a hideous menace to freedom"—for despite this menace, you find the Chinese intervention into Korea quite justifiable. Your comparison with how *we* would behave if a Communist army in Mexico marched towards our borders is patently preposterous. A Communist army marching towards our borders is, to use your own words, a hideous menace to freedom. A U.N. army fighting a military action to repel aggression marching in Korean territory toward Chinese borders is *not* a menace to freedom but a defense of it. One might have second thoughts about the wisdom of crossing the 38th parallel on strategic grounds—as Churchill did—but the grounds *you* gave are morally and politically indefensible. They are not the grounds of one who *seriously* believes that Communism is a hideous menace.

If I can shock you into rethinking your assumptions I shall not begrudge the time spent writing this letter. I am as insistent as anyone, as my writings will show, upon our basic freedoms, but believe that without the use of *intelligence* in thinking about problems those freedoms will be lost.

One minor point. It is not I who believes that the question of means can be left to a calculating machine. What I said was that if we cannot be reasonable about ends, as Russell[3] believes, then the question of means becomes only a technical question—which could be entrusted to a machine. I cited this as a *reductio ad absurdum* of the view I was criticizing.

1. Richard K. Washburn, Springfield, Massachusetts.
2. Syngman Rhee, dictator of South Korea.
3. Bertrand Russell.

124

Dear Professor Hastings,[1]   March 2, 1956

In conjunction with an analysis I am making of attitudes towards Communists and ex-Communists in the academic community, I am taking the liberty of writing you for clarification of some points in your interesting article in the *Key Reporter* of September, 1955.

Of the ex-Communists Chambers, Bentley, Budenz, etc., you write: "I do not question their sincerity, though they make me shudder." Nowhere is there an indication in your article that those who are still Communists affect you in the same way. This is not an unusual reaction, but I am a little puzzled by it since I naively assume that a Communist who has recognized that the Kremlin has betrayed the humanitarian ideas which originally led him to Communism should not be treated as a leper but only as an erring human being. And this not only out of charity but because it encourages other members of the Communist Party, torn by doubt and fearful that they will become the objects of shuddering aversion, to break with a conspiratorial movement controlled by the Soviet Union, and implacably hostile to all our institutions.

Humanity as well as intelligence points to the wisdom of making it possible for ex-Communists to rehabilitate themselves. The ethics of testifying against others must be judged case by case, and each individual must make such decisions for himself. Can we make wholesale judgments here? Once under subpoena a former Communist who has told the truth about himself cannot remain silent about others without risking a jail sentence. Would you have him remain silent if what he testified to has a bearing on the national security? Would your attitude be the same where racketeers, kidnappers, and narcotic addicts are involved? Is refusal to testify against others, refusal "to inform," no matter what their offense, always sound ethics, not to speak of citizenship? I wonder whether you have read Mr. Chambers' book *Witness* or Professor Almond's[2] *The Appeals of Communism* (Princeton University Press) which studies the complex of motives which lead to Communism and away from it.

And one final question in this, I fear, an already overlong and burdensome letter. You say, "If one's order of values is different from that of the society of which he is a member, he must take the consequences, but in the long view his integrity will not be in question." Quite right, if one is a heretic! But I am baffled to see how this applies to the conspirator who works by stealth outside the rules of the game, mislabelling the wares he offers in the market of free ideas, shirking the consequences of his *other* loyalties, but professing belief in democracy in order to destroy it by subversion, espionage, or sabotage. Where is the integrity? But perhaps you do not believe that the Communist movement today is a conspiratorial movement? That would explain some things that puzzle me.

At any rate, since I shall probably make reference to your interesting article, my observations are much more likely to be relevant if I have the benefit of your clarifications of the points I find troubling.

1. William T. Hastings, professor emeritus of English, Brown University.
2. Gabriel A. Almond, professor of international affairs, Princeton University.

125

Dear Dean Griswold,[1]   April 2, 1956

Thank you for your long and interesting letter of March 24th.[2] Please excuse my delay in replying since your letter arrived during our Easter vacation. I should like to begin by answering the question with which you conclude. "Will we not progress most soundly," you ask, "if persons who share these ultimate interests (in freedom) work together in a spirit of cooperation and mutual respect?" My answer is: most assuredly. I should be very happy to cooperate with you or Mr. Hutchins[3] or The Fund for the Republic in any joint enterprise bearing on the defense or study of civil rights. From the beginning I have sought to cooperate with the Fund. I met several times with Mr. Clifford Case[4] and we got along famously. He was kind enough to say that the position I took in my book on heresy and conspiracy was his too. I also met your colleague Professor Sutherland and found him very congenial. I was quite impressed with the sensible views he took on the matters we discussed and his dry sense of humor. I would have been very happy, indeed, to have continued the association in a voluntary capacity, but when Mr. Hutchins took over, all these relationships withered. When I saw that Mr. Hutchins' public pronouncements were prejudicing the position of the Fund not merely in the eyes of "conservatives" and "reactionaries" but intelligent people who could not be labelled, I was very much distressed. Although I had reason to feel aggrieved by Mr. Hutchins' scoffing reference to me before he assumed the presidency of the Fund, I consented to meet him as one of a small committee of liberals connected with the American Committee for Cultural Freedom in order to see whether we could find a common basis of belief and a common formulation of our belief which would not provoke misunderstanding. Mr. Hutchins professed agreement with my position and admitted only that his rhetoric was misleading. When I saw that his speeches continued to be rhetorically misleading, I wrote my article, sat on it for some time hoping against hope that Mr. Hutchins would take his position seriously enough as the face of the Fund to the world to express himself more judiciously. Finally, I published it to prove that Mr. Hutchins' views were not representative of what I regard as intelligent liberalism.

You will forgive, I hope, the appearance of overconfidence in my judgment that Mr. Hutchins was not helping the cause of liberalism and freedom. After all, I have been active on this front ever since I was a boy, long before many who have just recently awakened to the issues.

Further I want to say that on reflection I believe some of your criticisms are well taken. The title of my piece was unfortunate, but the title was not mine (in the U.S. as distinct from England titles do not belong to authors but to editors and publishers). Second, the reference and reply to Mr. Hutchins' unfair criticism of me in *Look*[5] was out of place. It detracted from the force of the argument. Third, I should have had less of a wind-up and edited out some of the sentences which gave the article in places a somewhat personal tone. These are serious shortcomings and I shall try to avoid them in future writing.

On the other hand, there are several strictures in your letter which are unjustified. I am convinced that you are demonstrably unfair to the *New Leader* and its editor.[6] You seem to know only those issues of the *New Leader* in which the Fund or Mr. Hutchins has been criticized. You are not familiar with those issues in which the work of the Fund in some of its specific projects is applauded—including the current issue. More important, you seem to judge the *New Leader* only with reference to the Fund. But surely this is no way to judge whether a periodical is genuinely liberal or genuinely devoted to freedom. Pick any ten or twenty or hundred issues at random during the last thirty years of its publication. I predict that you will

find that of all weeklies it is and has been the most consistently liberal, democratic, opposed to *all* varieties of totalitarianism. There is not a blot on its
escutcheon. It was critical of the Soviet Union when the latter was being
glorified. It was never fellow travelerish or Stalinoid. It fought the Liberty
League, the America First Committee, and Senator McCarthy's exaggerations.
Its contributors read like an honor roll of militant American liberalism.

I can assure you of what your own investigations will confirm. There is
no pattern of unfairness in the *New Leader* towards anything, including
Hutchins and the Fund. The one-page review it published on the bibliography on communism was handled in routine fashion by a reviewer actually
employed on a Fund project who did *not* say that the bibliography "was the
product of pro-Communist bias."[7] His last sentence—I am relying on my
memory—made some reference to possible anti-anti-communism which
showed how ignorant the reviewer was of Professor Sutherland. The main
impression it gave was of poor workmanship. The editor did not read the
review, nor would he feel called upon to edit it if he had done so. The
reaction to it came as much as a surprise to him as to anyone. (Many
reviews are featured on the cover; this was not.)

The second item you mention is a piece by the drama critic on one of the
judges in the Robert Sherwood awards of the Fund. Drama critics usually
enjoy a certain *Narrenfreiheit*[8] which editors are loath to destroy. But this
time the dramatic critic was not a fool but was raising what seemed to me a
very pertinent point about the eligibility of one of the judges. Surely you
wouldn't invite a member or ardent supporter of the Ku Klux Klan to judge
what work of Negroes contributes to improved race relations. Why should
anyone who, to mention only one thing, supported the Communist Waldorf
meeting be asked to judge a work that enhances the value of freedom? I
know something about the Waldorf "Peace" Conference since I organized
the counter-meeting at Freedom House. Every sponsor of the Waldorf
meeting received a personally signed letter from me containing the evidence that the control and the program was rigged and in Communist
hands. In what did the element of smear consist?

No, I fear very much that you are doing an injustice to the *New Leader*
rather than vice versa. But I am confident that if you will read it for any
consecutive period you yourself will acknowledge the truth.

And now as for Jerome Davis. It is strange—the things that are not
known in Ohio and Cambridge! Jerome Davis defended the Moscow Trials
in a signed statement published in the *Daily Worker* of April 28, 1938. Nor
was this the only one. A similar statement circulated in order to break up
the Commission of Inquiry into the Moscow Trials headed by John Dewey
was signed by Davis and published in *Soviet Russia Today,* March, 1937. I

exchanged several letters with him. He remained adamant in his position even after the two volumes published by the Commission of Inquiry containing the evidence that the Moscow Trials were frame-ups as far as their chief defendants were involved. There is much more to be said about Mr. Davis; some of it concerns certain aspects of the Robinson-Rubens case.[9] But whatever Mr. Davis may believe *now,* my characterization of him was accurate.

I am a little puzzled that you should believe this is all irrelevant to my criticism of Hutchins. The point is simple. I was giving an illustration of a situation in which *moral* guilt by association could legitimately be inferred. Anyone writing a preface to Davis' book was writing a preface to a party-line position (as Roger Baldwin recognized) by a party-line apologist. If Hutchins had any more sense he wouldn't have done it.

I wish to conclude by discussing one of your chief points—namely the fear that my criticisms of Mr. Hutchins may be exploited for their own purposes by reactionaries and other enemies of freedom. I must confess that I find this not very impressive. For consider. Your own writings on the Fifth Amendment, Hutchins' speeches, and Commager's[10] articles have all been picked up and given a great play in the Communist press. Would it not be unfair to blame you for that? Have not you yourself inveighed strongly against those who make capital of the fact that Communists sometimes agree with positions taken by non-Communists?

Why, then, even if the true things I say are picked up by a Fulton Lewis[11] or others should I be reproached? Perhaps I will convince Fulton Lewis that liberalism is better for America than his brand of conservatism. (I have a much better chance of doing that than you or Hutchins have of ever convincing the Communists!) I find this double standard very bewildering. If you are not responsible for the Communist use of your writings, why am I responsible for conservative use (or abuse) of mine?

Personally my own feeling is that there is so much confusion abroad in the land and downright ignorance of elementary political fact that one should hew to the line of the truth come what may. Unfortunately I have found just as much conformism and prejudice among many people who call themselves "liberals" as among followers of McCarthy.

Well, this letter is now longer than your own. But I hope it gives you an insight into the thinking of liberals who have been in the fight against obscurantism and reaction for a long time. I realize that you yourself are not responsible for some of the peculiar things done by the Fund, like the inequitable distribution of literature and the special award for hiring a librarian who had invoked the Fifth Amendment. And I also know that some of the critics of the Fund have been unjust, particularly with relation to

Freedom Agenda (the bibliography of those pamphlets seems one-sided but otherwise they are quite good).

However, there are very real and difficult problems on which liberals can disagree with mutual respect. One of them is over the implication of the use of the Fifth Amendment. It is probably no secret to you that I do not share your views on the matter. I hope, however, to get the benefit of your critical reaction to my analysis of your position.

P.S. Since you indicated I might show your letter to Mr. Levitas I am doing so together with a copy of my reply.

1. Erwin N. Griswold, dean, Harvard University Law School.

2. Griswold's letter was in response to Hook's article "Six Fallacies of Robert Hutchins," *New Leader* 39 (March 19, 1956): 21–24.

3. Robert Maynard Hutchins, president, The Fund for the Republic.

4. Clifford P. Case, Hutchins's predecessor as president of The Fund for the Republic, 1953–54.

5. Robert M. Hutchins, "Are Our Teachers Afraid to Teach?" *Look* 18 (March 9, 1954), 27–29. In this article, Hutchins attacked Hook by name twice, accusing him and Whittaker Chambers of being part of a repressive environment that discouraged teachers from discussing controversial topics in class.

6. Sol Levitas.

7. See letter 128, note 2.

8. Freedom to be a fool or to be foolish.

9. A Kremlin agent and his wife using the pseudonyms "Robinson" and "Rubens" had been reported under arrest in Moscow as American spies. The Trotsky defense committee feared that these supposed agents would "confess" to having received instructions from Trotsky via John Dewey to assassinate Stalin.

10. Henry Steele Commager.

11. Fulton Lewis, Jr., right-wing radio commentator and supporter of Senator Joseph McCarthy.

126

Dear Professor Hastings,[1]   April 4, 1956

Thank you for the patience and courtesy with which you have conducted our correspondence. I have found it a very instructive exchange. I am saddened, however, by what it reveals. You have no hesitation in passing firm judgment on ex-Communists about whom you confess to have no reliable knowledge; but on Alger Hiss, an unrepentant Communist, a convicted perjurer who is guilty of treason (a guilt established by three *independent* witnesses and unimpeachable documentary evidence), you have kept a "suspended judgment." Is this not bizarre?

You say you "would enjoy a weekend with Owen Lattimore." No doubt.

But what I find puzzling is this. If any individual had publicly defended the Nazi Reichstag Fire Trial in which the Nazis sought to frame Communists, and had applauded such trials as demonstrations of democracy, I am confident that you would have qualms in spending a weekend with him. Now it so happens that Owen Lattimore has publicly defended the monstrous frame-ups and purges of the Moscow Trials even after the John Dewey Commission of Inquiry had published the conclusive evidence that they were staged. (The Kremlin is presently on the way to acknowledging its past infamy.) Lattimore hailed these Trials as demonstrations of democracy. Why does moral complicity in Communist infamy count less with you than moral complicity in Nazi infamy?

Most puzzling of all is your reference to Micah.[2] I would have imagined that to "love mercy" was incompatible with a shuddering revulsion towards ex-Communists or any other person who had made a mistake of which he repented, particularly where there is no apparent feeling against unrepentant Communists. I would have imagined that to "do justly" requires careful examination of the evidence on which justice is based.

You refer to yourself as a "do-gooder." I had assumed that you were a liberal in the sense of James, Holmes, and Dewey, committed to a faith in the liberating power of the quest for truth. But there is nothing wrong in being a "do-gooder." The only difficulty I see is this: how do you know you *are* doing good if you refuse to investigate the evidence on which moral judgment must rest, and if you apply a double standard to actions of the same moral quality?

But enough of questions. You have already answered them in advance.

1. William T. Hastings.
2. Old Testament prophet who stressed righteousness and justice.

127

Dear Lovejoy,[1]   April 10, 1956

Would you join me in a public letter of resignation from the AAUP on the grounds that its present position abandons the standards of professional ethics which guided the foundations of the Association? Perhaps we can get a few additional signers. The report of the Special Committee on Academic Freedom and National Security[2] seems to me to be confused from beginning to end.

1. Arthur O. Lovejoy.
2. Hook's letter to Henry Luce of April 17, 1954 (letter 130), explains this report.

128

Dear Dean Griswold,[1]   April 11, 1956

Your letter of April 6th stirs me to a few comments. I am heartened to discover the area of our agreement. Perhaps we can even enlarge it.

1. I was not trying to justify the editorial policy of the *New Leader*. I was trying to explain that the Sessions review of the Sutherland[2] bibliography was not an attack on the Fund as such. Personally, as fond as I am of Mr. Levitas, I agree that the *New Leader* is a very poorly edited magazine. This is due to the fact that it has a poorly qualified because poorly paid staff. They were genuinely surprised that Sessions' review stirred up the fuss it did. What you attribute to editorial irresponsibility was due to ignorance. No one on the staff—believe it or not!—knew about Professor Sutherland. At any rate there is no pattern of hostility to the Fund as such.

2. There is more to the Davis[3] story than I revealed. Nor can he be explained in terms of his opposition to Hitler. He defended the Nazi-Soviet Pact. Norman Thomas can fill in the particulars.

3. Of course *before* one writes one must take into account the possibility that what one publishes will be wrongly used. But once the necessity for publication arises, then the relevant question becomes one of truth. In times of plague one posts notices even in houses of ill fame. I am not saying that the necessity of exposing Hutchins was as acute or that the *New Leader* is a disreputable organ. I am saying that if my analysis is sound it cannot hurt the legitimate activities of the Fund.

4. I look forward to reading the issue of the *Marquette Law Review* with your article and your address before the University of New Mexico. I am very much disturbed by the *reasoning* in the Slochower[4] Case—a man who committed perjury in 1941—he should have been given a hearing. (I don't believe in automatic dismissals.) The difference between us is that you believe no inference whatsoever can be drawn from the invocation of the Fifth Amendment, whereas I believe that *unless there is countervailing evidence,* including evidence of misinformation, harassment, or bad legal advice, there is some *presumption,* although not conclusive, of guilt or unfitness depending upon the question asked. I believe that this can be "demonstrated," remembering that we are dealing not with questions of pure logic but of psychology—individual and social. Harvard is right in asserting that invocation of the Fifth involves misconduct warranting investigation. In your view—strictly taken—there is no presumption of misconduct. The invocation in and by itself does not even warrant investigation. I

hope I have not misunderstood you. My view is that the invocation of the Fifth is sufficient, so to speak, morally to indict (if the question bears upon the performance of duty) but not sufficient to convict. We must always give a man a chance to explain why he took it.

In none of your writing so far do you seem to realize that in the overwhelming number of cases of those who invoked the Fifth Amendment there was *independent* evidence of membership in the Communist Party—and in most of the cases evidence much more concrete than that the Committee was told by someone that the witness was a member. The evidence is often documentary. The documentary evidence *plus* the invocation of the Fifth strengthens the presumption.

I worked the argument out in some detail and regret only that I have not previously published my studies. It will now be necessary to rewrite with an eye on the Clark[5] opinion which to my way of looking at things represents a sad day both for the defense of American freedom as well as for principles of justice. I am not surprised by the concurrence of Douglas and Black or of Warren[6]—of whom I do not share your high opinion. That Frankfurter[7] should have concurred despite his robust common sense did surprise me— enough for me to take fresh bearings and rethink my position once more.

1. Erwin N. Griswold, dean of Harvard University Law School.
2. John A. Sessions, review of *Bibliography on the Communist Problem in the United States,* in *New Leader* 38 (October 1955), 25–26. The bibliography was prepared under the general supervision of Professor Arthur Sutherland of Harvard University Law School.
3. Jerome Davis.
4. Harry Slochower, professor of German at Brooklyn College, took the Fifth Amendment when asked by the Senate Internal Security Subcommittee (the McCarran Committee) whether he had been a member of the Communist Party. He was dismissed from his position, was reinstated by the Supreme Court, and then dismissed again for taking the Fifth Amendment before another congressional committee.
5. In a 5–4 decision, the Supreme Court, speaking through Justice Tom Clark, ruled in *Slochower* v. *New York City Higher Education Board* (1956) that public officials may not be excluded from the protection of the Fifth Amendment and that exercise of the rights against self-incrimination is not a confession of guilt or a conclusive presumption of perjury.
6. Justices William O. Douglas, Hugo L. Black, and Earl Warren.
7. Justice Felix Frankfurter.

129

Dear Lovejoy,[1]   April 16, 1956

A letter to the *Bulletin* of the AAUP which the editors would bury somewhere in the back, sandwiched in between irrelevant comment and criticism, will do little good. My discussions with some of the members of the AAUP convince me that nothing but a public demonstration will make the Association entertain second thoughts on the question. (The passages on page 99 of the Committee report actually go so far as to say that unless members of the Communist Party teach in colleges Americans cannot learn objectively the nature of Communism.)

The only way to help the AAUP now is by shock treatment. If you do nothing which makes them reverse course, they will lose out gradually as more and more members discover the implications of the silly report. (I, too, am not concerned about the censures, although I believe full-scale investigations on the scene, instead of reliance on the public records, should be conducted.) Our resignations will hurt them less if it moves them to action than if we do nothing.

I know how important your writing is, but as a temporalist you know how essential action at the right time by the right person is. No one is in a better position than yourself to speak about what the AAUP was founded to achieve, especially in developing proper standards of professional ethics.

A letter from you and me in the *Bulletin* will be disregarded as a communication from a harmless old man and from a crank. Addressed publicly to the members of the profession over the heads of the Association, it may have a sobering effect.

1. Arthur O. Lovejoy.

130

Dear Mr. Luce,[1]   April 17, 1956

I am taking the liberty of writing you this personal letter in order to call your attention to a recent and grave event which may be momentous for the future of higher education in America and in relation to which the *TIME-LIFE-FORTUNE* publications may render a great public service.

On April 6–7 of this year the American Association of University Professors meeting at St. Louis adopted the report of its special committee on "Academic Freedom and National Security." This report laid down a policy to guide American colleges and universities which among other things proclaimed:

1) that members of the Communist Party should be permitted to teach in our institutions on the same terms as other teachers (despite the *official* instructions of the Communist Party to its teacher members to take advantage of their position to violate their professional trust), and

2) that in order to learn about Communist and ideological currents in the world, Communists should be employed as teachers. I quote the relevant sentences:

"To maintain a healthy state of thought and opinion in this country, it is desirable for adherents of Communism, like those of other forms of revolutionary thought, to present their views, especially in colleges and universities, so that they may be checked by open discussion. How else are Americans to know the nature of the ideological currents in their world? If representatives of Communism from abroad were to be employed under an exchange program in American institutions of higher learning, as has been proposed, the unwisdom of the present academic policy (barring Communist teachers) would quickly become evident." (*Bulletin of the AAUP*, Spring, 1956, p. 99)

The notion that in order to learn objectively about Communism it is necessary to employ members of the Communist Party to teach it is just as absurd as the notion that in order to give an objective report about Communist activities in the press it is necessary to hire members of the Communist Party as reporters. If we do not need to employ racialists to study objectively the claims of racialism, Fascists to study objectively Fascism, or bankrupts to study the laws of bankruptcy, surely it is not necessary to employ Communists in order to study the doctrines and conspiratorial practices of Communism.

The very nature of the official instructions given to members of the Communist Party show why they cannot be trusted to impart objective instruction in any field. I quote from the official Party organ:

> Party and Y.C.L. ("Young Communist League") fractions set up within classes and departments must supplement and combat by means of discussions, brochures, etc. bourgeois discussions and distortions in the regular curriculum. . . . *Marxist-Leninist analysis must be injected into every class.*
>
> *Communist teachers must take advantage of their positions, without exposing themselves,* to give their students to the best of their ability working-class (Communist) education. . . .
>
> Only when teachers have really mastered Marxism-Leninism will they be able skillfully to inject it into their teaching *at the least risk of exposure* and at the same time conduct struggles around the schools in a truly Bolshevik manner. (*The Communist*, May 1937, my italics)

Although often criticized for giving these instructions to its teachers, to this very day the Communist Party has not withdrawn them or qualified them in any way.

The Report of the Special Committee on "Academic Freedom and National Security" of the AAUP makes no reference to these instructions. It ignores the crass violation of *professional ethics* involved in membership in a group whose declared purpose is to subvert professional trust. Neither physicians, nor lawyers, nor any other self-respecting professional group would countenance membership of any of its practitioners in a secret organization dedicated to ends and activities which contravened the ethics of their profession. Only professors have achieved this distinction. The retort usually made that accepting these instructions is one thing, carrying them out another is quite specious. As well say that a boxer who has indicated his willingness to throw his fight or a student on a basketball team who has promised not to score is not morally culpable until it can be established that he actually carried out his instructions. The rules governing examination procedures in most colleges indicate clearly that evidence of *intent* to commit dishonesty is clear grounds for disciplinary action. Membership in the C.P., which issues specific instructions to act dishonestly, is certainly *prima facie* evidence of intent, warranting at the very least close inquiry. But not according to the AAUP. The ethical principles which teachers expect their students to follow they cast aside in assaying the professional misconduct of their colleagues.

The notion that teachers who have shown their willingness to join an organization which issues such instructions can be entrusted to teach Communism objectively is a measure of the naivete and professional irresponsibility of the committee of the AAUP, its council, and the majority of the delegates present at the St. Louis meeting.

The action of the AAUP is all the more to be deplored because it is almost certain to arouse a wave of public suspicion and irritation which can be capitalized on by Senator McCarthy and his friends. I am confident that a strong editorial statement by *TIME-LIFE-FORTUNE* will have a wholesome influence on the college teachers and educators generally. If in a public speech you can point up the problem of professional ethics—for *this* and not the political beliefs or opinions of Communist teachers is the chief issue—it will reinforce the salutary effect of the editorial.

P.S. There are other relevant documentary materials which I shall be glad to make available.

1. Henry Luce.

131

Dear Nicolas,[1]   April 20, 1956

In answer to your cablegram the situation can be very easily described. Russell's[2] letter was reported in the *N.Y. Times,* and was featured in full in the *Daily Worker* and other Communist Party publications. Since then the Communists have been making great capital of Russell's wholesale condemnation of the processes of American justice. There was great indignation against Russell not merely among the members of our Committee[3] but among liberal circles generally. It was widely felt that his action was tantamount to an endorsement of germ warfare charges against the United States for which actually there is "stronger" evidence, according to Russell's unjudicial logic, than that Sobell and the Rosenbergs were framed.

When it was learned that the sources of Russell's charges were Wexley, Kahn and Cameron[4]—all Communists—and Corliss Lamont, who is perhaps the most notorious fellow traveler in the U.S., the feeling was quite strong that Russell was lending himself unfortunately to another Communist campaign against the U.S.

There was no desire to embarrass the Congress[5] in this criticism of Russell. The reference to him as an "officer" was to his part as Honorary Chairman. Personally I was against sending him an official statement and proposed to write him myself, but I was in a minority of one on this point. I voted for sending the letter subsequently but was under the impression that it was to be sent to him, not released to the press.

However, our action here has been widely supported. There may be some question about the wisdom of the kind of letter and the tone of it which the American Committee Executive sent Russell. But I do not see in what way the American Committee breached any of the rules of the Congress. I can well imagine the Indian Committee or any other Committee criticizing some public statement of our Executive Committee members or of one of our Hon. Chairman without any repercussions.

My own judgment for which I have some evidence is that Russell was getting ready to resign anyhow, and that he would have given the Congress an ultimatum to endorse his plea for Sobell, *et. al.* or stand condemned as indifferent to cultural freedom.

P.S. This letter is not for publication but you may read it to the Executive Committee meeting. If I find the time I shall write an article on *Bertrand Russell's Credulity,* discussing the logic of his "case" but not mentioning either the Congress or the American Committee.

P.P.S. If there is a copy of the *Modern Monthly* for March, 1938 in Paris, you might consult my article on Corliss Lamont to understand better the character of Russell's witnesses.

---

1. Nicolas Nabakov, professor of composition, Peabody Conservatory, and secretary general, Congress for Cultural Freedom.

2. In March, 1956, Bertrand Russell published a letter in the *Manchester Guardian* accusing the FBI of atrocities and comparing the bureau to the Gestapo. The letter was an attempt by Russell to secure the release from prison of Morton Sobell, who had been convicted of being part of the Rosenberg spy ring. Sobell, Russell charged, was a victim of political hysteria along with Julius and Ethel Rosenberg.

3. American Committee for Cultural Freedom.

4. John Wexley, author of *The Judgment of Julius and Ethel Rosenberg* (New York, 1955); Albert E. Kahn, coauthor, with Michael Sayers, of *The Great Conspiracy: The Secret War against Soviet Russia* (Boston, 1946); Angus Cameron, Communist fellow traveler and co-founder with Kahn of Cameron and Kahn, a left-wing publishing house.

5. Congress for Cultural Freedom.

132

Dear Russell,[1]   June 18, 1956

This will acknowledge your letter of June 8. I was shocked to read your sentence:

> Corliss Lamont denied evils in Russia of which there was ample evidence; you deny evils in the U.S., of which there is equal evidence, except that they have not yet been publicly blazoned forth by Eisenhower.

This is utterly false and unfair and seems to confirm reports that have filled the Communist press here about your present political mood. From the time I was a boy of fourteen, when I first learned about the Tom Mooney case,[2] down to the present in my struggle against the excesses of the security program, I have consistently fought against evils in the United States. I mention this not as something deserving particular credit—it was part of the struggle of American liberals in which many participated. It was these struggles, particularly against the excesses of the first world war and post–world war period, against the Palmer raids and arrests, which contributed to the relative absence of civil rights violations during the second world war. We failed to prevent several evils then like the Minneapolis convictions[3] and the Japanese deportations from the West Coast—outrages enthusiastically hailed by those who now are hailing you as a comrade-in-arms—but it was not for lack of trying. We failed in your case too in fighting off the forces of reaction, but we roused the whole liberal community, and only the political ambition of the opportunist LaGuardia—another darling of those who now call themselves your friends—prevented the appeal from Justice McGeehan's decision.[4]

There are still plenty of evils in the United States but less than ever in the past, and there are still plenty of American liberals fighting these evils, and they are not helped in their struggle by the extremism of your statements. That you can draw an equation between Corliss Lamont and me, between the Moscow Trials with their tortures and faked confessions and the open trials of the Rosenbergs, between the independent judiciary of the United States (despite the occasional presence of a fool and bigot like McGeehan) and the Soviet courts which are ruled by the secret police, between Eisenhower and Khrushchev, is a measure of your passion and resentment against the United States and not of your rational judgment. It is like drawing an equation between Hitler's extermination of the Jews and British discrimination against West Indian Negroes in certain residential sections of Liverpool. I am confident that if one were to protest against this latter equation you would not charge him with defending segregation against Negroes in Britain. And yet this is the logic of your letter.

You ask me whether I have looked into the evidence concerning the Rosenberg and the Sobell cases. Until recently I knew only the evidence which appeared in the press at the time of their trials. I have now read the Wexley book[5] on the Rosenbergs. It leaves me utterly unconvinced that they were innocent of the charges made against them. Wexley's book is full of fantastic suppositions for which no valid evidence is given. The Communist bias is apparent on every page. This does not mean that I am convinced that it was the Mexican government that extradited Sobell. But neither am I convinced as yet that the F.B.I. kidnapped Sobell from Mexico and find implausible Wexley's explanation of the consistent failure of Sobell to state this in court where he could be cross-examined about it. There is an obvious distinction between the truth of the charge that Sobell's asylum was breached by the F.B.I. and the question of his guilt or innocent of the charge made against him. I am no special friend of the F.B.I. *If* they kidnapped Sobell from Mexico, I would be in favor not of a new trial but of his release to Mexico at once since I believe in the right of criminal asylum as well as of political asylum. (E.g., Gerhardt Eisler was undoubtedly one of the heads of the Communist espionage ring in the U.S., yet I would have opposed taking him off the Communist ship *The Batory* after he jumped bail, or his kidnapping, deportation, or extradition from England.)

I expect to do some more reading on the Rosenberg-Sobell case since I am not so certain in this matter as you appear to be, perhaps because having argued with Communists for so many years I am less gullible about them than you are. *If* an injustice has been done in the Rosenberg-Sobell case, that should be proclaimed, those responsible punished, and Sobell released. But that an injustice *has* been done has not been established; nor would it prove your thesis that the U.S. is a police state like Hitler's Germany and the Soviet Union, even if justice had miscarried in one case.

My reading shows me that all those who shouted charges about the United States using germ warfare in Korea (before examination, the evidence cooked up by the Communists for these charges was stronger than the evidence that the Rosenbergs and Sobell were framed!) are today shouting charges that the Rosenbergs and Sobell were victims of a conspiracy. I am not saying the converse is true.

The decision to make world propaganda out of the Rosenberg-Sobell case was a political decision in the Kremlin's campaign of political warfare against the United States. I am not saying that you should not make these charges if you believe them true. I am only trying, because of my esteem for you personally, to call your attention to the fact that the Communist build-up of you in their press is motivated neither by genuine regard for you nor by agreement with your ideals. You are being used—and effectively used—as a weapon in the Communists' political war against the United States. This is apparent from the interview of Belfrage[6] with you as reported in the Communist *National Guardian*.

Further, you are being systematically misinformed about America. What is less important, you are being misinformed about me. What is far more important, your statements about America and the use the Communist world press is making about them are hurting, not helping, American liberals fight for a freer America and a freer world.

I ask you only to remember about me that I am neither a Republican nor a Democrat, I have no official government post, I still regard myself as a democratic Socialist of the Labor Party sort. I hold the same ideas and ideals as I did when you knew me here and when we fought together against Catholic, Fascist, and Communist totalitarianism. This does not mean that I am necessarily right about the guilt of the Rosenbergs or Sobells. But it should spare me from being lumped together with apologists for Communist terror.

1. Bertrand Russell.

2. Tom Mooney, a socialist union organizer, was convicted of murder in connection with a 1916 bomb explosion in San Francisco. The governor of California pardoned him in 1939.

3. Reference to the trial of twenty-nine members of the Socialist Workers Party in Minneapolis in 1941 charged with sedition. Although acquitted of sedition, eighteen were found guilty of creating insubordination in the armed forces and received prison sentences ranging from sixteen months to a year and a day. See *New York Times*, December 2 and 9, 1941.

4. An offer to Russell in 1940 to teach at Queens College, a branch of the New York City University, was withdrawn because of Russell's unorthodox views on religion and morals. Judge John E. McGeehan's decision upholding the withdrawal was supported by Mayor Fiorello H. La Guardia, who was up for re-election in 1941.

5. John Wexley, *The Judgment of Julius and Ethel Rosenberg* (New York, 1955).

6. Cedric Belfrage, founder and editor of the left-wing *National Guardian*. He was deported to England in 1955.

133

Dear Russell,[1]   July 1, 1956

I am sorry my letter of June 18th gave you offense. None was intended. I do not believe, nor have I ever said anything which implied that you have a "pro-Communist bias." I am mystified by your statement that I believe such a thing. And all I meant by saying that "having argued with Communists for so many years I am less gullible about them than you are" is that during the last quarter century in the course of organizational conflicts to prevent them from capturing liberal groups and exploiting liberal causes, I have found them notoriously unreliable, utterly unscrupulous in misstating fact. I was not referring to political discussion or suggesting that you were ever taken in by Communist argument. I was referring to simple statements of fact to which we normally give credence when made by others. I found time and again that wherever it served their purpose Communists would invent facts. That is why I am distrustful of their key allegations concerning the Rosenberg-Sobell case until independent investigation confirms them. I assumed that you never had this kind of experience with them, but only ideological conflicts. My language, however, was unfortunate. I should have written that I was "more distrustful" than you rather than "less gullible." Please excuse the lapse and permit me to withdraw the latter expression.

The lapses are not all mine. You are mistaken about our having met in 1924. Perhaps you are confusing me with someone else. There is no reason why you should remember meeting me, but there is every reason why I should remember meeting you. The first time we met, I am confident, was at Calverton's[2] house in the thirties and the conversation was about strictly philosophical issues. I never put any stock in Soviet dialectical materialism. In our only public discussion about Communism in the *Modern Monthly*, I dissociated myself from the Communist movement in my very first sentence. I had always been a critic of orthodox Marxism and was accused of reading Dewey into Marx. I never criticized you for the statements you made about the Soviet Union on any ground, and certainly not on the ground that reactionaries were making use of them. I often made use of them myself, even when I was sympathetic for a brief period to the Soviet Union—out of fear of Hitlerism—and the only other people I knew who made use of them were not reactionaries but liberals like M. R. Cohen and Dewey.

Nor would I object to the Communists using your statements about the nature of American culture, the character of American justice, and the indirect reference to the U.S. as a police state if I thought those statements were true. In that case, it would be up to us to change things for the better, just as we are trying to do with the Negro problem and the excesses of the security problem. (I have never criticized, nor would I ever criticize anyone for exposing the evils of segregation and discrimination in the U.S. despite the use that *Pravda* and the *Daily Worker* make of the exposure. I use the fact that the Communists are exploiting it as an *additional* argument for removing the injustice.) It is because I believe that some of your statements are so exaggerated that they distort the truth about the state of American freedom—which is far from ideal—that I object to them. The use the Communists are making of your statements seems to me to aggravate your fault. You do me an injustice therefore in asserting that I object to your telling the truth about the U.S. because the Communists will make use of it.

Further, I am puzzled by your contention that the Court would have denied or refuted Sobell's statement that he had been "kidnapped" if it were in a position to do so. This is not the function of the Court according to rules of evidence and procedure in Anglo-American law. According to the same rules, this is what Sobell or his counsel should have proved or at least claimed at the time of the trial. I do *not* regard "the kidnapping" of Sobell as "trivial"—*if* he was kidnapped. But this has not been established. As important as this issue is, I presume the more important one is whether he actually is innocent of the charges made against him. And here I am puzzled by many other questions like why Sobell waited two and a half years after his conviction to raise the charge about kidnapping; why he used aliases in Mexico; why his mother and sister invoked the Fifth Amendment before the Grand Jury instead of telling then what they now claim is the truth about his flight. So far, I have found no plausible answers to these and other relevant questions on the hypothesis that Sobell is innocent.

I do not want to make this letter overlong since you are probably impatient enough with it already. But I do want to point out that I wrote you originally not to start an argument with you but to call your attention to the public record of an apologist[3] for the Soviet terror-regime whom you were quoting, so I was told, as an authority on the state of American freedom. He apparently has convinced you that he has never condoned the evils in the Soviet Union. I take the liberty of suggesting that the excerpts he sent you from his speeches are not representative, and his self-serving pamphlet, written to fend off criticism, not complete by far. They do not explain certain massive public facts such as his continued endorsement of the Moscow Trials; his attacks upon those who told the truth about them; his impassioned writings in defense of Soviet "ethnic democracy" as the solution of the minorities problem at a time when minority cultures and peoples were suffering brutal repressions; his resignation from the independent *Marxist Quarterly* to join the Communist Party magazine *Science and Society* on the grounds that he did not want to be associated with any periodical which was critical of the Soviet Union, of the Communist Party of the U.S., and of the Spanish Loyalist regime (the *Marxist Quarterly* in fact was consistently pro-Loyalist and opposed only the actions of the G.P.U. in Spain); his reference to the organizers of the old Committee for Cultural Freedom (not to be confused with the present committee of similar name)—Dewey, Kallen, Norman Thomas, and others—as "Fascists and allies of Fascists" for issuing a manifesto that the Soviet Union was just as much a form of totalitarianism as Nazi Germany—this denunciation appeared in the *Daily Worker* of August 14, 1939, a week before the Hitler-Stalin Pact which after some trimming Lamont endorsed; and finally, since I must stop somewhere although there is more, much more, just two or three years ago Lamont ran for state senator for New York state[4] as the official candidate of the American Labor Party which is owned lock, stock, and barrel by the Communist Party which ran no candidate itself—the Liberal Party in New York State came into existence in the early forties when the Communists took over the American Labor Party by infiltration.

There is some doubt as to whether Lamont was ever officially a member of the American Communist Party. I personally doubt it. He was more useful to the Communist cause outside than in. But there is no doubt that he was up until quite recently the leading Soviet apologist in the United States. All this and more I have said in print. If it were not true, it would be libellous.

I have no personal animus against Lamont, but you can now understand how distasteful I found the comparison you drew between us. During the war while you were still in this country Lamont would intone love-hymns to Stalin and the Soviet Union at the meetings of the Soviet-American Friendship Society of which he was for a long time Chairman. I recall one evening at the Rand School when you passionately inveighed against the notion that the victories of the Red Army testified to the superior validity of the Soviet way of life and its institutions. Lamont was the father of that argument.

1. Bertrand Russell.
2. V. F. Calverton.
3. Hook is referring to Corliss Lamont.
4. Lamont ran and lost in 1952.

134

Dear Mr. Polanyi,[1]   November 12, 1956

This is in answer to your letter of November 3. I very much fear that the circulation of Michael Polanyi's pamphlet *The Magic of Marxism and the Next Stage of History* behind the Iron Curtain may be construed by the intellectuals of Hungary, Poland, and other countries as a cruel mockery of their effort to liberate themselves from Communist oppression. There is a great danger that they may apply to their own radical demands for political freedom and national independence and liberation from Communist exploitation the following sentence:

> Unjust privileges can be reduced only by cautiously graded stages: those who would abolish them overnight would erect far greater injustices in their stead. (p. 19)

Although the context refers to Western institutions, the principle is stated in quite general form and reappears in *The Next Stage of History* as applicable to the Communist enslaved countries of Europe. Some readers may imagine that this principle sounds better in the mouth of a Communist commissar, urging workers and students to wait patiently for reforms from the Kremlin, than in a pamphlet circulated by the Science and Freedom Committee. It seems to me that the principle as it stands is false even for Western countries. If the July 20th [1944] putsch against Hitler and his system had succeeded overnight, there is no evidence that "far greater injustices would appear in their place." Sometimes a radical decision which makes a sharp break with the past like the Supreme Court desegregation decision may be necessary. Sometimes even a revolutionary step may be justified if the consequences of adopting this Metternich piece of wisdom, and waiting for cautiously graded stages, is war. If European Social Democracy had declared a general strike in 1914, the consequences could hardly have been worse than those which ensued. And they may have been better. The American Revolutionary War of Independence did not move by cautiously graded stages, and it was not replaced by far greater injustices than those it abolished. The same is true of the emancipation of the American slaves.

Recent events in Western Europe[2] make the section on *The Next Stage of History* seem anachronistic. Even before these events occurred, its sentiments, I fear, might be construed as encouraging the spirit of accommodation to tyranny in those countries and discouraging revolutionary movements against Soviet imperialism. E.g., on page 23 M.P. writes: "I do not regard the present form of government in these countries as an insurmountable obstacle to the liberation of thought." But the Communists, unfortunately, do so regard it and therefore it may be necessary to change the "present form of government" in order to liberate thought—at least this could be the reaction of intellectuals behind the Iron Curtain.

Nor is present evidence conclusive that history will "gratefully remember" Tito's abandonment of totalitarianism because history cannot remember what hasn't happened.

I doubt whether M.P. still holds to these views in the light of historical experience, or that he will be indifferent to the possible reaction of those whom we want to reach in Communist countries to his current formulations. They may say: "After all one can carry nostalgia for the Wilhelmine regime and the Francis Joseph[3] regime too far. There is no evidence that there exists Communist analogues to them."

It is absurd, of course, to assert that "freedoms are indivisible" when we look at the full sweep of history, since political freedom is a relatively recent phenomenon. But today the relationship between freedom is much more organic even if not total. Where totalitarianism destroys democratic political traditions, as soon as it is breached in one sphere of culture there is a tendency for the breach to extend itself to politics and economics, too. This did not happen in the past, e.g. Czarist autocracy could permit a relative freedom in the arts and sciences because no political democratic tradition had developed.

It is safe to predict therefore that in any Communist country genuine academic, literary, artistic, even economic freedom will express itself sooner or later in political form and move towards democratization, thus weakening the stability of Communist regimes which are everywhere terror regimes albeit in varying degree. M.P.'s apparent willingness to settle for a loosening of totalitarianism at the price of not "impairing the stability of a Communist regime" may be unfairly construed as a recommendation to intellectuals in Communist countries to support the regime, to make it more stable, in order to win some professional concessions from it.

Before circulating this pamphlet of M.P. in Communist countries which your letter indicates you are preparing to do, I strongly suggest that you test it on some intelligent Hungarian refugee intellectuals or on some of our Polish friends.

Please let me know what decision is taken and please circulate copies of this letter to members of the Science and Freedom Committee.

1. Michael George Polanyi, son of Michael Polanyi, professor of social studies, University of Manchester.
2. The Hungarian revolution.
3. Emperor of Austria, 1848–1916.

135

Dear Dr. Salant,[1]   November 13, 1956

You probably remember me as an old time colleague at N.Y.U.

I am writing you in puzzled indignation at the closing remarks of Howard K. Smith on this afternoon's Sunday CBS program "World in Crisis' (November 11, 1956). Smith's remarks go way beyond reporting and narrative comment: they are editorializing. His call for appeasement of the Soviet Union at the present time—for that is the purport of his remarks—would be appropriate in a debate or discussion, not in what presumes to be objective reporting.

Smith has been consistently wrong about the Soviet Union. Instead of eating his words or apologizing for his opinionated ignorance about the nature of Communism, he always ends up on a note of appeasement of the Soviet Union, implying that the only alternative policy is preventive war and overlooking the fact that it is precisely a policy such as he advocates which makes war with the Kremlin, as it did with the Third Reich, more likely.

At any rate, he has a right to his opinion but not smuggled in as contraband in a world report. He doesn't, I hope, speak for CBS. Why don't you put him face to face on a program with someone who has a different point of view?

I can nominate a dozen people.

1. Richard S. Salant, vice-president, Columbia Broadcasting Company.

136

Dear friend Jelenski,[1]   December 21, 1956

Thank you for your letter of December 10 commenting on my letter to George Polanyi re. Michael Polanyi's pamphlet. I shall not attempt to discuss your observations point by point because I look forward to thrashing matters out in discussion with you soon in Paris. But there are some things in your letter which indicate that we are talking past each other, so to speak, and I hasten to put them in proper perspectives.

Either you have misunderstood Polanyi's pamphlet and its main drift or I have. I wrote that it could be interpreted as encouraging a spirit of accommodation to tyranny in satellite countries, etc. To which you reply, "Are recent events in Poland the result of a spirit of accommodation to tyranny?"

(1) Polanyi's pamphlet was written long before recent Polish events. And if the Poles took it to heart they would *not* have gone *politically* as far as they did but restricted themselves to a gradual, oh! so gradual, loosening of *cultural* shackles. It may even be argued that the Russians would have

moved in on Gomulka[2] and his friends if the Hungarians had not gone all out. The very desperation of the Hungarian uprising probably saved the gains of the Polish "moderates."

(2) You say what else could be done except follow Polanyi's line in view of the betrayal of the Hungarian revolution in the West. Now, I am not responsible for American foreign policy, as you should know, and I can think of a great many things the West could have done to help the Hungarian revolution. But the trouble with the American policy is not that it is wrong but worse than that, there is no policy. This, however, may not always be true. At least some day I hope good sense and knowledge may prevail in high counsels here. The question I put to you is: suppose Washington were prepared to come all out in favor of the Hungarian (or Polish) people on the basis of the Yalta provisions of free elections and drag its reluctant allies with it, would *you* still take Polanyi's line? (I am assuming that for the sake of the discussion that you are supporting his real position.)

(3) You say that the reason Gomulka can develop his experiment is that "he acts on the *assumption* that communism can be compatible with these freedoms." If by "communism" you mean merely a socialized *economy*, why I believe that we should share that assumption, too. But if by "communism" you also mean *political* dictatorship, i.e., the absence of *political* freedom—that is something else again. When Polanyi says "that the Science and Freedom Committee is only concerned with freedom of science and thought," he means—or is certainly sure to be interpreted to mean—that not only should we be unconcerned with the economics of communism but with its politics. It is the politics which goes to the heart of the matter—because in the end, for reasons I have indicated, cultural and intellectual freedom, as Poland and Hungary both show, seek a political expression. When you say that "Gomulka is the Kerensky of Polish liberalism (Wiles),"[3] you are admitting this.

The important thing is perspective. Polanyi's perspective *psychologically* means capitulation. It means a physicist saying in the U.S.S.R. or elsewhere, "Just let me experiment freely and publish my technical stuff, and I have no principled objections against concentration camps for *political* heretics." It means an artist saying: "Let me paint like Picasso and I don't care how many Katyns are carried out against politically suspicious elements," etc.

I have no objection as a matter of *strategy* in a certain situation to someone giving lip-allegiance to communism in order to move towards cultural and *political* liberalization. At the present time until Washington can be induced to abandon Kennanism,[4] Gomulka's line of movement is the only sensible one. But I repeat, Polanyi's philosophy would paralyze such a movement wherever it turned out to be risky. You are muddying the waters by interpreting Polanyi's line as if it logically led to recent developments in Poland.

(4) As a matter of fact, Polanyi's line was defended long before Polanyi by Oskar Lange[5] (and also by Infeld[6]) who was a socialist prepared to welcome (as Polanyi does not) the economic structure of communism. But Lange and his miserable crew did not take Gomulka's line. They were passive, waiting, just waiting for events to bring the freer atmosphere that they privately hoped for.

Please try to understand that because one disagrees with Polanyi, one does not have to agree with current Western policy. These do not exhaust the alternatives. Polanyi has said in almost so many words that even if it were possible to overthrow a system of tyranny overnight, he would be opposed to such action (not because of the Kremlin's counter-action but because it necessarily would bring worse evils in its train). His slogan is gradualism at any price. This is as mystical and absurd as revolution at any price. The opposite of an absurdity can be every whit as absurd!

1. Constantin A. Jelenski, Congrès pour la Liberté de la Culture, Paris, France.
2. Wladislaw Gomulka, head of the Polish Communist Party, 1956–70.
3. Peter J. Wiles, professor of Russian social and economic studies, University of London.
4. Theory of containment of communism enunciated by George F. Kennan.
5. Polish socialist economist, who sought to reconcile socialism and the free market.
6. Leopold Infeld, physicist who was deported from Canada during the Cold War and resettled in Poland.

137

Dear Mr. White,[1]   April 23, 1957

I am sending you the substance of my Minneapolis address—but at Minneapolis I spoke from rough notes. The argument against pacifism is a simple one—what if absolutes conflict? If a conscientious objector is right in refusing to fight for his country on *grounds of conscience,* why has someone else not the right (who on grounds of conscience refuses to allow the conscientious objector the rights and privileges of citizenship in a country which might be destroyed by his refusal) to defend it in some way or other?

You might also look up something of Arthur Lovejoy's written concerning the conscientious objector around 1917. Drop a note of inquiry to Professor A. Lovejoy at 827 Park Avenue, Baltimore, Maryland. There is also a criticism of the pacifist position in an issue of the *Progressive* a few years ago in which Niebuhr and Macdonald participated.[2] Write to the *Progressive* for that number.

1. Jim White, Minneapolis, Minnesota.
2. Reinhold Niebuhr and Dwight Macdonald.

138

Dear Mr. Ettlinger,[1]   December 17, 1957

Apparently I misunderstood your letter.[2] Your concern with value judgments in the social sciences seems, judging by your communication in the *New York Times,* to be a concern with making *propaganda* for peace. But the problem of peace cannot be intelligently discussed without reference to *threats* to peace about which you say very little. The television program[3] you refer to was discussed, if I am not mistaken, by Mrs. Diana Trilling in the *New Leader*'s issue of some weeks ago. She contended with considerable plausibility that it was a one-sided, sentimental, unrealistic discussion of the problem precisely because it implied that peace depended only upon *our* position towards it, *our* way of thinking, etc., and not a word mentioned about the ever growing threats of Soviet aggression all over the world from South Korea to East Europe and Hungary. We are in far greater danger now from the Kremlin than we ever were from Hitler, but during the days when Fascism was on the scene a program similar to the one presented would have been met with outcries of indignation.

Pacifist programs used to play into the hands of Hitler. Today they play into the hands of the Kremlin by demoralizing our will to resist. Many who oppose the first do not unfortunately oppose the second.

Let us discuss value judgments by all means. If we shall recognize that those who want to surrender freedom for peace and make propaganda for peace at any price have already capitulated to the totalitarian hangman.

1. Adrian B. Ettlinger, New York.
2. Ettlinger's letter in the *New York Times,* November 14, 1957, argued that the proper application of modern social science can facilitate the abolition of war.
3. Reference is to the CBS television program "The Faces of War."

139

Dear Dr. Teller,[1]   January 7, 1958

I have just read your article in the current *Foreign Affairs.*[2] I cannot resist writing you to express my deep sense of appreciation for its uncommon common sense. You say precisely what needs saying, and I only wish that the 2500 American scientists who signed Pauling's and Condon's[3] declaration calling on the U.S. to discontinue testing all nuclear weapons could read it.

I have been baffled by the failure of so many leading American scientists from Einstein down to understand what we are up against. They seem to imagine that the best way to get thieves to reform is to remove the locks from our doors. They know this wasn't true for Hitler, why should they believe it to be true for the Kremlin?

1. Edward Teller, professor of physics, University of California, and "father of the hydrogen bomb."
2. "Alternatives for Security," *Foreign Affairs* 36 (January 1958): 201–8.
3. Linus C. Pauling, professor of chemistry, California Institute of Technology, and Edward U. Condon, professor of physics, Washington University (St. Louis).

140

Dear Dr. Bohn,[1]   February 25, 1959

I am catching up with my reading after a long absence and have reached the column you wrote that contained a letter from Scott Nearing.[2] Old propagandists never seem to fade away! Nearing's defense of the current terroristic regime in China reminded me of a debate I had with him in the thirties just after the Moscow Trials under the auspices of a student club in the School of Education at New York University. At that time he spoke in the teeth of the evidence as extravagantly of the joyful and happy life of the masses in the Soviet Union as he now does of China. He denied all allegations of Stalin's terror, the deportations, executions and tortures, cruelty, as anti-Soviet canards. I have not seen any retraction or disavowal on Nearing's part despite Khrushchev's partial revelations at the XXth Congress of the Russian Communist Party of how intense Soviet terror was at the very period when Nearing praised it for its humanity.

Scott Nearing saw in China what the Communists permitted him to see, just as the visitors to Hitler's Germany after 1934 saw only what the Nazis showed them. Nonetheless a sufficient number of victims had escaped from Germany to make the denial of these invited visitors that concentration camps existed in Germany sound very hollow indeed. Nearing could have learned the truth about the Chinese terror by talking with and interrogating Chinese refugee youth and scholars in Hong Kong, most of whom are non-political. They chose the bitter bread of exile rather than an uncertain and degraded life under the regimented terror of Communist China. By the time the Chinese get around to admitting the facts about their brutal repression, Nearing will probably be singing the praises of another totalitarian regime.

Nearing's concern with the children of the new China is very touching. He never showed the slightest signs of compassion for the Russian waifs made homeless by Stalin's deportation policy or for the Greek children deported by the Communist guerrillas or for the Chinese children organized by the Chinese Communists publicly to denounce their parents in mass murder trials.

Nearing's critical judgments are reserved only for the United States. I was told by Professor Takahashi of the University of Kuyushu who happened to be present at a talk Nearing gave at the International House in Tokyo last year that Nearing had characterized the U.S. as a Fascist state. He was unable to explain to Professor Takahashi why if the U.S. was a Fascist state he was permitted to travel abroad in order to denounce it. Whatever political criterion Nearing used to characterize the U.S. as a Fascist state would apply preeminently to the Communist states he admires.

I find on my return to the United States that since Mikoyan's[3] visit many of the old flock of party line appeasers and apologists are crawling out of their holes into which they crept after Khrushchev drowned the Hungarian Revolution in blood.

Years ago when Nearing was a distant neighbor of mine in Vermont I passed a gravel pit where he was wresting with a large stone. It was during the honeymoon period of the Nazi-Soviet Pact, when Nearing was consoling himself with the ouija board and spiritualism. I stopped to watch. Nearing looked up, expecting me to rub his nose in the dirty political news. I said nothing but kept watching. After a while Nearing said: "I feel honest when I work with stone. Words are such dishonest things. I can't bear to speak or write any more."

It is a pity that Nearing overcame his repugnance to the use of words. Words are no more inherently dishonest than stone. Or perhaps we should say that they are as honest as those who use them.

1. William E. Bohn, editor, *New Leader*.
2. In 1956.
3. Anastas I. Mikoyan supervised Soviet foreign and domestic trade during the reigns of Stalin and Khrushchev.

5

The 1960s and the 1970s

Sidney Hook remained a nominal member of the American Left during the 1960s and 1970s. He still proclaimed himself a democratic socialist and a supporter of the redistribution of wealth. These social democratic inclinations, however, increasingly appeared to be vestigial and an insignificant element in his political persona. The issues Hook most cared about put him on the Right side of the political spectrum. He supported the Vietnam War once President Johnson made the decision to commit American forces to the conflict, he rejected any modification of the principle of merit in higher education, he warned against any tampering with America's thermonuclear arsenal, and, although still a believer in the social welfare state, he no longer rejected out of hand the warnings of conservative economists regarding the dangers of government intervention in the economy.* It is perhaps not surprising, therefore, that the last three decades of Hook's life comprise less than fifty pages in his autobiography, *Out of Step,* which runs to over six hundred pages.

Especially shocking to some people was Hook's decision in 1972 to support Richard Nixon, the *bête noire* of the American Left, for president. This was not due to any love for Nixon or for the policies of the Republican Party. Rather, Hook was dismayed by the foreign policy pronouncements of George McGovern, the Democratic nominee. In an open letter to McGovern which appeared in October 1972 in the Los Angeles *Times* and *New America,* the organ of the Social Democrats, Hook regretted that he was limited to voting either for Nixon or for McGovern. He would have preferred voting for Norman Thomas, the long-time candidate of the Socialist Party, were he still alive. Absent Thomas, Hook could not vote for McGovern because of the South Dakotan's "appalling" foreign and educational policies.

---

*For Hook's doubts about socialism and the welfare state, see Hook, *Out of Step,* pp. 599–600.

McGovern's attitude toward the Soviet Union, Hook charged, resembled that of Henry Wallace and the 1948 Progressive Party, one of whose most enthusiastic members had been McGovern himself. With his call for a drastic reduction of the defense budget and the withdrawal of the bulk of American military forces from Europe, and his tendency to bend over backward when judging the Soviet Union, McGovern was echoing the Wallace of 1946–48, before the latter woke up to the reality of Soviet intentions. Hook charged that McGovern was both ignorant and naive when it came to the Soviet Union.

Hook also attacked the South Dakota senator's approach to the Vietnam War. He asked why McGovern's sympathy for the North Vietnamese desire for national independence did not also extend to the South Vietnamese. Did they not have the same right to national independence? Why, Hook asked, "is the Stalinist police state of North Vietnam more preferable?" "Your imagination seems to have a political bias," Hook accused McGovern, "and your sense of history seems color blind to Communist aggression." McGovern's foreign policy, Hook concluded, was one of "appeasement."*

Hook professed to be even more chagrined by McGovern's attitude toward the universities, particularly since McGovern was a former academician and should have known better. McGovern, Hook charged, had encouraged campus disruptions and would deny the right of supporters of American foreign policy to do scientific research of benefit to the American military. "Because I believe that the prospects of survival of our free society and of implementing the necessary social reforms on the road to a genuine welfare society will be weakened by your election," Hook told McGovern, "I am choosing the lesser evil. I am voting for Richard Nixon—the first time in my life I have voted for a Republican candidate for the Presidency."†

Hook maintained that, despite his support of Nixon, his political values had not changed. He continued to affirm the same things he had professed in the 1930s and 1940s. What had changed was the popular definition of "Left" and "Right," particularly the non-communist Left's willingness to stand up to the Soviet Union and Red China. Hook did respond on occasion when his left-wing *bona fides* were called into question. A good example was his reply to the widespread belief that he had become a neo-conservative intellectual.

In 1978, Hook addressed the national convention of the Social Democrats, U.S.A., on the topic "Social Democracy Means Human Freedom: A Response to the Conservatives."‡ Hook thought it strange that the attack on the welfare state was being conducted under the banner of "freedom." To oppose all government intervention into the economy as the libertarians did was to make a fetish of the free market. The problem was not to replace government intervention with no intervention, but to replace unwise intervention with sensible intervention.

---

*Sidney Hook, "An Open Letter to Senator George McGovern," *Los Angeles Times,* October 15, 1972.
†Ibid.
‡The speech was published in *New America* 16 (January 1979): 6–7, 12.

There was no necessary correlation between government intervention and the loss of freedom, Hook avowed. The socialist movement, for example, had begun as a protest "against the indignities of an industrial system that tied workers to fixed schedules and modes of conduct whose deadening monotony was felt to be incompatible with natural growth and the spontaneity of freely selected vocation." Freedom was a reality only when people were freed from the oppression of others. What kind of freedom did the poor man have in negotiating the conditions of his labor with a Rockefeller or a Carnegie? "The coercion of hunger or the fear of hunger can be just as persuasive, although different, as the coercion of physical violence or its threat."* Property meant power, and government action was necessary to ensure the freedom of those lacking power.

Government and not the free market had eliminated slavery and protected workers from the control of their employers. Hook argued that the modern task of government was to ensure equality of opportunity for everyone, and this necessarily meant that the government must provide a modicum of education, health, and employment so that each individual could develop to the best of his or her potential. The difficulty of this task was no excuse for not trying to cope with America's economic problems, "the chief of which are to provide full employment at an adequate wage level, economic growth, and minimal inflation."†

Although cogently argued, Hook's defense of the welfare state lacked his usual fire. There was a sharp contrast between the passion of his attack on McGovern and the detached tone of his defense of social democracy. He had made all the right arguments in behalf of government intervention, but one senses that his heart really was not in it, and that he would have preferred discussing the threats posed by neutralism and the movement to limit the West's nuclear arsenal.

---

*Ibid.
†Ibid.

141

Dear Mr. Fellows,[1]   March 7, 1960

Thank you very much for your thoughtful letter of March 2, 1960. I found your comments very pertinent and quite instructive. The draft of the letter was not mine.[2] The original mentioned only Sobell. I insisted first that clemency for Gold and then for Greenglass be included. And I see now that I should have objected to the discussion of the evidence in the Sobell case since we are all convinced that Sobell is as guilty as hell. But I got tired of making new points. The whole situation is complicated. The Communists and their dupes as well as well-meaning liberals are making strenuous efforts to start a campaign for Sobell's release and to make political capital against the U.S. out of it. By bringing in the cases of Gold and Greenglass, in addition to my sincere belief that they have already been sufficiently punished, I was trying to make the public aware that one-sided petitions for Sobell's clemency which omitted mention of Gold and Greenglass had a political motivation. I know that the Communists will never ask for clemency for Gold and Greenglass.[3]

There is some evidence from my mail that the non-Communists and genuine innocents who agitate for Sobell now feel they must make some mention of Gold and Greenglass. The Communists and their dupes are a little embarrassed—not much—when they have to be silent about them.

My feeling about Gold was established after reading his statement before the Senate Internal Security Sub-Committee which I reprinted on pp. 207–211 of my *Political Power and Personal Freedom.* If you have not read it, please do. In addition, I did feel the injustice of the ridiculously light punishment for Fuchs and May—both of whom deserved at the very least life imprisonment.[4] They both should have been shot. (Fuchs has now said that he would do what he did all over again—showing that his original statement of regret was insincere). Gold and Greenglass can be counted on to stay clean. Their real danger is from liquidation by the Communists. Incidentally, Robert Morris[5] feels as I do both about Gold's truthfulness in cooperating (after his initial attempt to hold back information) and the relative injustice of keeping him cooped up while Fuchs and May are free.

If Sobell is released and Gold and Greenglass not, every Soviet agent who is caught will argue that he will get better treatment if he clams up than if he cooperates in the exposure of others. If Sobell is released he can't do much harm. If he flees to a Communist country he will be exposing himself for what he is and perhaps teaching idiots something about Communist techniques. If he stays he can't do much: he will always be a marked man. My guess is that he will stay put—or he may go to England which is a refuge for quite a few American Communists.

As you see I harbor no doubts about Sobell's guilt. Democracies fight espionage with one hand tied behind their backs. Even so, if we were intelligent and could make the process of justice move faster, we might be able to be more effective as well as just. The Rosenbergs deserved their fate, but the delay in carrying out the sentence produces situations which must be politically and morally revaluated (e.g. the Chessman affair[6] shows that even a criminal case develops political as well as moral aspects if a deserved sentence is too long delayed). At the time of their execution the U.S. suffered a political defeat. It is not enough *to be* just: one must *appear* just.

This letter is confidential and not for publication. I wish I had the time to write these matters up in detail; any partial statement of my position lends itself to misunderstanding in a world where there is a positive will to misunderstand not only by the Communists among us but by the ritualistic liberals.

Your own letter suggests you have given these matters considerable thought. Why don't you try your hand at an article for *The New Leader*?

Thank you for writing me and by your criticism giving me a chance to clarify some points.

1. Robert Fellows, Jackson Heights, New York.
2. Reference is to a letter by Hook, Nathan Glazer, Irving Kristol, and Dwight Macdonald that appeared in the February 16, 1960, *New York Times*. It called for clemency for Harry Gold, Morton Sobell, and David Greenglass, members of the Rosenberg spy ring. Gold and Sobell each received a thirty-year sentence, while Greenglass was sentenced to fifteen years in prison.
3. Because Gold and Greenglass testified against the Rosenbergs. Greenglass was Ethel Rosenberg's brother.
4. For Klaus Fuchs, see letter 111, note 9. The Canadian Alan Nunn May was sentenced to ten years in prison. He served seven and was released in 1952.
5. Former counsel to the Senate International Security Subcommittee.
6. Sentenced to be executed for kidnapping, Caryl Chessman spent twelve years on death row in California arguing his case. He made numerous legal appeals and wrote four books. For some, he became a symbol of the barbarity of capital punishment, and his case became a *cause célèbre* among anti-American elements in Europe. He eventually was executed in the gas chamber at San Quentin in May 1960.

142

Dear Professor Kalven,[1]   April 7, 1960

I wish I had the time to reply to your letter at suitable length. There are about 57 points I want to make but they will have to wait. Some day I may get to Chicago and we can talk.

One basic difference between us is that you approach this whole case,[2] if you will excuse me for saying so, with extreme political innocence. For example, take a minor matter like what pleasant people the Sobells are. If this were an ordinary criminal matter like arson, rape, or murder—this would be relevant. But not when ideological espionage is involved. (Please look at my chapter on the subject.[3]) My dear Kalven—the hearts of many people have been broken who bet on their convictions that such pleasant persons like Fuchs and Hiss and Coplon[4] and every other agent couldn't be guilty of infamy. Those who think this way do not know that Communism is a disease of idealism. Most Communists in purely personal relations are better than most non-Communists, but you are dealing with idealistic fanatics who wouldn't hurt a kitten but yet who, if it were necessary for the cause, would sacrifice their own parents and children. Some have actually done so.

Secondly, you must understand the Communist movement and its psychology to interpret properly the reluctance of Communist defectors to testify, their failure to tell their whole story at the beginning (always their greatest mistake), their desire to shield their associates even after they have given up their faith which itself is a slow process. I am not privy to any government secrets but it is obvious to me that Elitcher[5] (like Chambers[6]) told as little as he possibly could. But what he said is true.

Thirdly, the behavior of a witness is very important to the jury who observes him. The evaluation of the true proceedings by judges on appeal is not lightly to be discarded. And despite what you say about the temper of the times, if I am not mistaken the very same judges who refused to grant the appeals of Rosenberg and Sobell granted the appeal of Coplon in the very same period of time. There was no judicial hysteria.

Fourthly, you are wrong in attributing these impermissible inferences to me. I do not draw any inference of espionage from mere membership in the Communist Party. Where in the world did you get that idea? (Please read what I have written about this.) I am simply making the commonsense observation that my initial credibility with respect to the charge that X committed murder is affected by the knowledge that X is a self-confessed member of Murder, Inc. Of course other people can commit murders, too, and some members of Murder, Inc. have not committed any. But the evidence *must be evaluated* in the light of the knowledge of what the functions of Murder, Inc. are. (Make your own substitutions.) Something that may be altogether innocent with respect to a man who is not a member of Murder, Inc. may not be so innocent in the light of knowledge of his membership. I approach these matters primarily from a scientific theory of evidence which, as you know, is different from a legal point of view according to which even compelling objective evidence of a man's guilt may not even be admissable. But I am here concerned with the question of truth.

As for the inference of consciousness of guilt. This is certainly justified. What you say indicates only that Sobell was inept. Things happened suddenly, and not all Communists are men of steel. Morton Sobell is a foolish alias but it is an alias.[7] Even if he was dragged back why didn't he come voluntarily? The commonsense inference about Sobell's not taking the stand is based not only on that fact alone, but *on that plus all the other evidence in the case.* If his attorney believed that the evidence was weak, no matter how fumbling his denial would have been, it would have helped him immensely. My experience with juries shows that if anything they are sympathetic to a gentle or frightened witness. Incidentally this doesn't apply to the refusal of the Sobell women to testify before the Grand Jury. *They* certainly had something to hide.

The difference between the Dreyfus and Sacco-Vanzetti cases and the Sobell case is this. The former were *not* members of an international conspiratorial political movement with a long and demonstrated history of successful perpetration of espionage. Dreyfus and Sacco and Vanzetti did not remain mute like Sobell when tried and for a considerable time thereafter. They shouted their innocence to the entire world. Of course even guilty people can do that, but I know of no innocent men who fail to do it in cases of such character. That is why if I were approached by any committee for Sobell, I should carefully examine the possibility that my good will and kindness of heart were being exploited—and exploited by people who endorsed some of the worst crimes in human history, the most recent of which were the massacres in Hungary, who have no compassion for the millions of men, women and children destroyed by arbitrary administrative whim in the Soviet Union. To this very day the Sobells and their political friends have remained mute about these things. Ask them.

I certainly believe that Sobell is entitled to due process. And I am convinced that he received it. In these matters I cannot claim anything more than a judgment based on great probability and in the legal aspects, evidence beyond reasonable doubt. But reasonable doubt must be an *informed* doubt, and without a close study of the Communist movement and how it operates, neither belief nor doubt can be informed.

If I am for Sobell's release at the present time it is only on grounds of mercy, not justice. I am sorely puzzled to observe how many ritualistic liberalists—I don't mean you!—find the quality of mercy strained when it comes to judging Nazis, Fascists, and totalitarians of other stripes but never when Communists are involved.

Well, I hadn't intended to go on at such length.

1. Harry Kalven, Jr., professor of law, University of Chicago Law School.

2. The Rosenberg case.

3. "Ideological Espionage," in *Political Power and Personal Freedom: Critical Studies in Democracy, Communism, and Civil Rights* (New York, 1959).

4. Judith Coplon, an employee of the Justice Department convicted in 1949 of passing FBI data to the Soviet Union.

5. Max Elitcher, a witness for the prosecution in the trial of Sobell.

6. Whittaker Chambers.

7. Hook is wrong here. Sobell's aliases included M. Sowell, Marvin Sand, and Morton Solt. Sobell was his real name.

143

Dear Ben,[1]   April 8, 1960

Here is my frank and well-considered opinion about the questions you ask.

There is no official policy of discrimination against anti-Communists in colleges and universities. Here and there pockets of antagonism exist on the part of administrative officers, and I have no doubt that *some* injustices have been done by some ritualistic liberals and pro-Communists to militant anti-Communists. But not only is this episodic but very difficult to prove. It would be worth a man's professional reputation to make the public charge that it was widespread. And it would be extremely inadvisable for a Congressional Committee to announce any investigation of this theme as such. The outcry would be as strong as was encountered by Matthews' attempt to list infiltrations into churches.[2]

There is no objection to a quiet or mute anti-Communist. But if he is outspoken and militant like me, for example, he will find the going hard—unless he has achieved some professional eminence. I was the first person elected to the presidency of the American Philosophical Association (Eastern Division) by a canvassed poll of the membership (for nominations) *before* the actual meeting. At first I didn't want to stand because I was sure that the Party boys and their friends would gang up with all my personal enemies against me. They didn't have the nerve and although I was away in India, I was elected. Nonetheless, I have suffered for being an anti-Communist—honors denied me, not being invited to certain lucrative lectures, cut out of all Fund for the Republic projects—what a gravy train that is!—etc. But this is nothing to get excited about. I am happy to pay such a small price for my beliefs and am prepared to pay even a higher one if necessary.

The key to the situation is that the great majority of the American professoriate are still ritualist liberals. They don't approve of *Communism*. But the Communists and fellow travelers they know are personally ingratiating, with a perpetual fawning popular front psychology. On the other hand, militant anti-Communists like me, who are always sounding off, are as popular as porcupines. God knows I'd like to keep my mouth shut and pen quiet for a while, but unfortunately when I do nobody else does (with a few exceptions, of course). The result is that even when my colleagues agree with me, they don't like me.

P.S. If any case of discrimination against anti-Communists comes to your attention, the best procedure is first to get them to write up and publish their story in the *New Leader*. Then they can if they wish be brought in as witnesses in connection with an appropriate measure of legislation the Committee is deliberating about. Very few people who want to remain in teaching can afford the publicity. Remember that the people who fired Fuchs and refused to rehire him considered themselves 100% Americans.

With respect to the whole Communist problem in this country, I am inclined to believe that we have suffered as much if not more from stupidity in the ways of exposing, handling, and combatting Communism as from the actions of the Communists themselves. The hostility towards anti-Communists among non-Communists is one sign of this, the cultural vigilantism which calls every socialist, even a liberal, a Communist is another, and the willful ignorance and/or innocence of ritualistic liberalism still another.

P.S.S. I never did get that collection of documents on Communism which one of the Committees published some years ago.

1. Benjamin Mandel, director of research for the House Committee on Un-American Activities and Senate Internal Security Subcommittee.
2. Joseph B. Matthews, a columnist for the Hearst papers, wrote "Reds and Our Churches," *American Mercury* 77 (July 1953): 3–13; and "Red Infiltration of Theological Seminaries," *American Mercury* 77 (November 1953): 31–36.

144

Dear Bert—wherever you are![1]   August 25, 1960

I am taking the liberty of endorsing a letter from *Boris Souvarine*[2] which is self-explanatory. I don't know anybody at the Hoover Institute. If you do—I remember you were there—would you be willing to write in Boris' behalf? He is highly qualified to participate in, advise, and cooperate in the project—and he also has a remarkable collection of books and documents.

It is a pity that a man of his gifts is reduced to doing chores just to keep alive and has not the wherewithal to devote himself to completing the creative work of which he is capable.

The summer has flown, and I have accomplished very little. The Berlin Congress was a bust—more of an occasion for Western breastbeating and lamentation over our deficiencies than for a firm and definite response to the ever-present and ever-growing Communist danger. The initiating Congress in 1950 was much better. If I have to fight Communist despotism— I'll take Koestler and Kennan[3] any time although Koestler today is more interested in Yogi and God than is good either for him or the cause of freedom.

Ann and I trust you and Ella are well and that you have had a refreshing summer.

1. Bertram D. Wolfe, a former Communist who became an intense anti-communist and wrote *Three Who Made a Revolution* (New York, 1948).
2. Pseudonym of Boris Lifchitz, a former Bolshevik who became a supporter of Trotsky and was expelled from the Communist Party in the 1920s. He wrote *Stalin: A Critical Survey of Bolshevism* (New York, 1939).
3. Arthur Koestler and George F. Kennan.

145

Dear Mr. Porter,[1]   February 24, 1961

Your long letter of February 15th reached me just as I am about to depart for the West to deliver the Matchette Lectures at Purdue University. Forgive me therefore for writing so briefly in reply to your "thoughtful" comments. I put thoughtful in quotes because much of what you say is based on a lack of knowledge of my views on Communism, on Fascism, and on related subjects. I have expounded these views over a long period of years. The most relevant of my writings in this connection are *Heresy, Yes—Conspiracy, No!* and *Political Power and Personal Freedom.* Perhaps you can procure these volumes in Spain from the USIS or from colleagues at home.

My overall reaction to your letter is that, paraphrasing Thomas Mann, "nothing separates us but an abyss" in our understanding of the nature of the Communist movement, democracy, and civil rights. (Incidentally as a life-long opponent of Fascism in all its varieties, you don't have to agitate me about Salazar.[2] Among the varieties of Fascism, I include certain forms of political Catholicism. See my *Reason, Social Myths and Democracy* and my article on "The New Failure of Nerve" in *Partisan Review* [1943].)

I list here a few items to explain my feeling.

1. The question of Communist Party teachers is fundamentally a question of *professional ethics*. The commitment to flagrant violation of professional ethics is spelled out in the directives of the C.P. to its teacher-members. Here in the East the Communists ran wild in some institutions. You seem to be unfamiliar with the evidence. There is good reason to believe that indifference to this question of professional ethics, where Communists were concerned, who were clearly guilty of unprofessional conduct, played into the hands of cultural vigilantism just as the indifferences of many ritualistic liberals to the demonstrated presence of members of the C.P. in government services contributed to the rise of McCarthyism. (See my chapter on "Freedom and Security" in *Political Power and Personal Freedom.*)

2. I have read the entire record of the hearings on the Institute of Pacific Relations. It beats me how anyone who claims to understand the Communist movement can deny that Lattimore was an ardent Communist fellow traveler who had every right to teach at a university but should never have been an official advisor of the State Department. Lattimore wrote a defense of the infamous Moscow Trials as an expression of democracy!—even after the report of the Commission of Inquiry headed by John Dewey which presented the documentary evidence that these trials were frame-ups. (Even Khrushchev in his report to the XXth Congress of the C.P. of the U.S.S.R. has admitted substantially the truth of some of the Commission's Inquiry.)

3. You systematically confuse the protection that a member of the C.P. should receive under the Bill of Rights where his legal freedom is concerned, with his "rights" of employment, etc. where it is not a question of depriving him of his freedom or sending him to jail. Where others besides Communists are concerned I am confident you see the point. A policeman who, charged with graft, refuses to reply to a legitimate departmental inquiry to explain the source of $200,000 found in his account can stay out of jail by invoking the Fifth Amendment, but does this give him the right to stay on his job? *Mutatis mutandis,* the same considerations apply to members of the Communist Party.

4. Your remarks about Castro[3] are a little disquieting to me. They bring back echoes of "liberal" apologists for Hitler who pointed out that after all Hitler solved the unemployment problem, raised the standard of living of the German workers, etc. and lifted them out of the depths to which the Weimar Republic had permitted them to fall—and echoes of "totalitarian liberal" apologies for Stalin's purges and enforced collectivization. When Castro stepped in to reverse the judgment of his own courts which refused to convict innocent persons, this was enough for me. Nor have I or any

other sensible person ever held that Communism is the source of *all* the world's troubles. Neither was Hitler. But at a certain time he was the worst and most dangerous problem and exacerbated all the others. The same is true for Communism today.

5. No informed person can separate, as you seem to do, the American Communist Party from the international Communist movement. If there were no Kremlin, American Communists would be no more a danger than other varieties of dissident Communists today who are fanatics. But granted that guilt is personal, everyone who joins the C.P. has been guilty of an *act* of joining an organization which is part of an international apparatus for the conquest of power.

If I stop at this point it is only because I must catch a plane. But I cannot resist saying as I glance through your enclosure that anyone who relies on Somerville's[4] transparent sophism and attempts to explain away what the Communist Party is, is in need of further study. I suggest in this connection that you consult Theodore Draper's two volumes[5] on Communism and Frank S. Meyer's *The Moulding of a Communist,* prepared under the auspices of The Fund for the Republic. Also, if you will pardon a further reference to my writings, my *Marx and the Marxists* and, if it is accessible to you, my review of Somerville's *Soviet Philosophy* in the *Nation,* during the year the book was published (1945?) and the ensuing correspondence.[6]

1. Denton Porter, New York.
2. Antonio de Oliveira Salazar, dictator of Portugal.
3. Fidel Castro.
4. John Somerville, professor of philosophy, Hunter College, and author of *Soviet Philosophy: A Study of Theory and Practice* (New York, 1946).
5. *The Roots of American Communism* (New York, 1957) and *American Communism and Soviet Russia* (New York, 1960).
6. Review appeared in the *Nation* 164 (February 15, 1947): 188–89.

146

Dear Mr. Porter,[1]   April 10, 1961

I have just returned from Berkeley where I gave the Thomas Jefferson Lectures at the University of California (in which I discussed some of the issues you are concerned with) and found your letter of March 29th.

For many years I have made it a point, out of simple courtesy, to reply to the letters I receive from correspondents. This has been an arduous task, and I am beginning to feel as the letters mount that it is too much for me. When

I got your long letter and its enclosure I had the choice of disregarding it, waiting until I returned from my trips (the California trip followed the one to Purdue), or answering it briefly. I had no time to read carefully the hardly decipherable memorandum and literally just glanced at it on the assumption that the accompanying letter was a sufficient indication of your views.

I am truly sorry if I mistook your position, all the more so because the bitter tone of your reply suggested that my well-intentioned haste, for which I apologize, blocks any avenue of communication between us which may still be open. I surmise that you have plenty of leisure, but I must ask you to stretch your imagination a bit to grasp the difficulties under which as teacher, scholar, writer, administrator, committee man—to mention only the public sector of my life—I labor. At the moment I have scores of unanswered letters facing me.

In what I say now I shall assume that you are not a Communist fellow traveler but a principled democrat.

1) I haven't overlooked "the practical consequence of our having anti-Communist but non-democratic bedfellows." I do not know whether you see the English *Times* and (Manchester) *Guardian.* They carried a communication from me protesting the recent persecutions by the Spanish government of its political opponents. Nor is this the first time I have condemned Franco. I began on the very first day of his revolt against the Loyalist regime. But as a democrat I am prepared, *if it is necessary,* in order to contain Communism to approve joint military action even with non-democratic powers on the same grounds that I supported our help to the Soviet Union (our non-democratic bedfellow in World War II) in withstanding the assault of Hitler, or our help to Tito, another totalitarian tyrant, in preventing Yugoslavia from being destroyed by the U.S.S.R. But just as I exercised the freedom to criticize Stalin for his terror, during our alliance with him, so I criticize Tito for his imprisonment of Djilas,[2] and Franco for his persecution of democrats and socialists.

Whether we need "military bases in Spain" to defend the remaining bastions of freedom in Europe I don't know. If the military experts say they are necessary, I should prefer to regard Spain as a possible co-belligerent in a defensive action than an ally—just like the Soviet Union. Unfortunately many people thought that because the Soviet Union was a co-belligerent she was a democratic ally! I know of none who make that mistake with respect to Franco.

2) I never said that Lattimore wrote a book on the Moscow Trials. He wrote a famous article which I assumed you saw in the I.P.R. hearings since it was reproduced in the record. I believe Congress had every right to investigate the conditions under which we lost China. I believe that Latti-

more was disingenuous in denying his pro-Communist sympathies, of which the article together with other items was sufficient evidence. He published his article after the John Dewey Commission, which investigated the truth of the charges made at the Moscow Trials, issued its report.

3) I nowhere implied that all the volumes in the Fund for the Republic Series were of equal worth.[3] Iverson's book[4] is very inadequate at key points—precisely on the situation in the City Colleges which you will find documented in my *Heresy, Yes—Conspiracy, No!*

4) But now to matters of more substance—the bearing of Communist membership and/or Communist ideas on a man's right to employment. With respect to government employment, I agree with the maxim of Roger Baldwin, former head of the A.C.L.U., that superior allegiance to a foreign government disqualifies a man from serving his own. This covers the case of membership in the C.P.

Now as for a man's ideas. I think on reflection you will agree with me that a man's ideas are relevant to his employment if they bear upon the character of the work he is doing, the nature of the trust involved, etc. For example, a man who believed that the Marshall Plan was a capitalist plot to enslave Europe is not qualified for a job which requires him to implement the plan; a man who is sympathetic to Nazi ideology has no right to a job in the State Department—nor has a man who welcomes the idea of Communism as the wave of the future; an anti-Semite has no right to complain if he is fired from a job in the Anti-Defamation League; and Robert Hutchins to the contrary, a man who doesn't believe in civil liberty but approves of dictatorship, of any variety, has no right to a job in the American Civil Liberties Union or The Fund for the Republic. As I have said elsewhere—this is a matter of common sense. I am a devoted member of the Euthanasia Society. But if I were a physician and applied for the job of superintendent of a Hospital for the Hopelessly Diseased, I could very well understand why my ideas on euthanasia could be considered as disqualifying me.

5) You misunderstand the case of the policeman and the Fifth Amendment. The $200,000 in the box of the policeman who earns $5,000 a year is not by itself evidence of graft. He is asked: "Where did you get it? Is it graft?" and answers, "I refuse to reply on the ground that a truthful answer would incriminate me." He can stay out of jail but would you keep him in his job—after giving him a hearing, of course? A member of the C.P. is asked: "Did you follow out the instructions of the C.P. to take advantage of your position in the classroom and indoctrinate for the Party line without exposing yourself?" He makes a similar answer. Would you not say that this, too, is a violation of professional trust? Would you permit a nurse to practice who, if asked whether she gave a lethal dose to a patient, invoked

the 5th Amendment even though the evidence is not sufficient to convict her?

The entire question of the Fifth Amendment is very complicated, and if I can lay my hands on my book[5] I shall send it to you. I assume you have read Griswold's book[6] which states an opposing view.

Since you are in the army I assume you are a very young man, and I don't expect you to have read stuff of mine which was published before you were born and while you were a child. But I do hope you will entertain the possibility that the problems you are concerned with have been thought about before—even if you find subsequently that you are dissatisfied with the answers. I am still puzzled to understand what your objections are to my article on Political Pretenders[7] which was written on the request of a liberal editor to help readers understand when a person on the international political scene (Castro, Lumumba, Gizenga, Toure,[8] et al.) was a Communist or not. The references to the domestic scene were incidental. As it is, the article brought forth charges that I was myself a Communist or a secret sympathizer from some crackpot group in California where everything grows.

I close with renewed expressions of regret for having merely "glanced" at your enclosure before writing you and at my unintended sharpness of tone. (I had no time to read my letter to you before I went off.) But even so I certainly didn't mean to impugn your "good faith."

I am always prepared to rethink any position I take and to learn from my critics even if I am not convinced by them.

1. Denton Porter.
2. Milovan Djilas. Yugoslav anti-communist dissident and author of *The New Class: An Analysis of the Communist System* (New York, 1957). Djilas spent many years in Tito's prisons.
3. Hook is referring to the series of books on communism in American life sponsored by The Fund for the Republic.
4. Robert W. Iversen, *The Communists and the Schools* (New York, 1959).
5. Hook, *Common Sense and the Fifth Amendment* (New York, 1957).
6. Erwin N. Griswold, *The Fifth Amendment Today* (Cambridge. Mass., 1955).
7. Hook, "Political Pretenders and How to Tell Them." *Saturday Review* 43 (December 13, 1960): 6–8, 29.
8. Fidel Castro, Patrice Lumumba (first premier of the Republic of the Congo), Antoine Gizenga (a supporter of Lumumba), and Sekou Toure (first president of Guinea).

147

Dear Mr. Bryant,[1]   May 24, 1961

Your letter to me of May 2 was mistakenly addressed to Columbia University. Hence it has just reached me. I have noted your sentiments and have concluded that you were in favor of permitting Hitler and Eichmann to take over the entire world and imposing their infamies upon mankind rather than resisting them by military means. Under the circumstances, I am not much impressed by your alleged concern for humanity. If we had followed your policy, we would by now be either dead or enslaved.

Those who resisted Hitler and wish to resist Khrushchev if he attacks are just as much devoted to the ideals of peace as you profess to be. But they are more sincerely interested in freedom, and far more intelligent about the methods by which to insure peace *and* freedom. Even if the free world capitulated to Communist terror, there is no guarantee that Khrushchev and Mao will not nuclear bomb each other and you out of existence. So not only will you become a slave but before long a dead one.

The willingness to fight for one's life is sometimes the best way of preserving one's life and of preventing the fight.

You ask me what I mean by a free world. Most simply put, it is one in which a person like yourself who disagrees with the policies of his government is free to speak, no matter how absurd or irresponsible he is. Under Hitler's regime and in Khrushchev's empire, you would be shot or first brain-washed and shot for your disagreements. That is the kind of world which your policy, if it were followed, would bring about.

I think it is worth fighting, if necessary, to prevent that world from becoming universal. I believe just as strongly that we will not have to fight if Khrushchev knows that we are prepared to do so.

1. Ernest Bryant, Boston, Massachusetts.

148

Dear Corliss,[1]   July 14, 1961

Your hysterical letter of May 31 has just reached me here. In it you accuse me of pursuing you with demonic fury for twenty years, charge me with committing "a frame-up" against you, and demand an apology from me. You enclose a memorandum dated Dec. 1, 1958, which I don't recall having seen before.

You are really lucky that I didn't see this piece of disingenuous pleading before. For it would have decided me to do something which I should have done in the public interest long ago. Now I am going to write a little book called *The Case of Corliss Lamont.*[2] You won't be able to fool the public any more with your paid advertisements and circulars about where you disagree with the Commmunists—without mentioning the more important issues on which you have agreed with them and, in effect, done their work for them. For I shall tell the truth about you, quoting from your words— your books, articles, and letters. Personally, of course, you don't rate all this attention, but I shall discuss you as an illustration of a social-political phenomenon and the use the Communist movement has made of you.

As for the charge that you called us (the organizers of the Committee for Cultural Freedom) Fascists and allies of Fascists, I shall prove it to the hilt—not only by printing the text of the *Daily Worker* letter of August 14, 1939 (large portions of which were taken word for word from your other writings—that is why we held you responsible), but by printing the interpretation placed on your text by the *Nation* editorially (even though they *opposed* us) and by other publications. The cream of the jest, however, is what you don't know. It was *Dewey himself* who read your letter as accusing us of Fascism. Dewey, despite his title of Honorary Chairman, was actually as active, if not more so, than any of us. He was still full of the Moscow Trials. It was he who sparked our indignation. I have in my possession the original manuscript of the letter he drew up, unsolicited by anyone, after the Soviet-Nazi Pact was signed on August 23, 1939, barely a week after your infamous letter was signed. He asked that we send it out *under his signature* to all whose names appeared as signers in the *Daily Worker* (he specified even whom *not* to send it to), asking them whether in the light of the Nazi-Soviet Pact, they still thought the Committee for Cultural Freedom, which had practically predicted this pact, were "Fascists and allies of Fascists." This is only one piece of evidence of (1) how keenly Dewey himself felt about your letter, and (2) that it was *he* himself who interpreted your letter as charging us with being Fascists—which, of course, was its clear intent, despite the sly attempt at ambiguity. The fact that you didn't mention us by name was immaterial. Everybody knew who the leading spirits behind it were—just as they knew, until you got scared, who the head of the F.S.U.[3] was without mentioning your name.

Despite your pretence *now* that these charges were far from your mind, let me remind you that you never *publicly* dissociated yourself from the letter's charges or *publicly* repudiated the interpretation you call grotesque—despite my challenge to you to do so and my pointing out to you in various letters that this was the accepted public interpretation. Even the Board of the A.C.L.U. read your Open Letter that way! Dewey told me about your personal letter to him. He was, for him, quite bitter about it. He said you were one of those individuals—I know others, too—who insult people in public and write sugared notes to them in private. Why didn't you make your letter public? The very fact that you sent it is *prima facie* evidence that there was a general public understanding that you had charged us with the same thing that the *Daily Worker* had. The *Nation* was widely read those days. Why didn't you correct their reading of your letter?

So where, my dear Corliss, is the frame-up? Even if Dewey and all of us were mistaken, and the insinuation was more a matter of your stupidity than of your artfulness, where is there any attempt at a frame-up? All we did is to call attention to the public record. Don't you feel a little abashed when you use a term like "frame-up"?—you who defended the torture and execution of those innocent men, who mouthed the slanders about Trotsky being a Hitler agent and all the other Stalinist filth? You have not even had the gumption to repent publicly for the role you played in that affair. In the memo you send me, you refer to the fact that Dewey proved more "realistic than I" about violations of civil liberty. How delicately and disingenuously put! I shall certainly quote it together with your characterization of the Soviet invasion of Finland as an "error"—subsequently revised. And since you profess such great admiration for Dewey, I hope you won't object to my quoting from your letters to me what you said about him during the war when you were on your knees before Stalin. There wasn't a thing Khrushchev revealed about Stalin and the Moscow Trials which Dewey and our Committee didn't call your attention to at the time they were happening.

Under the circumstances I hope you will not think it rude of me if I say that a protest against frame-ups by you sounds very much like Webster's words after 1850 to Emerson.

Before you call me a liar again check your facts. Try to recall who wrote the article on Dewey's *Common Faith* in the *New Masses* under the contemptuous title "The Right Reverend Re-Defined," which oddly enough was *not* mentioned, even in a footnote, by the author of "Fresh Light on Dewey's *Common Faith*" in the *Journal of Philosophy*.

You also insult my colleagues on the Dewey Committee when you say I "vetoed" the appointment of Russell[4] to the organizing committee.[5] What am I—a Commissar? How could *I* veto—I was only one out of many? If my memory serves me, it was Schneider,[6] supported by Kallen,[7] who proposed that the members of the organizing committee, national and international, be individuals who were actively interested in Dewey's philosophy and who were in some way associated with his work in education or some other discipline. *That* was why Russell wasn't invited, particularly since someone mentioned his Columbia lectures in which he practically associated the philosophy of pragmatism with the use of force. Kallen was particularly sore about that and so was Kilpatrick.[8]

Russell's mistakes are his own—they are not of the nature of political crimes. You are in a class by yourself. I am going to focus some beams of analysis on you so that you won't be able to deceive anybody or even yourself. And I am going to tell the truth about the resignation of the *Humanist* editors, the firing of Priscilla Robertson, and some other incidents of general interest.

P.S. As an indication of my fair-mindedness I should like to make the following proposal. Under the auspices of the Tamiment Institute and the Chairmanship of Norman Thomas (or some other mutually agreed on figure), let us have a public debate on any of the following topics.

1. Were the Moscow Trials a Frame-Up?
2. Is (or was) Corliss Lamont a Communist Fellow Traveler?

I am prepared to take the affirmative on either or both of these topics.

1. Corliss Lamont.
2. Hook never wrote this book.
3. Friends of the Soviet Union.
4. Bertrand Russell.
5. Hook refers here to the committee organized to honor John Dewey posthumously.
6. Herbert W. Schneider, professor of philosophy, Columbia University.
7. Horace Kallen.
8. William Heard Kilpatrick, professor of education, Teachers College, Columbia University.

149

Dear Professor Teller,[1]   October 30, 1962

Thank you very much for your letter of October 16th about *Fail-Safe*.[2] I have already read the book and confirm your judgment of its political tendency and especially its likely political effect. I am planning to review it for the *New Leader* in hopes that *Time* magazine will comment on the review.[3] I shall use shamelessly the technical points you make, but my main criticism will be of the authors' political ignorance.

What I found contemptible about the book was the picture painted of American civilian experts on nuclear affairs. The authors have learned everything they know from these experts, including the fact that no weapon system can be infallible. They then turn around and paint them as monsters, and attribute to them positions they have never held. It is clear, as Burdick asserted in his interview with Norman Cousins, that the authors believe or profess to believe that some such accident is "inevitable," the word is Burdick's. To say that an accident of this kind is inevitable is just as absurd as to say it is impossible.

I, too, am sorry that we didn't have a chance to meet more often last year. There is a chance that I may be in the Bay area late in January. I shall take the liberty of looking you up if you are on the scene at that time.

1. Edward Teller, nuclear physicist.
2. A novel by Eugene Burdick and Harvey Wheeler about human extinction resulting from nuclear weapons.
3. "The Politics of Science Fiction," *New Leader* 45 (December 10, 1962): 12–15. This was expanded into *The Fail-Safe Fallacy* (New York, 1963).

150

Dear Professor Kimura, [1]   January 30, 1963

It is always a pleasure to hear from one of Japan's most distinguished thinkers whose wisdom shines through every line of your communication. What I also deeply appreciate is something which alas! I have found much rarer than wisdom, viz., a passion for human freedom. Today, more than ever in the past, true wisdom about human affairs and especially about the preservation of a peace worthy of man, requires the presence of this passion for human freedom and a readiness to defend it whenever it is threatened.

I agree heartily with many of the points you make, but I wish to supplement them by making some more specific proposals concerning the question of how to achieve a stable and permanent peace. Before making these proposals I should like to offer a few comments on your own observations.

I maintain that there already exists a common interest between the United States and the U.S.S.R. This is a common interest in survival. The peoples of the United States and the U.S.S.R. desire peace as fervently as the people of Japan. The leaders of the United States also desire peace. The best proof of this is that when the United States had a monopoly of atomic weapons and could have imposed their will on the U.S.S.R., they refused to follow the policy advocated at that time by Bertrand Russell who urged that these atomic bombs be dropped on the Soviet Union if it rejected the American proposal to turn over all atomic power and weapons to an international authority. (I am attaching a copy of this letter of Bertrand Russell which has since been published and which indicates that he was prepared to sacrifice the entire population of Western Europe in order to destroy Communism.)

Now it has been obvious that until recently, when Khrushchev abandoned the Leninist-Stalinist doctrine that war between the democratic and Communist worlds was inevitable, that the Soviet leaders did not believe that peace was possible. They sometimes professed a belief in coexistence, but at the same time they insisted that capitalism inevitably breeds war. One cannot sincerely believe both that capitalism can coexist with socialism and that capitalism inevitably generates war. Lenin was fond of quoting the Prussian General von Clausewitz that "war is the continuation of politics by other means." And although it is true that on occasions Stalin and Lenin also talked about how much they loved peace, they probably had in mind another famous dictum of von Clausewitz. "The conqueror is always a lover of peace: he would like to subdue our state unopposed."

The development of nuclear weapons has finally convinced Khrushchev and the Kremlin that war is so deadly that no one can win it. One does not have to believe that all human life will be destroyed in a nuclear war or that the survivors will necessarily envy the dead. Whatever the costs, they are too high. Everyone loses. Khrushchev's realism on this issue in contradistinction to the irresponsibility of the Chinese Communists on this point cannot be praised too highly. Mao-Tse-tung cannot forgive Tito for revealing the fact that Mao told him some years ago that the Chinese Communists were prepared to lose three hundred million lives in a nuclear war if they would win it. I have never been able to understand the confidence which some of the left-wing Japanese Socialist leaders place in a person capable of such cold-blooded inhumanity. Perhaps they are not really Socialists!

Why, then, if the U.S. and the U.S.S.R. have the common interest in survival have they not worked out a program of disarmament and suspension of all nuclear experiments? The reason is clear. The leaders of the U.S.S.R. have refused to accept reasonable inspection and controls. An agreement on disarmament without adequate control and inspection is not worth the paper it is written on. Why? Because unfortunately the world has had a very sad experience with the systematic violation of its treaties by the Soviet Union. Again and again the West signed agreements, and again and again when it suited the Kremlin they were broken. The last and most glaring instance was the violation by the U.S.S.R. of its public pledge not to resume nuclear testing after the U.S. had ceased all tests. Then suddenly the Kremlin announced tests which to be carried out properly required preparations of many months. This proved that the Soviet Union had been cheating.

The U.S. has continually reduced the margin of safety in inspection and tests in order to induce the Kremlin to accept controls, but it cannot jeopardize the liberties of the remaining free nations of the world, including those of Japan, by abandoning the indispensable precautions.

I do not exaggerate the danger of the Soviet violation of its pledges. There is not only the overwhelming evidence of history, there is the evidence of its own ideology. I certainly agree with you that all nations should faithfully "observe the principle that no country is allowed to interfere in the internal politics of any other country." The Kremlin has signed such declarations hundreds of times. Yet it has organized a fifth column which is actively working in its behalf in almost every country on the face of the globe.

In this connection there is a well attested incident which testifies to the way in which Communists think. Harry Hopkins was complaining to Stalin about the difficulties in the course of negotiations with the Japanese at the end of the war. The Japanese rightly insisted that they should be permitted to keep their Emperor if they wished. They made this a condition for peace. The Americans were negotiating with them in good faith. All this made Stalin impatient. He told Harry Hopkins it was all a waste of time. "Promise the Japanese anything they ask for," Stalin said, "in order to get them to lay down arms. Then after they surrender, you do what you want." This is exactly how Stalin and the Kremlin negotiated. This position follows from their ideology. It reinforces the absolute necessity of having adequate controls when disarmament conventions are drawn up. Have we forgotten the promises the Kremlin made to the Hungarians if they surrendered? They did not even abide by the sacred promise of a safe conduct to Nagy[2] who had taken refuge in the Yugoslav embassy.

Since I believe that Khrushchev and the Kremlin now understand the dangers of any type of nuclear war, I have hopes that in time they will accept multilateral disarmament under adequate controls. I agree with you that it will take time.

What else should the U.S. and the U.S.S.R. do to build common interests? Here you have pointed the way by suggesting that they cooperate in aiding the underdeveloped countries. This is a very complex problem. The underdeveloped countries might resent it, preferring to play off one nation against another. Perhaps all aid should be channeled through an international authority. I am concerned about the effects of uncontrolled aid on the economies and work habits of these countries. If this aid comes too easily, and proper safeguards are not adopted against waste and inefficiency, the people who live in these countries may become dependent on perpetual relief and not develop habits of self-aid. The economy of Japan in the past started from levels lower than those of some countries today. Japan transformed herself into a great industrial power primarily by its own efforts. Is it too much to expect that something of the diligence and conscientiousness, the patient craftsmanship and exquisite sense of workmanship exhibited by the Japanese people in their evolution be manifested by the peoples of other undeveloped countries? The Japanese people know that it is not healthy either for one's character or for one's welfare always to receive and never to give. The underdeveloped countries may have few things to give for what they receive, but their citizens should give of themselves for the public good. I should like to see economic aid internationalized and distributed with an eye on the necessity of aiding peoples to aid themselves. Aid should be educational rather than only in the form of a global soup kitchen.

I come finally to a proposal for achieving stable peace which you do not touch on, but which I believe of the highest importance. The leaders of both countries claim that the peoples of the other side needlessly distrust them, that popular opinion is misled by the propaganda of the press, radio, and television facilities. Very well, let us make a beginning and a common quest for the truth about each other.

Let us begin by raising the Iron Curtain in the field of culture. Let each government permit the leaders of the other side to talk to its own side in complete freedom. Let the U.S. turn over to the U.S.S.R. one radio channel for its exclusive use and *vice versa*. Let the same be done with a television channel, then a theater, a school, and possibly a column in a newspaper. The leaders of both sides will be in a position to address themselves directly to the populace of the other country. The mechanism of exchange—of fair and equitable exchange can be worked out. As the Iron Curtain slowly lifts there will be a surge of new confidence in the possibilities of peace.

In addition I should like to see the exchange educational program extended not only in the technical and engineering and agricultural disciplines but in the arts and humanities. Let a Soviet professor of philosophy give a course in a leading American university and an American professor of philosophy at the University of Moscow or Leningrad. Let the students have free access to these professors not only in philosophy but in economics, history, literature, art, law, sociology, and anthropology. Some may object that the U.S.S.R. will send only party people and trained propagandists but that the U.S. will send only reputable scholars. No matter. I think the U.S. would be willing if only reciprocity in essential matters is honestly carried out.

Many of my proposals may not be practicable. It will be hard to overcome Soviet suspicion. But since the Kremlin professes to have the truth in all these matters, it should not fear open and honest debate. The eyes of the world will be on the two countries, and in time some progress may be made. If these proposals are unacceptable, I am prepared to make others. The important thing is to keep the two sides talking together even vehemently or belligerently rather than fighting each other.

I must confess that I am not an optimist in politics, and because the worst may be avoided it does not mean that the best will be achieved. But as long as the worst is avoided—that is a [next two words are illegible]. And the worst is war.

I believe that the Kremlin may slowly become more receptive to the reasonable proposals which you and I have made. I know that I shall exercise my privileges as a free citizen of a free country to criticize my government if it refuses to consider them. Perhaps as the Soviet people understand the significance of Peking's attack upon Khrushchev as a revisionist, as they reflect upon Red China's invasion of India, as they hear the Chinese Communists loud boast that *they* are the heirs of Stalin and his concentration camp economy, they will draw closer to the American people out of a common interest and a common fear.

You are correct in referring to a fantasy which Thomas Masaryk[3] once projected. All the peoples of the world would forget their differences if the earth were threatened with an invasion from Mars. It may be that what will bring the peoples of the U.S. and U.S.S.R. closer together will be the emergence of Red China as an aggressive nuclear power. But China has already twice endangered the peace of the world. Tomorrow she may be even a greater danger to peace. But that is another problem.

1. Takeyasu Kimura, professor of economics, University of Tokyo.
2. Imry Nagy, head of the Hungarian government during the 1956 revolution. He was executed in June 1958.
3. Founder of the Czech Republic in 1918 and president of Czechoslovakia, 1918–35.

151

Dear Mr. Fulton,[1]   January 30, 1963

I am replying to your letter of January 23, 1963.

You can work concretely for international peace by thinking more about what you can say to your son, Timothy, when he is old enough to ask questions about the heritage we leave him. It is a heritage of many things and traditions. The most precious aspect of that heritage are the ideals and institutions of freedom which permit him to grow into a person, with the power to exercise his judgment, and the right to say "No" to tyranny. It is a heritage which will enable him, in your own words, "to grow into a considerate person," acquiring a dignity by recognizing the dignity of other human beings.

You must also tell your son, Timothy, that this heritage was won for him by tens of thousands of human beings who died in the fight for freedom, who suffered, and bled and underwent such torture in dungeons and concentration camps that they prayed for death as a release from pain and indignity. These were the men who refused to take as their motto survival at all costs and at any price, and therefore refused to live a life of infamy, compounding the evils of cowardice with those of betrayal.

The world that Timothy and his father inherit today would not be in existence if at the time that Hitler threatened to overrun the world, the citizens of that day had asked: how can I preserve peace?, instead of asking: how can I preserve freedom? Indeed, had their leaders asked the second question early enough and answered it intelligently, they would also have found the way to preserve peace, too.

Tell your son, Timothy, that you and he owe a debt to all those who fought and died so that both of you can breathe the air of freedom; that you can discharge that debt only by fidelity to the same faith which inspired them; and that this allegiance is part of the great humanistic tradition which teaches that it is not life itself that is worth living but the good life.

Tell your son, Timothy, that intelligence and courage and compassion are the three pillars of the good life, that when freedom is threatened by oppression and tyranny, he should scorn those who would frighten or woo him into capitulation by slogans such as: "It is better to live on one's knees as a slave than die on one's feet," or "that it is better to be a live jackal than a dead lion." To the last, let your son, Timothy, and the Timothies everywhere reply:

"Yes, it is better to be a live jackal than a dead lion—for jackals but not for men; that those who are willing to live like men, to fight and if necessary to die like men, have the most excellent prospects of surviving as free men and escaping the fate of both live jackals and dead lions."

If the Timothies of this world are inspired by this attitude, we will have both a free *and* a peaceful world. For Timothy to believe it, *you* must believe it. Do you?

---

1. Leonard V. Fulton, El Corrito, California.

152

Dear Mr. Lawler,[1]   April 30, 1963

I have received a copy of *Continuum*[2] and your letter of invitation to contribute to it. I would sooner write for the *Daily Worker*.

I read your editorials and reviews with growing amazement. All my life I have fought Catholic authoritarianism, but *your* variety of Catholicism I find morally vile. This is *not* because your position of unilateral disarmament is an invitation to Communist aggression and disarms the free world in its struggle against the extension of Communist terror. Here you are merely politically naive and historically ignorant. What I find morally vile is your aspersions upon the character and personality of those like Herman Kahn[3] and others who are concerned with the preservation of both peace *and* freedom, your studied avoidance of their arguments, your jeers and denigration of their motives. On the other hand, you have nothing save kind words for appeasers and unilateralists—to which I do not object—but not a critical line in assessing the yawning weaknesses of their position, to which I do object.

You dare to speak of moral atrophy in referring to Kahn, Teller, and critics of appeasement. But it seems to me that your own writing exhibits an atrophy of the centers of critical intelligence. And in our complex world a morality without intelligence leads to disaster. One expects a certain degree of hypocrisy in a purely secular journal. Its presence in a religious periodical is nauseating.

1. Justus George Lawler, editor, Herder and Herder, a New York Roman Catholic publishing house.
2. A new Catholic quarterly.
3. Herman Kahn, defense analyst and author of *On Thermonuclear War* (Princeton, N.J., 1960).

153

Dear General Harris,[1]   January 2, 1964

Thank you very much for your letter of December 28 commenting so generously on my small book *The Fail-Safe Fallacy*. That the Strategic Air Command is devoted "to the preservation of an honorable peace" is apparent to any knowledgeable person but, unfortunately, books like *Fail Safe* transmit a badly distorted image among millions who are not reached by refutations like mine.

It seems to me a perfectly legitimate aspect of the educational activity of the United States Air Force to counteract misleading impressions about itself—beginning with the immediate families and friends of the personnel and extending to ever-widening circles. Ours happily is an essentially civilian tradition, but every soldier, sailor, and airman is a citizen who, as a citizen, is justified in participating in discussion of problems of common concern.

If I could afford it I would send a copy of my little book to every member of the United States Air Force with my compliments in the hope that they would read it and pass it along to others.

1. Lieutenant General Hunter Harris, vice–commander in chief, Headquarters Strategic Air Command, Offutt Air Force Base, Nebraska.

154

Dear Vetter,[1]   January 21, 1966

Your note of January 10th was forwarded to me and has just come to hand. Although you wrote it in cold but toothless malice, I found it hilarious. It really brightened my day. I cannot tell what occasioned your missive, since the only statement I have recently signed was the Freedom House Appeal in support of the South Vietnamese struggling against the aggression by the North Vietnamese and your friends the Viet Cong. It is the same kind of statement I signed at the time of the attack against South Korea, and earlier when Western Europe was threatened by Hitler—defensive actions which, if I recall correctly, you also opposed. Had we followed your political line we would all be dead or enslaved by now.

I do not know who Hargis[2] is and the only Schwarzes[3] I am acquainted with are all New Yorkers and all democrats with a small "d."

Yes, your note did indeed bring back some memories, but I am afraid not very pleasant ones. Two stand out. I remember you positively slavering over your collection of pornography to the obvious disgust of your wife and embarrassment of your guests. And even more vividly your boasts about how much of this and that you were hoarding during the war against Fascism—and this even after you changed your line when Hitler invaded the Soviet Union.

I am glad to see that your interest is on higher matters, however mistaken and hysterical you may be about them. But one thing I can't permit you to get away with—your trying to pass yourself off as someone who was critical of Stalin! At the time of the Moscow Trials you gave no evidence of it, jeered at those who opposed it, and contemptuously refused to sign any statement calling for an inquiry or denouncing Stalin's purges and terror.

Finally, I am puzzled by your jubilation that Communist Russia and China pay hard cash for Western wheat while "free-enterprise India" gets it free. What have you got against India? You really should inform yourself about these things. Your colleagues and students used to say you were ignorant of psychology—the joke of your department!—but one would expect you to know *some* things of general knowledge.

India is *not* a free enterprise country as her succession of five-year plans show. Her dominant Congress Party is socialist. Her agricultural troubles are the result of drought and especially population problems which would be still there even if there were no Rajahs. China's and Pakistan's attacks have also contributed. The fact that Russia must buy wheat shows the failure of her agricultural policies, while China's famines are induced *both* by population pressure and repression (forced collectivization).

Personally I am in favor of sending surplus American wheat free not only to India but to Russia and China, too, provided a UN team supervises its distribution so that all elements of the population get it, and bread is not permitted to become a weapon against dissenters. There is a precedent for this—the Hoover Relief Mission in the twenties which the Russians accepted.

I close in the hope that at your age you have permanently outgrown your early interests and are prepared to do some serious reading.

1. George B. Vetter, professor of psychology, New York University.
2. The Reverend Billy Hargis, anti-communist evangelist.
3. Frederick C. Schwarz, head of the Christian Anti-Communist Crusade and author of *You Can Trust the Communists* (Englewood Cliffs, N.J., 1960).

155

Dear Corliss,[1]   July 8, 1966

Voltaire once remarked that everyone has a natural right to be stupid, but that beyond a certain point it was a privilege that should not be abused. Your letter of June 30 replying to my attempt to reason with you has gone far beyond that point.

I did not suggest that you hang yourself. Nor did Max Eastman. He merely expressed the fear that you would do so after Khrushchev's revelations of the crimes of Stalin whom you had so zealously supported against the criticisms of John Dewey, Norman Thomas, and other democratic and socialist thinkers. Your thunderous silence as our charges against Stalin were being confirmed seemed to indicate a state of despair. That you should read this fear as a suggestion on our part is such an obvious projection of your own state of mind that it is tantamount to an acknowledgment. I predict that more revelations about Stalin's barbarities will come to light. The longer you live—and I hope you live a long time because personally I bear you no ill, objecting only to your defense of terror—the greater will be your punishment.

Nor is it true that I have defended "Johnson's war of aggression in Vietnam." I have defended the joint America–South Vietnam war of defense against the Communist North Vietnamese efforts and that of their Viet Cong agents to impose by force a Communist terror regime on the South. And although exercising the privileges of a citizen of a free society to criticize some features of American policy, I have been opposed to a withdrawal of American forces before UN supervised and guaranteed elections could be held. Otherwise this would lead to the massacre and/or enslavement of millions of South Vietnamese. Even the Buddhists are opposed to the Viet Cong!

But you cannot shed your guilt as an apologist for Stalin's terror—have you read the books the Soviets themselves have published on life under Stalin?—by making false charges about Johnson and pretending he is like Stalin. You wouldn't be alive if he were or enjoy the right under our Bill of Rights to defend the terror of the Viet Cong.

No, you don't believe that silly stuff yourself! In your heart of hearts you yourself know how deeply you committed yourself to Stalin's regime, and how lucky you are to live in a free culture that does not purge by concentration camp, frame-up trials, and death those that were proved wrong, not even those who like you betrayed its ideals by pleading Stalin's cause. Bless your stars you live in the U.S. and not the U.S.S.R.!

Whenever your name is mentioned, some one is sure to ask: what did he say when the Russians themselves exposed Stalin? I bet members of your own family don't mention Stalin's name for fear of embarrassing you!

1. Corliss Lamont.

156

Dear Corliss,[1]   November 16, 1966

The next time you visit your analyst I suggest that you discuss with him the phenomenon of projection. Your letter is a perfect textbook case of projection. Having passionately defended the Moscow Trial Frame-up in the teeth of the overwhelming evidence adduced by the Dewey Commission, evidence confirmed by Khrushchev's speech before the XXth Congress of the Russian Communist Party, you are now claiming that *you* have become the victim of a frame-up. It really is to laugh! Those whose frame-ups you defended were tortured and killed, their dependents sent to concentration camps, their lives blasted. But you are thriving comfortably on the unearned increment of a culture whose free institutions you would destroy.

In order to live with yourself you must imagine that *you* are the victim of an imaginary plot. Your analyst will tell you that your projection is the defense by your "unconscious" to blot out the memory of your long years of apologia of Stalin's terror.

Even without the "mythology" of psychoanalysis the situation is clear enough. Far from hounding you, I have never written you except in answer to your own jeering letters. And I have never uttered anything about you which is as condemnatory as what John Dewey said about your conduct in his letters and conversations to me.

You have been wrong about a thousand things. But so have others and, despite the McCarthys, in a free society one has a right to be wrong. What is unforgettable and unforgivable about you are three things: (1) your defense of the Moscow Trials despite the evidence we offered you, (2) your enthusiastic encomiums of Stalin at a time when his hands were still sticky with the blood of innocents, and (3) your calumny against those who opposed Stalin and sought to expose the truth about his terroristic rule.

Your silence about the Moscow Trials and your role in defending them during the ten years which has elapsed since Khrushchev's speech is so deafening that it drowns out your protestations about anything else. Your name has become a byword among those who remember the past.

Despite all this I do not believe that the gates of compassion should be shut in the face of anyone who sincerely regrets his evil actions. And I would like to make a proposal which can serve as a test of your good faith. Instead of spending money on advertisements for yourself and your books as a great humanist thinker, I suggest that you take a page in the *NY Times* in which you declare to all and sundry that study of the evidence presented by the Dewey Commission in the light of Khrushchev's speech and subsequent revelations in the Soviet Union and elsewhere (e.g. the rehabilitation of many who were liquidated, etc.) has convinced you that you were mistaken about the Moscow Trials, ashamed of calling John Dewey a red-baiter, etc. etc.

Only an act of this kind will free you from your imaginary obsessions about being the victim of a frame-up, and give you enough peace and tranquility to live with yourself. The longer you delay, the greater the burden of your guilt. Every politically conscious person whom I have met and who knows that I know you has asked me in the course of the last ten years,

"Say, what did Lamont do after he read Khrushchev's speech?" Some even feared that you would not survive the shock.

The last time I was asked the question, I replied: "Lamont wrote me implying that he may have made a mistake—comparable to a mistake I made in saying that Darrow addressed a jury rather than a judge in the Loeb-Leopold case." The rejoinder was not difficult to anticipate: "Why, the s.o.b. is sticking to the old line despite everything. I'll bet he's having nightmares!"

You close your letter "in pity and anger." You fool yourself again! Pity and anger don't mix. If you feel one, you can't feel the other. The truth is, dear Corliss, that you may be angry with me but you don't pity me. You are angry with me because you know I am right, disinterestedly right, about you. You are really pitying and feeling sorry for yourself—for having lost the intellectual and moral respect of your fellows, you have lost your own sense of self-respect. Self-respect cannot be bought or won back by money but only by moral courage.

I propose an act of moral courage to you. What about it?

1. Corliss Lamont.

157

Dear Professor Morrison,[1]   October 10, 1967

Thank you for your letter of October 3rd. I am surprised that you have drawn such sweeping conclusions about my position from my exchange with Mr. Arnoni.[2] I have regarded our involvement in Vietnam originally as a mistake but do not believe that we can pull out now without a negotiated peace that would save at least millions of people who resisted Communist aggression with our encouragement from extermination. I have publicly opposed escalation in the war on *both* sides.

I am completely unconvinced by "the evidence" that the U.S. is deliberately making war against civilians unrelated to the military efforts. If that were our policy, all of North Vietnam would have been laid waste by now. There are, of course, errors. We have bombed our own troops and South Vietnamese troops many times!

I have a vivid memory of the Communist charge that the U.S. conducted germ-warfare in Korea! Visiting delegations, not all of whom were Communists, were taken in by manufactured evidence. After the hostilities ceased, even the Communists dropped the charge. It was an elaborate hoax.

None of the evidence you cite is at all persuasive to sustain such serious charges as you are prepared to believe. The circumstantial evidence about the extent of our bombing is far from conclusive. It may take ten times as many bombs to put a hidden battery of guns above the de-militarized zone out of commission, especially at a hardened protected site, than to destroy an entire city.

This letter is necessarily inadequate to do justice to all the issues, but I am under the impression that you have assumed too much about my position which differs in important respects both from the hawks' and doves'.

1. Chaplain W. Morrison, professor of history, Youngstown University.

2. M. S. Amoni and Hook debated Vietnam in letters published in *New Republic* 50 (September 25 and October 23, 1967).

158

Dear Sir,[1]   August 5, 1968

I have time only for a brief response to your request for a comment on the interview with William Sloane Coffin,[2] the tearsheets of which have just reached me.

The only principle that can justify William Sloane Coffin's appearance in your salacious pages is that in times of plague it is necessary to post notices everywhere—even in whore houses. Reverend Coffin apparently believes we live in times of plague.

What is intellectually more objectionable is to have him queried by a stooge who instead of engaging in an honest and searching examination of his views feeds him leading questions, to which Mr. Coffin makes carefully rehearsed answers without having to meet the obvious rejoinders to the glaring errors of fact and logic in his argument, and the deficiencies and inconsistencies in his moral position.

An honest exchange would have consisted of a spontaneous, critical dialogue between Mr. Coffin and someone who was not a gaping, worshipful admirer but who had a sober control of the relevant facts. To cite only one instance. One of Mr. Coffin's key assumptions is that American foreign policy is based on the conception of Communism "as a monolithic world force"—with one face, one ideology, and one danger. We do not have to agree with all aspects of American foreign policy—as I do not!—to know that this assumption is absurdly false, shattered on a hundred hard rocks of facts. We have distinguished over and over again between Tito, Stalin, Khrushchev, Gomulka, Mao, Castro, and Kosygin.

Morally Mr. Coffin stands compromised by his retreat from the declaration of October 20, 1967 in which after *citing* as the law of the land "anyone who knowingly counsels, aids or abets another to refuse or evade registration of service in the Armed Forces . . . shall be liable to imprisonment" etc., he went on to add,

> We hereby publicly counsel the young men to continue in their refusal to serve in the Armed Forces . . . we pledge ourselves to aid or abet them in all the ways we can. This means that if they are arrested for failing to comply with a law that violates their consciences, we, too, must be arrested; for, in the sight of that law, we are now as guilty as they.

At that time Mr. Coffin did *not* contend that the law was unconstitutional; he did *not* give that as grounds for his defiance. When the government finally and reluctantly took him at his word, he shifted his ground. Not only did he plead that the law violated his rights to free speech but that he didn't make the speech [next several words are illegible] by the law, that he did *not* counsel or aid or abet draft evasion. It is one thing to say "I made the speech and it is unconstitutional to punish me." It is altogether different to say, "I deny I made the speech and therefore should not be punished."

The only extenuation I can find for Mr. Coffin's role as a gravedigger of the freedoms he exploits in his crusade against an imperfect American democracy, struggling to survive and improve in a sea of troubles, is that he cannot see the truth for his tears—about the world, his country, and himself.

P.S. This letter must be printed entire, if printed at all.

1. Auguste C. Spectorsky, editorial director, *Playboy* magazine.
2. Chaplain, Yale University.

159

Dear Mr. Sherson,[1]   November 3, 1970

I have read and reread your letter of October 28th. Feeling as you do about me it must have required patience and forbearance for you to write it. But in that fact I see the glimmer of hope that you are still open to reason. You are suffering from one of the diseases of idealism—and when you admit that you are ready to condone murder and that if you had the courage you would engage in it, I am moved to compassion for you and to tears for your anguished parents. Ideas like yours have led the Brandeis students to kill an innocent father of nine children—and once killing begins of this kind, the perpetrators become hardened and end up as moral maniacs.[2]

So try to think through the position once more. It may save your life and the life of others.

1. First of all, it is possible to oppose the U.S. involvement in Vietnam and still be opposed to the student violence you condone. The student violence will *not* shorten our involvement. It only makes more likely internal repression for which, if it comes, you and those who think like you and act on their thoughts will be *mainly* responsible. If I were a John Bircher[3] and favored repression, I would hire the Weathermen[4] to do just what they are doing. For they are indistinguishable in their role from agents provocateurs.

2. Secondly, your comparison between the terrorism of student extremists and American actions in Vietnam is completely illegitimate. There is little difference between the things that happen in Vietnam and what happens in any war. During the war against Hitler and his Japanese allies, hundreds of thousands of non-combatants were destroyed at Dresden, Hamburg, Hiroshima. But what would you have had—if Hitler and Fascism had not been opposed? Not merely 6 million people incinerated[5] but probably 60 million! You are alive, and all your family, only because Hitler was defeated. You can speak freely today as well as the foolish pacifists you so much admire only because others were *not* pacifists and died to prevent the extension of Fascism. All politics in a world where interests conflict—and they will always conflict!—is a choice of lesser evils. You will not mature politically unless you understand that.

3. You have your opposite numbers in the ranks of fanatical anti-Communists. What answer would you make to someone who addressed you as follows:

> You who profess a concern for human life and freedom: What about the millions who have been tortured and slaughtered by the terroristic Communist regimes of the world? What about the hundreds of thousands killed or exiled in North Vietnam? Authentic documents of defectors from the Viet Cong report that 15 categories of individuals numbering 2 millions are scheduled for liquidation if and when the Communists take over in the South. What are you doing to save *their* lives? You are a blatant hypocrite, completely indifferent to the fate of past, present, and future victims of Communism. Actually, you are a collaborator by your silence and an accomplice by virtue of your criticism and actions. So long as you tolerate Communist liquidations (read the grisly accounts of the torture and beheadings by the Viet Cong), you yourself deserve to be liquidated.

The logic of this fanatic is the mirror image of yourself. You say you would be glad to see Nixon dead if you thought it would save the life of one Vietnamese peasant. But you recognize that even if Nixon were dead, it wouldn't save the life of one Vietnamese peasant. However, if you love Vietnamese peasants so much, what about the tens of thousands of Vietnamese peasants slaughtered by General Giap who refused to pay tribute or disagreed politically with him and his group. Would you say—shouldn't you say if you are clear-headed—about your sincerity I have no doubt—(all of the Nazi students I argued with in the 20's were sincere), "I would be glad to see General Giap shot if I thought it would save the life of one Vietnamese peasant."

4. The fact that you don't say it shows that you are woefully uninformed and misinformed. I am no admirer of the South Vietnam regime, but there is incomparably more freedom and dissent permitted there than in North Vietnam, which is a total dictatorship—more freedom than in our own Civil War, much more than in the U.S. at the time of Valley Forge, etc. There is an opposition press, a supreme court, we hear of dissent, etc. The plain truth is that the people of South Vietnam don't want to be ruled by the Communist North.

Despite all this I think it was a mistake for the U.S. to get involved when it did, since a victory would be possible only by risking a war that would result in worse evil. But it is obvious to all but fanatics that we are trying to get out—even Nixon (whom you would kill), too. But you can't undo a mistake by just saying it is a mistake. You can't leave precipitately and turn over to the tender mercies of the Viet Cong butchers the hundreds of thousands our presence encouraged to fight. It is like the mistake of a bad marriage. You can't walk out just like that leaving the children uncared for. You must make provision for them.

Your ignorance about the state of the world cannot be explained merely by your youth but by your deficient political education. You write like one who has suddenly discovered poverty and deprivation. You talk about *The Grapes of Wrath*, but you really don't know what you're talking about. I grew up under the *urban* conditions equivalent to the scenes Steinbeck described and in many respects worse. Together with Norman Thomas, A. J. Muste (before he became a pacifist), and others I fought to transform those conditions. In large measure we succeeded—but we have raised our sights and must do much more. But the progress made counts for nothing in your eyes.

How explain then that it is the Okies[6] of the 30's and their descendants who feel that they must defend the country against you and your paranoic violence-prone friends? How explain the fact that Steinbeck spent the last 10 years of his life in large part combatting just such attitudes like yours? How explain that you seem ignorant of the fact that the Federal Government has recognized in *principle* its responsibility for a floor of welfare (and income) below which no human being should be permitted to sink? The floor is much too low, but we can raise it by successful coalition politics and wipe out poverty overnight.

The cure for democracy is a better and more intelligent democracy, not the mindless violence which you approve in a kind of emotional infantile indulgence. Recognize the truth. With all of society's many and gross imperfections, you and your SDS[7] friends have nothing to put in its place. At least we democratic socialists know the direction in which we want to move, and we know what we don't want. We don't want the terroristic dictatorship of a minority of self-appointed and self-annointed leaders whether Kremlinist, Maoist, Castroite, Marcusian,[8] etc. We don't want a police state or even the temporary suspension of the Bill of Rights as it exists in Canada today.[9]

But don't you see that *your* thinking and the actions that logically follow from it would bring about the police state that you profess to fear, and foolishly claim already exists despite the fact that dissent, non-violent dissent, was never wider and more tolerated—even encouraged—in the entire history of the U.S.?

I have paid you the only compliment I can pay to an honest seeker after clarity and political wisdom—to wit, of taking your argument seriously, rethinking my own position, as I ask you to rethink yours.

P.S. This letter is not for publication—in whole or part.

Since I have kept no copy, will you please be good enough to return it to me?

1. Marc S. Sherson. Sherson's letter defended the Viet Cong and attacked American involvement in the Vietnam war.

2. In 1970, Katherine Anne Power, then a senior at Brandeis University, took part in a robbery in Boston of a branch of the Street Bank and Trust Company. During the robbery, a policeman was shot and killed. The small group involved in the robbery planned to use the money to finance their radical activities. Power surrendered to authorities in 1993, after having been a fugitive for twenty-three years. She pled guilty to charges of manslaughter and armed robbery and received an eight- to twelve-year sentence.

3. Member of the John Birch Society, a radical right-wing organization.

4. Weathermen (Weather Underground) were a violent offshoot of the student activism of the 1960s.

5. A reference to the Jewish Holocaust during World War II.

6. Migratory workers from Oklahoma during the 1930s.

7. Students for a Democratic Society.

8. Followers of the Marxist philosopher Herbert Marcuse.

9. Pierre Trudeau, the prime minister of Canada, assumed emergency wartime powers in October 1970 in order to combat the terrorist activities of radical French Canadian separatists.

160

Dear Mr. Silvers,[1]   April 14, 1972

I have just returned from an Easter vacation and found your letter of March 22. Normally I do not read *Esquire* nor have I seen recent issues of the *New York Review*. The quotation attributed to me in *Esquire* was made in the course of a telephone conversation with the writer of the article whom I do not know and have never met. Nonetheless, I do not believe that what I said was wrong and unfair and am sorry you think so.

1) As for your view on "the necessity for democratic rights under all regimes," I do not recall reading anything in the *New York Review* in criticism of the totalitarian repressive practices either in North Vietnam or Cuba—practices much worse than those criticized in some other non-totalitarian countries. Your support of revolutionary groups in this country, including the Black Panthers, can certainly not be justified on the basis of allegiance to democratic values and principles.

2) My reference to Stone[2] was probably elicited in reply to a query of the interviewer. When I referred to his support of the Moscow Trials, I was not thinking of the letter in the *Daily Worker* of April 28, 1938, but the letter of August 14, 1939. I have a very vivid recollection of that letter since it was directed primarily against John Dewey and me, and specifically mentioned the Committee for Cultural Freedom, which we had organized, as among the "Fascists and their friends" who were smearing the Soviet Union as totalitarian. I have the thirteen single-spaced pages of the supporting material that was sent out with that letter and which solicited signatures to the statement that "from the standpoint of cultural freedom" the Soviet Union had made the most far reaching cultural, educational, and scientific advances. This was at a time shortly after the third Moscow Trial and when the worst purges were in progress in every field of the arts and sciences.

The signatories of that letter were endorsing not only the Trials but the purges, too, since they could not have honestly characterized the Soviet Union as they did without approving the horrible repressions that were taking place. Nor could they claim that they were unaware of what was going on because the press was full of reports, and the Committee for Cultural Freedom was holding protest meetings against cultural repression in the Soviet Union (and in Nazi Germany, too).

I had not read Stone's articles in the issues you sent me and was unaware of their existence. How then could I imply that his "views then are reflected in his work for us now?" The context of my remarks makes unmistakably clear that I was referring to the *past*.

I am delighted with Stone's articles and that he understands what is happening in the Soviet Union now. But much worse than what he condemns today was occurring in the Soviet Union during the period in which he was proclaiming the quality of the cultural freedom that existed there, and denouncing us for protesting these outrages.

I am perfectly willing to write to the editors of *Esquire* clearing up any ambiguities and explaining specifically what I had in mind, viz., that at the very time that the Moscow Frame Up Trials were held and the purges raging in the Soviet Union, Stone was endorsing the "cultural freedom" that prevailed in that unhappy country. Had I known of his articles I would have congratulated him on his discovery of what had been going on in the Soviet Union for at least 35 years. Early in the very year he signed the letter Professor Berg and Koltsov[3] were liquidated for their belief in Mendelism.

1. R. B. Silvers, founder of the *New York Review of Books.*
2. I. F. Stone, radical journalist and publisher of *I.F. Stone's Weekly.*
3. Leo Simonovich Berg and N. K. Koltsov.

161

Dear Mr. Madon,[1]   October 24, 1972

Your letter of October 15th has just reached me. If you ever were a student of mine you should have learned to inquire as to the *reasons* for a decision before judging it. Since you have not done so your condemnation means as little to me as your admiration.

I do not discuss the simple-minded question you raise in the enclosed but the ethical issue is much more complex than you realize—even more complex than Sir Robert Thompson[2] believes it to be. As one who believes it was a mistake to get involved in Vietnam, I still recognize that we cannot walk out precipitately anymore than a man who has made a mistake in his marriage can simply walk out on his wife and children. Certain conditions must be met. It is quite clear to me that Senator McGovern's[3] position has prolonged the war. Why should the North Vietnamese agree to any reasonable concessions or conditions when they are assured by McGovern that in the event of his victory, he will completely capitulate to them without asking anything in return and just hope for the return of the prisoners? If you were negotiating with X, and Y, his opponent, tells you he will give you anything you want if and when he wins, wouldn't you hold out?

In philosophy as in other disciplines there is no substitute for common sense. Use it!

1. Roger H. Madon, Riverdale, New York, an opponent of the Vietnam War. Madon wrote Hook to protest his support of the re-election of President Nixon.
2. Robert G. Thompson, British authority on counter-insurgency warfare.
3. Senator George McGovern, Democrat from South Dakota and 1972 Democratic candidate for president.

162

Dear Mr. Mont,[1]   May 9, 1973

Thank you for sending me a copy of your letter to Michael Harrington[2] of December 15th last.

You are perfectly right! My chief reason for not supporting McGovern was his views on, and attitude towards, communism—much more irresponsible than those of Henry Wallace in 1948. In retrospect, I should have ended with a call for a symbolic protest vote for the S.L.P.[3] as I did in 1964. But I didn't believe the polls and thought the election would be close like the one between Humphrey and Nixon in 1968 when I actually campaigned for Humphrey.

Personally I believe and have publicly so declared that Nixon should now resign. But I cannot understand how any democratic socialist can support anyone like McGovern whose views about communism could prove so disastrous to the islands of relative freedom that still exist in the world. Those socialists who are indifferent to McGovern's views about communism remind me of their prototypes who declared that the enemy of the American working class in the early 1940s was in their own country and that foreign policy was dependent on domestic policy.

Of course there are differences—polycentrism, the China-Soviet conflict, etc.—but I consider myself sufficiently an internationalist to worry about Western Germany and Europe, etc. Why did Brandt, why did the socialist gov't. of Israel prefer to see Nixon elected rather than McGovern? The answer is obvious. If only Jackson[4] or Humphrey[5] or even Muskie[6] were running. Despite the detente with Mao and the Kremlin which is one way of curbing both, I still believe that if either power moved against the remaining free countries of the world, or threatened to do so, Nixon probably would do more to resist them than McGovern, and that a McGovern victory would probably encourage whatever aggressive designs they had.

I may be wrong but the above explains my vote, and I still oppose Nixon's domestic policy.

1. Max Mont, Jewish Labor Committee of Los Angeles.
2. American socialist, and author of *The Other America* (New York, 1963).
3. Socialist Labor Party.
4. Senator Henry "Scoop" Jackson, Democrat from Washington.
5. Senator Hubert H. Humphrey, Democrat from Minnesota and 1968 Democratic presidential candidate.
6. Senator Edmund S. Muskie, Democrat from Maine and 1968 Democratic vice-presidential candidate.

163

Dear Ms. Saluk,[1]   February 1, 1975

I have received your letter of January 23 which was forwarded to me here[2] where I am doing some research. Although I am immersed to my neck in other writing commitments, I was struck by the thoughtfulness of your inquiries. I must answer briefly and because of that with an appearance of dogmatism which would be dissipated if I had the time really to do justice to the issues you raise.

1) No, the present economic crisis does not strengthen the Marxist economic position. First because present-day "capitalist" society is a mixed economy, and some economists argue that the difficulties flow from government interference with free market forces. Secondly, the current recession flows from efforts to stem inflation whose causes had nothing to do with the functioning of the economic system *per se*—the Vietnam expenditures that were not covered by increased taxation and by the purely political Arab oil embargo that could bring even a purely socialist economy, dependent upon foreign sources of energy, to its knees. Thirdly, what is valid in Marx's theory of historical development of capitalism remains so regardless of the present economic difficulties.

2) Far from vindicating Lenin's theory of imperialism, recent political and economic events invalidate it. Has your university library access to *Survey*—an English periodical? There is an article by Lewis Gann on "Lenin's Theory of Imperialism" in the winter issue, 1973 (reprinted in Vol. I, #1 of the 1973–74 *Intercollegiate Review*) which explodes its key assumption. I have a reprint somewhere. If I find it I shall send it on. But my books and papers are scattered across the country.

3) Now for a perspective on China—the source today of a new crop of illusions even greater than those generated by the U.S.S.R. in the Thirties—illusions even more prevalent in the academy than among trade unionists.

  a) First of all remind your fellow trade unionists that when Hitler came to power in 1933, he increased the real wages of the German workers, improved their social conditions, welfare benefits, etc. The Nazi trade unions even had a limited right to strike except in defense industries. Would they have endorsed Hitler's political program?
  b) The real contrast is not between the economic state of the Chinese workers and peasants today and what it was 50 or a 100 years ago (technological changes make such comparisons difficult), but between

their present lot and that of the workers and peasants on Taiwan, whose economic status is far and away superior to that of the workers and peasants on Mainland China, and who although not enjoying the political freedom of workers who live in the U.S. nonetheless have much more political freedom than the Chinese or in their own past.

c) Thirdly, the real dimensions of the internal Chinese Communist terror are largely hidden and unknown, but having been in Hong Kong several times and spoken to hundreds of refugees I can assure you that the terror is immense. Some of it leaked out when the Cultural Revolution of 1965–68 took place. Every visitor to China is carefully guarded. They see only what the Chinese want them to see. It is not for nothing that Mao and his followers glorify Stalin.

d) When I am told that the Chinese masses support Mao and the Communist dictatorship I ask why then does the regime fear even the semblance of free and secret elections. I ask why it is that when the gates were open to Hong Kong a few years ago, the rush of millions to get out compelled China to shut them down again. Finally at the only occasion when Chinese were permitted a choice—tens of thousands of Korean War prisoners were given a choice between returning to Mainland China or going to Taiwan (only the Chinese Communists were permitted to harangue, cajole and threaten them because the Indians in charge were making up to Mao)—the overwhelming majority preferred to eat the bitter bread of exile than return to Communist Red rule. Why? Ask your colleagues that.

1. Eleanor Saluk, Gainesville, Florida.
2. Hoover Institution, Stanford University.

164

Dear Bill,[1]   October 23, 1975

I was glad to hear that you, Anita, and Robin are well and in good spirits.

Apparently I was misinformed about your attitude toward Hiss' reinstatement to the Massachusetts bar. I was told that you were up in arms at the prospect.

However I find your observations on his reinstatement and on my criticism of the Court's reasoning singularly unpersuasive. Having had a chance now to read all the documents in the case, it seems clearer than ever to me that the Court's opinion is not only incoherent but rather scandalous, and I hope to show this in an article for a law review as soon as I can find time to do it. The Court overrode the controlling case on the issue of reinstatement—the Keenan case—which declared, in denying reinstatement, that to overcome the original disbarment "requires little less than absolute assurance of a complete change of moral character." In effect then in its opinion on Hiss the Court held that although Hiss' 1950 conviction was "conclusive evidence of his lack of moral character at the time," he had now furnished conclusive evidence of a complete change of moral character.

But even assuming that the probability that Hiss was still knowingly lying in asserting his complete innocence and that he was a victim of a judicial frame-up is only 50% (i.e. even if the judges are completely ignorant of the evidence), how in heaven's name can they assert that the fact that Hiss is now of good character is beyond reasonable doubt?

I really am puzzled, Bill, by several points in your letter—some minor, and others major. The minor ones first.

What has "merely" got to do with the decision to reinstate Hiss? He doesn't expect to practice. Neither his living nor his freedom is at stake. The reinstatement is the first step towards his rehabilitation in the eyes of the world on the authority of the courts or other official body.

Secondly, I never expected you to remind me that Hiss was convicted only of perjury, not espionage or treason. What was the perjury about? If Hiss had not committed espionage or treason, at least one of the two counts on which he was convicted could not have been filed. Even the Board of Bar Overseers in referring to Hiss' conviction of the crime of perjury adds "involving breach of public trust and espionage." The only reason Hiss was not indicted for espionage or treason was because of the statute of limitations.

And now for the main point. You urge me to use my mind to influence "the too many people who think that Hiss was framed" instead of flogging a dead horse. What do you think the effect of Hiss' reinstatement has been not only on the "too many" who think that Hiss was framed but on the many more who were in doubt about whether he was guilty or framed? Inquire about you, read the *New Yorker* comment, the *New Republic,* etc. and you will find that Hiss' reinstatement is widely regarded as a vindication—especially among the young, and even among young lawyers.

Consequently if I am to do as you suggest, influence those who think Hiss was framed, criticizing the decision to reinstate him is among the first things to do. There are other things I am doing, too.

This is hardly the place to touch on your other comments. You evidently have not read my article published in *New America,* the official organ of the Socialist Party, indicating why Nixon was the lesser evil to McGovern. My mistake was to judge the country's sentiment by the ritualistic liberals' response to McGovern in the universities. If I had known that McGovern's position (which was worse than that of Henry Wallace's in 1948), would be so heavily repudiated, I would have come out for the Socialist Labor Party candidate as I did in 1964 when Johnson—as crooked as Nixon anytime— and Goldwater were running. As it is, I gather that some people close to Meany[2] gave my article wider circulation (the NY *Times* didn't print it).

About the *New Leader*. My only regret is that I resigned quietly and killed the front page story the NY *Times* was preparing to run. That would have fulfilled my obligations to Sol Levitas. The readership and influence the *New Leader* once had no longer exists. Had I remained I would have had as much influence on it as you have had on *Partisan Review*. (Aside from the *Encounter* episode, it seems obvious that *P.R.* has used you more than you have influenced it. I shall pay my respects to *P.R.* and some of its editors at the proper time and place.)[3]

The whole question "whom to influence" seems unimportant to me in the twilight of my life, especially since I am not active politically. The critical judgment of a select few on the validity of my ideas means more to me than the plaudits of any crowd. And as you know there are crowds and crowds.

Well, this is longer than it should be, but I hope it's legible (I had difficulty in reading your light pencilled lines).

1. William H. Fitelson, an anti-communist New York lawyer and a friend of the Hooks.
2. George Meany, president, AFL-CIO.
3. See *Out of Step*, ch. 31, "Inside *Partisan Review:* The Radical Comedians."

165

Dear Norman,[1]   May 4, 1976

Lillian Hellman[2] is getting away with murder in her *Scoundrel Time*. She was a fanatical defender of the Moscow Trials and all the associated Stalinist infamies. She viciously attacked even the efforts of the Dewey Commission to discover the truth about the Trials. She was the keynote speaker of the Communist Waldorf Peace Conference in 1949 etc., etc.

She keeps silent about those who without extenuating the behavior of the Communists criticized both the HUAC[3] and the McCarthy committees. Whatever injustices were the result of the excesses of the Congressional committee inquiries do not begin to compare with the genocidal Stalinist practices that Lillian Hellman staunchly defended up to a few years ago.

There is more—much more to be said—to put the picture in balance. Just about three years ago she attacked Kusnetzov[4] (who had defected to England) on the grounds of a rumor that he had given the KGB information about other dissidents as the price for his own safety. In the course of her remarks she admitted that in her visit to the Soviet Union she had become aware of the persecution of the dissidents. But neither in the Soviet Union nor in the U.S. did she open her mouth in protest.

I have not seen a critical word anywhere about her book. Have you assigned it for review to anyone? The Lord knows I have many more important tasks but if you lack a reviewer, I shall be glad to do it.[5]

1. Norman Podhoretz, editor, *Commentary* magazine.
2. American playwright.
3. House Un-American Activities Committee.
4. Anatoly Kusnetzov, Soviet writer who defected to England after becoming disenchanted with communism. The Soviet Union branded him a traitor. Prior to his death in 1979, Kuznetsov was a broadcaster for Radio Liberty.
5. This review ultimately appeared in *Encounter:* "Lillian Hellman's *Scoundrel Time,*" *Encounter* 48 (February 1977): 82–91.

166

Dear Mr. Cohen,[1]   March 19, 1978

Is the piece from *Esquire*[2] you mailed me a spoof? If it isn't how can anyone who is knowledgeable take it seriously?

As for my own views, I am asking the editor of *New America* to send you the issue containing my address criticizing the conservative and neoconservative revival.[3] The December issue of *New America* contains a very brilliant essay by the Polish philosopher Leszek Kolakowski, now at All Souls College, Oxford, which I strongly recommend. It bears on the same theme but with much greater profundity.

You must really stop calling people "nuts" with whom you disagree.

As for your own views on foreign policy and the Soviet Union, they seem to me to be very questionable. What Russian economist called Cuba "our Vietnam?" It is not a question of who is liked but (a) who is more powerful, (b) who is prepared to violate the borders of other nations and (c) for what purpose. The Russians were not liked in Czechoslovakia, but that didn't prevent them from moving in and extending the *Gulag Archipelago.* Hitler was not liked by any country except Germany and Austria, but that didn't prevent him from taking them over.

Look at the Map of Freedom published by *Freedom at Issue* at Freedom House and you will observe that the area of the free world is shrinking.

No one I know is asserting that the USSR is planning to attack the U.S. today or tomorrow. Many are saying that if the USSR acquires a great preponderance of strength, the Kremlin will call the turn on any disputed issue. Already George Kennan has revived Russell's[4] slogan "Better Red than dead," and urged capitulation in the event that any threat of war arises. Those who disagree say that it is possible to avoid *both* war and capitulation, provided the Kremlin realizes that it cannot be certain of victory. Peace has been preserved, in Churchill's phrase, under the "balance of terror." Let us keep that balance until hopefully there are changes within the totalitarian countries.

1. Mortimer T. Cohen, New York.
2. Article in *Esquire* described Hook as one of the founding fathers of neo-conservatism.
3. "Social Democracy Means Human Freedom: A Response to the Conservatives," *New America*, 16 (January 1979): 6, 12.
4. Bertrand Russell.

167

Dear Dan,[1]   August 23, 1978

As usual—you ask the searching questions.

About Berle[2] whom I got to know quite well for a short period of time. We were both on the Board of the Strasbourg College of Free Europe of which he was the leading spirit. As you can imagine, I pumped him about the past, especially the Chambers-Hiss episode. At the time and until the end of his life, Berle was as anti-Communist as I. He offered two varying versions of the Chambers-Levine visit in '39.[3] The first was something along these lines: "The world was falling apart around us and suddenly this improbable-looking man appears with an improbable, horrendous story.[4] How could we be expected to take it seriously with icebergs looming up on all sides of the ship of state," etc. The second version: "Despite the chaos and confusion in Washington, I realized how serious Chambers' charges were and although I found them shocking and almost incredible, I sent a memorandum to the White House but Admiral McIntyre,[5] Roosevelt's advisor on security, refused to pass on the silly tale to Roosevelt." I got the impression from Berle that he believed that until he died Roosevelt remained uninformed about the Hiss charges.

All this was colored by Berle's bitter remarks about Acheson's[6] initial naivete about Communism. He told me that Acheson had pushed him out of the State Department because he, Berle, had an intelligent (called "hard" by those who didn't share it) line on the Kremlin.

More serious is the fact which I didn't know until I read Weinstein's book that Berle under oath at first swore that Chambers had not charged Hiss *et al.* with espionage, despite the existence of Berle's handwritten notes of their meeting which indicated that Chambers had mentioned it in passing. I was out of the country at the time and didn't see any newspaper account of Berle's HUAC[7] testimony in which he also recollected that Chambers had not even identified the Washington group as members of the Communist Party. Technically this was perjury but I believe, though Weinstein does not, that Berle really misremembered. He even denied that Levine was present at the meeting with Chambers. Also he kept telling me that McIntyre was in charge of internal security in 1939 when, according to Weinstein, McIntyre was only appointments secretary to Roosevelt while he, Berle, was ostensibly himself in charge of internal security. I haven't read Berle's diaries which must be taken *cum grano salis*[8] if they have been edited.

Now about Chambers' attitude towards Hiss. You are wrong about there being any element of entrapment towards him; you are right about Chambers' streak of cruelty which was ideologically motivated. And you must get the time period in context to allow for Chambers' ideological shift.

I know that Chambers felt closer to Hiss than to all his other Washington brethren from the time that Herbert Solow[9] came to me in 1938 to help C. come up from under ground. Herbert reported a special relationship to Hiss. So did Meyer[10] who knew that the Chamberses and Hisses had been meeting socially. Someday if and when Meyer tells everything he knows about the principals this will be confirmed, but please don't quote me about this. Not that Meyer knew everything. Actually, after *proving* in his review of Zeligs' book[11] that Chambers was not a homosexual, he was surprised to learn of Chambers' own admission of homosexual incidents. When I kidded him about his analysis, he said that he had roomed with Chambers and traveled by ship to Europe with him, and he saw no sign of this tendency in Chambers. As you know, I don't subscribe to the Freudian mythology, but it seems reasonable to me that Chambers at the time was drawn, at least unconsciously, to Hiss. And Hiss was in every way a likeable fellow in those days, truly idealistic. How else explain C.'s effort to break him away from the Party line when C. was planning to defect. Also remember that the persecution of Chambers began *after* he gave his public testimony. Judging from what Herbert told me about C.'s feelings toward Hiss, they changed markedly after Hiss filed his suit. Herbert was convinced that Hiss had broken with Stalinism, if not Communism, by the time of the HUAC hearings. Chambers was convinced that he had not, and that like other idealistic fanatics his character had been transformed in the political crucible. I do not believe he ever "hated" Hiss, partly because he felt some remorse at exposing him. Despite what Hiss was prepared to do to him, Chambers couldn't help feeling some pity. Actually all of us who were convinced from the outset that Chambers was telling the truth about Hiss felt some pity for Hiss. Over the years when, despite the revelation of the ghastly crimes of the Gulag Archipelago and Hiss' leader,[12] he still persisted in brazening it out, this feeling of pity turned to disgust.

About Chambers' attitude toward Lionel.[13] Chambers, like most of L.'s bright undergraduate Columbia friends, had an intellectually patronizing attitude towards Lionel. This was true of Herbert, Meyer, M. Adler.[14] The only exception I knew was Henry Rosenthal. They all liked him but mistook his gentleness for weakness. It was apparent to me at the meeting L. arranged for me to meet Chambers to set him right about the theory of Social-Fascism (a meeting which Diana Trilling[15] and apparently you, too, doubt ever took place—I assure you it did. In the thirties, although always a follower and not a leader, Lionel was more interested in politics than when you got to know him at Columbia), Chambers was hostile to me on political grounds but affectionately contemptuous to Lionel. You must also remember that by the time the incident related by Pearl[16] took place, Chambers was moving ideologically very far away from the kind of secular rationalism that had originally put him, as he thought, on the road to communism. He became a real heresy hunter, smelling out secular rationalist contraband. Saul Bellow[17] (you may check with him) told me a story a year or so ago about his attempt to get a job at *Time* as a reviewer about the same time that Pearl was there. He cleared all the preliminaries and was sent into Chambers for the final O.K. According to Bellow, Chambers questioned him about Wordsworth's poems and was displeased because B's explanation didn't reflect an appreciation of Wordsworth's turn to orthodoxy. I'm not sure I got the nuances right.

My impression is, although I may be wrong, that at this time and especially after he quit *Time*, C. *hat sich distanziert*[18] from most of his unbelieving Jewish acquaintances. He even seems to have kept Meyer at arm's length during this time. According to *Witness*, of course, we are all *trafe*.[19] If he were alive today he would underwrite Solzhenitsyn's Harvard speech[20] with both hands. He would hate my guts as much as ever, remain cool towards Meyer, and probably welcome your and Irving's[21] intimations of the transcendent as a healthy development. I think he would be astonished at the attempt to make a cult or a deep thinker of dear, gentle Lionel—I suspect Lionel himself would too. But I mention all this because whatever C.'s feeling of *ressentiment,* as you call it, against Lionel, its source has nothing to do with his feelings about Hiss—which given the times, the changing political climates and the personalities involved, are perfectly explicable as much when C. admired Hiss in the full flower of H.'s idealism as when he turned reluctantly against him, and then in the agony of his pain and disillusion vented, and this only in private, his fury against him.

Finally, you are right in saying "there is so much of *The Possessed* in all of this." But Chambers is much more interesting and plausible than any of Dostoyevsky's characters.

1. Daniel Bell, professor of sociology, Harvard University.

2. In a September 1939 meeting, Chambers told Adolf A. Berle, Jr., then assistant secretary of state, of the activities of a clique of pro-Soviet federal employees. For Berle's role in the Hiss–Chambers case, see Allen Weinstein, *Perjury: The Hiss-Chambers Case* (New York, 1978).

3. Meeting of Chambers and the journalist Isaac Don Levine with Berle in September 1939.

4. In 1948, Whittaker Chambers testified before the House Committee on Un-American Activities that while he was a Communist, during the 1930s, Alger Hiss, then a high-ranking State Department official, had provided him with secret government documents to be transmitted to the Soviet Union. After Hiss denied having spied for the Soviet Union, Chambers produced the "pumpkin papers." These were copies of the documents Chambers claimed he had received from Hiss. Hiss was ultimately convicted of perjury and sentenced to five years in prison. After being released from prison in 1954, Hiss launched a campaign of vindication. Two elements in this campaign were restoration of his right to practice law and a reversal by the courts of his conviction. In August 1975, Hiss was readmitted to the Massachusetts Bar. This was the first time in its history that the Massachusetts Bar had ever readmitted a lawyer who had been convicted of a major crime. Hiss's suit, to have his conviction overturned, however, was not successful.

5. Marvin H. McIntyre, appointments secretary to President Roosevelt.

6. For the relationship between Berle and Dean Acheson, see Weinstein, *Perjury,* 63–66.

7. House Committee on Un-American Activities.

8. With a grain of salt.

9. Herbert Solow, friend of Chambers from undergraduate years at Columbia University.

10. Meyer Schapiro. Schapiro was a friend of Chambers since their undergraduate days at Columbia University, and Chambers confided in Schapiro during Chambers's confrontation with Alger Hiss in 1948. For the relationship between Chambers and Schapiro, see Weinstein, *Perjury.*

11. Meyer A. Zeligs, *Friendship and Fratricide: An Analysis of Whittaker Chambers and Alger Hiss* (New York, 1967).

12. Stalin.

13. Lionel Trilling, professor of English, Columbia University, and a friend of Chambers since the 1920s, when they were undergraduates together at Columbia Uni-

versity. Trilling's novel *The Middle of the Journey* (New York, 1947) has a major character modeled on Chambers.

14. Mortimer J. Adler.
15. See letter 195, note 3.
16. Bell's wife.
17. Author of *Herzog* and other novels.
18. "Has distanced himself."
19. Hebrew word for non-kosher.
20. Alexander Solzhenitsyn gave a speech at the 1978 Harvard commencement attacking Western secularism and humanism.
21. Irving Kristol.

168

Dear Mr. Snell,[1]   December 29, 1978

I feel very guilty in provoking you to write such a lengthy letter, but I hope you will forgive me for saying that you seem to have missed the main point of my position. Please try to understand that I don't want a nuclear war with the Kremlin. I want to avoid that war, and without surrendering to Communism.

What I am saying is:

1) The Kremlin will never go to war unless its leaders are convinced they will win it.

2) Our strategy is to make them unsure that they will win such a war or that their losses will be so unacceptable that a victory will be hardly worthwhile to them.

3) They will not be tempted to take even a slight chance of defeat because

   (a) They are winning the world, as they see it, without war.

   (b) They worship at the altar of History—it makes no sense to them to go down fighting for a "lost cause."

   (c) They have always prided themselves on their Bolshevik realism.

   (d) Their satellite populations in all likelihood would revolt in a nuclear war whose fallout would decimate them, etc., etc.

4) At present—no matter what caused it—*your* proposal that we disarm is practically an invitation to them to take over.

5) My proposal is to remain strong enough to make them understand that they cannot destroy our retaliating capacity by a first strike.

Now which one of these propositions do you reject and why?

With all our past faults and irresponsibilities, we are still strong enough to make the Kremlin hesitate to risk nuclear war—and with a little more effort and money we can increase the risk for *them*. I think I know how the Bolshevik mind works. I have been studying it for more than sixty years.

You should be devoting your efforts to describing what the Gulag Archipelago would look like in America if and when we surrendered to the Communists. There will be no ports anywhere to receive the refugee vessels of Americans trying to escape the Communist concentration and extermination camps. I am confident that if the American citizenry grasp what is surely in store for them in the event of a Communist takeover, they will willingly bear the burden of a defense strong enough to *deter* the Kremlin from making war.

At present by preaching a gospel of despair you are without realizing it helping to bring about a universal Gulag Archipelago. Neither Solzhenitsyn, or Mihajlov, or Sakharov[2] preach unilateral nuclear disarmament for the West. I can't believe that you will persist in this foolish view when you think hard about it.

1. Dewitt S. Snell, Schnectady, New York.
2. Mihajlo Mihajlov, Yugoslav political dissident and writer; Andrei Sakharov, Russian dissident and human rights spokesman.

169

Dear Mr. McGillicuddy,[1]   January 1, 1979

This will acknowledge your kind letter of recent date enclosing some photographs of New York. They should have been accompanied by a calendar of 1979.

I am writing, however, to express my puzzlement and distress at what I regard as a disservice not only to your customers, of whom I have been one for almost half a century—since I joined the faculty of New York University—but of the general public.

From time to time I have seen episodes of the television series *The Unknown War*[2] which you have sponsored. Each time I have been appalled by the blatant Soviet propaganda that pervades both the film and the text. I have studied this period and am familiar with most of the episodes described. The distortions, omissions, and outright fabrications are truly horrendous. How could you have been conned into lending your name and resources to such a perversion of the historical truth? Whoever advised you about this matter has abused your confidence, and to some extent undermined the confidence of your own customers in your own judgment.

1. John F. McGillicuddy, president, Manufacturers Hanover Trust Company.
2. This series on the war between the Soviet Union and Nazi Germany presented an overly favorable picture of the Soviet Union and Communist leadership. See Edward S. Shapiro, " 'The Unknown War': Fairy-Tale Version," *Congress Monthly* 45 (December 1978).

170

Dear Mr. Cohen,[1]   March 26, 1979

The periodical in which that absurd list appeared is *Esquire*. By this time you should have received my article from *New America* criticizing the revival of conservatism.

Your letters to others strike me as being more cogent than your letters to me. You write, "If you want to beat Communism, improve conditions in the USA." Improve them we must—regardless of Communism—but no amount of improvement will stand in the way of an expansionist totalitarianism. You remind me of those fools in England who shouted—"If you want to stop Hitler, improve conditions in England, wipe out slums, etc." Well, actually Hitler wiped out the slums with his bombs! Czechoslovakia in 1948 and 1968 actually improved conditions but it did not help them.

But you show real wisdom in your letter to Ira Glasser![2] You put your finger on the basic issue, "The Rights of the Victims," but do not go far enough. I shall send you a copy of a commencement address I gave at the University of Florida on "The Rights of the Victims."

Your retort to the woman who said she thought you were crazy even though you taught her 30 years ago was inappropriate. The fact that it took Ms. X 30 years to find out that you are crazy does not prove that she is crazy but that she is stupid. There is a profound difference between the two states of mind.

You must be middle-aged by now, but you still sound like a bright young freshman trying to impress his teacher. This is a pity. Some of your observations show real insight and wit. Why not develop them into essays—and then possibly a book?

Or after excising needlessly offensive remarks that hurt you more than your targets, why not publish a collection of your letters?

1. Mortimer T. Cohen.
2. Lawyer with the New York branch of the American Civil Liberties Union.

171

Dear Henry,[1]   April 16, 1979

Thank you for your kind words about my contribution to the Hiss discussion in the March issue of *Encounter*.[2] My piece on Caute[3] in the January issue is even more important because the myth about the terror in America during the McCarthy era is being revived.

I am still an unreconstructed Social Democrat who regards the Communist danger as the main threat to human freedom and who believes that the partisans of the free market and the so-called libertarians who would trade with the Kremlin for *profit* are not dedicated to freedom first. But I have always admired your courageous publishing program and regard it as a damn shame that you lost control of your old firm.

Speaking of your books:

1) That Lipper book[4] was and is very important. I remember how uncomfortable Einstein was when I sent him a copy of the German edition, and recently young Joseph Shattan[5] who just read it at my suggestion was as moved by it as he was by Solzhenitsyn.

2) Have you still a copy of my book on the Fifth Amendment?[6] I have no copies and would appreciate one, either paperback or hard cover.

3) Also all my copies of Chambers' *Witness* have been "stolen"—by people who borrow them and refuse or "forget" to return them. Can you send me a paperback?

The older I grow the more formidable grows the challenge to freedom and enlightenment. The historical ignorance of the young is appalling. The situation is too serious to allow oneself to be discouraged. One must keep on fighting.

1. Henry Regnery, founder of Henry Regnery Company, publisher of conservative books.

2. Hook's article "The Case of Alger Hiss," *Encounter* 52 (August 1978): 48–55, provoked several responses which he, in turn, answered in the March 1979 issue.

3. Hook, "David Caute's 'Fable of Fear and Terror'," review of Caute, *The Great Fear: The Anti-Communist Purge under Truman and Eisenhower,* in *Encounter* 52 (January 1979): 56–64. Caute is quite critical of Hook's stance on the matter of Communists in academia.

4. Elinor Lipper, *Eleven Years in Soviet Prison Camps* (Chicago, 1951).

5. Joseph Shattan, neo-conservative intellectual.

6. Hook, *Common Sense and the Fifth Amendment* (New York, 1957).

6

The 1980s

Sidney Hook concluded his autobiography with these words: "The greatest and most enduring source of happiness in my life—aside from the bitter-sweet joys of personal and parental life, about which I am sure few would care to hear—has been the experience and excitement of clarifying ideas, of battling in a good cause, and of teaching a bright and questioning class of students." Hook continued clarifying ideas and battling in the cause of freedom until his death in July 1989. Appropriately enough, the final chapter of *Out of Step* is titled "Reaffirmations." In it he wondered whether "the open society will survive the assaults of its enemies within and without" (*Out of Step,* 596).

Hook's cause was freedom, and much of the last decade of his life was taken up with the defense of academic freedom on the campus. He was not optimistic about its future. "I would lack candor," he noted, "if I did not say that there has been a widespread erosion of the academic ethic itself in American universities even as the defenses of academic freedom against intrusion from outside forces have been strengthened" (*Out of Step,* 591–92). Working at the Hoover Institution on the campus of Stanford University, Hook had a firsthand view of the impact of political correctness and multiculturalism in academia. He was appalled by what passed for advanced thinking, personified by the parade of overwrought Stanford collegians, led by Jesse Jackson, shouting, "Ho, ho, ho, western civilization must go."

Hook's contribution to the defense of academic freedom was helping to found the Center for Rational Alternatives (CRA). This was established in the aftermath of the wave of campus disruptions during the 1960s that was initiated by the Free Speech movement at Berkeley in 1964. The CRA's influence was limited. Its most significant undertaking was sponsoring several national conferences. Its example did, nevertheless, encourage several academicians in the 1980s to create the National Association of Scholars. The NAS succeeded where the CRA had failed in attracting foundation support. Within a few years the NAS had a substantial membership, including some of America's leading academicians. Its quarterly journal, *Academic Questions,* took the lead in exposing the threat to academic freedom, and its annual award for the defense of academic freedom bears the name of Sidney Hook.

172

Dear Mr. Cohen,[1]   January 11, 1980

Your letter of January 2 has just come to hand. . . .

You really ought to be ashamed of yourself. The Kremlin disappointed you—so instead or rethinking your position—you cry "down with Brzezinski"[2] and "to hell with Afghanistan." For your part, you write, the Communists can take over "Mexico, Mississippi and the South Bronx." What would you fight for to prevent them from taking over? It is obvious— nothing. Your position is even more extreme than that of the neo-Nazi isolationists who in a debate with me in 1941 said, "I am prepared to defend the free society from Hitler in the streets of the Bronx."

No, on your view we really need not fear war as the Kremlin expands and builds up its power and puts itself in a position to cut off vital lines of communication throughout the world. When it is strong enough and issues an ultimatum on any issue, "Yield or Fight," the logic of your position will be, "of course we must yield. We can never have the same kind of Gulags here." I can hear you saying—indeed you have come near saying it—"After all, its better to be Red than Dead." As if that was the only alternative! You forget that in a world in which the Kremlin (Khrushchev) has threatened to H-bomb Red China, you may end up by being Red *and* Dead.

There are some things that are too important to be exhibitionistic about. You may not believe that the Afghans are fighting for their freedom. But they are fighting for their country, their religion, their right to be Afghans! Why spit on them? Why cry "to hell with them!"? Why in effect cheer on the same power that trampled on the Hungarians and the Czechs and that would threaten the Israelis and any other group that refuses to accept their yoke.

Shame on you! and shame again! If I were a religious man, I would urge you to pray for God's forgiveness.

1. Mortimer T. Cohen.
2. Zbigniew K. Brzezinski, national security adviser to President Carter, and professor of public law and government, Columbia University.

173

Dear Dr. Brzezinski,[1]   January 8, 1981

I was very much impressed by the incisive, intelligent way you handled your interrogators on the McNeil/Lehrer Report last night. The restraint imposed on yourself by the necessities of your post will not, I hope, operate in the future when you return to scholarly life. Even to the politically unsophisticated mind it should be obvious that the partisans of former Secretary of State Vance's[2] policies are seeking to make you a scapegoat of his bankrupt course. Having heard Vance give his assessment of the international situation according to which the Soviet Union has been suffering defeats everywhere, I am convinced that he was better qualified to be a Minister of the Gospels than a Minister of State.

One of President Carter's few virtues in this area is that he selected and retained you as his advisor. Would that he had followed your advice more often.

1. Zbigniew K. Brzezinski.
2. Cyrus T. Vance, secretary of state under President Carter.

174

Dear Professor Miller,[1]   January 26, 1981

I want to congratulate you on your article "Demystifying Mao" in the current *Humanist*. It is the most illuminating analysis of the Chinese situation I have read, balanced, historically knowledgeable and politically sophisticated—far and away superior to the plethora of journalistic accounts coming from the pens of literary tourists. It deserves a much wider circulation. I suggest you develop it into a small book.

What you say (and some translations from recent Chinese fiction—short stories adapted from life—reinforce the point) suggests that the "excesses" of the Cultural Revolution constitute a kind of Chinese Gulag Archipelago parallel to the Soviet Gulag Solzhenitsyn has been writing about. I put excesses in quotes because the ordinary procedures that were involved together with the actions at the time of the "Let a hundred blossoms bloom" episode would fill many times more than the three volumes that Solzhenitsyn devoted to the Soviet Gulag.

If and when you do the book—or failing that perhaps in an extended article—I hope you will examine the glowing reports of Chinese life and culture during the years of the Cultural Revolution with which the American public, lay and academic, were regaled not only by the Galbraiths[2] and Shirley MacLaines[3] but by scholars under the influence of Fairbank[4] at Harvard. The whole subject warrants an independent study—a project funded perhaps by the NEH or one of the major foundations.

I don't usually write letters like this, but I was so impressed by the perceptiveness of your article—all the more startling because of the locus of its appearance[5]—that I felt it was only appropriate to express my appreciation for its clarity and suggestiveness.

1. Lynn Miller, professor, Temple University.
2. John Kenneth Galbraith, professor of economics, Harvard University.
3. Hollywood actress.
4. John King Fairbank, professor of history, Harvard University, and dean of American Sinologists.
5. In the past Hook had been angered by what he perceived to be the *Humanist*'s tendency to bend over backward when discussing the Soviet Union and communism.

175

Dear Martin,[1]   January 27, 1981

If the doctors give me permission to travel I am planning to attend a Conference on the Crisis in Social Democracy at the end of April in Copenhagen. I am heart-sick at the way Brandt, Kreisky, and Palme[2] are lining up the Socialist International behind Castro in Central America, opposing European efforts to strengthen their defenses, and criticizing the U.S. for intervention in Poland because of our offers (actually the AFL-CIO offers) to give moral and economic support (meager as that is) to the Polish trade unions. I am thinking of writing a paper "In Defense of the Cold War" (which prevented a hot war)—one that the Kremlin has never stopped waging.

What a disaster Carter's foreign policy has been! When you get stronger—you are still young enough!—I propose to write to Reagan telling him who I think should be his foreign policy advisor.

1. Martin F. Herz, State Department official, historian of the Cold War, and friend of the Hooks.
2. Willy Brandt of West Germany, Bruno Kreisky of Austria, and Olaf Palme of Sweden.

176

Dear Senator Percy,[1]   March 23, 1981

As my many writings show, the most recent of which is *Philosophy and Public Affairs* (Southern Illinois University Press), I have been a strong partisan of the policy that concern for human rights should be an integral element in American foreign policy. Because of that, I am writing to you concerning the nomination of Dr. Ernest W. Lefever[2] as Assistant Secretary of State for Human Rights and Humanitarian Affairs.

I have been a close reader of Dr. Lefever's writings on the subject and have found that he is a courageous and intelligent defender of the basic concepts of human rights. I have been appalled by the evidence of a veritable campaign of misrepresentation of his position by those who are more hostile to current American foreign policy than dedicated to the even-handed defense of human rights. Dr. Lefever is being criticized because he is not an absolutist about human rights and recognizes that human rights must be given priority over the expression of a particular human right in a specific place and time. For example, when the United States was critical of Nazi Germany and then went to war with Germany, Joseph Goebbels, the Nazi propaganda chief, denounced the United States for its hypocrisy on the grounds that the violations of human rights in the United States, particularly against our Negro citizens, rendered our criticisms of the Nazi system invalid. Similarly, when Nazi Germany invaded the Soviet Union and the United States supported the Kremlin, the Nazi propagandists had a field day about the Four Freedoms we were ostensibly defending—everyone of which was being violated by Stalin.

Our reply at that time was not to deny the existence of our own violations of human freedom or the abominations against human rights in the Soviet Union, but to point out that what was at stake was the whole structure of human rights which required the elimination of the greater evil or threat at the time.

The logic of this position cannot be gainsaid. It is the logic that has guided Dr. Lefever's reflections and advocacy, and it should be sufficient to expose the unfairness and intellectual dishonesty of those criticisms of him that impugn his dedication to the philosophy enshrined in our Bill of Rights. Dr. Lefever's merit warrants his confirmation.

1. Senator Charles Percy, Republican from Illinois.
2. Founder, Ethics and Public Policy Center, Georgetown University.

177

Dear Norman,[1]   April 13, 1981

Yes, I have read your piece on "The Future Danger."[2] I hope you will not misunderstand or regard me as immodest—I intend it as a tribute—

when I say I felt like sub-titling it "Sidney Hook Brought Up to Date."

Only on one point do I believe you could have put more stress. This is the alarming revival and strength of the mood of neutralism, pacifism and in effect anti-Americanism in Europe which may prevent redressing the nuclear balance there. Even if it does not prevent the necessary rearming, it may paralyze the will to resist if and when the crunch comes.

Despite the revelations of Solzhenitsyn and others, the "Better Red than Dead" position, with its false antithesis, is much stronger today than when I debated the issue with Bertrand Russell twenty years ago.

How to reverse this mood is a formidable and pressing task which is not receiving the attention it deserves. Arms without the will and courage to use them are useless—they create the illusion of a readiness which is not there. It is a theme worth pondering—and should result in an education program for action that may require the concerted efforts of many of us.

The prospects for the future—barring contingencies no one can forecast—are grim. I fear that even the resolve to go down fighting may be dismissed as a rhetorical affectation by those who are prepared to come to terms with the new wave no matter what.

1. Norman Podhoretz.
2. In "The Future Danger" (*Commentary* 71 [April 1981]: 29–47), Podhoretz warned against the growth of Soviet power and the decline of American power and stated that the United States must hold the line against the "Soviet desire for imperial hegemony."

178

Dear Dr. Schrecker,[1]   November 30, 1981

Having read your letter and your reprint from the *Antioch Review* (which I had not previously seen), I am frankly puzzled as to why you want to interview me. And why now at the end of your research and not before? Your mind is already made up and, I suspect, was fixed on your conclusions when you undertook your inquiry. Every page of your reprint suffers from grievous sins of omission and commission, and it would require a lengthy brochure to expose them in detail. You are obviously unfamiliar with the way a Communist Party cell functions on a campus, unaware of official Communist Party literature on the subject of education, and unaware of actual Communist Party activities on the campuses. You say that you have read my works on the subject. Your comments do not indicate any familiarity with the material and argument contained not only in my *Her-*

esy, Yes—Conspiracy, No! but my *Common Sense and the Fifth Amendment, Education for Modern Man,* and *Political Power and Personal Freedom,* or even my *Saturday Evening Post* article.[2]

When you say that "even the most dedicated Communists drew a line
(against indoctrination) at the classroom door," your naivete is touching,
even somewhat pathetic. How do you know they drew a line? Did the
Communists tell you this themselves? How would you go about determining the truth of what they told you? The official party instructions were
clear enough. Would any zealot, regardless of his views, admit that he
"sought to impose his own political views on his students" rather than that
he taught the truth to them? Have you had any experience with classroom
teaching? Surely as an historian you would like to find empirical evidence
that Communists as dedicated professional scholars always followed the
lead of evidence and not the party line. Show me a Communist Party
member who in his writings or speeches or teaching criticized a position
taken by the Communist Party in any field—if a political scientist, e.g., that
Roosevelt was not a Fascist when the Communist Party said he was; and
that he was a reactionary when the Communist Party hailed him as a great
progressive; or if a philosopher that Mach and/or Carnap[3] were not reactionary idealists as Lenin claimed; or if English professors that Thomas
Wolfe[4] was not a Fascist when the literary organs of the Communist Party
decided he was; or even mathematicians or scientists. (One of them, Dirk
Struik,[5] glorifying the Communist Party dogma about dialectics, flagrantly
suppressed Einstein's judgment about the scientific worthlessness of
Engels' writings on the subject—see my *Reason, Social Myths and Democracy* for the story.)

I notice also the absence of Harry Gideonse,[6] and any of the ex-Commu-
nist teachers who defected from the ranks, among those you interviewed. I
wonder whether Bernard Grebanier,[7] who was expelled from the Communist Party cell at Brooklyn College as a "Trotskyite-Fascist" for condemning the Moscow Trials after first endorsing them, was alive when you began
your inquiries. He was the first honest-to-goodness Communist Party member identified, although the existence of the cell was known by its anonymous publications.

You probably were not born at that time, but during the major period you
write about the United States was actually at war with Communist powers, and
the threat of war with the Soviet Union hung ominously over the events—a
war in which the leaders of the Communist Party publicly declared their support for the Kremlin. In that kind of atmosphere it was amazing that there were
not even greater excesses as lamentable as any excess was. Anyone having
lived through a real reign of terror during the post–World War I years, in the

academy and without, would have a sense of relief that things weren't worse than they were. A sense of proportion and balance is completely missing in your pages. It is as if you were born yesterday.

Finally, since I haven't the time to write that brochure, I sense your strong compassion for the horrible fate suffered by "the victims" of McCarthyism. I wonder whether you ever inquired of the Communists you interviewed how much compassion they ever felt or expressed for the much worse fate of the innocent victims and their entire families at the hands of the Communist system they actively supported—and more specifically the professors who were dismissed, exiled, deported to concentration camps and sometimes shot? After all, they were actively supporting a program for a system which openly stood for the abolition not only of academic freedom but of all freedoms for dissenters. I disagreed with redoubtable philosophers like Arthur O. Lovejoy, T. V. Smith, and Brand Blandshard,[8] with whose writings on the subject I assume you are familiar, since my view was one based primarily on the question of professional ethics, but given the commitment of members of the Communist Party to destroy the very system whose values they were invoking and their support of, at the very least their failure to protest against, the ruthless terror of Communist regimes against dissenters, *they* do not have justified moral grounds for complaint. So it seems to me. Abuses of academic freedom are the concern of those of us who believe in it.

And ask *yourself* this question. If these victims had been members of a Nazi party and as fervent supporters of Hitler and his practices as they were of Stalin and Stalin's practices, would you still feel the same compassion for them? I assume of course you are a liberal and a democrat.

P.S. I note your reference to me in your reprint. I recall having dinner with Allen[9] once in New York and exchanging some letters, copies of which I do not have. But I have no memory of "helping him write" (how?) articles and speeches. If you have any data or documents on this I shall be glad to see them. He was a pretty articulate man.

1. Ellen W. Schrecker, author of *No Ivory Tower: McCarthyism and the Universities* (New York, 1986). Schrecker had sent Hook her article "Academic Freedom and the Cold War," *Antioch Review* 38 (Summer 1980): 913–27. In both her article and her book, Schrecker made clear her disagreement with Hook regarding the employment of Communists on the campus. See especially *No Ivory Tower*, pp. 105–9.

2. "What Shall We Do about Communist Teachers?" *Saturday Evening Post* 222 (September 10, 1949): 33, 164–68.

3. Ernst Mach, professor of philosophy, University of Vienna. Lenin accused Mach of being part of a bourgeois conspiracy. For Carnap, see letter 65, note 1.

4. Author of *Look Homeward, Angel* (1929) and other novels.

5. Professor of mathematics, Massachusetts Institute of Technology.

6. President of Brooklyn College.
7. For Grebanier, see Hook, *Out of Step*, p. 253.
8. Professor of philosophy, Yale University.
9. Raymond B. Allen, president of the University of Washington.

179

Dear Martin and Elisabeth,[1]   February 6, 1982

I don't know what the prospects are for me, but I shall struggle to stay alive to rejoin the fight for all I hold dear at a time when the odds of defeat are growing for the free world. I close with a word or two on the current issue. Of course we never consigned Poland to Russia at Yalta. In the eyes of Roosevelt and the useful idiots around him—*we* sincerely negotiated a compromise with Stalin, but in their ignorance about Communism and Stalin, despite what we did to disillusion them, they deceived themselves.

My illness dulled the immediate impact of the blows of the West's reaction to what happened in Poland.[2] On television Kennan[3] sounded worse than Chamberlain,[4] and as justified as Kissinger's[5] complaint was, he should have had the grace to make public apology for the policy he initiated whose legitimate fruits we now have seen.[6] I still remember my critical discussion with Sonnenfeldt[7] here in which, defending Kissinger, he said, "we shall tie the Soviet Union with ropes of silken trade to prevent her from undermining the status quo."

I myself never believed in the rollback theory after 1953 and especially after 1956 when the Kremlin, doubtful about what to do in Poland and Hungary, was taken off the hook by the invasion of Egypt and Eisenhower's passivity in Europe.

The last and lost opportunity of a rollback was at the time of the Berlin blockade. Stalin was not ready for war. The air lift proved that. The blockade should have been broken by armored trains and tanks. When I asked General Clay in Berlin whether he had been surprised by the blockade, he denied it and said elaborate plans had been made to break it on all fronts. When I asked him, "what happened, then?" he replied, "The State Dep't. vetoed our plans." Those were the days when we had the atomic monopoly. Stalin would have retreated.

Containment became the only alternative, but as Africa, the near-East, and Cuba and Central America show, we are *not* containing the Soviet Union. Reagan's tough talk counts for less than the immediate commercial gains of the farmers, bankers and stupid Republicans who do not understand what the real issue is and what we are up against. The *Ost Politik* was a disaster, and the French will no more oppose the Kremlin in a showdown than they did Hitler. Washington doesn't realize that the world is a far more dangerous place than even you pointed out to them.

1. Herz.
2. Soviet repression of the Solidarity labor movement.
3. George F. Kennan.
4. Neville Chamberlain, British prime minister identified with the policy of appeasement during the late 1930s.
5. Henry Kissinger.
6. A reference to the policy of "détente" with the Soviet Union initiated when Kissinger was secretary of state under Nixon.
7. Helmut Sonnenfeldt, a Kissinger assistant and one of the architects of détente.

180

Dear Rabbi White,[1]   February 13, 1982

What is one to conclude from the fact that you devote your entire column in the February 12th issue of the *San Francisco Jewish Bulletin* to reproducing, without any comment from you, quotations from the *Partisan Review* asserting that both the U.S. government and that of the Soviet Union are interested primarily in preserving the status-quo? That you agree with it? One would be interested to learn, if so, on what grounds?

The passages you quote[2] are typical New Left propaganda. Only yesterday it compared the treatment of the Air Controller's union by the US government to the treatment of Solidarity in Poland by its government. As a critic of the inadequate response of the American government to recent Polish events, I still believe it is cheap and untrue to equate the positions of Washington and the Kremlin as dedicated merely to the defense of the *status quo*. Does the Soviet invasion of Afghanistan, its penetration through Cuban janissaries in Africa, and its attempt to destabilize the situation in the Near East at the expense of Israel indicate a fidelity to the status quo? As mistaken and naive as American policy has been, is there any doubt that the US would favor free elections in Poland as the Yalta agreements provided or the fulfillment of the Helsinki commitments to which the Soviet Union is pledged but which it systematically violates throughout its empire?

The hospitality and freedom enjoyed by the Czechoslovakian dissident at Bloomfield College is evidence enough of the absurdity of the equation he draws between the US government and its fumbling but democratic policy, and the terroristic regime of the Soviet Union. Compare the position of the Soviet and Czechoslovakian dissidents in their own countries with that of the Chomskys, I. F. Stones, and Ellsbergs here.[3] For very shame! It is as intellectually stultifying and morally obscene as to equate anti-Semitism in the U.S. with anti-Semitism in the Soviet Union or Nazi Germany.

1. Saul E. White, rabbi, Congregation Beth Shalom, San Francisco.
2. Passages were by John Mason, a Czechoslovakian dissident, which appeared in Dick Howard and John Mason, "Dissident in Czechoslovakia: An Interview," *Partisan Review* 49 (1982): 119–31.
3. Noam Chomsky (professor of modern language and linguistics, Massachusetts Institute of Technology), left-wing journalist I.F. Stone, and Daniel Ellsberg (the person who provided the Pentagon Papers to the Senate Foreign Relations Committee and to the *New York Times*).

181

Dear Mr. Meese,[1]   March 30, 1982

A message for the President! It seems to me, Ed Teller, and many of us here[2] that the President should deliver a filmed fireside chat to the American people on the whole question of the nuclear freeze. He should not oppose it but stress that he wants to go further in actual reduction of nuclear armament. In the course of his speech he should say that if the Kremlin refuses his reasonable alternative proposals, he would be willing to consider the option of a nuclear freeze *providing that fool-proof verifiability involving on-site inspections* are a feature of it. He should cite the difficulties of checking compliance in a closed society and cite past cases of violations by the Soviets of agreements on testing, use of chemical warfare, etc. There are many instances.

This is really a must!

1. Edwin Meese, counselor to President Reagan and future attorney general of the United States.
2. Hoover Institution.

182

Dear Bill,[1]   May 21, 1982

It was Elmer Davis[2] at the time of Hitler who said "Better no world than some worlds" in reply to obsessed One Worlders like Robert Hutchins.

And as you know, for years Bertrand Russell and I exchanged heavy shot and shell over his proposition that if the Communists refuse to accept reasonable terms for mutual disarmament, the West should disarm unilaterally even if that meant universal domination of communism "with all its horrors" (interview with Joseph Alsop).[3] I argued that it was both wiser and nobler to announce that we were prepared to go down fighting for freedom even at the risk of world destruction, whatever that meant.

Elmer Davis and I are liberals. Why, then, do you arrogate only to conservatives this view that some things are worth dying for? (*Wall Street Journal,* 5/21/82) It seems to me that in situations of this kind the terms "conservatism" and "liberalism" are irrelevant. A thumbnail expression of my philosophical testament reads:

"It is better to be a live jackal than a dead lion—for jackals, not men. Men who have the moral courage to fight intelligently for freedom have the best prospect of avoiding the fate of live jackals and dead lions. Survival is not the be-all and end-all of a life worthy of man. Under some conditions, the worst thing we can know about a man is that he has survived. Those who say that life is worth living at any cost have already written for themselves an epitaph of infamy, for there is no cause or person they will not betray to survive. Man's vocation should be the use of the arts of intelligence to defend and extend human freedom."

This is the credo of a free man and transcends the differences about a market economy, the specific forms of the welfare state, the validity of the arguments for the existence of God, and other political, economic and educational issues that divide us.

1. William F. Buckley, Jr., founder and publisher of the *National Review.*
2. Radio commentator and author of *But We Were Born Free* (Indianapolis, 1954).
3. Newspaper columnist.

183

Dear Mr. Sheldon,[1]   November 15, 1982

Thank you for your good wishes. Yes, I remember our correspondence. You need not feel that not being a native American has any relevance to the matters on which we may differ. The laws of logic and evidence are not national in character.

First of all about China. I hope you can read Richard Bernstein's recent book on China or Fox Butterfield's.[2] Both of them were students of Fairbank[3] at Harvard and on the basis of their firsthand experience in China have concluded that Fairbank shamelessly misled the American public about the nature of the mainland Chinese regime, especially the state of affairs at the time of the "Cultural Revolution." It was no news to me since I had spoken to Chinese refugees in Hong Kong who fled for religious reasons (they were Christians) and had no axe to grind.

My views on Vietnam were not adequately reported in the story. I always believed that the US should have brought the same pressure on France as it did on the Netherlands to surrender their colonial possessions in Asia. DeGaulle did promise the Vietnamese their national independence. I thought it was a bad mistake to get involved, but once we were involved I argued that unless we could win the right of the South Vietnamese who certainly didn't want Communist rule to be left alone (which was the essence of the Paris accords), our withdrawal would be followed by a genocidal attack on the population. What happened in Vietnam and Cambodia after our withdrawal was predictable. Getting in was a mistake, but getting out and denying the South Vietnamese the means to defend themselves was a crime.

The situation in those countries today is infinitely worse that what it was under Diem or Thieu.[4]

I used to say that because a man makes an unwise marriage that doesn't justify him later walking out on wife and children without making some provisions for them. The same logic applies to the Vietnam action. The word that gets out from the Vietnamese concentration and re-education camps is that conditions are so bad that all the inmates ask for is poison to shorten their life and suffering.

My position on intervention when free or independent nations are threatened by intervention from despotic or totalitarian outside regimes is like that of John Stuart Mill—whom I quote in my chapter on "Bertrand Russell and Crimes Against Humanity" in my *Philosophy and Public Policy.*[5]

1. Walter A. Sheldon, New York.
2. Bernstein, *From the Center of the Earth: The Search for the Truth about China* (Boston, 1982); Butterfield, *China: Alive in the Bitter Sea* (New York, 1982).
3. John King Fairbank.
4. Ngo Dihn Diem, president of South Vietnam who was killed by the South Vietnamese military in November 1963. Nguyen Van Thieu headed the anti-communist South Vietnam government until its collapse in April 1975.
5. See letter 197, note 2.

184

Dear Mr. Sheldon,[1]   November 22, 1982

I was never an advisor to the American government on foreign policy, and I am no expert on China. Even if I had visited China I doubt I could speak with authority on what was going on. Actually I was in the Soviet Union in the summer of 1929 but was so isolated doing my research at the Marx Engels Institute that I really didn't know what was happening in the country until I left it.

The conditions you describe as having seen with your own eyes in China during the days of Chiang Kai-shek I saw with my eyes in India—in Calcutta, in several other regions, and in Bombay, too. But not even those who suffered seemed willing to support a totalitarian despotism that promised to alleviate their condition—except for those who supported the two or three Communist groups.

You say that in 1949 the Chinese Communists desired contacts with the U.S. What is the evidence for that? At the time the Chinese Communists were staunch Stalinists. Their intervention into the Korean War was not motivated by any threats to their hegemony.

One thing was clear to me although I was not a Chinese expert, that the Chinese Communists were *not* agrarian reformers as some of our officials and Edgar Snow[2] reported. The Chinese Communists came to power by virtue of the actions of the Kremlin, which violated all the pledges it gave in the Sino-Soviet Treaty of 1945, and the ineptitude of the American gov't. which insisted that the Nationalist regime enter into a coalition gov't. with the Communists. Marshall[3] was completely taken in by Chou En-lai and Stilwell.[4] I have seen a letter he wrote in which he declared the Chinese Communists to be genuine democrats. But I don't want to rehearse the events of those years and the record of the gruesome measures conducted by the Chinese Communists in every region where they came to power under the pretext that they were destroying the handful of landowners, etc. I was never an admirer of the Nationalist regime and accepted the criticisms made of it by my teacher John Dewey, and even by Huh Shih who later became its ambassador. I was always looking for a Third Force to support but in the absence of a Third Force knew that the Communists would be the greater evil.

Granted that the conditions which existed in pre-Communist China were as bad as you say. How do you account for the fact that when the Chinese prisoners of war, at the close of the Korean War, were given an opportunity to choose, even though the Indians in charge of the matter refused to let any one speak to them except the Chinese Communist representatives, who alternately threatened their families and promised them everything—the overwhelming majority chose the bitter bread of exile and poverty rather than repatriation to China? If the Chinese masses were permitted to speak and vote would they support the Communist regime?

I believe I am aware of the differences between Chinese and Russian totalitarianism. The Chinese are currently more pragmatic but *au fond* have a tighter control over the population than the Kremlin. The way they control their population is evidence of that. Genetically they are a remarkable people—hardworking, family centered, education-loving. Under a free society, they would soon put Japan and the U.S. in the shade.

Personally I am all for giving the Taiwanese control of their island. But *if* the choice were limited between the present system and its incomplete liberties and the Mainland system which one would the Taiwanese choose? The Taiwanese students here who hate the Nationalists tell me they hate and fear the Communists more. And if the Chinese masses on the Mainland were given a choice how do you think they would choose? Do you remember what happened when for a few days China lifted the Bamboo Curtain in South China? The entire population was getting ready to move.

But this letter is already overlong and I don't want to re-argue my position on Vietnam. It was a mistake to become militarily involved but once in it was worse *for the Vietnamese* for us to withdraw as we did. That proposition is demonstrable. Nothing you have written disproves it. Nor do I agree with you that Chinese logic and American logic are different. Logic is the same. What is different are the moral outlooks of Communist and Western democratic regimes.

1. Walter A. Sheldon.
2. Edgar P. Snow, author of *Red Star over China* (New York, 1937).
3. General George C. Marshall, President Truman's special envoy to China after World War II.
4. General Joseph W. Stilwell, chief American military adviser to the government of Chiang Kai-shek during World War II. He detested Chiang.

185

Dear Nat,[1]   November 30, 1982

Thank you for your note of November 19 which just reached me yesterday. I would have been very happy if you and your wife had attended the dinner which was more than "the party"[2] I thought I had let myself in for—what with the President's letter and Pat Moynihan's[3] grandiloquent telegram, touched with traces of the Blarney stone. But at least Pat composed it, but I suspect that the White House letter had several draftees—one of whom made the President knowledgeable about my role in helping to establish the Dewey Commission.

Actually letters like yours mean more to me than public tributes, and I am really grateful that you consider yourself a student of mine in any sense—or more accurately as someone who has been influenced by me. That is a tribute to me because of the high regard I have had for your own work, your intellectual independence, freedom from cant, and the inspired common sense you bring to the discussion of controversial issues. (So far as I can recall my only point of difference with you—if it was a difference— was over Vietnam. I thought it was a mistake to get involved but thought it was also a mistake to get out unless we could guarantee either by victory or agreement that the South Vietnamese whom we had encouraged to resist were safe from what we feared would befall them and actually did after we withdrew.)

Last night I read your piece in the *Festschrift*[4] volume on the Rosenberg case. My main interest in the case was in the evidence. I always opposed the death sentence in that case (and later signed a petition for the commutation of Sobell's sentence on condition that it be linked with a petition for Harry Gold's[5] commutation, too). In fact everyone I knew was against the death sentence with one exception. Perhaps you are unaware that the Executive Committee of the Congress for Cultural Freedom publicly petitioned Eisenhower to commute the Rosenbergs' death sentence—and this despite its funding,[6] an additional piece of evidence that the Congress was really independent in all its activities and enterprises.

The only exception was Philip Rahv[7] who told me, and probably others, that he was against commutation because their survival would perpetually fuel a world-wide Communist propaganda campaign to "Free the Rosenbergs." I said, "Even so . . ." that would be better than making them martyrs sanctified by death. Rahv was cagey and didn't publish his view although he firmly held it. Later when he reverted to his Leninist phase in his attack on *Commentary* and the anti-Communists, I was told that he listed the Rosenbergs' deaths in his litany of denunciation of U.S. imperialism.

I don't know whether I ever told you this. I once gave a paper on church-state relations before the Judicial Conference of the Ninth Circuit Court which was held at the Rockefeller Tetons resort. Kaufman[8] was there and was much impressed with my paper and ensuing discussion. He sent several hours with me giving me a harrowing account of the persecution to which he and his family had been subjected. The details were indeed rather grim. He was in a highly nervous state. He implored me to write an extensive analysis of the Rosenberg case "like the kind you have written about the Hiss case." When I raised the question about the sentence, he told me—and I am certain of this—that "under the statutes governing espionage during war-time I had no alternative." "But what about Greenglass,[9] then?" I asked. "He was a cooperative government witness," he replied. Every lawyer I have asked tells me that Kaufman was wrong. I gave Kaufman an evasive answer. Later I got a long communication and then a telephone call from ex-Judge Simon Rifkind who had been a classmate of mine at CCNY before he went off to Yeshiva. He asked me to go into the procedural aspects of the case and reply to Vern Countryman's[10] attack on Kaufman which he thought unjustified. By this time I had become reluctant to take up the case and, pleading the burden of other work, suggested he get in touch with *you* to undertake the assignment.

The reason for my reluctance was that I was reading some of Kaufman's opinions in several cases and discovered that at every opportunity he had he was taking an extreme, ritualistic liberal line that seemed to me if not more extreme than the ACLU, now in the hands of the New Left, just as extreme. It was clear to me that Kaufman was hoping to purchase immunity from continued attacks from "the Left" by donning the mantle of Black and Douglas[11]—even more so. He seemed oblivious to the fact that it was not the verdict for which he was not responsible but the sentence for which he was being attacked, and that he would never be forgiven for that. I confided my impression of what Kaufman was doing and why to Rifkind who surprised me by saying: "I think you are right. Why don't *you* tell him what you think."

I almost published an attack on Kaufman after reading his dissenting opinion in the case of the Brooklyn teacher who because of his conservative political views had a ten-minute telephone conversation with the CIA on his return from Israel where he had studied PLO terrorism. Scheduled for promotion, when his political enemies discovered this information which he did not keep silent, they withdrew the recommendation for promotion and voted to deny him tenure. He sued the Board of Higher Education and his colleagues, and won $460,000 damages in a jury trial. The City appealed, and the Second Circuit Court reversed on a pure technicality 2 to 1 with Kaufman writing a supplementary opinion, purely gratuitous, attacking the teacher as a CIA espionage agent, etc. The City settled out of court for $200,000, but I lost any sympathy I had for Kaufman.

The matter of the *evidence* in the trial still interests me. I am still convinced that Rosenberg was guilty, and even Philby[12] has a passage in which he discusses the evidence in the Fuchs case "which led to Gold and then to Rosenberg"—and Philby should know. He is more of an authority, Caute[13] to the contrary notwithstanding, than Doctorow.[14]

I think you are correct in assessing the public reaction at the time, but you don't mention the *cumulative* impact of the series of espionage trials and confessions during the previous years and the feeling that we were at war.

I was not aware of the role Douglas played. What an s.o.b.! I had a debate with him at the Brooklyn Law School on the First Amendment and his *Points of Rebellion*. When it came to his turn to speak, he just introduced his young wife to the boys and they cheered her. He did admit to me that the famous sentence he quoted from Hitler denouncing student disorders in the German universities during 1932 (ostensibly a speech at Hamburg) in words very much like *our* criticism of student violence in the USA, was fraudulent. He didn't know that the student disrupters of the German universities against Weimar, Jewish professors, and students were Nazis!

Well this has become some screed! I am enclosing a copy of my response to the overgenerous remarks made at the dinner.

Ann joins me in wishing both of you best wishes for a refreshing and productive year.

1. Nathan Glazer, professor of sociology, Harvard University.
2. In celebration of Hook's eightieth birthday.
3. Senator Daniel Patrick Moynihan, Democrat from New York.
4. Glazer, "The Death of the Rosenbergs," in Paul Kurtz, ed., *Sidney Hook: Philosopher of Democracy and Humanism* (Buffalo, N.Y., 1983), pp. 65–76.
5. Harry Gold. See notes to letter 141.
6. Reference is to revelations that the C.I.A. helped finance the Congress for Cultural Freedom.
7. Editor, *Partisan Review*.
8. Judge Irving R. Kaufman. He presided at the Rosenberg trial.
9. David Greenglass. See notes to letter 141.
10. Professor of law, Harvard University law school.
11. Hugo L. Black and William O. Douglas, Supreme Court justices.
12. Kim Philby, British spy for the Soviet Union.
13. David Caute.
14. E. L. Doctorow, author of the novel *Daniel* (New York, 1971) which deals with the Rosenberg case.

186

Dear Ms. Rose,[1]   February 5, 1983

History is *not* "always a question of whom to believe" if you mean by that that there are no objective facts or truths. It is true that it is often difficult to ascertain the truth, but I am confident that you would never agree that anything said about you or anyone else is as true or false as anything else.

The U.S. offered to surrender its monopoly of atomic weapons to an international authority years *before* Vishinski (who was the prosecutor of the notorious frame-up Moscow Trials in the 30s) introduced his resolution.[2] At that time the USSR did not have the atomic bomb. It would have been stupid for the U.S. to destroy its atomic weapons *before* the International Commission was established because in that event when the Kremlin developed its atomic bomb (with the help of Fuchs, Harry Gold, and other Soviet spies) it would have had the Western world at its mercy.

Had the Kremlin accepted the Baruch-Lilienthal proposals, it would have been part of the International Commission supervising the transfer of all atomic energy and bombs to the international authority. The Vishinski proposal was an obvious dodge.

When you write that you do not believe either side is responsible for the cold war you must come to terms with the fact that after World War II the U.S. withdrew all of its forces from Europe while the U.S.S.R. kept them in Central and Eastern Europe, that the U.S.S.R. violated the specific provisions of the Yalta, Teheran and Potsdam agreements calling for *free* uncoerced elections in the territories it occupied, the Communist putsch in Czechoslovakia engineered by the Kremlin, the refusal to permit its satellite regime in Poland and Czechoslovakia to accept the Marshall Plan, its blockade of Berlin, and many other incidents.

I hope that in addition to the *Village Voice* you have access to other publications as well. You may be amused by the piece in the *New Republic* on the *Village Voice,* and interested in the other enclosures.

There was a time when the N.Y. Public Library reported that all of my books had been stolen or defaced by those who apparently disagreed with the views expressed in them. Some of them, however, have been replaced.

1. Patricia Rose, New York.
2. Refers to the 1946 Soviet United Nations resolution to outlaw atomic weapons. This resolution made no provision for international control and inspection of these weapons.

187

Dear Mr. Jeffords,[1]   May 2, 1983

I am appalled by your reply of April 22 to my letter urging that you support the President's position on El Salvador. Have you asked yourself what the consequences for human rights will be if the Communist guerrillas triumph? Look at Cuba, Nicaragua and Vietnam! In every one of these countries the situation with respect to human rights is immeasurably worse both quantitatively and with regards to the intensity of terror than the situation as it existed before the Communist insurgency.

Granted that the land reform program is making slow progress. But it is progressing, and the AFL-CIO has applauded the efforts made to implement it. These efforts are being impeded by the ruthless destruction of the economy and agricultural infrastructure by the guerrillas. The suggestion for unconditional talks with guerillas who have refused to participate in the negotiations undertaken by Venezuela, Colombia, Mexico, and Costa Rica, and refused to engage in elections, is really an invitation to unconditional surrender by the legally elected regime of El Salvador.

Granted that the justice system needs improvement both in the military and civilian sectors. Have you asked yourself what kind of system of justice would prevail when the Communist guerrillas take over—and they surely will if the policy you advocate is followed? Do you know the realities of the Cuban and Vietnam Gulags where the chief request of the inmates reaching the outside world is for poison to put an end to their prolonged suffering and degradation?

Why should you expect more exemplary conduct on the part of the El Salvador regime in the midst of a civil war abetted and funded by foreign powers than our own conduct during the Civil War?

I cannot help thinking that you are being unduly influenced by noisy, unrepresentative pacifist elements who focus on the motes in the eyes of those who are *resisting* Communist aggression but are blind to the murderous activities of the enemies of human freedom.

1. Congressman James R. Jeffords, Republican from Vermont.

188

Dear Mr. Sheldon,[1]   June 30, 1983

I can't recall now whether I ever replied to your letter of last December which has just surfaced in a mass of papers that follow me around the country. But if I haven't I have just one request to make. Please buy, borrow or steal a copy of *Son of the Revolution* by Heng & Shapiro (Knopf)[2] and then ask yourself whether the Chinese Communist genocide of the so-called middle class in the cities and country was so different from Hitler's genocide of the Jews, except that many more millions were involved in China.

I agree with you that our policy should be based on the Declaration of Independence, the Constitution, etc. But when Hitler invaded the Soviet Union, I supported all-out aid to Stalin who, as far as we knew, had killed by 1941 more innocent people than Hitler, because Stalin was the choice of the lesser evil. What would *you* have done? What is the choice of the lesser evil in Central America?

1. Walter A. Sheldon.
2. Heng Liang, *Son of the Revolution* (New York, 1983). Liang and Judith Shapiro were husband and wife, but Shapiro is not listed as coauthor of *Son of the Revolution.*

189

To the Members of the Los Angeles County   December 30, 1983
Board of Supervisors,

I wish to unqualifiedly endorse the proposal before you to submit to the voters of Los Angeles County the referendum on Bilateral Nuclear Weapons and Human Rights Declaration. Many reasons for this referendum may be given, but the strongest among them is that the very effectiveness of a nuclear freeze and the likelihood of international peace depends upon the recognition and enforcement of human rights by the signatories of the pact. The indivisibility of these two issues has been recognized by Dr. Andrei Sakharov and other proponents of human freedom in a peaceful world. Such a referendum does not constitute unjustifiable intervention into the domestic affairs of nations since all are on record as endorsing the provisions of the UN Declaration of Human Rights and the Helsinki Accords.

190

Dear Mr. Sheldon,[1]   Jan. 4, 1984

A happy New Year to you and your family, too.

If I live to deliver it the Jefferson lecture will be delivered not only in Washington on May 14 but in New York on May 17 at NYU. The particulars will be announced later.

I am a little puzzled by your enthusiasm for Blaustein's letter which I read on publication.[2] Whenever anyone wants to export the Declaration of Independence to the Soviet Union or any Communist country, they are denounced—in the past by individuals close to Blaustein—as cold warriors who want war. They have no objection to exporting the Declaration of Independence to non-Communist countries, whose governments are not hostile to the U.S., even if the destabilization of those governments leads to the victory of Communist movements in those countries that strengthen the over-all position of the USSR and/or Mainland China. After that the export of the Declaration of Independence to those countries is denounced as Yankee imperialism, e.g. Nicaragua.

I note that *Commentary* did carry your letter last summer and Podhoretz discovered the Achilles heel in it. Prudence or "seichal"[3] is part of intelligent morality. Unless we had allied ourselves with France of the Bastille against the far less despotic Great Britain of those years—there would have been no Declaration of Independence or a U.S. to give asylum to refugees.

1. Walter A. Sheldon.
2. Letter of Albert P. Blaustein, professor of law, Rutgers University law school (Camden, New Jersey), published in the *New York Times,* August 12, 1983. Blaustein argued that the advocacy of freedom and democracy should be a fundamental principle of American diplomacy.
3. Hebrew word meaning common sense or wisdom.

191

Dear Mr. Moyers,[1]   January 13, 1984

You probably may not recall our correspondence a year or two ago when I protested your departure—to my great disappointment—from the standards of fair editorial supervision of the panel on Jacobo Timerman's book.[2] I was taken aback by the heat of your rejoinder and your consigning me to the netherland of reactionary thought.[3]

The point that I was making and that some of the other members of the panel were also making was that the distinction between authoritarian and totalitarian regimes, even if one detested both, was intellectually tenable even though it was not by itself sufficient always to guide practice.

The enclosed column[4] gives the point even greater topicality and suggests that those who have taxed Dr. Jeane Kirkpatrick[5] with illiberalism because she has made the distinction have been guilty of great injustice to her.

1. Bill D. Moyers, television journalist.
2. *Prisoner Without a Name, Cell Without a Number* (New York, 1981). This book describes Timerman's torture while in prison in Argentina and his antagonism to the military government of Argentina and its campaign against left-wing terrorists. Moyers hosted a panel discussion on CBS on the controversy surrounding Timerman and his book.
3. On October 8, 1981, Moyers responded to a letter from Hook complaining that the panel discussion had been biased against Timerman's critics. Moyers denied that the panel was as one-sided as Hook claimed, and he noted that Irving Kristol and Michael

Novak, critics of Timerman, had been invited to appear on the panel but canceled at the last moment. Moyers also declared his own sympathy for Timerman. In a letter to Moyers on October 19, 1981, Hook expressed "pained incredulity" regarding Moyers's letter, claimed that Moyers had confirmed that lack of objectivity of the panel discussion, and declared that Moyers had been unfair to both Jeane Kirkpatrick and Irving Kristol.

4. Column was by Arnold Beichman, a long-time associate of Hook in the war against communism.

5. Jeane J. Kirkpatrick, American ambassador to the United Nations during the first years of the Reagan administration. She made the distinction between authoritarian and totalitarian governments in "Dictatorships and Double Standards," *Commentary* 68 (November 1979): 34–45.

192

Dear Owen,[1]

February 3, 1984

The answer to your question is involved in a section of my talk. The existence of a *legally recognized political opposition* with an electoral process which makes it possible for a minority to peacefully become a majority is a rough and ready criterion to apply to a nation evolving towards democratic rule.

I was heartened to find when I was in Taiwan a legally recognized political opposition which I gather won some seats. Some organizations (like Freedom House) that make a list of free countries do not yet consider Taiwan to have measured up fully to the criterion because so many members of the chief legislative body are in effect selected rather than elected to represent provinces on the Mainland. If the Mainland does not make war against Taiwan, I anticipate that in time the growing interrelation and absorption between the Taiwanese population and the mainland-born Chinese will ultimately make all seats in the legislative chamber elective. This of course must be *a gradual* process.

To be perfectly frank I greatly fear the Machiavellian perfidy of the Chinese Communist warlords given the naivete of American statesmen and the cynicism of the Europeans who would write Taiwan off for a trade-deal. The Communist behavior in Tibet and their schemes and traps for Hong Kong show what is in store for Taiwan. So common sense dictates that Taiwan must consider itself in a state of siege. The lot of the Taiwanese population *compared to the population on the Mainland* has, even under the Japanese, been fortunate. If the Chinese Communists take them over, their present life in Taiwan, to those who survive, will appear like life in Paradise.

This seems to me to be the grim truth and must be given first consideration in establishing a viable democracy. Best regards to all our friends in your office.

1. Owen Lippert, Asia and World Institute, Taiwan.

193

February 21, 1984   Dear Mr. Moyers,[1]

Thank you for taking time out of your busy life to write me on February 8 replying to my letter.

You will recall that the occasion for my writing was the column by Mr. Beichman reporting that developments in Argentina had disproved Mr. Timerman's contentions about the future of that country's regime, and confirmed the distinctions and predictions of his critics whom he, Timerman, consistently abused by calling them totalitarians, notably Irving Kristol. He also called Jeane Kirkpatrick a totalitarian, who had never discussed his case but elaborated on the distinction between authoritarian and totalitarian regimes in her article in *Commentary.*

I shall not enter into a further discussion now about this distinction. I am hoping to receive soon from the Wilson Center of the Smithsonian Institution the text of my discussion of this issue with Michael Walzer[2] and shall be glad to forward it to you.

The point I originally made was that in the television program you chaired on the Timerman affair his critics were given the short end of the stick, and the introduction of biased questioners at the end, one of whom was Timerman's son, wasn't cricket. In the light of that discussion, and of the articles that appeared in *Midstream,* the *Wall Street Journal, Commentary,* etc., I am truly at a loss to understand the concluding paragraph of your letter.

> As for the Timerman affair, I still have trouble understanding why so many advocates of the distinction between authoritarianism and totalitarianism attempted to discredit him personally instead of joining the debate on the issue. The conduct of some of his detractors, who ignored his experience in prison and attacked his character, struck me as evidence of the inexplicable malice of some intellectuals who look out on a tormented world from a safe distance, and then cannot tolerate anyone whose reality contradicts their ideology. There was something about the attack on Timerman that was ugly and unbecoming. To my knowledge you did not participate in it. Perhaps you can help me to understand it. I would be most grateful.

Not a single member of the television panel attacked Timerman personally. No one on that panel nor any one else defended the way he was treated or extenuated the conduct of those who arrested and abused him. They disputed his characterization of the character of the regime as totalitarian, his accusations against the Jewish community as complicitous by its silence in his treatment, and similarly demonstrably false statements. Indeed, almost at the very time or shortly after the panel, Timerman's book was on the best-seller list in Buenos Aires! Further, in articles in *Midstream* and the *Wall Street Journal* Timerman's statement that he was being persecuted *only* because he was a Jew was contested. He was charged with concealing the fact in his book that *he himself* had supported the military coup and dictatorship against the Argentinian democratic regime, that rightfully or wrongfully he was taxed with collaboration with his commercial partner who had allegedly served as money-man for the terrorist guerrillas. Even if he had been guilty of all this, it would not constitute a justification of the bestial treatment he received. That was not the point. The point was that he was passing himself off as a victim of a kind of pogrom against the Jews, which was a premonitory sign of the fate of all the Jews in Argentina, and which the Jewish community (like the German Jewish community before them in Germany) was cowardly accepting. When some reporters asked him whether he did have any relationship with or knowledge of his partner's alleged activities he refused to answer, and responded only: "That's the kind of questions *they* asked!," implying that anyone who asked that kind of question was like them. But in his book he does *not* indicate that this type of question was asked since it might raise doubts whether he was arrested *because* he was Jewish.

There is of course no reason why the victim of injustice should be a moral hero; and he may very well be an insincere and dishonorable person. Some of Timerman's critics criticized him because by not telling the truth he was imperilling the position of the Jewish community in Argentina, and strengthening the hands of anti-Semites who might be tempted to increase their harassment of the Jews.

I know of no one who ignored Timerman's experience in prison or denied the truth of his report about that experience; nor of anyone motivated by malice against him. Timerman's conduct after that experience, his denunciations of critics of his position as Fascists and totalitarians, his behavior and remarks in Israel and after leaving Israel, have raised legitimate questions about his intellectual and moral integrity. He has yet to acknowledge that he was mistaken about his contention that Argentina was a totalitarian regime whose political character was irreversible, and that he was unjust to those who pointed out that its movement towards a more democratic nature was possible.

This letter already overlong is not the place to discuss at length the situation in Central America. But first, I recall no one deploring Carter's naivete on the grounds of his intervention on behalf of human rights in Argentina. It was Carter's view of the nature of communism, and his belief that the American people were unduly fearful of it, that was declared naive. All neo-conservatives I know, as well as conservatives like President Reagan, are *strongly* in favor of intervention on behalf of human rights in all countries, including South America. The arrest of Timerman took place while Carter was President; the return to democracy took place while Reagan was President. On the other hand, the intervention of the American government to protect the horrible persecutions of members of the Helsinki Watch Committee in the Soviet Union and its satellites has been fruitless.

The real issue is what should the attitude of the U.S. government be towards governments whose policies we disapprove of on democratic grounds, which are threatened by totalitarian movements, allied to Cuba and the Soviet Union, in an area vital to our national interest. With respect to El Salvador, the existing regime, disapprove of it as we will, has the support of a greater portion of the electorate than our own, in a vote in which participation was more than 80% of those eligible, in an election that had many hundreds of international observers. Although Robert White[3] charged the CIA had a hand in it, it turned out that all the CIA did was to provide the Duarte[4] regime with machines to thumb-print voters to prevent fraudulent voting. The Duarte regime, which I and my friends in the AFL-CIO supported, counted the ballots. Unfortunately, Duarte lost. The election was honest. But there is overwhelming evidence that the elections being planned in Nicaragua will be rigged unless the persecution of the opponents of the Marxist-Leninist camarilla ceases. I am in favor of *international* supervision of the elections in both countries.

I am not as familiar with the situation in Guatemala, but I do know we are urging moderation on the regime, and that the prospects of our success are immeasurably greater than they would be if the Communist guerrillas seized power. Have you ever examined the papers discovered in Grenada which revealed the extent to which that seizure of power became the focus of Communist plans for further advance? Even the North Korean Communists were on the scene.

For a democrat and a believer in a free society, the choice is ultimately one of common sense and prudence fortified by relevant knowledge. If it hadn't been for Batista, there would have been no Castro. But as bad as Batista was, if the only choice was between a regime like his or Castro's, which would be the lesser evil? Not long ago—was it you or someone else?—someone quoted Burke[5] to the effect that "our choice sometimes is between the acutely disagreeable and the altogether intolerable." As almost a life-long opponent of communism, when Hitler invaded the Soviet Union I advocated support of Stalin against him (as did you, I presume), even though Stalin had slaughtered far more people than Hitler at the time, because Hitler's victory would be more prejudicial to the survival of the free society at that time than Stalin's triumph. If one could bring oneself to support a totalitarian regime like Stalin's against an even more monstrous one, what objection can there be in supporting an authoritarian regime against a totalitarian one, if those are the only alternatives, while bringing to bear whatever influence we can on the regime we support, to abide by moderate procedures, and gradually with the onset of peace to move towards a more democratic regime? After all, can we in all decency expect other countries locked in a life and death civil war struggle to behave much better than the North and South did in our own Civil War?

1. Bill Moyers.
2. Michael L. Walzer, professor, School of Social Sciences, Institute for Advanced Study.
3. Robert E. White, Carter administration ambassador to El Salvador.
4. José Napoleón Duarte, president of El Salvador.
5. Edmund Burke.

194

To the Editor of the *Village Voice*,[1]   March 13, 1984

Paul Berman's article on my views and their development teems with errors, distortions and outright fabrications. Despite the tributes with which his vituperative attributions of McCarthyism are interlarded, I feel very much like the Irishman who was tarred, feathered and ridden out of town on a rail by local bigots, who remarked: "Begorrah, if it wasn't for the honor of the thing, I'd just as soon have walked."

One illustration that stands for a hundred. As my *Heresy, Yes—Conspiracy, No!* makes clear, I have defended the right of qualified teachers to profess *any* heretical doctrine, communist, fascist or whatnot. I maintained, however, that persons who are members of any group that gives them instructions to take advantage of their position in the classroom to indoctrinate for a party line are unfit on *professional grounds* to serve as teachers. This is the official position of the New School for Social Research. Even so, I have not argued that such membership is a ground for automatic exclusion, only of careful inquiry, not by the state or Congress, but by the teacher's peers. At no time have I advocated that the Communist Party be outlawed. (cf. my *Political Power and Personal Freedom,* pp. 307–310).

The scurrilous references to me as a leading intellectual McCarthyite is in the best Stalinist tradition. It exemplifies what I long ago characterized, even before Orwell, as "the degradation of the word." Berman arbitrarily redefines a McCarthyite as anyone who is opposed *both* to Communist conspiracy and to Senator McCarthy's demagogy. This is comparable with saying that "if by murder we mean character assassination, then Paul Berman is guilty of murder." I make no such accusation. I charge him only with being guilty of character assassination.

On May 8, 1953 when Senator McCarthy was at the height of his power and influence, I published the following letter in the *New York Times* calling for the organization of a national movement to retire Senator McCarthy from political life. In the interest of truth I am requesting that you publish the letter so that your readers may determine the accuracy of Mr. Berman's account.

To the Editor of the *New York Times:*

Even those who for reasons of their own are inclined to be silent about Senator McCarthy's methods must be aware of the incalculable harm he is doing to the reputation of the United States abroad. The evidence mounts daily that he is a heavy liability to the friends of American democracy and international freedom, and an obstacle to all efforts to counteract Communist lies about the true nature of American society.

But even more significant than the deplorable effect abroad is the new tack that Senator McCarthy has taken on the domestic scene. He seems to have turned from investigating Communists, while making reckless and exaggerated statements about them, to hounding former Communists who are now actively engaged in the defense of liberty against the totalitarian threat. Oddly enough, while he pursues men who discarded years ago the passing Communist illusions of their youth and whose integrity is now unquestionable, Senator McCarthy extends his blessings to certain other former Communists, some of whom remained faithful to the party long after those whom he is attacking had left it. The only explanation for this peculiar behavior is that the objects of Senator McCarthy's wrath have dared to question the intelligence and effectiveness of his methods of fighting communism.

Senator McCarthy evidently considers agreement with his own fantastic views about how best to resist communism as the acid test of democratic loyalty. Yet it can easily be shown that Senator McCarthy's behavior has strengthened sympathy for communism and decreased friendliness to American democracy all over the globe. In the light of the facts it is legitimate to interpret Senator McCarthy's actions as motivated less by an interest in combating communism than by a desire to exploit the authority he possesses as a Senator.

As one who has been active in anti-Communist work for many years, I believe I am in a position to evaluate the validity of the charges Senator McCarthy has brought against two of his recent targets, Theodore Kaghan of the High Commissioner's Office in Germany, and James Wechsler, editor of the *New York Post*.

Whatever his youthful fellow traveling may have amounted to, Mr. Kaghan has in the past decade proved to be a formidable opponent of the Communist movement. The record of his work in Austria and Germany is as unambiguous as it is honorable. The letters of praise and commendation he has received from Chancellor Figl of Austria and Mayor Reuter of Berlin express sentiments which are concurred in by all informed observers. To impugn his loyalty because of honestly avowed errors of his youth is a sign either of obtuseness or of calculated political insincerity.

The case of James Wechsler is an even more outrageous instance of senseless persecution. Senator McCarthy recently addressed a telegram to him, using Mr. Wechsler's party name of the Thirties. (It is safe to assume that Senator McCarthy, who knows the party names of his present associates who were once Communists, does not address them in this way.) He has gone so far as to insinuate that a fierce attack on Mr. Wechsler by the *Daily Worker* was either written or inspired by Mr. Wechsler himself.

One does not have to agree with Mr. Wechsler about everything to recognize the valuable services he has performed in exposing Communist pretenses and duplicity at a time when the then Mr. McCarthy was vegetating in peaceful somnolence. It appears that Mr. Wechsler's unforgivable sin in Senator McCarthy's eyes is not his youthful communism, for otherwise Senator McCarthy would have to treat Messrs. Budenz, Rushmore, et. al. in the same way. Mr. Wechsler has been guilty only of criticizing Senator McCarthy, and the latter is abusing his political position to carry on a personal feud.

The issue, however, is not personal. After all, sooner or later all intelligent Americans concerned about freedom will have to criticize Senator McCarthy's irresponsibilities. Are they therefore to be slandered or pilloried?

The time has come to organize a national movement of men and women of all political parties to retire Senator McCarthy from public life. This is one movement in which we shall not have to fear infiltration by Communists. For the day Senator McCarthy leaves the political scene the Communists throughout the world will go into mourning.

1. Hook never mailed this letter.

195

Dear William,[1]   March 14, 1984

The other chapters in my autobiography are just as long or longer.

I shall be glad to consider cuts but not on Lasch.[2] His book and his quotation about my alleged statement that the Communist system is based on "total error" are still being cited as evidence of *my* absolutism. Because of his persistence in refusing to see any distinction between theoretical error and political terror, I cannot in justice to myself ignore what he said.

I know he is an editor of some kind at *PR* and he probably will want to reply—in the next issue—but what I say is within the amenities of civilized discourse.

As distinct from Diana Trilling[3] and others, I am proud of being "a cold war liberal" and have always argued that a vigorous defensive cold war is the best way of preventing a hot war in Western Europe. The pejorative associations of the phrase can be overcome by pointing out that the origins of the Cold War originated by the Kremlin with the organization of the Comintern in 1919, suspended during World War II, and resumed when the Soviet Union rejected the Baruch-Lilienthal Plans for the internationalization of atomic energy, rejected Marshall Plan aid to Czechoslovakia and Poland, and attacked the Atlantic Alliance.

Cf. my chapter "In Defense of the Cold War" in my *Marxism and Beyond.* Will enclose it if I can find a copy.

You probably have seen the attack on me in the *Village Voice* of March 13. The pictures are lovely. I have drafted a reply but before sending it, I would like to find out who Paul Berman is and what political group he's associated with. Do you know? Someone said he belongs to the *Nation* crowd. If he is C.P. or Trotskyist I won't dignify it with a reply since his rejoinder will consist of more slanderous and libelous statements.

1. William Phillips, editor, *Partisan Review.*
2. Christopher Lasch, professor of history, University of Rochester, and author of *The New Radicalism in America, 1889–1963:The Intellectual as a Social Type* (New York, 1965). In this book, Lasch claimed that Hook had said the Soviet Union was based on a system of "total error." Hook actually had said it was based on a system of "total terror." See Hook, *Out of Step,* pp. 568–69.
3. Wife of Lionel Trilling and a social and literary critic in her own right.

196

Dear Paul,[1]   March 30, 1984

Delighted to get word from you. Just yesterday I had a visit from a very unhappy Mexican whose Instituto de Investigaciones Sociales y Económicas, A.C. had just been shut down by the President of Mexico. His name is Augustin Navarro and he unfolded a tale of corruption, cowardice, and ineptitude which makes that country seem absolutely hopeless. I know nothing about Mexico. But if only one tenth of what he says is true, the situation is very bad. If you are doing studies on Mexico he is someone to talk to. He says he knows where all the skeletons are buried in Mexico from way back.

As for the foreign critiques of America, especially in Europe, I don't believe it is necessary to invoke the concept of decadence to explain them. They are all easily explainable as the blue funk of fear of war. The Kremlin puts on a convincing *act* that they are in a state of paranoia about the U.S. because of *our* provocative posture in response to *their* SS20's[2] and most of NATO is scared witless that the Soviets will move, and the U.S. has become the scapegoat because it costs nothing to blame it and it is dangerous to criticize the Russians. The resultant surge of isolationism in this country from all sides will sooner or later, to the delight of the Kremlin, dissolve NATO. Europe will fall into the Soviet orbit, without war.

As you can see from the April issue of *Encounter* in which you have a piece, Straight[3] is threatening to sue.

Yes I would be glad to see your piece on Kennan. Meanwhile have a fruitful visit to Europe, give our best to your wife and we look forward to seeing you in Vermont where we hope to be by mid-June if, if, if. . . . My days are full of ifs.

1. Paul Hollander, professor of sociology, University of Massachusetts.
2. Soviet long-range missiles.
3. Michael W. Straight, former editor of the *New Republic,* speechwriter in the White House, and deputy chairman of the National Endowment for the Humanities. Straight's autobiography, *A Long Silence* (New York, 1983), revealed that he had known of the activities of the English spies Guy Burgess and Anthony Blount during the early 1950s and yet had not said anything to the authorities until a decade later. Burgess and Blount were friends of Straight. The magazine *Encounter* had received a letter from Michael Straight's attorney demanding an apology for publishing Sidney Hook's essay "The Incredible Story of Michael Straight" (*Encounter* 61 [December 1983]: 68–73). The attorney claimed that Hook's essay was full of errors. His letter and Hook's response are in *Encounter* 62 (April 1984): 77–78.

197

Dear Mr. Cohen,[1]   May 1, 1984

I find very puzzling and somewhat offensive your characterization of my letter in the *N.Y. Times* of April 25[2] as "casuistical" since you employ that term to suggest something Jesuitical.

Mill's argument is perfectly straightforward and I suggest you read his essay in its entirety. Intervention by those who believe in freedom to prevent or frustrate the intervention by those who wish to destroy the freedom or independence or democracy of another nation is *in principle* always justifiable. As I understand it, that is the situation in El Salvador. Cuba and Nicaragua, with the support of the Kremlin, are attempting to overthrow the legally elected government of El Salvador. We are justified in preventing that intervention providing that the cost is not too great.

When Franco revolted against the legally elected gov't. of Spain in 1936, Hitler and Mussolini intervened to help him. When the [next line is missing] the U.S. adopted the Neutrality Resolution which made the sale impossible. The Madrid gov't. then had to turn to the Soviet Union, which gave them arms only on condition that the NKVD run the war in Spain, which led to a civil war among the opponents of Franco and the fall of the Republic.

In Vietnam it is clear that North Vietnam sent its regular troops into South Vietnam to help the Viet Cong which was largely its own creation to overthrow the Saigon regime. Either we should not have gone in—because of logistic or other reasons—or, having gone in, we should have fought it with Congressional approval to a point where the independence of South Vietnam was assured.

The U.S. has in recent years never intervened, nor should it, in the affairs of a Communist country that does not seek to subvert or overthrow non-Communist regimes, e.g. Albania. We should have left Cuba alone until Castro began to export his revolution to other non-Communist countries.

The West has never had a Jeffersonian or democratic International devoted to overthrowing Communist countries. But the Communist Int'l. was organized by the Soviet regimes to overthrow non-Communist countries regardless of how democratic they were.

Of course principles must be intelligently applied to each case. They are not recipes or prescriptions to be mechanically applied. This is not casuistry but reflective action.

1. Elliot A. Cohen, Pomona, New York.
2. Hook's letter to the *Times* reads as follows:

> To the Editor:
>
> Senator Patrick Moynihan is to be commended for insisting that moral considerations should always be an element in the determination of American foreign policy. In applying them to the current question of intervention in the affairs of other nations, however, he has strangely ignored the moral principles outlined by John Stuart Mill, the great liberal philosopher, in his essay on "Non-Intervention" in *Fraser's Magazine* (1859).
>
> I am confident that the Senator agrees with Mill's first point:
>
> "To go to war for an idea, if the war is aggressive not defensive, is as criminal as to go to war for territory or for revenue; for it is as little justifiable

to force our ideas on other people, as to compel them to submit to our will in any other respect."

But Senator Moynihan seems strangely indifferent to the second and main point Mill makes in his essay, which is just as topical today as when it was written:

"The doctrine of non-intervention to be a legitimate principle of morality must be accepted by all governments. The despots must consent to be bound by it as the free states. Unless they do, the profession of it by free countries comes but to this miserable issue, that the wrong side may help the wrong side, but the right may not help the right. Intervention to enforce non-intervention is always right, always moral, if not always prudent."

Prudence, of course, must always enter into the determination of an intelligent policy. It is to be hoped therefore that Senator Moynihan, who is as much of a liberal as a conservative as these terms are currently defined, will rethink his position.

198

Dear Rebecca,[1]   December 12, 1984

Thank you for your good wishes. I shall be 82 in a few days and my vision (physical) is growing dimmer by the day. Although I was glad to hear from you, I was somewhat puzzled by your letter. I can't make out what your attitude is towards Mainland China. I have gotten to know Heng Liang and Judy Shapiro. She is very bright, started out like you as a Maoist but learned the hard way what Stalinism is. When I met her I immediately thought of you—a ten-year-older and wiser edition. But she and her husband are dedicated people to the cause of freedom and democracy, and are making sacrifices for it. Against my advice they are both sacrificing academic careers for it.

You should write to the XXth Century Foundation and get a copy of their report on the "State of Freedom on Mainland China with Special Reference to 1983." If only the American newspaper people (including Flora Lewis[2]) would read it. They would understand that it means nothing to say that the economic ideas of Karl Marx have been abandoned in China. They were really abandoned a long time ago. But what has *not* been abandoned in China is Leninism—the dictatorship of the Party or the Political Committee of the Party. Deng Xiaoping is as much a dictator as Mao and the Gang of Four, only more foxy with more factions to contend with.

I am terribly ignorant of China and envy you your linguistic capacities. But I am seeing quite a number of mainland Chinese students who are studying here. Their stories sicken me with horror—all variations of Heng Liang's but not told with the consummate artistry of Judy Shapiro's prose.

Oddly enough, my writings on Marx, socialism and allied themes are being discussed by some of these young politically minded Chinese and they seem excited by them. A piece I wrote long ago, actually a speech delivered in monosyllables to a Japanese audience on "Pragmatism and Existentialism," translated and published in the first issue of *The Chinese Intellectual,* has been enthusiastically received. It seems that there is a strong interest in American pragmatism and European existentialism in present-day China among what has emerged as an intellectual class.

Do you see *Freedom at Issue*? There is an excellent piece by Miriam London and Ta-Ling Lee on the current state of political affairs in mainland China. A post card to Freedom House, 20 W. 40th St., NY, NY 10018 will bring you the issue.

Many Americans I know have visited China. They are impressed by the sights but horrified when they learn how primitively people live and still in what fear. A pity more of them do not visit Taiwan before they return to the US. Those that do are overwhelmed by the differences. Some say that the Mainland must destroy Taiwan, or come to terms with Taiwan and then reduce it to the common state that prevails in the Mainland because if the Chinese masses really understood the level of prosperity that exists in Taiwan—which from our point of view is low—and the relative degree of freedom that exists there (which as we know is crippled and uncertain), they would become ungovernable, even if they didn't move to overthrow the regime. What do you think?

My advice whatever it is worth is for you not to go to China or Hong Kong or back to Taiwan until you clear your mind as to what you believe and what you want to do. If you become a participant in events abroad you run great risks. If you remain in the US and become an interpreter of Chinese life, politics and culture, you may carve out a career of significance. More and more people are going into Chinese studies and in a few years the competition will be rife.

And as a last piece of evidence of how reactionary I am, my advice is don't wait too long to find a husband and raise a family.

1. Rebecca Karl.
2. Foreign affairs columnist, *New York Times.*

199

Personal & Confidential

Dear Professor Boyer,[1]   February 21, 1985

I am glad to answer your letter of February 11, although my eyes are giving me great trouble. Almost against hope I look forward to finding someone who can tell the true and objective story of the roles of American scientists, of the most activist of the scientists, on the political scene. *It will require great courage to do so.* The situation I described thirty-five years ago[2] is essentially the same—even more so—today.

The plain fact is that the American government in unprecedented fashion followed the lead of American scientists in offering to internationalize atomic weapons of which the US had a monopoly. The Baruch-Lilienthal proposals were so generous that when the USSR turned them down, no less a severe critic of the US than Bertrand Russell urged that the Kremlin be given an ultimatum and atom-bombed if it refused to accept the US proposals. I cite this only as evidence of the generosity and genuine desire for peace behind the offer.

One would have thought that the scientific American community would learn something about the Soviet Union from this and other episodes, like its refusal to permit its satellites to accept the Marshall Plan aid and other events. On the contrary, it has persisted in adopting a policy according to which there is a moral equivalence between the US and USSR, one that views the USSR as any other great power, in complete ignorance of, or indifference to, the domestic and foreign consequences of its Communist belief, strategy and tactics. What is worse, *some* sections of the scientific community expressed, e.g. in the political stance of the *Scientific American,* owned and edited for many years by Piel,[3] an ardent follower of Henry Wallace, their criticisms against American defense initiatives, never once criticizing the Soviet Union in the same way. I don't see *Science* these days, but some of my colleagues tell me that it is being edited by a small activist group whose foreign policy and defense orientation are neutralist, if not anti-American.

I don't know about that but I do know about the Pugwash meetings.[4] Notice almost every representative of the American side is someone who has *publicly* attacked American foreign and domestic policy. No Russian representative has ever murmured a criticism of the Kremlin or of its barbarous treatment of scientists who do not come to heel at the Party's command. How can in such circumstances the declarations issuing from that group be given credence? Eugene Rabinowitch once told me that at every Pugwash meeting he attended he could always spot the KGB operators in attendance. Yet the Americans ignored all this as inconsequential.

Notice also how hostile large sections of the scientific community almost automatically become to official scientific advisors of the American government, their character assassination of Edward Teller, not so much for the Oppenheimer incident[5] in which he told the truth about his own judgment, as because of his weapons research.

All this is preliminary to answering your three questions: 1) It is a myth that anyone thought, dreamed or *advocated* the imposition of a *Pax Americana* on the world as a result of the American monopoly of the atom bomb. I challenged Einstein to tell me who these scientists were. He could not. His passionate belief in *collective* guilt of *all* the Germans except those in Hitler's jails and outside Germany was clear evidence that he wanted them punished and didn't care at all if the Kremlin took all of Germany. We used to ask those like Hutchins[6] who believed in World Government whether it was to be the government of a free world or an enslaved world. After all, Hitler believed in World Government, too; and I remember in 1940 when it looked as if Hitler would devour all of Europe, some of my colleagues at Columbia consoled themselves with the thought that we now would have a United States of Europe!

No, there were no *Real Politik* groups that wanted a *Pax America*. There was another important group you omitted. Those of us around Clarence Streit,[7] who believed in a Federal Union of all the Western democracies, liked Churchill's offer to France in 1940 to become a joint commonwealth with England. That was and is, less so today, an important movement. It would be open to any nation with a democratic political system of a genuine kind to join.

2) No, I did not neglect this political dimension. I interpret it quite differently from you. What were "the external events" which you claim made a difference to the scientists' views? What happened in Poland, what happened in Berlin, the blockade, the whole series of Soviet actions in *direct contravention to their pledged word and treaties?* But the scientists drew no inference from this. They reacted critically to *our own defensive measures* and then blamed the US for the necessity of taking these measures, disregarding their causes. Linus Pauling and others like him were even loath to believe that North Korea had invaded South Korea in 1950.

I attributed then and still do the American scientists' critical attitudes toward US government policy on almost every issue affecting the Soviet Union to nothing more sinister (but in its consequences as harmful) than ignorance, stubborn ignorance, sometimes compounded by a refusal to examine the evidence, of the nature of Communism. Documentary evidence exists that every Soviet scientist on an exchange program must sign a pledge of loyalty to the KGB or its equivalent to further its work if called upon to do so. This is shrugged off by most American scientists, and any attempt to restrict the range of operation of Soviet scientists in the US is met with loud outcries, usually orchestrated from Cambridge and the Union of Concerned Scientists. And this despite the fact that the movements of American scientists and scholars in the Soviet Union are severely limited.

3) Yes, about Dewey.[8] His views on these issues were very much like mine although by temperament he avoided controversy and was inclined to trust anybody until he had evidence they were untrustworthy. What he learned about the Stalinist regime and its murderous rule when he was Chairman of the Commission to Investigate the Truth About the Moscow Trials led him to systematic distrust of the direction of Soviet foreign policy. As you know, in several long letters to the *New York Times* during the height of the euphoria about the Kremlin as our great democratic ally when Hitler double-crossed Stalin, he warned about the danger of Stalin's resumption of the cold war and urged that we agree on conditions of peace and freedom for Eastern Europe before pouring unlimited aid to the Kremlin.

In an article in *Commentary* in the late 40s or early 50s Dewey criticized the anti-scientific movement that began in reaction to the atom bomb, by pointing out that the decision to use the bomb was a political one and had to be evaluated in political terms. I defended the use of the atomic bomb at Hiroshima, not Nagasaki, because (1) it brought the war to an end; (2) saved the millions of Japanese and Americans lives that would probably have been lost if the American troops had to storm the beaches of Japan (after Iwo Jima we knew what to expect). I can't say Dewey *explicitly* agreed. I know that when he heard me talk this way to Robbie, the second Mrs. Dewey, he did not demur.

Finally, I was in Vermont when the *New York Times* arrived with its blaring headlines about the bomb. The war in Europe was over, and I feared that as a result of Roosevelt's political naivete, transmitted to Truman through Mrs. Roosevelt until Truman learned better, we would yield to Soviet pressure to engulf first West Germany and then France and Italy. I was happy the war in the East would be over and not so fearful that if the Soviet armies moved we would cravenly retreat. At the time we were already in the midst of bringing our boys back home. The Kremlin kept their boys where they were.

P.S. Some of Albert Wohlstetter's articles on defense may be useful. In one of them he cites the case of a leading scientist who is on record saying that it is unworthy to imagine that the Communists would violate any test ban on weapons. A few months after that it was clear that the Communists had been violating the ban at the very time this trusting declaration was made. Did the scientist learn better? Not yet any evidence.

1. Paul Boyer, professor of history, University of Wisconsin, and author of *By the Bomb's Early Light: American Thought and Culture at the Dawn of the Atomic Age* (New York, 1985).

2. Hook, "The Scientist in Politics," *New York Times Magazine,* April 9, 1950.

3. Gerard Piel, publisher of *Scientific American.*

4. Meetings between Soviet and American scientists at the summer home of Cleveland industrialist Cyrus Eaton to discuss nuclear disarmament proposals.

5. Teller's testimony questioned nuclear scientist Robert Oppenheimer's political reliability and was a factor in the government's decision to remove Oppenheimer's security clearance.

6. Robert M. Hutchins.

7. Clarence K. Streit, president, Federal Union, and editor of *Freedom and Union.*

8. Boyer asked Hook about Dewey's attitude toward nuclear weapons.

200

Dear Mrs. Erdmann,[1]   February 22, 1985

Thank you for your letter of February 19. How did you happen to see my credo *Belief in Action?* You are much too kind in your judgment. One of course is not the best judge of his or her own writing, but I believe I have written better things.

Space of course did not permit me to develop my views on freedom adequately. But I have never defined freedom as the right to do anything, insisted that the desire for freedom is always *specific,* that one freedom limits others, and that freedoms conflict, making intelligence the supreme value—(*not* the only one) in a cluster of other desirable values. I am enclosing two reprints—one that bears on this issue, and another "In Defense of the Cold War" that bears on your questionnaire.

I am not very optimistic about the prospects of the survival of the free and open society—the state of European public opinion, the dominant *ritualistic*—not realistic—liberalism in our universities, the widespread failure to understand the democratic ethos are among the reasons for my lack of optimism. But of course the struggle must continue—even against odds.

1. Erika Erdmann, professor of biology, California Institute of Technology.

201

Editor: *Northern Californian Jewish Bulletin,*   April 1, 1985

I was startled to find in Mr. Kamin's story on "The Jewish Voice for Nuclear Freeze" (March 29) a quotation from Jeffrey Dekro in which he links "the gas chamber slaughter of Jews in Nazi Germany and the deaths and mutilations of Japanese citizens by U.S. atomic bombs" as both technological horrors of modern times. This outrageous piece of anti-American propaganda echoes the line of the Kremlin's disinformation specialists. The slaughter of the Jews in the Nazi holocaust, no matter how achieved, was a monstrous crime. It involved no special technology. The bombing of Hiroshima, on the other hand, was an act approved by President Truman, designed to end the war, which it succeeded in doing, and to save millions of lives that would have been lost on *both* sides had American troops been compelled to storm the beaches of Japan.

Deliberately to ignore this difference is to equate the arch-criminal Hitler with Truman, the leader of American democracy and friend of Israel. One expects to find this amalgam in the pages of *Pravda* where it is conjoined with the bombing of Dresden, actually undertaken at the behest of the Kremlin to facilitate the offensive of the Red Army. In its campaign to turn the Germans against the American nuclear policy, the Kremlin cites the bombing of Dresden together with Hiroshima as evidence of American inhumanity. Waskow[1] and Dekro are disseminating this canard.

It is incomprehensible to me that Mr. Dekro's linking of the Nazi holocaust of the Jews and Hiroshima should escape editorial criticism. It is indeed odd that Mr. Dekro should refer to the "deaths and mutilations of Japanese citizens" by American bombs and not to the deaths and mutilations of German citizens at Dresden and Hamburg whose consequences in dead and injured were more dreadful and numerous than at Hiroshima. All of these acts of war were brought on by Japanese and Nazi unprovoked attacks against the U.S. They have nothing in common with the criminal atrocities of Hitler against the Jews.

Just as misleading is the headline of your story—"Shalom Center: the Voice for Nuclear Freeze." There is no such thing as a Jewish voice for nuclear freeze or for any specific strategy for preserving peace. There are only wise or unwise voices, politically informed or politically illiterate voices—Jewish or non-Jewish. The American defensive nuclear deterrent has so far prevented a Third World War.

There are several weighty reasons for questioning the wisdom *at present* of a nuclear freeze. Among them is one that should be of special interest to the members of the Bay Area Council for Soviet Jews and to all human beings concerned with the fate of Soviet Jewry. No agreement on a freeze can be self-monitoring. Nor can it be completely verifiable by mechanical means alone. Much can easily be concealed from any satellite eye. Were the U.S. to violate any freeze agreement, our free culture makes it possible for thousands of whistle blowers to expose such an action. In the complete absence of a free press or media in the USSR, how could a Soviet violation be known? The most essential element in any agreement is the good faith of its signatories. What is the record of compliance of the Soviet Union with its past agreements—particularly the Helsinki agreement? Every member of the Soviet Helsinki Watch Committee is in a concentration camp or psychiatric institution. What assurance have Waskow and Dekro and those they have misled that the Kremlin will live up to any nuclear freeze agreement any more faithfully than they have honored the Helsinki agreement?

1. Arthur I. Waskow, author of *The Worried Man's Guide to World Peace* (Garden City, N.Y., 1963).

202

Dear Ms. Anderson,[1]   April 3, 1985

In reply to your inquiry of March 25, 1985 about Valery Chalidze,[2] I wish to stress the fact that I am familiar only with his efforts and publications in furthering human rights, particularly in the Soviet Union. He has devised a singularly effective method of defending and furthering human rights in the Soviet Union by mobilizing public opinion to plead for the fulfillment of Soviet law itself by the authorities. Without professing any revolutionary or counter-revolutionary doctrines, Chalidze has made it more difficult for the Soviet authorities to violate their own standards of legality. He has deprived them of the rationalization that they cannot recognize the rights of outside nations or forces to interfere in Soviet domestic affairs. All Chalidze and those whom he has influenced have asked of the Soviet authorities is that they obey their own laws.

It is obvious that the Soviet regime and its sympathizers throughout the world have made it difficult for Valery Chalidze to survive and continue his educational campaigns. A MacArthur Fellowship grant would permit Chalidze to continue a mission which is of deep concern not only to citizens of the USSR but to enlightened citizens everywhere who agree with Sakharov, Chalidze's mentor and friend, that the cause of peace is strengthened wherever the cause of human rights is defended.

1. Mirdza Berzins Anderson, assistant director, MacArthur Fellows Program.
2. Soviet physicist and human rights advocate. He was deprived of Soviet citizenship in 1972.

203

Dear Mr. Mazer,[1]   April 4, 1985

Thank you for your note of March 27 and your reflections on US-Soviet trade. I wrote an article on the subject two summers ago at a conference on the subject that remains unpublished in which I urged that we restrict our trade to consumption goods primarily—leaving the question of wheat sales open.

My chief critics—very vehement—were heads of heavy technological hardware companies who turned out to be extreme libertarians who put profit first, not freedom first.

I found your article surprisingly moderate, and you do admit that we certainly have not much to gain by trade. It doesn't take sufficiently into account the importance of trade, especially in technology, to the Kremlin and the fact that almost all of it has potential military uses. It ignores the evidence now being published in *Le Monde* from Soviet sources (described in several stories in the *NY Times*) of the billions of dollars saved by the theft and transfer of military patents, research techniques and related discoveries of the West through the alleged business dealings of the Soviet trade representatives which are actually organized by the GPU, the KGB, and the Kremlin's military staff. In addition, the danger that our banks will lend the Kremlin as it has its satellites billions of dollars of credit, puts a dangerous political card in the hands of our enemies. And that they are our enemies, in a sense in which we are not theirs, is something I hope I don't have to prove. And if you have any lingering doubt about that I suggest that you read Shevchenko's *Breaking with Moscow*. Even the anti-American Conor Cruise O'Brien[2] was shaken by it, consoling himself with the claim that they are probably bungling and inefficient enemies. If our trade makes them more efficient, there is no reason to believe that they will become less hostile.

1. Richard Mazer, New York.
2. Irish writer, diplomat, and politician.

204

Dear Mr. Wright,[1]   May 6, 1985

Thank you for your letter. Your analysis seems to me to be quite sound.[2] There is only one element I should like to suggest in addition which you yourself have probably thought about but so far not stressed. That is her[3] obvious infatuation with Dashiell Hammett[4] who got the Communist religion in a big way and who would undoubtedly have broken with L.H. if she had become even slightly critical of the Communist Party or the Soviet Union. Hammett was a functionary of the C.P., the hardest of hard liners, proud of his superficial knowledge of Communist theory and practice, Lillian Hellman's guru about all matters political. Hammett was uncomfortable about the way he had made his living and of his sensationalistic detective story writing which in the early days was looked down on contemptuously by the literati, especially the Party guardians of proletarian literature. To compensate he became more Stalinist than Stalin.

Lillian Hellman was not an attractive woman but an intelligent one. Her love affair with Hammett was central to her life. Praise from him on political matters was balm to her heart. I have seen this syndrome time and again in the Communist movement. A man's love for a woman and especially a woman's love for a man, or more recently a parent's love for a wild political extremist child, will lead to a reorientation of point of view. Even the justices of our courts, local and national, are influenced in their political juridical judgment by the desire to ingratiate themselves with rebellious children and grandchildren to prove they are "with it" and not reactionary mossback liberals.

Yes, you are right. My essay on Hellman[5] has been universally ignored and neglected by authors and reviewers of books on L.H. I guess I am not very popular with any of these groups. I have it on reliable authority that Mary McCarthy was pleased that L.H.'s suit[6] didn't come to trial because her lawyer told her that the most powerful evidence for the defense was my piece which would be exhibit #1 at the trial. Mary McCarthy, knowing what I think of *her* going to North Vietnam and pressuring the young American prisoners of war to betray their sworn oath, making fun of them, and telling their captors of their refusal to cooperate—leading to their punishment—was relieved that I wouldn't be called as a witness. That was the only way she could have won her case. But had I testified the truth about L.H., I would have also testified the truth about M.M., and I don't believe the judge would have stopped me.

Good luck on your book—and more power to you in the struggle to tell the truth. You will need courage, but I am confident that you will do well.

1. William Wright, author of *Lillian Hellman: The Image, the Woman* (New York, 1988).

2. Wright wrote to Hook concerning his research on Hellman. Wright stated that Hellman had lied about her politics and had maintained her political prejudices in the face of overwhelming contrary evidence.

3. Lillian Hellman, playwright.

4. Dashiell Hammett, mystery writer.

5. Hook, "Lillian Hellman's *Scoundrel Time*," *Encounter* 48 (February 1977): 82–91.

6. In February 1980, Hellman filed a defamation suit against Mary McCarthy, Dick Cavett, and the Educational Broadcasting Corporation for $2,250,000. She sought compensation because in January 1980 McCarthy, a guest on Cavett's television show, had

called Hellman a bad writer and a liar. See William L. O'Neill, *A Better World: The Great Schism: Stalinism and the American Intellectuals* (New York, 1982), pp. 359–65.

205

Dear Mr. Jacobs,[1]   June 11, 1985

Your letter in the *New York Times* of May 27th stating "There are no Thomas Jeffersons in Nicaragua" reveals such startling political naivete that I am taking the liberty of writing you at the request of some of your constituents in the hope that I may contribute to your enlightenment. Dr. Silber[2] did *not* assert that the contras in Nicaragua are followers of Thomas Jefferson. His simple point is that the likelihood of establishing a society that will be minimally democratic as well as in our national interest is immensely greater if the contras prevail than if the Communists do. The historical evidence for this is overwhelming. Not a single Communist dictatorship has been followed by a democratic society. But right-wing dictatorships sometimes are, e.g. Spain, Portugal, Greece, Argentina, Brazil.

You assert "the contras are right-wing dictators: the Sandinistas are left-wing dictators." This seems to exhaust your political wisdom. But there are gaping holes in your position. Have you ever asked yourself, in any specific case, deplorable as both forms of dictatorship are, the triumph of which one is a greater danger to the American national interest and the cause of freedom?

Batista was and Castro is a dictator. The Shah of Iran was and the Ayatollah Khomeini is a dictator. According to you, it is a matter of indifference to the national interest whether Batista or Castro (who invited Soviet nuclear missiles to be set up in Cuba) rules in Cuba. The Shah of Iran certainly did not treat Americans as the Ayatollah did.

The Wilhelmine Empire of Germany and the Third Reich were certainly dictatorships as were the Czarist and the Leninist Communist regimes. According to your simplistic thinking, this makes it a matter of indifference to the national interest which prevailed. Such a view seems to me to constitute a definition of political illiteracy.

Moral judgment should always enter into the formulation of American foreign policy. But the consequences of what we do or leave undone for the preservation of democratic institutions are always relevant. There were people like you who in June, 1941, when Hitler invaded the Soviet Union, held that since both were dictatorships, we should be neutral and not send aid to the Soviet Union. Roosevelt properly disagreed. In many ways the Stalinist dictatorship was much worse than the Czarist dictatorship that preceded it. In the oppressive twenty-year rule of the last Czar, a handful of political dissidents were hanged for acts of violence (there was no capital punishment for civil crimes). Under Stalin's twenty-year rule, an average of 20,000 innocent persons a month were either shot or perished in concentration camps (see Conquest's[3] *The Great Purge*).

Nonetheless, intelligent democrats supported American aid to the Soviet Union. Why? Because on the evidence a victory by Hitler would constitute a greater ultimate danger at the time to the American national interest and democratic institutions.

I am not comparing the magnitude of the danger to the American national interest from the triumph of the Sandinistas, *to which your vote contributed,* with the danger of a Hitler victory. But I am appealing to you as an American Congressman who is responsible to his constituents to consider the *consequences* to American freedom and security of establishing another Cuba in central America. This as contrasted with the consequences of a victory for the contras, many of whose leaders led the fight against Somoza.

1. Congressman Andrew Jacobs, Jr., Democrat from Indiana.
2. John R. Silber, president, Boston University, and a member of the National Bipartisan Committee on Central America.
3. Robert Conquest.

206

Dear Mr. de Onis,[1]   ca. June 21, 1985

I am very puzzled by the story appearing under your byline in the *NY Times* of June 19. The headline and first sentence indicate that the State Dep't. issued a detailed defense of its report on Communist arms shipments to El Salvador's guerrillas, a subject that interests me greatly. But before even telling readers what the State Department said, you publish at considerable length the criticisms of that statement not only by Mr. Barnes[2] but by other critics of the Administration. As much or more space is given to the critics of the statement and the administration's policies as to the document you are reporting—a document which I presume is quite lengthy. Indeed, only in the conclusion of the story do you quote two snippets from the document. By that time the reader has been overwhelmed by refutations and criticisms—so that no clear picture emerges as to the precise points at issue.

You have a right to your bias and opinions but they belong on the editorial pages, not in what purports to be an objective news story. By citing the response or rejoinder first, you convey your bias without having to own up to it openly. It is a transparent stratagem which violates the ethics of journalism. When you give accounts of Communist or other left-wing movements in Central America and elsewhere you do not proceed this way. All that intelligent and fair-minded readers require of journalists is an objective presentation of the relevant facts. Granted that complete objectivity is impossible, some evidence should be provided that the journalist is striving to be as objective as possible instead of practicing "advocacy journalism."

1. Juan de Onis, reporter for the *New York Times*.
2. Congressman Michael D. Barnes, Democrat from Maryland, and a leading critic of the Reagan administration's Central America policy.

207

Dear Mr. Solarz,[1]   June 27, 1985

I have been very puzzled by your Op-Ed piece in the *New York Times* of June 20 proposing that the Democratic Party firmly reject any military assistance to the contras of Nicaragua. After some reflection, I do not know whether to conclude that you are politically naive and misinformed or blatantly hypocritical for electoral purposes. I confess to a reluctance to draw either conclusion because on the basis of your discussion on *Firing Line,* I was under the impression that you were both politically well-informed and politically sincere.

But what am I or any other knowledgeable person to think? A resolute opposition to aggressive Communism whose central target is the U.S.A. obviously includes opposition to Communist Cuba which is supported and allied with the Soviet Union. But the evidence is overwhelming that the Nicaraguan Communists, who have betrayed the ideas of the democratic Sandinista revolution, are converting Nicaragua into another Cuba. Do I have to rehearse all the relevant evidence? From the very beginning, even when the Carter regime was foolishly supplying the junta with millions, it endorsed, together with Cuba, the Soviet invasion of Afghanistan and "the living nightmare," your words, it has imposed on the Afghan nation. The newly adopted anthem of the Nicaraguan Communists proclaims that the U.S. is the enemy of mankind. The Soviet Union and Cuba have built up their Nicaraguan ally to a point where it has the most powerful fighting force in Central America. The Ortega regime has made a charade of the Contadora peace process. Even now the Nicaraguan regime can threaten the strategic sea lanes of the Caribbean if we ever became involved in that area of the world or if the Warsaw Pact nations ever attacked Western Europe.

It is purely demagogy on your part to charge that the U.S. "embraces authoritarianism." You know perfectly well that it is only when *there are no other alternatives* do we support authoritarian regimes when they are threatened by totalitarian movements, because in such situations this is the policy "of the lesser evil" to the national interest and the prospects of human freedom. Name one Communist country which has ever peacefully developed into a minimally political democracy. Some authoritarian countries have. Spain, Portugal, Greece, Argentina, etc.

Sometimes the policy of the lesser evil justifies support even of a totalitarian regime; that is why the U.S. sent aid to the Soviet Union when Nazi Germany invaded in 1941. That is the key to our present policy toward China.

I am a Social Democrat who supported Scoop Jackson's[2] foreign policy because it was bi-partisan. The dominant foreign policy influence in the Democratic Party today is set by McGovern and House Speaker O'Neill[3] who hate Reagan more than the Communist enemy leaders. McGovern's remarks on Andropov's death in which in effect he said "Pity it wasn't Reagan instead of this great lover of peace" is a sad indication of what many Democrats think.

I thought you recognized the difference between a Batista and a Castro, the Shah and the Ayatollah, even though as democrats, we oppose both. Your equation between martial law in Taiwan and martial law in Poland is absurd, even though both can be criticized.

You will not be taken seriously as a resolute opponent of Communism so long as you oppose the contras in Nicaragua whose leaders are *not* followers of Somoza but are as democratic as Duarte. Some of them were leaders of the revolt against Somoza.

1. Congressman Stephen J. Solarz, Democrat from Brooklyn.
2. Senator Henry Jackson, Democrat from Washington.
3. Congressman Thomas P. "Tip" O'Neill, Democrat from Massachusetts.

208

Dear Mr. Jacobs,[1]   June 28, 1985

I am planning to circulate my letter to you commenting on your defense of your refusal to aid the contras in their opposition to the Communist Nicaraguan dictatorship.

May I have your permission to circulate your reply?

No insult to you was intended or contained in my communication. Political naivete is not a crime or even a personal vice, but hardly a recommendation for political office, certainly not for continued political office. Nor is political simplism illustrated in your charge that I am confusing civil war and invasion. What you fail to understand is that civil wars and invasions are often interrelated. For example, when Franco revolted against the democratic Spanish regime, Hitler and Mussolini sent troops to aid him. Congressmen with the same simplistic mentality you show argued that we should not send arms to the democratic Spanish regime to defend itself. Cuban troops and Soviet advisors are just as much invaders in countries where civil wars are raging as were Hitler's and Mussolini's troops in Spain.

There are invasions and invasions. You opposed our intervention in Grenada and our military aid to the contras as forms of invasion without taking note of the presence of Cuban and other Communist forces there or proposing ways of stopping them.

I take the liberty of citing the wisdom of John Stuart Mill, the great liberal philosopher, on the logic of intervention. Perhaps it will reduce somewhat your political naivete.

> The doctrine of non-intervention, to be a legitimate principle of morality, must be accepted by all governments. The despots must consent to be bound by it as well as the free states. Unless they do, the profession of it by free countries comes but to this miserable issue, that the wrong side may help the wrong side but the right may not help the right.
> Intervention to enforce non-intervention is always right, always moral, if not always prudent.

I assume that you regard Communist aid (Cuban, Soviet, etc.) to sustain Communist dictatorships as wrong. If so, why do you regard American military aid to those who resist Communist dictatorships as unjustified? Especially in the light of the evidence that Nicaragua is becoming another Cuba openly allied to and supported by the Soviet Union whose declared purpose is the destruction of our free society.

1. Andrew Jacobs, Jr.

209

Dear Mr. Kim Dae Jung and Kim Young Sam,[1]   July 1, 1985

I have received your communication of May 18, 1985 and was startled to find no mention of, no less a condemnation of the occupation of the library of the USIS building in Seoul.[2] This outrageous action justified by the presumptuous claim that the US government was responsible for the Kwangju incident[3] has alienated a large group of Americans, of whom I am one, who consider themselves friends of Korean democracy.

I do not know whether you were on the scene when I visited Korea in the last year of the rule of Syngman Rhee. I was the only American he would see because of my writings on Communism, and I went directly from his residence to the largest group of students I have ever addressed, in which I defended the extension of democracy to South Korea and the curtailing of Syngman Rhee's benevolent despotism. He regarded himself as the George Washington of South Korea and showing me his tortured hands, he complained about the ingratitude of both the Americans and the Korean students.

Since that time, I have kept abreast of developments in South Korea and especially of the many attempts of Kim Il Sung[4] to destroy it. No one in the US approves of anti-democratic coup d'etats in South Korea. But the US has tried not to interfere in Korean domestic affairs in order not to give substance to the Communist charge that the South Korean regime is merely a puppet government. The U.S. is damned if it interferes, and damned if it doesn't.

A few more anti-American demonstrations will reinforce the growing feeling among Americans that we should withdraw our military forces from South Korea and leave it to Peking to bridle, if it can, Kim Il Sung who will pounce on you as soon as the US forces depart. What happened in Taiwan can easily happen in South Korea. Rest assured that once American troops are withdrawn, they will not return. Deny this and you will be living in a fools' paradise, but not for long.

You should make this clear to the student leaders. If they are indifferent to the fate of South Korea when Kim Il Sung's hordes invade, that will justify the present regime's charge which I do not *now* believe that these leaders responsible for the sit-in and other anti-American actions are not only in effect playing North Korea's game but intend to do so.

1. Co-chairmen, Council for the Promotion of Democracy, and prominent South Korean dissidents living in exile in the United States.
2. Hook's comment was unfounded since the occupation of the library occurred on May 22, 1985, after the Kims had mailed their letter.
3. A peaceful anti-government demonstration in 1980 in the South Korean city of Kwangju turned violent when the military intervened in a brutal fashion. The Chun Doo Hwan government then imposed military rule.
4. Communist leader of North Korea who died in 1994.

210

Dear Mrs. Barlow,[1]   July 8, 1985

Your open undated letter has been forwarded to me.[2]

You write that you respect my work and background. It is obvious you are familiar with neither, and with not much else.

It is simplistic merely to say that "support for democracy has been the linchpin of our foreign policy." The linchpin of our foreign policy has been to contain the aggressions and expansions of totalitarian powers in their struggle for world domination and the destruction of "free societies" (by which I do not mean necessarily free-enterprise societies). Sometimes in behalf of this policy we may have to support by military and economic aid not only military domestic despotisms whose internal policies we abominate, but even totalitarian regimes like present-day China or the Soviet regime under Stalin when Hitler invaded Russia, June 22, 1941. This was even *before* Russia became a co-belligerent in World War II.

I am confident on the basis of what I have been told of your political tendencies and the internal evidence of your letter, that you certainly approve the action of the U.S. in supporting the Soviet Union when Hitler invaded even though *at the time* Stalin had killed many more innocent victims, including Jews, than Hitler. The reason? A victory by Hitler would have been a greater threat to the prospects of free society and our national interest.

Sometimes, as Burke[3] once put it, our choice is limited between the "politically intolerable and the politically impossible"—as, e.g. between the Shah and the Ayatollah.

It is not necessary to visit a country to get a reliable account of what is transpiring there.

I didn't have to go to Uganda to find out what happened under the regime of Idi Amin. On the other hand, many persons like you have visited the Soviet Union and even Nazi Germany, and come back with first-hand reports of what a wonderful and free culture existed there.

I supported the revolution against Somoza. The U.S. government, at the beginning, supplied to the revolutionary junta more aid of various kinds than Somoza ever received. But the first thing the Ortegas did was to endorse the Soviet invasion of Afghanistan, and their actions since then complete the picture of a consolidation of a Communist guerrilla dictatorship. How symbolic is it that the new national anthem characterizes the USA as "the enemy of the human race."

I am not a Catholic, but I am a firm believer in religious freedom. Even *you* should have been outraged by the action of the Communists in stripping a Catholic priest naked, driving him out of doors and photographing him with an innocent nude woman and distributing pictures to defame the church.

You are also mistaken about how political democracy was restored in Argentina. The reason was that in contradistinction to Communist totalitarian dictatorships, the military dictatorship tolerated certain islands of religious and cultural and economic freedom which permitted the organization of an opposition. You will not agree with Jeane Kirkpatrick's book,[4] but you may learn from it.

Every sentence of your letter radiates political duplicity. Nicaragua is important because it is rapidly becoming another Cuba, a spearhead of the Soviet Union directed against the U.S. Even if the situation in other Central American countries was as deplorable as you state—which is far from being the case—that is not true of them. I am in favor of political democracy in all countries, and if you will join me in protesting the absence of political democracy in Nicaragua, I will join you in protesting the absence of democracy anywhere in the world. I have already done so without you.

1. Harriet P. Barlow, Blue Mountain Lake, New York.
2. Mrs. Barlow had written a three-page criticism of a June 2, 1985, advertisement in the *New York Times* supporting the Contra campaign against the Sandinista government. The advertisement was signed by Hook, among others.
3. Edmund Burke.
4. *Dictatorships and Double Standards: Rationalism and Reason in Politics* (New York, 1982).

211

Gentlemen,[1]   August 21, 1985

Thank you for your letter of August 6 in reply to my response to your earlier communication. I am happy to learn that you do not approve of the student occupation of the USIS building, and am pleased that you helped persuade the students to leave voluntarily. But I am puzzled by your statement that a *condemnation* of the action would have been counterproductive. How are you going to persuade the students from repeating their performance if you do not condemn their occupation?

Even more puzzling not only to me but to many of my colleagues is the sentiment expressed in your statement that "it is not an unreasonable thing to ask for an apology from the U.S." You have admitted that the U.S. had nothing to do with the Kwangju massacre. Why then should it apologize?

The years you have spent in the U.S. apparently have taught you very little about the American psyche. An apology presupposes guilt, and the American people would turn out of office any government which apologized for something it was not guilty of. The only country in which people apologize for something that they did not do and are not responsible for is Japan. Unfortunately the Japanese mentality must have left a lasting impression on the psychology of the Korean people if your statement expresses the general feeling.

One final point. Don't take too lightly the growing feeling that perhaps the U.S. should withdraw its troops from Korea. It is not true that American troops are in Korea *primarily* to serve American security interests anymore than American troops were in Vietnam to protect American security interests. Furthermore, some military people now say that China under Deng[2] will have an inhibiting effect on Kim Il Sung and that the U.S. is no longer needed.

Finally you ask: "Even if the American troops were there solely to protect Koreans, does that deprive the Korean people of their right to dissent?" The answer is of course not. And you ought to apologize for asserting that anything I wrote made any such implication. All peoples have a right to dissent. All I protested was the way in which the students expressed their dissent by invading the premises of the U.S. whose soldiers were there to protect South Korea from the totalitarian North Korea where absolutely no dissent of any kind is permitted. I wonder whether the students who invaded the USIS premises and engage in other forms of dissent, however limited, would enjoy the same freedoms if and when Kim Il Sung and his son took over.

I hold no brief for the South Korean regime whose unnecessary repressive measures I strongly disapprove of. But I don't see what the U.S. can make it do without opening itself to the charge that we are imposing our will on a weak country.

1. Kim Dae Jung, Kim Young Sam, and You Jong Keun, Korean Institute for Human Rights.
2. Deng Xiaoping.

212

Dear Joan,[1]   November 8, 1985

I was quite taken aback by many things in your letter of November 1st but will comment on only a few. The most important was my shock in discovering that you apparently have lost your faith or belief in democracy, for if you are a democrat, then you *must* believe in the right to dissent. And without intellectual and political freedom there is no dissent. That there are other values in life is beside the point where one is discussing democracy. Or are you saying, as I suspect, that there are other kinds of democracy and freedom than political freedom—the kind of political freedom you are enjoying in the U.S. and which you would *not* enjoy if you were living in the

USSR, Cuba and other Communist countries, even Hungary and Romania and China?

1. Where does one begin with you? It is as if the record of the Gulags has passed you by. For me political democracy may be *incomplete* without other forms of democracy, educational, ethnic, industrial, racial, etc. *But without political democracy no other kind of democracy is possible.* Without the freedom to speak, assemble, publish, etc., how can any other freedom be protected against abuse? Of course without means, health, etc., I am not free to travel. But when we talk of the *freedom* to travel, as distinct from the ability to travel, e.g. to leave the country, we are not talking about ability, we *are* talking about the freedom to leave countries like the U.S., Britain, West Europe and the absence of freedom to leave countries like the USSR, East Germany, etc. even when one has the means and will to do so. There is no freedom of travel in any of the Iron Curtain countries. It is a penal offense to try to leave, and many hundreds have been shot trying to leave. Doesn't the existence of the wall that runs through the whole of Europe built to pen people in mean anything to you?

2. But you seem to be indifferent to this basic freedom. You sent me a clipping with a familiar story—very familiar to me—of unhappy Russian Jews in the U.S. What has that got to *do with the basic issue?* I am not a religious person, but I believe strongly in religious freedom. These Jews are free to believe or not to believe here in the U.S.—to be Jews or not. But they all feel that they were *not* free in the Soviet Union. Can you deny that? Doesn't the fact that the experience of these Jews, like most escapees and "permitted emigrants" (at great cost), is to turn them in vast numbers against *any* kind of socialist society tell you what they have endured? The Jews are almost all staunch followers of Reagan! Further, as bad as their current economic plight is, it is much better than that of the great majority of people in my early days. They and their children will get out of the ghetto as soon as they acquire sufficient facility in the language. How many of them would go back to the USSR if they could?

3. On what basis do you assert that I cannot conceive of any improvement in Communist countries? Of course there can be, and there has been some *economic* improvements here and there, especially where capitalist incentives (China, Hungary) have been introduced. But that is relatively unimportant to any freedom-loving democratic person. *Even under slavery there have been variations in the economic position of slaves.* The question of more or less of capitalist or socialist elements in the economy is completely subordinate to the question whether the population is free to make its political choice. I have been waiting for decades to see a Communist dictatorship transform itself peacefully into a democracy or some form of

genuine political pluralism. Some authoritarian and fascist countries have returned to some form of political democracy—Spain, Greece, Argentina. Name one Communist country where such a change has occurred. Does this evidence, since you do talk of evidence, mean anything to you?

What really worries me is that there is evidence in the material you sent me that you no longer believe in a pluralist democracy, that you are inclining to the view that a one-party dictatorship is satisfactory if its despotism is benevolent (to whom and how judged you do not make clear). I hope I am mistaken about this.

4. What was really painful was to read your flip remark "a poet who was once imprisoned in Cuba." So what! He wasn't merely imprisoned, he was tortured for twenty years. It isn't only a poet who was jailed and tortured but thousands of workers and peasants. The Cuban terror against dissenters has grown. You refer to Cuban crimes as "mistakes," just as heirs of Stalin today in the USSR refer to Stalin's "mistakes," even as they send individuals who are *less critical of the USSR than you are of the U.S. into insane asylums.* How can you be so callow? And how can you compare the costs you have suffered for your dissenting views to what dissenters have experienced in Communist countries? Your costs have been the usual costs of unpopular opinion. You have not been beaten, starved, drugged. Your children have not been taken away from you, you have not come anywhere near suffering the deprivations of individuals whose genuine moral impulses have led them to protest the corruptions of power in non-democratic countries.

5. I am bewildered when you say you regard yourself as part of "a humanistic and liberating strand in American life." I am afraid you are using these words "humanistic" and "liberating" in the same way as the Communists use the term "democratic." My experience, broader than yours, shows that most students are not *bombarded* by views like mine to which *you* are counterposing another point of view. Most students I know are ignorant about or have been misinformed about the actual history of the Soviet Union and conditions that exist there today. Judging by your letter, you have become *in effect* an apologist for the terroristic regimes that miscall themselves socialist in the world. As a teacher, your function in the classroom is *not* to combat what you *assume* the students are being subjected to outside the classroom but to present *both* sides of controversial issues fairly. That is required by the academic ethic. I had always assumed you would agree about this. Now I don't know. I would hate to think that you are purveying one-sided criticisms and diatribes about the shortcomings of democracy, which certainly are many, on the grounds that you are merely counteracting alleged indoctrination of a contrary kind. No one has an academic justification to use the classroom as a bully pulpit.

6. In comparatively small measures as in large, you reveal the same loose thinking. What in the world do you mean when you say that "the decision as to what is properly within a subject cannot be decided by an authority?" What authority besides your peers' judgment do you need to decide that a teacher of math or French or political science has no business discussing in class techniques of birth control, sex experience, or enrolling students in campaigns against abortion, etc. When I was a student we often would protest, at our peril, that the teacher was not discussing what was relevant to the subject matter of the course. At that time our teachers were mostly conservative and reactionary, politically speaking. Today the evidence seems to be that individuals whose views are conventionally called New Left or more extreme are abusing the academic ethic.

No one can intelligently believe that anything goes in the classroom, that anyone is qualified to teach anything. And if you believe *that,* you must acknowledge an authority or method of determining qualification, competence, etc. Of course there are border-line cases in which it is difficult to decide, but because there are twilight zones doesn't wipe out the difference between high noon and midnight. Can there be any doubt where Ollman[2] or Alan Wolfe[3] belong?

And how can you bring yourself to write that the SSRC[4] cannot be neutral in determining what falls within the legitimate boundaries of a subject because the SSRC is financed by the Ford and Rockefeller Foundations? What specific decision has the SSRC made that you can reasonably attribute to the fact that they got their money from Ford and Rockefeller? Why, anyone who gets money from Ford, Rockefeller or Guggenheim is usually subject to less, if any, restraint than when he or she gets money from tax or government sources.

You can get a copy of the awards made by the Rockefeller, Ford and Guggenheim Foundations, and the projects they fund. Why don't *you* look at the evidence instead of merely talking about evidence. As a matter of fact, all of these foundations are under attack for supporting left-wing causes. Really, you surprise me.

Well, I must stop. You probably have been as much angered by what I have written as I was pained by finding my courageous freedom fighter and temperamental rebel sounding like an apologist for the current varieties of totalitarianism. You end with a question, whether my mind is open to new evidence and argument. I think I am. Try me.

1. Joan Roelofs, professor of government, Keene State University.
2. Bertell Ollman, professor of politics, New York University, and inventor of the board game "Class Struggle."

3. Professor of sociology, Queens College.
4. Social Science Research Council.

213

Dear Harry,[1]   November 25, 1985

Thanks for sending me your article on Soviet psychiatry. Better late than never. It was published more than four years ago. Unfortunately the conditions you deplore have not improved. According to Peter Reddaway[2] they have, if anything, grown worse. Since you are a declared sympathizer and admirer of the Soviet Union, more articles along the line you have written may contribute to the Kremlin's abandonment of the barbarous practices you describe.

I was puzzled by your reference to the fact that "millions of Jewish lives were rescued by the sacrifice of millions of Russian lives." Do you mean that the Kremlin had a policy of rescuing Jewish lives by sacrificing Russian lives, or do you mean that as a result of the Soviet defeat of Hitler, Jewish lives, among others, were saved from destruction at the hands of Hitler? You can hardly mean the former because we know that after the Nazi-Soviet Pact was signed, Stalin turned over to Hitler more than a hundred German-Jewish Communists who had fled to the Soviet Union after Hitler came to power. Among them were Margarete Buber-Neumann and Alex Weissberg. (The books by Margarete Buber-Neumann and Weissberg[3] relating to their experiences were among those I sent to Einstein.)

There is no evidence that beginning with the advent to power of Stalin that the USSR was friendly to Jews. Indeed the anti-Trotsky campaign in the USSR was marked by a great deal of anti-Semitic sentiment. Even Bukharin before he became a victim of Stalin refused to protest the use of anti-Semitic slurs in the campaign against Trotsky.

Indeed, it seems clear that Stalin *helped* Hitler come to power by his theory of social-fascism which split the German working class and enabled Hitler to consolidate his power without any open resistance by the working class. On January 30, 1933 it became clear to me that Stalin was willing to let this happen in Germany because he hoped that Hitler would become involved in war with the West while the Soviet Union picked up what was left of post-war Europe. When he saw that this strategy wouldn't work, he signed his pact with Hitler, got back all the Baltic states as well as large parts of Poland and Romania, and supported Hitler loyally, until Hitler double-crossed him.

Despite the fact that the Jews were the first target of Hitler's bestiality after the war began, Stalin also turned against them. Have you forgotten the Jewish doctors' plot in 1952? If Stalin had not died in 1953 the entire Jewish population in the Soviet Union would have been dispatched to the Siberian wastelands.

By this time you must have read Khrushchev's speech before the 20th Congress of the CPUSSR about Stalin's many crimes (in which Khrushchev had participated) and which the Soviet system under Stalin made possible. Why should you be more anguished by the treatment of dissidents in 1960 and 1970 than you were by the trial and execution of the old Bolsheviks (who were not even dissenters) in the frame-up Moscow Trials of the 30s and by the literally millions of innocent people destroyed in the purges? (See Robert Conquest's *The Great Terror.*)

I can well understand how your own work in psychiatry would make you more sensitive to the issue of the abuse of psychiatry, but as fundamental, perhaps even more so since there may have been genuine errors of classification, is the abuse of other elementary human rights. More gruesome than reading about these events is speaking about them with the victims who managed to get away or be exchanged, Bukovsky, Volpin, Amalrik[4] (before he was killed), etc. In addition, there is a considerably larger group of persons who are receiving the same treatment, sometimes worse, than the Jewish refuseniks and dissenters—Ukrainians and other ethnic groups who cannot organize appeals to the conscience of the world because the international organization of their co-religionists or countrymen are so weak. Only Amnesty International occasionally writes about them.

So I hope you continue to write about these outrages in publications of larger circulation than *Jewish Currents.*[5] I know that like all of us you are very much concerned to keep the world at peace, but the problem of peace is not unrelated to human rights. The world could have had peace had it submitted to Hitler. One doesn't have to go so far as Kant as to believe that a world in which dissent—even the mere *verbal* dissent of protest—brings with it a life sentence in the cells of psychiatric hell is hardly worth preserving.

Your piece in *Praxis* (1978) raises another set of questions. I was never impressed with Picasso's *Guernica,* and regard most political interpretations of aesthetic themes as irrelevant. It seems to me quite a liberty to regard Picasso as a Fascist because of it. And although I despise Ezra Pound, it seems to me quite possible that *some* of his Cantos may be considered good poetry, as is T. S. Eliot's *Murder in the Cathedral.* My political judgment of Picasso is based on his politics, not on his painting. It is bad enough that like Sartre he was a Stalinist and once denied that the Gulag was a Soviet reality. Sartre had the grace, which Picasso lacked, to admit he was wrong before he died.

1. Harry Slochower of the Association for Applied Psychoanalysis. This was the Slochower of *Slochower* v. *New York City Board of Higher Education* (1956). After being academically blacklisted, he became a Freudian therapist and the editor of a psychoanalytic journal devoted to the arts.

2. Coauthor, with Sidney Bloch, of *Psychiatric Terror: The Abuse of Psychiatry in the Soviet Union* (New York, 1977).

3. Buber-Neumann, *Under Two Dictators* (London, 1949), and Weissberg, *The Accused* (New York, 1951).

4. Vladimir Bukovsky, Russian writer, scientist, and human rights advocate. He left Russia in 1982 for Stanford University. Aleksandr Volpin, Russian mathematician, philosopher, and political dissident. He emigrated to Israel in 1972. Andrei A. Amalrik, Soviet dissident historian, and author of *Will the Soviet Union Survive until 1984?* (New York, 1970). Amalrik spent seven years in a Soviet labor camp. He died in an automobile accident in Spain in 1980.

5. A small left-wing magazine.

214

Dear Mr. Colby,[1]   February 19, 1986

You have indeed put your finger on a key point. One of the language difficulties we have with the Soviet regime is that when it serves their interest they give a new and perverted meaning to the terms of discourse. But my contention is that in every specific case of difference with them this is demonstrable. For example, they will say that their press is "free" and therefore we cannot claim they have censorship. But note if we were to discuss whether the press was "free" in Germany under Hitler or in Spain under Franco, they would emphatically deny that the press was free. In such cases we can show that the very same criteria they use to establish the fact that the Nazi and Fascist press was not free, if applied to the Soviet press would compel us to reach the same conclusion.

In the end if they are not engaged in "good faith" negotiations, they usually will stalk out or break up the negotiations. But sometimes they will compromise and look for some other phrasing. The point is that they wish to exploit the emotive association of the vocabulary of "democracy" and "freedom." Why? Because *they do know* the *proper* meaning these terms have in world opinion. So they kidnap the "terms" of the free world and fill them with a different content. But it should not be difficult for negotiators who understand the ethics and logic of democracy to expose their practices.

Unfortunately too many of our officials are not sufficiently sophisticated intellectually to do this.

1. Roy Colby, Colorado Springs, Colorado.

215

Dear Peter,[1]   March 10, 1986

Please excuse this scrawl since I am just recovering from a second cataract operation. I'm going on to 84 and what with the multiple hazards of a contingent world this is to be expected.

I certainly petitioned the President (Eisenhower) to call that conference,[2] but it was in the form of a personal letter to him. But I do not believe that it was ever reported in the press, and in retrospect I am not surprised that Eisenhower didn't follow up on my suggestion. Whatever his standing as a military figure about which I have no competence to judge, his political understanding of Communism, its ideology and internal regime was sadly deficient. His reference to his inability to reply to Gen. Zhukov's contrast between the moral basis of the USSR and USA (Zhukov claimed that citizens are required to serve the country in the USSR but in the USA everyone serves only himself) shows this. Eisenhower seemed to be unaware that citizens in the USSR have the primary responsibility of serving the *minority political Communist Party or its ruling faction*, and not their own conception of the public welfare or the good of the country. Eisenhower reported that he didn't know how to reply to Zhukov. This incident occurred before Stalin eliminated Zhukov from the scene.[3]

It is more and more apparent to me that many scientists who certainly are not sympathetic to Communism and even disapprove of the treatment of Sakharov are *politically* unaware of the dangers of Soviet expansion and the operative influence of Leninist ideology on Soviet practice. It is a sad and difficult problem, and in many ways a repetition of the appeasement mood of the late 30s, intensified of course by the fear of nuclear war. Many scientists do not understand that the Kremlin will *not* initiate a war with the West unless it is practically sure to win it. Our defense strategy is to make them uncertain of such victory to begin with and then work for the abolition of nuclear weapons and if possible an effective shield against them.

1. Peter Coleman, author of *The Liberal Conspiracy: The Congress for Cultural Freedom and the Struggle for the Mind of Postwar Europe* (New York, 1989).
2. In January 1958 Hook published an article in the *New Leader* which mentioned that he had urged President Eisenhower to convene a conference of scientists to explain the dangers facing the free world.
3. Georgi K. Zhukov, commander of the Soviet armies that fought in Poland and Germany in 1944 and 1945. In March 1946, he was relieved of his position as commander of Soviet forces in Germany.

216

Personal

Dear Mr. Chapman,[1]   March 28, 1986

Having once criticized you for having improperly characterized my position—I am a Social-Democratic Daniel among a lion's den[2] of mainly Republicans and Jacksonian Democrats[3]—it is only fair for me to commend you for the logic, incisiveness and brilliant writing of your column today on the inconsistencies of those who tried to wriggle out of their embarrassment at the Nicaraguan raid into Honduras.

I write as one who believes that my fellow American citizens who disagree with my view that we ought to give aid to the Contras are just as good democrats as I am, and that *opponents* within the democratic process should *not* be regarded or criticized as *enemies* of the democratic process.

But it is perfectly legitimate as your column illustrates to question the *validity* of political assertions and actions by their consequences. Some facts may be in dispute and sometimes we may have to suspend judgment. But regardless of the degree, strength and depth of penetration of the Nicaraguan invasion of Honduras, it is *not* "a figment of the imagination."

If, as some leading Democrats now admit, the Sandinistas are "Marxist-Leninist Communists," why should they have been surprised? Or why should they have taken at its face the pronouncement of the Nicaraguan official representative in the U.S. that our officials were deliberately lying?

At any rate, even when I find myself—as is likely—in disagreement with you again, I shall on the basis of what I have just read, re-examine my own position more carefully. I have been wrong about many things but I am not too old, even approaching 84, to learn.

1. Stephen Chapman, journalist.
2. Hoover Institution.
3. Supporters of Senator Henry Jackson.

217

Dear Raziel,[1]   March 30, 1987

I hope that when my chapters on NYU are read my book will not be removed from the bookstore window.

I haven't followed the details of the Iranian arms scandal. It is obvious that Reagan like Carter before him does not understand that compassion, however genuine, for the lives of a few American hostages in the hands of the enemies of a free society must not be permitted to interfere with a firm and principled foreign policy. What disgusts me is the spectacle of journalists who had played up the pleas of families of some of the hostages for the President to do something to get them released—contrasting what was done for Daniloff[2] with their pitiful plight. They were foremost in attacking Reagan for yielding to their hysterical laments and accusations that he was not doing enough for the hostages.

Unfortunately the fallout of all this stupidity will be the abandonment of the Contras and the emergence of another and stronger and closer Cuba, increasing the likelihood ultimately of greater American involvement when the Bolshevik-Leninists act true to form.

I am not a Zionist, although sympathetic to Israel from the perspective of the global struggle for the survival of a free society. I am a firm believer in the death sentence for spies whether their name is Walker or Pollard[3] (or whether they are white or black) with some provision for clemency.

1. Raziel Abelson, professor of philosophy, New York University.
2. Nicholas A. Daniloff, American journalist seized in August 1986 by the Soviet Union and exchanged for Gennadi F. Zakharov, a Soviet spy captured in the United States.
3. The Walker spy family operated from 1968 to 1985. It sold the Soviet Union classified reports on the tracking of Soviet submarines and surface ships. This did incalculable harm to the navy's intelligence operations. During the 1980s, Jonathan J. Pollard, a Navy Department employee, provided Israeli representatives with classified information on Iraq and other matters.

218

PERSONAL AND URGENT

Dear Mr. Tisch,[1]   May 26, 1987

I have written to several people at CBS News without receiving any acknowledgment of my letters or a courtesy of a reply. I am now writing to you.

On March 30, 1987, Mr. Dan Rather reported that a Soviet military publication had charged that the AIDS disease was the consequence of a leak from a "U.S. Army laboratory conducting experiments in biological warfare." Several months before that this story had been denounced at a State Department meeting as a piece of Soviet KGB disinformation propaganda. Freedom House, of whose board I am a member, has circulated a memo from a Soviet defector who participated in disinformation propaganda against the U.S. of this character.

I wrote to ask under what circumstances did Mr. Rather acquire and broadcast this disinformation, and why he made no mention of the State Department's explicit disavowal and condemnation of it. I am now asking you for answers to my queries. For some months I have been struck by the tendentiousness of Mr. Rather's newscasts but have encountered nothing as blatant as this. It seems to me that CBS's public responsibility is affected by its vulnerability to disinformation planted by a totalitarian power. At any rate I shall be obliged if you can throw any light on this incident.

1. Lawrence A. Tisch, chairman of the board and chief executive officer, CBS.

Index

Page numbers in *italic* refer to letters to the addressee.

About the Editor

Educated at Georgetown University, the University of North Carolina, and Harvard University, Edward S. Shapiro teaches American history at Seton Hall University in New Jersey. He is the author of numerous essays and reviews, and his most recent book is *A Time for Healing: American Jewry since World War II* (1992).